D1422538

NEW PERSPECTIVES ON MALTHUS

Thomas Robert Malthus (1766–1834) was a pioneer in demography, economics and social science more generally whose ideas prompted a new 'Malthusian' way of thinking about population and the poor. On the occasion of the two hundred and fiftieth anniversary of his birth, *New Perspectives on Malthus* offers an up-to-date collection of interdisciplinary essays from leading Malthus experts who reassess his work. Part One looks at Malthus's achievements in historical context, addressing not only perennial questions such as his attitude to the Poor Laws, but also new topics including his response to environmental themes and his use of information about the New World. Part Two then looks at the complex reception of his ideas by writers, scientists, politicians and philanthropists from the period of his own lifetime to the present day, from Charles Darwin and H. G. Wells to David Attenborough, Al Gore and Amartya Sen.

ROBERT J. MAYHEW is Professor of Historical Geography and Intellectual History in the School of Geographical Sciences at the University of Bristol. He is the author of highly acclaimed *Malthus: The Life and Legacies of an Untimely Prophet* (2014) and of a new edition of Malthus's *Essay on the Principle of Population and other Selected Writings* for Penguin Classics (2015). He was a Fellow of Corpus Christi College, Cambridge and was awarded a Philip Leverhulme Prize for his contributions to historical geography. He has also held awards from the British Academy and the ESRC and is a Fellow of the Society of Antiquaries of London.

NEW PERSPECTIVES ON MALTHUS

EDITED BY

ROBERT J. MAYHEW

University of Bristol

CAMBRIDGE
UNIVERSITY PRESS

CAMBRIDGE
UNIVERSITY PRESS

University Printing House, Cambridge CB2 8BS, United Kingdom

Cambridge University Press is part of the University of Cambridge.

It furthers the University's mission by disseminating knowledge in the pursuit of education, learning, and research at the highest international levels of excellence.

www.cambridge.org
Information on this title: www.cambridge.org/9781107077737

© Cambridge University Press 2016

This publication is in copyright. Subject to statutory exception and to the provisions of relevant collective licensing agreements, no reproduction of any part may take place without the written permission of Cambridge University Press.

First published 2016

Printed in the United Kingdom by Clays St Ives plc

A catalogue record for this publication is available from the British Library

Library of Congress Cataloguing in Publication Data
Names: Mayhew, Robert J. (Robert John), 1971– editor.
Title: New perspectives on Malthus / edited by
Robert J. Mayhew, University of Bristol.
Description: Cambridge, United Kingdom : Cambridge University Press, 2016. |
Includes bibliographical references and index.
Identifiers: LCCN 2016008440 | ISBN 9781107077737 (hardback : alk. paper)
Subjects: LCSH: Malthus, T. R. (Thomas Robert), 1766–1834. |
Demographers – Great Britain. | Demography – History.
Classification: LCC HB863.N49 2016 | DDC 330.15/3092–dc23
LC record available at http://lccn.loc.gov/2016008440

ISBN 978-1-107-07773-7 Hardback

Cambridge University Press has no responsibility for the persistence or accuracy of URLs for external or third-party Internet Web sites referred to in this publication and does not guarantee that any content on such Web sites is, or will remain, accurate or appropriate.

For Clara: avec les tendres excuses de son Père pour ce qui va suivre

Table of Contents

List of contributors   *page* ix
Acknowledgements   xiii

Introduction
'Alps on Alps arise': revisiting Malthus   1
Robert J. Mayhew

PART I   MALTHUS IN HISTORICAL CONTEXT

1   Who were the pre-Malthusians?   25
     Ted McCormick

2   Malthus and Godwin: rights, utility and productivity   52
     Gregory Claeys

3   Malthus and the 'end of poverty'   74
     Niall O'Flaherty

4   Malthus and the new world   105
     Alison Bashford and Joyce E. Chaplin

5   Island, nation, planet: Malthus in the Enlightenment   128
     Fredrik Albritton Jonsson

PART II   THE RECEPTION OF MALTHUS

6   Malthus, women and fiction   155
     Ella Dzelzainis

7   Finding a place for the anti-Malthusian tradition
     in the Victorian evolution debates   182
     Piers J. Hale

8 Imagine all the people: Rockefeller philanthropy,
   Malthusian thinking and the 'peasant problem' in Asia   208
   David Nally

9 The publication bomb: the birth of modern
   environmentalism and the editing of Malthus's *Essay*   240
   Robert J. Mayhew

10 Malthus today   267
   Derek S. Hoff and Thomas Robertson

   Afterword   294
   Karen O'Brien

Bibliography   301
Index   327

List of contributors

FREDRIK ALBRITTON JONSSON is an Assistant Professor of British History at the University of Chicago. He has published extensively on eighteenth-century political economy and natural history. His first book is entitled *Enlightenment's Frontier: The Scottish Highlands and the Origins of Environmentalism* (Yale University Press, 2013).

ALISON BASHFORD is Vere Harmsworth Professor of Imperial and Naval History at the University of Cambridge and a fellow of Jesus College, Cambridge. Most recently she is author of *Global Population: History, Geopolitics, and Life on Earth* (Columbia University Press, 2014) and editor with David Armitage of *Pacific Histories: Ocean, Land, People* (Palgrave, 2013). With Joyce E. Chaplin she is co-author of *The New Worlds of Thomas Robert Malthus: Rereading the Principle of Population* (Princeton University Press, 2016).

JOYCE E. CHAPLIN is the James Duncan Phillips Professor of Early American History at Harvard University. She is the author, most recently, of *Round about the Earth: Circumnavigation from Magellan to Orbit* (Simon & Schuster, 2012); she is also editor of *Benjamin Franklin's Autobiography: A Norton Critical Edition* (W.W. Norton, 2012). With Alison Bashford, she is co-author of *The New Worlds of Thomas Robert Malthus: Rereading the Principle of Population* (Princeton University Press, 2016).

GREGORY CLAEYS is Professor of the History of Political Thought at Royal Holloway, University of London. He is the author of numerous studies that have addressed the history of Malthusianism in its conjunction with utopianism, Owenism, social Darwinism and, most recently, John Stuart Mill in his *Mill and Paternalism* (Cambridge, 2013).

ELLA DZELZAINIS is a Lecturer in Nineteenth-Century Literature in the School of English at Newcastle University. She is the co-editor of

Harriet Martineau: Subjects and Subjectivities (Manchester University Press, 2011) and *The American Experiment and the Idea of Democracy in British Culture, 1776–1914* (Ashgate, 2013). She is the author of several articles on aspects of nineteenth-century literature, feminism and economic history and is currently completing a book entitled *Commerce Between the Sexes: Feminism and Political Economy in Industrial Fiction, 1832–1855*.

PIERS J. HALE is Associate Professor of the History of Modern Science in the Department of the History of Science at the University of Oklahoma. He received his PhD in History from Lancaster University in England. He has written a number of articles on the politics of evolution in the second half of the nineteenth-century. His book, *Political Descent: Malthus, Mutualism and the Politics of Evolution in Victorian England* was published by University of Chicago Press in 2014.

DEREK S. HOFF is Associate Professor of History, Lecturer at the University of Utah, specializing in the history of economic ideas in the United States. He is the author of *The State and the Stork: The Population Debate and Policy Making in US History* (University of Chicago Press, 2012), which won the Pacific Coast Branch of the American Historical Association's award for best the first book in 2013, and, with John Fliter, of *The* Blaisdell *Decision: The Contract Clause, and the Great Depression* (University Press of Kansas, 2012).

ROBERT J. MAYHEW is Professor of Historical Geography and Intellectual History at the University of Bristol. He is the author of *Malthus: The Life and Legacies of an Untimely Prophet* (Harvard University Press, 2014) and has edited Malthus's selected works for Penguin Classics (2015). His work on Malthus has been funded by the British Academy and the Leverhulme Trust. He is also the author of *Enlightenment Geography* (Palgrave, 2000), *Landscape, Literature and English Religious Culture, 1660–1800* (Palgrave, 2004) and the co-editor of *English Geographies, 1600–1950* (St John's College, Oxford Research Centre, 2009).

TED MCCORMICK is Associate Professor of History at Concordia University. His first book, *William Petty and the Ambitions of Political Arithmetic* (Oxford, 2009), won the 2010 John Ben Snow Foundation Prize, awarded by the North American Conference on British

Studies. His current work examines the relation between quantitative approaches to population and ideas about providence, nature and government in Britain and colonial America from the Tudor period through the eighteenth century.

DAVID NALLY is University Senior Lecturer in Human Geography at the University of Cambridge and a Fellow of Jesus College, Cambridge. His research focuses primarily on the political, economic and cultural dimensions of colonization, the geopolitics of subsistence crises, the politics of disaster relief and the political economy of agrarian change. He is the author of a monograph, *Human Encumbrances: Political Violence and the Great Irish Famine* (University of Notre Dame Press, 2011). Recently he has been studying the emergence of American philanthropy as a moral and political force shaping global relations, particularly in the fields of population control and food production.

KAREN O'BRIEN is Vice-Principal (Education) and Professor of English Literature in the Department of English, School of Arts and Humanities at King's College London. Her publications include the British Academy's 2000 Warton Lecture in English poetry ('Poetry against Empire: Milton to Shelley'), *Narratives of Enlightenment: Cosmopolitan History from Voltaire to Gibbon* (Cambridge University Press, 1997, awarded the British Academy's Rose Mary Crawshay Prize) and *Women and Enlightenment in Eighteenth-Century Britain* (Cambridge University Press, 2009).

NIALL O' FLAHERTY is Lecturer in the History of European Political Thought at King's College London. His research explores the changing relationships between theology, science and social thought in Britain in the late eighteenth century, as well as questions relating to the secularization of social discourse in the period. He is currently in the final stages of completing a book entitled *The Doctrine of Utility in the Eighteenth Century*. The work offers a genealogy of Lockean moral thought in England, situating William Paley's philosophy in relation to that of his predecessors in the theological utilitarian tradition: John Gay, Edmund Law and Abraham Tucker, while also reflecting on its afterlife at the start of the nineteenth century, and particularly the contribution of Thomas Robert Malthus. He has published a number of articles on the moral and religious thought of William Paley, specifically on his engagement with David Hume. He also has an essay forthcoming in the Yale University Press edition of Malthus's *Essay on the Principle of Population*, entitled 'Malthus and the History of Population'.

THOMAS ROBERTSON is an Associate Professor of History at Worcester Polytechnic Institute in Worcester, Massachusetts. He is author of *The Malthusian Moment: Global Population Growth and the Birth of American Environmentalism* (Rutgers University Press, 2012). His new research uses archival and ethnographic data to illuminate the environmental history of US development projects in Nepal during the Cold War.

Acknowledgements

David Nally acknowledges a Philip Leverhulme Prize as well as a Rockefeller Grant-in-Aid award and extends his thanks to the staff at the Rockefeller Archive Center – and to Nancy Adgent in particular – in Sleepy Hollow, New York. He also thanks David Beckingham, Philip Howell and Robert Mayhew for comments on an early draft and Stephen Taylor for his able research assistance.

Ella Dzelzainis thanks the British Academy for the award of a Postdoctoral Research Fellowship (2007–10) to research Malthus. Thanks are also due to Carolyn Burdett, David Feldman, Cora Kaplan and Robert Mayhew for their generous insights regarding earlier drafts and to the participants in the Malthus Reading Group at King's College, London (2009–12).

Niall O' Flaherty is very grateful to the editor and to Richard Bourke for insightful comments on earlier drafts of his chapter. He also thanks the Malthus Reading Group at King's College, London and Isabel Rivers for her helpful reading suggestions.

Robert Mayhew as a contributor thanks Philip Appleman for his reflections on editing Malthus for W.W. Norton. Thanks are also due to W.W. Norton for offering sales figures for Appleman's edition of Malthus. He also thanks Simon Winder and Joanna Prior at Penguin for sales figures and authorization to access the Penguin Archive at the University of Bristol respectively. For guidance in that archive, thanks are due to Michael Richardson and Hannah Lowrey.

As editor, Robert Mayhew would like to thank Linda Bree at Cambridge University Press for commissioning this collection of essays and also the two readers for the Press who gave such helpful comments on the project at the proposal stage. Also at Cambridge University Press, thanks go to Isobel Cowper-Cowles, David Morris, Chloé Harries and Anna Bond. Thanks also to Jenny Slater at Out of House Publishing for her speedy and diligent work at the proof stage. Thanks also to Karen O'Brien, not only for offering the 'Afterword' for this collection, but for suggesting the approach to Cambridge in the first place with the germ of this project. Above all, he must thank all the contributors. When putting together his 'wish list' of contributors for a collection of essays showcasing contemporary scholarship about Malthus, he had no right to dare to hope that they would all take up the offer to contribute with such alacrity and enthusiasm. All contributors were given a tight deadline for the submission of essays in order to make publication in Malthus's anniversary year possible, but all replied by sticking closely to the schedule agreed while still offering work of an outstanding quality, which has made his task as editor both pleasant and easy.

Introduction

'Alps on Alps arise': revisiting Malthus

Robert J. Mayhew

> Fir'd at first Sight with what the *Muse* imparts,
> In *fearless Youth* we tempt the Heights of Arts,
> While from the bounded *Level* of our Mind,
> *Short Views* we take, nor see the *Lengths behind*,
> But *more advanc'd*, behold with strange Surprize
> New, distant Scenes of *endless* Science rise!
> So pleas'd at first, the towring *Alps* we try,
> Mount o'er the Vales, and seem to tread the Sky;
> Th' Eternal Snows appear already past,
> And the first *Clouds* and *Mountains* seem the last:
> But *those attain'd*, we tremble to survey
> The growing Labours of the lengthen'd Way,
> Th' *increasing* Prospect *tires* our wandring Eyes,
> Hills peep o'er Hills, and *Alps* on *Alps* arise![1]

Thomas Robert Malthus, like most educated men of his generation, could routinely cite the poetry of Alexander Pope and did so in the book that made his name, *An Essay on the Principle of Population* (1798), where he drew on the *Essay on Man*.[2] To the student of Malthus, it is perhaps Pope's image of the benighted young scholar from *An Essay on Criticism* that is more apposite. Malthus's ideas, notably in their first expression in 1798, seem to exhibit a stark simplicity and a crystalline clarity that makes them easy to comprehend, and that leads to prompt acceptance or pre-emptory rejection. And yet scholars attending to Malthus's work find 'with strange Surprize' that the origins, intentions and impact of his ideas in their historical context are far more complex and contested than their beguiling simplicity of exposition might lead them to anticipate. The same dynamic applies to the reception of Malthus's ideas. It is easy to begin with the sense of a simple binary between admirers such as Darwin who found in Malthus a 'theory by which to work' and critics such as Marx who dismissed Malthus's work as a 'superficial plagiary' in support of the bourgeoisie. And yet here as well we find 'endless Science rise', in that such simple binaries are soon broken down on closer inspection. Marx, for example, drew on Malthus's analysis of under-consumption in his political economy, while Darwin's filiations with Malthus's ideas underwent complex changes over time and were carefully stage-managed as he sought acceptance in the Victorian scientific community. Throughout the 200 years since Malthus wrote, simple responses of acceptance or rejection have shaded into more nuanced intellectual engagements.

New Perspectives on Malthus traces new lines of scholarly surprise in understanding the ideas and legacy of Thomas Robert Malthus. The essays in Part I show that there are still important new things to say about where Malthus's ideas came from, about his intentions in framing them and about the ways in which they were understood and debated in his own age. The essays in Part II show new aspects of the vast panoply of responses to Malthus over the past two centuries. In so doing, the essays in *New Perspectives on Malthus* inevitably both chart the peaks of Malthusian scholarship and, *ipso facto*, add new ones to the landscape. And yet, of course, this book can inevitably only make selected surveys of the range of Malthus scholarship. As such, the aims of this introduction are threefold. First, to provide a simple introduction to Malthus's ideas and their evolution over time. Second, to give a sense of the broad swathe of reactions to Malthus's ideas over the decades down to the present. These two parts, therefore, provide the reader with an inevitably brief small-scale map of Malthus's ideas and their reception, of the broader landscape into which the subsequent essays can be placed as more detailed, large-scale charts of various peaks in Malthusian scholarship. And lying behind all of this is the third issue, which will be addressed in concluding this introduction: why, exactly, has Malthus had such a staggering impact on the ideas of his own age, on modern understandings of that age, and on every subsequent era down to our own?

Malthus's ideas: a small-scale map

Malthus tends to be memorialized as the first writer about population, a sobriquet as misleading as that which makes Samuel Johnson the first author of an English dictionary. As Ted McCormick charts, Malthus in fact stood on the shoulders of centuries of previous work on demography and its implications for statecraft, most notably drawing on a complex set of debates in the generation immediately preceding him. Since the first appearance of Malthus's *Essay* in 1798, allegations have been made that Malthus plagiarized the ideas of Joseph Townsend's *A Dissertation on the*

Poor Laws (1786). As McCormick shows here and elsewhere, it is more plausible to suggest that Malthus drew on his predecessors but built a new argument, something the opening chapter of the *Essay* acknowledges as Malthus explains that his argument is 'not new' but draws on David Hume, Adam Smith and Robert Wallace.[3] And yet to understand why Malthus's contribution to debates about the nexus of population and politics became so notorious as to eclipse the work on which it drew and to which it contributed, thereby creating the misleading sense that Malthus was the father of demography, one needs to look both at the content of his *Essay* and at the heightened anxieties of the moment at which it emerged.

Malthus's *Essay* was published at the peak of the Irish Rebellion of 1798, this being the moment when English society faced the most serious threat it ever would of an invasion bringing the principles of the French Revolution to its shores. It was the counter-revolutionary ambitions of Malthus's *Essay* that gave it a notoriety no previous work about the politics of demography had achieved, ambitions that became clear by the end of an opening chapter advertising the book's achievement as being an 'argument [that] is conclusive against the perfectibility of the mass of mankind'.[4] Malthus hoped the conclusiveness of his argument would come from its logical construction. True to his mathematical training at Cambridge University, Malthus argued from a set of axioms, via empirical evidence for what he saw as quasi-Newtonian 'laws of nature,' to what he believed was an unavoidable conclusion whose acceptance would explode revolutionary utopianism.

Malthus's axioms are laid out in the opening chapter of the *Essay*: that 'food is necessary to the existence of man' and that 'the passion between the sexes is necessary, and will remain nearly in its present state'.[5] The second of these axioms was highly controversial because radical writers, most notably William Godwin who was Malthus's prime target in the *Essay*, had argued that sexual desire would wither with the progress of civilization. And yet, as Gregory Claeys shows in this volume, Malthus's relationship with Godwin's ideas was not one of mere hostility, the filiations between their ideas on utility and social productivity being far more nuanced. Taking Malthus's axioms as read, they do not in and of themselves create a problem until the addition of a second set of arguments; namely, the claim that population tends to grow at a faster rate than food supply: 'population, when unchecked, increases in a geometrical ratio. Subsistence increases only in an arithmetical ratio. A slight acquaintance with numbers will show the immensity of the first power in comparison of the second.'[6] If one accepts this imbalance between the rates of increase of population and food, an ongoing societal problem has been uncovered, namely how to balance population and food resources. And yet Malthus was aware that his two ratios needed to be substantiated by evidence. For this reason, he presented evidence from around the globe to show that at each stage of social development one found evidence of a need to control population increase to make it balance with available food resources. Malthus envisaged this control in terms of what he called 'checks' and singled out two types. 'Positive' checks were natural forces that adjusted population growth downward and thereby brought it back in line with available food resources, these checks being famine, disease and warfare. It was here that Malthus pioneered the naturalistic explanation of famine as the product of food shortage that was one of his most important legacies and whose modern ramifications are traced in David Nally's chapter in this volume. 'Preventive' checks were human or social forces that achieved the same balancing act by less violent means; Malthus was aware that with societal advance people had come to limit procreation by delaying marriage or by practising sexual restraint within marriage, each of which actions would reduce fertility levels. He was also aware that families could seek to balance family size against standard of living, choosing to reduce the number of children they had to ensure their relative affluence. Preventive checks, of course, opened up a social interpretation of food scarcity, the other side of the genealogy Nally traces, and one that is normally posited as a critique of Malthusian reasoning however much it was in fact imbricated in his argument from the outset. On Malthus's account, over time preventive checks had become more important and ensured that the aegis of positive checks was weakened. Even allowing for social advance, however, the world Malthus inhabited was one where poor harvests could lead to food riots such as those that wracked Britain in the 1790s, and where epidemics and 'sickly seasons' were occasional reminders of the more than merely vestigial power of positive checks.

Malthus had laid out his conceptual and historical case about the propensity of population to outstrip food resources by the conclusion of Chapter 7; the rest of the *Essay* went on to plot the political, economic and religious consequences of accepting his argument. We can identify four main lines Malthus pursued. First, and as already implied, the principle of population exposed the optimistic manifestos of radical personal and societal development that had been flowing from those enthused by the French Revolution as mere delusions. Second, Malthus saw in his principle of population grounds for scepticism about the ways in which poverty was alleviated by the state.[7] For the better part of two centuries, the Elizabethan Poor Laws had operated in England to relieve extreme distress when the price of bread rose above a certain threshold. Malthus had two objections to the Poor Laws. First, he argued that 'they may be said ... in some measure to create the poor which they maintain'.[8] The Poor Laws decoupled the ability to have children from the ability to support them as the state would aid *in extremis*, and as such weakened the power of Malthus's preventive check, the exercise of foresight in determining when and whether to have children. Reducing the power of the preventive check de facto increased the number of children people had, hence the claim that the Poor Laws created those they supported. Second, Malthus noted that giving the poor more money to buy food could not in the short term increase food supply and therefore would lead the price of foodstuffs to increase. Such increases would lead those who were just above poverty to be drawn into a reliance on poor relief: as a result the Poor Laws 'may have alleviated a little the intensity of individual misfortune, [but] they have spread the general evil over a much larger surface'.[9] For these reasons, Malthus advocated the abolition of the Poor Laws and their replacement with a system of workhouses where people would labour for their entitlement to food. He also argued that state incentives should be focused on the increase of tillage and food production as only an increase in food supply could alleviate want rather than redistribute it. It was Malthus's ideas about poverty and the Poor Laws that galvanized opponents in a spectrum from Christian moralists through Romantic poets to Karl Marx to vitriolic denunciations of Malthus in various idioms, and yet as Niall O' Flaherty shows in his chapter, Malthus's ideas about poverty evolved to be far more nuanced and systematic than their critics allowed and were anything but mere cronyism towards the wealthy.

Attending to food production as the core of economic wellbeing also explained the third consequence Malthus detected in his principle of population, the need to correct Adam Smith's definition of wealth.[10] Malthus came in the generation after Smith's epochal economic treatise, *The Wealth of Nations* (1776), and was a lifelong supporter of, and advocate for, Smith's ideas. Malthus was as keenly aware as Smith that he wrote at a time of massive change in the economic structure of British society, as agrarian production came to be far less dominant in the face of rapidly expanding commercial and manufacturing sectors. And yet for Malthus, far more than Smith, this diversification of the economy was not an unbridled good if it did not bolster food supply. Just as the Poor Laws could not increase the quantity of food, so for Malthus merely monetary wealth of the sort that manufacture and trade could create might only lead to increased nominal wealth. In taking this line, Malthus was in some ways drawing on the earlier economic ideas of the Physiocrats, but he was more immediately drawing out a consequence of his own principle of population: if food is necessary for survival, only the production of more food can create the conditions in which more people can survive, in which the same number can survive in greater comfort or in which both processes can take place simultaneously. This question of the relationship in Malthus's work between political economy and its grounding in the physical environment is taken up by Fredrik Albritton Jonsson's essay in this volume.

The fourth and final set of consequences Malthus drew from his principle of population related to religion, the topic addressed in the final two chapters of the *Essay*.[11] For an ordained clergyman to see in God's dispensation to humankind a system of laws that could, in Malthus's own words, 'be fairly resolved into misery and vice'[12] was to pose a dilemma. How could the existence of a wise and good Christian God be reconciled with such laws of population? In a response that many would condemn on its publication but that derived from the rationalist Anglicanism of his Cambridge education, Malthus argued that as 'the first great awakeners of the mind seem to be the wants of the body',[13] so the principle of population in fact spurred the individual to greater efforts and societies in aggregate to civilizational advance. As such, the misery and vice of the principle of population 'produces much partial evil; but ... a great overbalance of good'.[14] The human ability to plan coupled to nature's niggardliness meant that for Malthus a timeworn truism had new truth to it: 'necessity has been with great truth called the mother of invention'.[15] There is no evidence that the closing theological chapters of the *Essay* were mere 'window-dressing'. On the contrary, they appear to have been a deeply felt expression of Malthus's beliefs, and yet he removed them from all the later editions as they were received with great nervousness on publication. Where the intention of the *Essay* had been to oppose revolutionary fervour at the crisis point that was 1798, the final two chapters smacked too strongly of a similar radicalism in the eyes of many readers.

The *Essay* made Malthus's name as a writer and yet he was clearly dissatisfied with it from the outset. One of the first traces we have of Malthus after the publication of the *Essay* is a letter to his father requesting a raft of books about demography and an array of travel writings.[16] No sooner was the *Essay* published, then, than Malthus started working to deepen his knowledge and strengthen his arguments. And the trip Malthus took with friends to Scandinavia in 1799, while clearly recreational, was also part of this project. Malthus's travel diaries are filled with comments on crop yields, food prices and manufacturing, and as such they betray the interests of the economist on the road. Malthus also showed himself keenly alert to the impact of weather on social and economic activity (hereby reverting to the environmental groundings of economic activity), travelling as he did in the wake of the exceptionally hard winter of 1798, the consequence of which had been to test preventive checks to the limit and even see a reversion to positive checks in some places. Above all, however, what is important about the Scandinavian travel diaries is that they witness a transition from Malthus the abstract philosopher of social laws to Malthus the empirical observer more concerned with the nuance and complexity of the links between population, production and policy than with simplifying them for political purposes.[17]

The first published product of Malthus's increasing preoccupation with the complex interactions of nature, politics and economic activity was a pamphlet on the heated debates about high food prices in the England to which Malthus returned from his continental sojourn. Malthus's *Investigation of the Causes of the Present High Price of Provisions* (1800) might seem a continuation of the anti-revolutionary rhetoric of the 1798 *Essay*, arguing as it does that high prices are not due to landowners or merchants storing food to cash in on high prices by artificially limiting supply. On the contrary, for Malthus 'the sole cause' of prices having been inflated so greatly relative to the dip in food supply is the impact of the Poor Laws artificially inflating the entitlements of the poor. And yet it is at this point that the more nuanced approach of the later Malthus is witnessed. For all his continued theoretical hostility to the Poor Laws – '[which] I certainly do most heartily condemn' – he is prepared to accept that pragmatically in the context of 1800 they have alleviated extreme need and that this is a material good. This essay was also Malthus's most sophisticated exposition of his ideas about the naturalistic origins of food scarcity, a theme that echoed down to the twentieth century, as David Nally chronicles. At the end of the *Investigation*, Malthus advertised that he was working on a new edition of the *Essay* and that it would be made 'more worthy of the public attention, by applying the principle directly and exclusively to the existing state of society, and endeavouring to illustrate the power and universality of its operation from the best authenticated accounts that we have of the state of other countries'.[18]

In a sense, Malthus somewhat misled his audience by retaining the title from 1798 for the so-called 'great quarto' or 1803 *Essay*, for it was stretching credibility to see it as merely a new edition of an extant book. The topic remained the same, as did the central focus on the principle of population, its history and socio-economic ramifications, and yet the 1803 *Essay* was four times longer than its predecessor, being a massive tome of 200,000 words despite the removal of the theological sections from 1798. Taken as a whole, the changes Malthus made took the *Essay* of 1803 in the direction of a detailed empirical investigation of the principle of population and away from being an abstract argument about Newtonian laws of social mechanics. Malthus's advertisement of his intention to produce a new version of the *Essay* as quoted above from the *Investigation* was extremely fair in its foreshadowing of the new balance of that work, picking out as it did two key changes. First, just as Malthus had said he would use the best accounts, so Books I and II of the 1803 *Essay* conducted an exhaustive survey of the operation of the principle of population, both in 'the less civilised Parts of the World, and in Past Times' (as the heading to Book I had it), and then in the 'different States of Modern Europe' in Book II, starting from Malthus's own experiences of Norway and Sweden before proceeding around the continent and ending with Britain. These two books, far longer than the entirety of the 1798 *Essay*, replaced the short 'global tour' of the first edition and evidenced Malthus's longstanding interest in historical and geographical writing. Taken together, Books I and II were the illustration of the principle of population 'from authenticated accounts' that the *Investigation* had promised. These sections of the 1803 *Essay* have been neglected in terms of their argumentation and implications by scholars, a neglect rectified in this volume by Alison Bashford and Joyce Chaplin's engagement with Malthus's treatment of colonial and indigenous knowledge. The second key change for the 1803 *Essay* was its greater attention to the political and economic implications of the principle of population for modern societies. While the *Essay* still criticized Godwin and thereby continued to betray its genesis in the tensions of 1798, this was overwhelmed by greatly expanded discussions of the definition of wealth (itself a continuation of Malthus's jousting with Adam Smith), of the impact – baleful or otherwise – of the Corn Laws on food supply, by the new and somewhat less astringent approach to the Poor Laws that O' Flaherty analyses in this volume and, most importantly, by a more sanguine analysis of the power of the preventive check to population. On this last topic, Malthus conceded that he had been overly pessimistic in 1798; European demographic data showed the power of moral restraint and economically motivated forethought in checking fertility. While the power of population to outstrip food supply remained a basic predicate of Malthus's reasoning, he accepted that in modern European societies, the preventive check was effective in staving off the imbalance of food and population on a long-term basis. As such, Malthus was reaching towards an awareness of an epochal change in the interrelation of population growth and economic growth whose reality economic historians have endorsed statistically.

Malthus spent the rest of his life adjusting details of the argumentation of the 1803 great quarto, with further editions emerging in 1806, 1807, 1817 and 1826.[19] After 1803, and building on his reputation as the foremost political economist in the generation after Adam Smith, Malthus engaged in pamphlet commentary on the key economic issues of the age, each of them deriving from the interests he had first addressed in the 1798 *Essay* – issues around bullion and whether Britain should go back onto the Gold Standard, the economic condition of Ireland and the likely impact of emigration on that condition, and the definition of value and the valuation of commodities. In many ways, the most highly charged issue Malthus addressed was the Corn Laws, a topic about which he wrote two pamphlets. The Corn Laws were a system of state intervention in the operation of the market, and to that extent were akin to the Poor Laws, and yet Malthus was far more positive about their worth. The reason for this lay in his continued belief that the land and its produce was the only true source of real wealth. Where many liberals, following what they saw as Adam Smith's lead, argued that the Corn Laws were an expensive and inefficient intervention in the operation of market forces, Malthus argued for their importance on two grounds. First, and as he said in his 1814 pamphlet on the topic, 'security is of still more importance than wealth'. The maximization of nominal wealth was, for Malthus, meaningless if it endangered our ability to feed our population; political embargoes, warfare and the increased wealth of corn exporting countries such as the USA and Russia could all block food supplies flowing to Britain and at that point the country would face crippling food scarcities regardless of its ability to pay for food. And resting behind this concern with food security was the second reason to support the Corn Laws; without food security there could be no political security. The turmoil of 1798 that had first engaged Malthus stayed with him as a concern throughout his life; as he put it in 1815, the labouring classes are 'the foundation on which the whole [social] fabric rests'.[20] And if those classes could not feed themselves – something that both the increased price volatility of a free market in corn and the increased vulnerability to political and economic changes elsewhere in the market rendered more likely – then the maintenance of peace and prosperity could be endangered by loosening the protectionism the Corn Laws enshrined.

Malthus's interventions on the Corn Laws once again pointed to his caution about markets. And this caution was also a strong vein running through his final great work, *Principles of Political Economy* (1820). *Principles* addressed many of the same themes as the *Essay* but from a different angle: Malthus argued that the *Essay* had 'endeavoured to trace the causes which practically keep down the population of a country to the level of its actual supplies', while his *Principles* aimed to show 'what are the causes which chiefly influence these supplies, or call the powers of production forth into the shape of increasing wealth'.[21] At its simplest, then, Malthus depicted the *Essay* as focusing on the demand side of the interrelationship between food and population while *Principles* attended to the supply side. While the *Principles* is Malthus's great engagement with the economists of his day, especially David Ricardo, what is most lastingly important about it is its claim to make Malthus one of the first great analysts of market failures. Emerging as it did after a long period of economic depression in the aftermath of the Napoleonic Wars, *Principles* was preoccupied with the fact that demand and supply could be chronically out of kilter. Emerging from Malthus's analysis of the Corn Laws and the Poor Laws was an awareness that a mere need for goods was not synonymous with an effective demand for them. And likewise from the supply side, the mere existence of un- or under-utilized resources in terms of land or labour did not mean they would be used. Finally, and putting these two things together, one could have a need for goods alongside underutilized resources, but a market would not put these two things together productively without the lubrication of effective demand.

The last decade or so of Malthus's life saw him propelled to public fame. Thus he was twice called to give evidence to parliamentary Select Committees, one concerning machinery and its impact on the labouring classes in 1824 and one concerning the likely impact of a scheme of Irish emigration on that country's economic prospects in 1827. In the same decade, Malthus was a founding member of the Political Economy Club, a dining society that has been seen as the first attempt to give some scholarly coherence to the study of economics; was elected as a Fellow of the Royal Society; and was given a stipendiary prize by the Royal Society of Literature. In the final year of his life, Malthus was also instrumental in the establishment of the Statistical Society of London (the forerunner of today's Royal Statistical Society) and his name was inextricably linked with the passing of the New Poor Law, although his actual influence on that law was indirect at best.[22]

Malthus's reception: a small-scale map

Malthus's ideas attracted support and vilification in equal and extreme measure in his own lifetime and this capacity to polarize has remained at the core of his reception ever since. Spanning the last years of Malthus's life and the early Victorian age, among his most important defenders was Harriet Martineau whose *Illustrations of Political Economy* (1834), as she put it in her *Autobiography*, 'exemplify Malthus's doctrine'.²³ Martineau's tracts were remarkably popular in their own age, their monthly instalments selling at least 10,000 copies and they are at the heart of Ella Dzelzainis's examination of Malthus's impact on the literary treatment of the Condition-of-England question. On the other side from Martineau was William Cobbett who denounced 'the monster MALTHUS' in his most famous work, *Rural Rides* (1830).²⁴ Charles Dickens's evocation of Malthus in *A Christmas Carol* (1843) was equally scathing albeit less acerbic. In the opening stave of the book, Scrooge is visited by two 'portly gentlemen, pleasant to behold', who ask him for a little Christian charity for the poor. Scrooge replies that he already pays towards the workhouse and that this is sufficient. When pressed that many would rather die than be consigned to the workhouse, Scrooge's infamous reply is couched in deliberately Malthusian terms: ' "If they would rather die", said Scrooge, "they had better do it, and decrease the surplus population." '²⁵

Perhaps the most sophisticated and violent response to Malthus that originated in his lifetime but ran on for decades afterwards was that of the English Romantics.²⁶ In 1798, as Malthus produced the *Essay*, Coleridge and Wordsworth published their *Lyrical Ballads*, a poetic manifesto for Romanticism that, in its celebration of the numinous and nutritive status of nature, was set on a collision course with the Malthusian image of nature as niggardly. It was the 1803 edition of Malthus's *Essay*, however, that witnessed that collision, Coleridge scribbling on a copy of 'the stupid Ignorance of the Man!' while his friend the poet Robert Southey added tersely that Malthus was a 'fool', an 'Ass' and a 'booby'.²⁷ And if Southey's comment in a letter that Malthus was a 'voider of menstrual pollution' might be seen as a private excess, in a published essay of 1812 he called Malthus's work 'a colliquative diarrhoea of the intellect'.²⁸ Southey was the first Romantic to take up the cudgels against Malthus publicly, but he was by no means the last, William Hazlitt penning a 400-page *Reply to the Essay on Population* (1807). The later generation of Romantics shared this hostility to Malthus, Shelley dismissing him as 'a priest of course, for his

doctrines are those of a eunuch and of a tyrant', and Byron targeting satir-
ical flak at him in the English cantos of *Don Juan*.[29] Victorian social critics
influenced by the Romantic vision took on the hostility to Malthus. Thus
Thomas Carlyle coined the denigration of economics as the 'dismal science' in direct reference to Malthus: 'the controversies on Malthus and
the "Population Principle", "Preventive check" and so forth, with which
the public ear has been deafened for a long while, are indeed sufficiently
mournful. Dreary, stolid, dismal, without all hope for this world or the
next.'[30] In the generation after Carlyle, John Ruskin constructed a very
similar criticism of Malthus: 'in all the ranges of human thought I know
none so melancholy as the speculations of political economists on the
population question.'[31]

The force that tied the criticisms of Coleridge and Carlyle was a
Christian one that saw in Malthus's vision of the inevitability of human
suffering a fundamental impiety. The greatest secularizing project of the
nineteenth century, the political economy of Marx and Engels, shared a
hostility of equal vigour towards Malthus. It was in the 1860s that Marx
levelled his sights on Malthus's *Essay* in *Capital*, dismissing it as 'nothing
more than a schoolboyish, superficial plagiary', the fame of which was
'due solely to party interest' – Malthus's 'party' being that of his own class
as a 'parson of the English State Church'. For Marx, Malthus had correctly
seen the 'disharmonies' capitalism created by its inevitable tendency to
cycles of boom and bust, but by packaging this as a law of nature, he had
mystified its social origins. Engels, in a letter of 1881, looked forward to the
day when communism arrived, convinced such a society would be able to
'regulate the production of human beings ... without difficulty'.[32] To the
extent that this hostility towards Malthusian reasoning became embedded
in the state socialisms of the twentieth-century world, it became important to global population debates. This is particularly apparent in the case
of China where Mao in 1949 dismissed the idea that 'food cannot keep
up with increases in population' as 'the absurd argument of bourgeois
Western economists like Malthus', preferring instead the slogan 'Ren Duo
Liliang Da' ('With many people, strength is great'). And while the Great
Chinese Famine of 1958–62 and its death toll of 45 million or more cannot
be directly attributed to this policy, it was certainly instrumental in the
emergence of a far more stringently Malthusian policy of family limitation in the form of the one-child policy thereafter.[33]

If Romantics and Marxists alike were hostile to Malthus, two other
great strands of nineteenth-century thought were explicit in acknowledging their indebtedness to Malthus: Darwinism and economics.

Commemorating the fiftieth anniversary of the publication of *Origin of Species*, Alfred Russel Wallace claimed that the impact of Malthus's ideas on himself and Darwin 'was analogous to that of friction upon the specially prepared match, producing that flash of insight which led us immediately to the simple but universal law of the "survival of the fittest," as the long sought *effective* cause of the continuous modification and adaptations of living things'. Darwin made similar if more plain comments in his *Autobiography* about reading Malthus in 1838 'for amusement' but finding here 'a theory by which to work'.[34] That this was not a mere retrospective fabrication by Darwin and Wallace is made clear by a perusal of Darwin's notebooks, which show that he did in fact read Malthus as he was drawn into the circle of the ardent Malthusian Harriet Martineau.[35] Malthus is also directly referenced in *Origin of Species* (1859), the struggle for existence being styled as 'the doctrine of Malthus applied with manifold force to the whole animal and vegetable kingdoms'.[36] And yet how Malthus was to be read in evolutionary terms was the subject of great controversy, even between Wallace and Darwin, and it is to the landscape of this contestation that Piers Hale attends in his chapter in this volume. Darwin read Malthus's perpetual struggle between the power of population and the abilities of food to sustain it as still active in the human world, as had Malthus himself, where Wallace argued that Malthus's ratios still applied in the natural world but had been superseded in the human world by the powers of our reasoning. In this, Wallace was true to the socialist utopianism he had imbibed as a child and points the way towards various 'non-Malthusian' versions of evolution that circulated in the late nineteenth and early twentieth centuries.[37]

Darwin went on to extend his vision of natural selection to human beings more explicitly in his later writings, notably *The Descent of Man* (1871), and in this he was part of a far broader current of thinkers applying evolutionary ideas to mankind. This set of doctrines is often dubbed 'social Darwinism', and then and now Malthus has often been deemed its progenitor. Indeed, it has even been suggested that 'social Darwinism' is a misleading label, and that 'scientific Malthusianism' may more accurately encapsulate the efforts to apply evolutionary ideas to society.[38] This application of Darwinian ideas back into the human world from which they had initially sprung in Malthus's thought led to two main currents of debate either side of 1900 that Malthus himself could not have anticipated. First, there was the emergence of groups advocating contraception as a preventive check to ease the pressure of population growth. These groups were often labelled 'Malthusian', the adjective coming to be a synonym for 'contraception' from the 1870s despite the fact that Malthus as an eighteenth-century clergyman had viewed such methods of birth control with horror, only ever alluding to them by oblique reference to 'improper arts'.[39] The Malthusian League in Britain, for example, was founded in 1877 and was extraordinarily active, printing an estimated three million pamphlets between 1879 and 1921, publishing a regular journal entitled the *Malthusian*, and encouraging the formation of sister societies across the globe, an enumeration of 1911 suggesting that Malthusian Leagues now existed in 'Holland, Germany, France, Austria, Spain, Brazil, Belgium, Switzerland, Cuba and Portugal'.[40] It was no accident then, that when Aldous Huxley imagined his dystopian future in *Brave New World* (1932), its mode of contraception was called a 'Malthusian belt'. It is one of history's terminological ironies that Malthus's name became a global brand in the service of a doctrine he abhorred in his own age. The second set of ideas was at some odds with the doctrine of Malthusianism, arguing as it did that societies must encourage selective breeding to ensure that evolutionarily favourable human traits were preserved. In the struggle to survive, only those who demonstrated advanced intelligence should be encouraged to breed. As such, the poor should be treated as Malthusian Leagues across the globe suggested; that is, encouraged to use contraception or, in more extreme arguments, forcibly prevented from procreating by sterilization and the like,[41] but a different approach was needed for the rich and the intelligent, encouraging them to procreate. This doctrine, known as eugenics, was most clearly advocated by Darwin's cousin, Francis Galton, from the 1870s, and was hostile to Malthusianism, which it saw as recklessly indiscriminate in encouraging the more developed groups to limit their fertility. And yet eugenicists also claimed Malthus as their intellectual forbearer, notably on the basis of his comments on selective breeding in Chapter 9 of the 1798 *Essay*, Galton calling him 'the rise of a morning star before a day of free social investigation', while in 1923 the first issue of the *Annals of Eugenics*, founded by Galton's pupil and successor Karl Pearson, lauded Malthus as 'Strewer of the Seed which reached its Harvest in the Ideas of Charles Darwin and Francis Galton'.[42] Well into the twentieth century then, whichever side of arguments about population control and social Darwinism one took, Malthus remained a key inspiration, striking the match as assuredly as he had done for Darwin himself.

Throughout this ferment of debates to which Malthus's ideas had been subjected in the century after his death, economists had unsurprisingly remained respectful of Malthus as one of the trio of classical economists who had given shape to their discipline. Indeed, the great nineteenth-century economists – John Stuart Mill, Stanley Jevons and Alfred Marshall – all made positive reference to Malthus's demographic work. And yet none saw Malthus as a vital interlocutor as had the Darwinians, Romantics and Marxists, for all their mixed response to him. It was only with the emergence of John Maynard Keynes that Malthus was once again deemed relevant. Malthus has been described by Keynes's biographer as his 'favourite economist', a judgement that was more wittily endorsed by Keynes's Cambridge undergraduates who nicknamed him 'Jeremiah Malthus'.[43] Above all, in two sharply separate engagements with Malthus in the aftermath of World War I and then in the Great Depression, Keynes would make Malthus relevant to the modern era, reworking the meaning of Malthus's ideas to accord with the needs of the times as he perceived them. In 1919 in *Economic Consequences of the Peace*, Keynes argued that the trauma of World War I could be viewed in Malthusian terms as a struggle for scarce resources created by population pressure in Germany. A decade later, in the throes of the Depression, Keynes turned again to Malthus, but this time to Malthus the economist rather than Malthus the demographer, arguing that Malthus had shown why economies fail to generate demand even when there is spare labour and underutilized capital in his *Principles of Political Economy*. In 1933, Keynes passed a celebrated judgement that would be echoed closely in his *General Theory of Employment, Interest and Money* (1936), perhaps the most politically influential economic tract of the twentieth century: 'if only Malthus, instead of Ricardo, had been the parent stem from which nineteenth-century economics proceeded, what a much wiser and richer place the world would be today.' The core insight that Keynes offered to substantiate this claim was Malthus's discovery of the principle of effective demand, which would become the lynchpin of Keynes's *General Theory*.[44]

Keynes died in 1946, just as his ideas were becoming the founding tenets of government fiscal policies across the advanced world. Interest in Malthus remained undimmed, but shifted back to Malthus the demographer. In particular, economists, scholars, novelists and ecologists started to speak of a parallel between the atomic bombs that had ended World War II and a 'population bomb' that needed to be defused. As the philosopher Bertrand Russell noted in 1964 in what was already becoming a hackneyed formula, there were 'two antithetical dangers', those of the H-bomb and of the population bomb, continuing that, although antithetical, they were linked: 'nothing is more likely to lead to an H-bomb war than the threat of universal destitution through over-population.'[45] Behind this lay a fear of a possible Malthusian third world war generated by a global struggle for access to food and resources, exactly the understanding of World War I offered by Keynes half a century earlier, a fear that united governments and the global philanthropic foundations that David Nally scrutinizes in this volume. Especially important to the so-called 'neo-Malthusianism' that emerged from this in the 1960s and 1970s was a new ecological perspective, arguing that the sheer proliferation of human beings on the planet would lead to the breakdown of the ecological systems on which life on earth was predicated, this being a new and ultimate form of Malthusian positive check. The most famous proponent of ideas of ecological neo-Malthusianism was (and is) Paul Ehrlich, whose 1968 book *The Population Bomb*, a work dubbed 'the most famous population treatise since Malthus', sold in the millions and catapulted its author to fame via numerous television appearances.[46] Ehrlich's high-flown rhetoric attracted implacable critics such as Julian Simon who in their rebuttals of neo-Malthusianism ensured that Malthus remained a household name during the postwar decades.[47] And key to Malthus's visibility in this era was the emergence of mass market editions of his *Essay*, the topic that Robert Mayhew addresses in his chapter that seeks to question the lines of connection between Malthus, neo-Malthusianism and the rise of modern environmentalism.

All of the strands of postwar Malthusianism just mentioned – development economics, global population policies, ecological doom-saying – remain active in our age. Thus Jared Diamond's controversial *Collapse* (2005) framed the Rwandan conflict as a Malthusian war of resource scarcity in the context of mushrooming population growth.[48] Similarly, with still-rapid population growth in many parts of the world and a reverse demographic decline in many developed nations, scholars and political analysts have been quick to speak of 'new population bombs' ready to explode in our contemporary world, ascribing political and religious fundamentalism and radicalization to this demographic juxtaposition in trying to explain the events of 9/11.[49] And yet Malthus's ideas are also being recycled and reused in new ways today, which are canvassed in Hoff and Robertson's chapter. In particular, where Ehrlich and his critics focused on whether population growth would lead to ecological catastrophe and resource depletion, recent decades have seen the terms of debate shift to the question of whether both population increase and escalating per capita consumption will lead to Malthusian positive checks via climate change undermining the habitability of the earth as a home for humankind. This vision received global attention thanks to a 2009 speech by the United

Kingdom's chief scientific advisor, Sir John Beddington, anticipating 'a perfect storm of global events', which led, as he said, to people asking 'am I now a second Thomas Malthus?'[50]

Alps on Alps arise

From Byron to Beddington, from poets to scientists, from the French Revolution to our present-day anxiety about climate change, Malthus has retained his vitality, his ability to inspire and infuriate. Why has the intellectual history of the past two centuries been so densely marked with peaks of Malthusian interest? While no definitive answer can be offered, we can perhaps see in Malthus a threefold significance facing towards the past, towards his own age and towards ours. First, on the analysis pioneered by Wrigley and Clark, Malthus was essentially right in his analysis of the functional interaction between population, resources and wealth for all pre-industrial societies predicated on organic energy as opposed to fossil fuels.[51] As such, students of all the societal formations until Malthus's own age are indebted to Malthus's analysis. And yet as Wrigley and Clark note, there is a certain irony that Malthus was the anatomist of a socio-economic system that was being eclipsed even in his own lifetime; the owl of Minerva flew at dusk. Malthus's fame or indeed notoriety in his own age rested not on whether he was 'right' about its socio-economic dynamics, but on the exact moment at which he made his intervention about population and politics, the high point of post-revolutionary anxieties that was 1798. While drawing on an established body of demographic discussion, Malthus catapulted it and himself to prominence by applying it to build a counter-revolutionary argument. And the reception of this argument in his own age by radicals such as Godwin and Cobbett ensured that Malthus was at the heart of debates about politics, population and economic policy throughout his lifetime, his later editions of the *Essay*, his *Principles of Political Economy* and his other pamphlets showing a flexible mind keenly debating the most important issues of the age. Malthus then, was quite simply one of the most important intellectuals of his era, a fact that is often obscured by the obliquity that surrounded his name. Finally, why have Malthus's ideas remained a touchstone of debate throughout the past two centuries? One reason must be the adjectival mutations of his name in the service of ideas he did not hold; if 'Malthusian' as a euphemism for contraception made Malthus a household name in the decades either side of 1900, 'neo-Malthusian' performed the same function for three or more decades after World War II. And yet it would be wrong to frame Malthus's enduring relevance in purely nominal terms. On the contrary, behind the recycling of Malthus's name to new causes rests a far more important substantive perpetuation of his ideas. For even if Malthus anatomized a socio-economic system in its death throes, this does not entail the irrelevance of his ideas to industrial and post-industrial societies. On the contrary, Malthus in the *Essay* and his *oeuvre* more generally built the discursive parameters of modern social discussion, bringing into one frame of reference as he did population, economics, resources and politics. Different elements of this nexus have been highlighted in different engagements with Malthus over the past two centuries, with Keynes responding to Malthus the economist, for example, while the neo-Malthusians of the past few decades meshed his ideas about population with an ecological understanding of the concept of resources. Examples could be multiplied, but Malthus's enduring relevance emerges from his drawing of these ideas into a systematic, interlinked frame of reference, and from the flexibility with which his delineation of these categories has proved capable of redeployment and redefinition in different ages.

Giving an address in Cambridge on the centenary of Malthus's death in 1934, Keynes closed by suggesting that 'a century hence, here in his Alma Mater, we shall commemorate him with undiminished regard'.[52] As we mark the quarter millennium since Malthus's birth, there is no reason to gainsay Keynes's judgement about Malthus's enduring importance both as a locus of historical inquiry and as a touchstone for modern debates, only to suggest that it can be extended still further into the future.

Notes

1 Alexander Pope, *An Essay on Criticism*, lines 219–232, in John Butt (ed.), *The Poems of Alexander Pope* (London: Methuen, 1963), p. 151.
2 John Harrison *et al.*, *The Malthus Library Catalogue* (Oxford: Pergamon Press, 1983), pp. 136–7 lists nine separate sets of works by Pope in Malthus's library. Malthus cites the *Essay on Man* three times in his 1798 *Essay* in Chapters 9, 18 and 19: Thomas Robert Malthus, *An Essay on the Principle of Population*, in E.A. Wrigley and David Souden (eds.), *The Works of Thomas Robert Malthus*, 8 vols. (London: Pickering and Chatto, 1986), vol. 1, pp. 62, 122 and 137. Further references in this chapter are to this edition.
3 Malthus, Essay, p. 7.
4 Malthus, *Essay*, p. 10.
5 Ibid., p. 8.
6 Ibid., p. 9.
7 On this question generally, see Gareth Stedman Jones, *An End to Poverty? A Historical Debate* (London: Profile Books, 2004).

8 Malthus, *Essay*, p. 33.

9 Ibid., p. 30.

10 For Malthus's ideas as an economist, see Samuel Hollander, *The Economics of Thomas Robert Malthus* (Toronto: University of Toronto Press, 1997). For those ideas in the context of political economy, see Donald Winch, *Riches and Poverty: An Intellectual History of Political Economy in Britain, 1750–1834* (Cambridge: Cambridge University Press, 1996).

11 On Malthus and religion see A.M.C. Waterman, *Revolution, Economics and Religion: Christian Political Economy, 1798–1833* (Cambridge: Cambridge University Press, 1991).

12 Malthus, *Essay*, p. 38.

13 Ibid., p. 124.

14 Ibid., p. 126.

15 Ibid., p. 125.

16 John Pullen and Trevor Hughes Parry (eds), 2 vols. *T.R. Malthus: The Unpublished Papers in the Collection of Kanto Gakuen University* (Cambridge: Cambridge University Press, 1997–2004), vol. 1, pp. 63–5.

17 For which see Patricia James (ed.) *The Travel Diaries of T.R. Malthus* (Cambridge: Cambridge University Press, 1966).

18 Wrigley and Souden, *Works of Malthus*, vol. 7, pp. 5–18, quotes at pp. 6, 13 and 18.

19 For all these editions, see Patricia James's variorum edition of the Essay (Cambridge: Cambridge University Press, 1989).

20 Wrigley and Souden, *Works of Malthus*, vol. 7, pp. 100 and 162.

21 T.R. Malthus, *Principles of Political Economy*, ed. John Pullen, 2 vols. (Cambridge: Cambridge University Press for the Royal Economic Society, 1989), vol. 1, p. 344.

22 See Peter Mandler, 'Tories and Paupers: Christian Political Economy and the Making of the New Poor Law', *Historical Journal*, 33 (1990), 88–103; and Peter Mandler, 'The Making of the New Poor Law Redivivus', *Past and Present*, 117 (1987), 131–57.

23 See James P. Huzel, *The Popularization of Malthus in Early Nineteenth-Century England: Martineau, Cobbett and the Pauper Press* (Aldershot: Ashgate, 2006), pp. 55 and 57.

24 William Cobbett, *Rural Rides*, ed. George Woodcock (Harmondsworth: Penguin, 1985), p. 298.

25 Charles Dickens, *A Christmas Carol and Other Christmas Writings*, ed. Michael Slater (Harmondsworth: Penguin, 2003), pp. 38–9.

26 See Maureen McLane, *Romanticism and the Human Sciences: Poetry, Population and the Discourse of the Species* (Cambridge: Cambridge University Press, 2000) and Philip Connell, *Romanticism, Economics and the Question of 'Culture'* (Oxford: Oxford University Press, 2001).

27 Coleridge and Southey's reactions to the 1803 edition are contained in H.J. Jackson and George Whalley (eds.), *The Collected Works of Samuel Taylor Coleridge, Marginalia Volume III: Irving to Oxlee* (Princeton: Princeton University Press, 1992), pp. 805–9.

28 Kenneth Curry (ed.), *New Letters of Robert Southey*, 2 vols. (New York: Columbia University Press, 1965), vol. 1, p. 357. I quote Southey's 1812 *Quarterly Review* essay from Robert Southey, *Essays, Moral and Political*, 2 vols. (London: John Murray, 1832), vol. 1, p. 246.

29 Percy Shelley, *A Philosophical View of Reform*, ed. T. W. Rolleston (1914; reprinted Honolulu: University of Hawaii Press, 2004).

30 Thomas Carlyle, 'Chartism' (1839) in *Selected Writings*, ed. Alan Shelston (Harmondsworth: Penguin, 1971), p. 229.

31 John Ruskin, *Unto This Last and Other Writings*, ed. Clive Wilmer (London: Penguin, 1997), pp. 207–9 and 222–6.

32 All these comments can be found in Ronald Meek (ed.), *Marx and Engels on Malthus* (London: Lawrence and Wishart, 1953). For Marx and Engels's veiled indebtedness to Malthus, see John M. Sherwood, 'Engels, Marx, Malthus and the Machine', *American Historical Review*, 90 (1985), 837–65.

33 For the attack on Malthus, see Judith Shapiro, *Mao's War against Nature: Politics and the Environment in Revolutionary China* (Cambridge: Cambridge University Press, 2001), pp. 21–48, whence Mao is cited p. 31. Estimates of death tolls in the Great Chinese Famine are from Frank Dikötter, *Mao's Great Famine: The History of China's Most Devastating Catastrophe, 1958–1962* (New York: Walker, 2010).

34 Andrew Berry (ed.), *Infinite Tropics: An Alfred Russel Wallace Anthology* (London: Verso, 2003), pp. 68–9; Charles Darwin, *Autobiographies*, ed. Michael Neve and Sharon Messenger (Harmondsworth: Penguin, 2002), p. 72.

35 Adrian Desmond, *The Politics of Evolution: Morphology, Medicine and Reform in Radical London* (Chicago: University of Chicago Press, 1989).

36 Charles Darwin, *The Origin of Species*, ed. Jim Endersby (Cambridge: Cambridge University Press, 2009), p. 58.

37 For these debates in England, see Piers Hale, *Political Descent: Malthus, Mutualism and the Politics of Evolution in Victorian England* (Chicago: University of Chicago Press, 2014). For the Russian strand to the same debate, see Daniel Todes, *Darwin without Malthus: The Struggle for Existence in Russian Evolutionary Thought* (New York: Oxford University Press, 1989).

38 For social Darwinism as scientific Malthusianism, see Gregory Claeys, 'The "Survival of the Fittest" and the Origins of Social Darwinism', *Journal of the History of Ideas*, 61 (2000), 223–40.

39 Malthus's reference to improper arts is from the 1803 edition of the *Essay*: James (ed.), *Essay*, vol. 2, p. 97.

40 See Rosanna Ledbetter, *A History of the Malthusian League, 1877–1927* (Columbus: Ohio State University Press, 1976).

41 On which topic see Matthew Connelly, *Fatal Misconception: The Struggle to Control the World's Population* (Cambridge MA: Harvard University Press, 2008).

42 For Galton on Malthusianism and Malthus, see Richard Soloway, *Demography and Degeneration: Eugenics and the Declining Birthrate in Twentieth-Century Britain* (Chapel Hill: University of North Carolina Press, 1990), pp. 92–3. For

the *Annals of Eugenics*, see Allan Chase, *The Legacy of Malthus: The Social Costs of the New Scientific Racism* (New York: Knopf, 1977), pp. 82–3.

43 Robert Skidelsky, *John Maynard Keynes: The Economist as Saviour, 1920–1937* (London: Macmillan, 1992), p. 416; and John Toye, *Keynes on Population* (Oxford: Oxford University Press, 2000), p. 205.

44 John Maynard Keynes, 'Thomas Robert Malthus: The First of the Cambridge Economists' (1933), in *The Collected Writings of John Maynard Keynes: Volume 10: Essays in Biography* (London: Macmillan, 1972), pp. 71–103. Keynes's judgement of the relative merits of Ricardo and Malthus was rehearsed again in John Maynard Keynes, *The General Theory of Employment, Interest and Money* (London: Macmillan, 1936), p. 32.

45 Bertrand Russell, 'Population Pressure and War,' in Stuart Mudd (ed.), *The Population Crisis and the Use of World Resources* (The Hague: W. Junk, 1964), p. 1.

46 For Ehrlich as most influential population treatise since Malthus, see Derek S. Hoff, *The State and the Stork: The Population Debate and Policy Making in US History* (Chicago: University of Chicago Press, 2012), p. 165.

47 Paul Sabin, *The Bet: Paul Ehrlich, Julian Simon and Our Gamble Over Earth's Future* (New Haven: Yale University Press, 2013).

48 Jared Diamond, *Collapse: How Societies Choose to Fail or Survive* (London: Penguin, 2005), the chapter being entitled 'Malthus in Africa: Rwanda's Genocide'.

49 Jack Goldstone, 'The New Population Bomb: The Four Megatrends That Will Change the World', *Foreign Affairs*, 89 (2010), 31–43.

50 Beddington's speech is quoted from the online version, which can be accessed at www.govnet.co.uk/news/govnet/professor-sir-john-beddingtons-speech-at-sduk-09.

51 E.A. Wrigley, *Continuity, Chance and Change: The Character of the Industrial Revolution in England* (Cambridge: Cambridge University Press, 1988); Gregory Clark, *A Farewell to Alms: A Brief Economic History of the World* (Princeton: Princeton University Press, 2007).

52 John Maynard Keynes, 'Robert Malthus: A Centenary Allocution,' in *Collected Writings 10*, pp. 104–8 at p. 108.

PART I

Malthus in historical context

CHAPTER I

Who were the pre-Malthusians?

Ted McCormick

For historians versed in the nuances of context and contingency, this might seem an embarrassing question. Embedded in the practices of whiggish disciplinary history – as witness C.E. Strangeland's 1904 *Pre-Malthusian Doctrines of Population* – the very label 'pre-Malthusian' suggests a series of bungled attempts to grasp and express (or, conversely, to suppress) the fundamental truths that Malthus published in his *Essay* of 1798.[1] In Strangeland's case, the list is long indeed, beginning with primitive fertility cults and running through classical philosophers, medieval scholastics and early modern reason-of-state theorists, to English mercantilists and French Physiocrats. Still more significant is the object of Strangeland's history: *doctrines* of population. These doctrines emerge as a congeries of politics, science and ideology. They require a state conscious of itself over against the governed. They imply an understanding of the causes of human multiplication and a set of assumptions about the power, and the right, of the state to intervene therein. But they manifest themselves principally in an attitude toward population and population growth: either as an unmixed good, a measure of wealth and strength, or as potentially threatening to the welfare and stability of the state. Complex *doctrines* of population gain political and cultural traction by reflecting or sustaining rather simpler *attitudes* toward population. This is not Strangeland's argument, but it colours not only the story he chooses to tell but also the stories of population still told today.[2] To be a pre- (or anti- or neo-) Malthusian is, above all, to have a certain attitude toward population. By extension, it is to favour or oppose interventions that promote or hinder population growth.

The most common understanding of what it meant to be pre-Malthusian might thus be called 'attitudinal'. Within this frame, early modern thinkers – especially those who emphasized population as a source of labour or military strength – tend to be seen as favouring maximal growth in virtually all circumstances, or else as aiming at an optimum population or population density, somewhere above the then-perceived current level.[3] A similar demographic 'optimism', predicated on a different social vision, is seen to have tinged the writings of the Enlightened and revolutionary dreamers Malthus would confront at the end of the eighteenth century.[4] Since the *Essay*, on the other hand, 'pessimism' about the earth's capacity to support large numbers, as well as about the destabilizing effects of unchecked growth on individual states – has been the dominant mode, to some extent in scholarship and to a great extent in popular and political discourse.[5] Exceptions are, of course, to be found on both sides of the Malthusian divide: pessimists promoted colonial emigration as a safety-valve for England's teeming poor in the early seventeenth century; present-day scholars dismiss popular anxieties about fertility in the developing world as superstitious, faddish or racist.[6] But in either case, and whatever the particular anxieties or interpretative frameworks in play in a given instance, it is the attitude towards large and increasing numbers of people that supplies the fundamental organizing principle for analysis – and that ultimately assigns the ideas and people analysed to the right or the wrong side of history.[7]

Of course, no one was a pre-Malthusian at the time; nor, if Malthus ushered in a wholly new pessimism, can his predecessors usefully be understood in terms of their optimism. To complicate the idea of pre-Malthusians, we can take as a starting-point Robert Mayhew's recent biography, which is at once resistant to the optimism/pessimism binary and alert to continuities as well as ruptures between Malthus and his precursors. According to Mayhew, Malthus's salience lay in his rejection of three widely received assumptions: the association of good government with maximal population; the denial of effective or imminent rather than hypothetical limits to growth; and the belief in an endlessly bountiful nature, or what is sometimes called 'cornucopianism'.[8] On this account, Malthus's predecessors were defined not simply by a positive attitude toward growth but by a complex and coherent worldview – essentially providentialist if not always strictly Christian, Enlightened and committed to the capacity of human agency, and in particular policy, to shape society. This is at once a richer and more historically specific framework than the bare consciousness of population that Strangeland requires to start his story and a suppler one than the labour-hungry pro-natalism that animates many accounts of demographic thinking in the century or two before Malthus. Moreover, as A.M.C. Waterman has shown, it was a framework with which Malthus shared common ground, even as he modified it.[9] In Mayhew's account, it gathers together the revolutionary trio whom Malthus took on by name – Richard Price, William Godwin and the Marquis de Condorcet. But who else were pre-Malthusians in this more fleshed-out sense? And how, exactly, did Malthus depart from them?

In fact, the framework in question informed most English discourse on population throughout the early modern period. The reason for this is not far to seek. That 'the multitude of people' was 'the king's honour' was enshrined in scripture, as was the injunction to 'be fruitful, and multiply'; the affirmation of rapid human multiplication since the Creation, recommencing after the Flood, was a standard feature of sacred history; the idea of a fundamentally anthropocentric cosmos watched over by a solicitous divinity structured the worldviews of educated and uneducated alike.[10] Nor did these convictions differentiate England from the rest of Christian Europe – or the early modern period from the Middle Ages.[11] What does seem to have marked England out, however, was the emergence and development of a discourse on population that underwent substantial alterations and elaborations even as it remained ensconced within the shelter of these organizing assumptions about government, multiplication and nature. Inasmuch as these assumptions were matters of deep-seated belief as well as learned scholarship – theology and sacred history, and later natural philosophy – rather than of demography or political economy per se, the key context for interpreting changes in early modern demographic thinking is not disciplinary but moral, religious and, increasingly from the mid-seventeenth century, scientific.[12] Seen in the context of seventeenth- and eighteenth-century English demographic thinking, Malthus's *Essay* was more a departure from within than a rejection of tradition.

'In the beginning,' Sir John Elliott recently said of the study of population, 'there was Botero.'[13] The new *ragion di stato* Giovanni Botero pioneered towards the end of the sixteenth century was arguably the first discourse to assert, in one breath, both population's importance as a political-economic resource and its limitation by other resources, in the first instance territory.[14] At approximately the same time, another major theorist of sovereignty, Jean Bodin, outlined in his *Six livres de la république* the importance of both population and of quantitative demographic knowledge to effective rule. Viewing demographic thought through the lens of the emergent centralized state, it is a short step from these preliminary identifications to more elaborate programmes of planned migration and naturalization and the plethora of seventeenth- and eighteenth-century pro-natalist projects – some drawing on classical or medieval precedent, others outlandishly novel – incentivizing marriage and procreation. Opinions might differ considerably on the most

productive policies and the best distribution of people across a territory or
an empire, as well as across the sectors of an economy; pro-populationism
was compatible with divergent views of the state's scope and the body
politic's shape. In practice, too, the populations in question were riven
by confessional, national or ethnic distinctions that further complicated
their government. (Indeed it was often just such distinctions that spurred
thought about populations as such.) But these disagreements seem to have
occurred within a common and enduring problematic of population,
according to which – absent territorial constraints most political thinkers
and economic writers thought so distant as to be effectively imaginary –
the augmentation of numbers was both legitimately and feasibly the work
of policy. Into this happy garden Malthus would slither.

Yet before and after Bodin and Botero were 'Englished' in 1606, English
authors engaged in demographic discussions of a somewhat different
order.[15] Rather than dealing with total populations, whether of city-states
or colonial empires, these writers focused attention on particular, functionally defined 'multitudes'; rather than exploring how territory limited
absolute numbers, they posited a mixture of moral, political and environmental causes for the relative rise and fall of these subpopulations.[16]
One of the best-known progenitors of this discourse was Thomas More,
the first part of whose *Utopia* (1516) outlined both the moral causes and
the demographic consequences of rural enclosure. In a process More pith-
ily summarized as sheep eating up men – but that other sixteenth- and
seventeenth-century authors simply labelled 'depopulation' – the landlords' greed motivated the enclosure of arable lands and their conversion
to more profitable and less labour-intensive use as pasturage; the husbandmen and families evicted in consequence took to the roads and the towns,
driven to vagrancy, crime and, ultimately, the gallows.[17] In other words,
a landscape reshaped by human passions transformed one multitude –
husbandmen – into another: vagrants. This was a moral process, but it
was at the same time an environmental, economic and demographic one.
The population politics it implied was less one of absolute augmentation of national numbers and more one of maintaining a fragile balance
between qualitatively distinct, locally rooted and functionally interrelated
subpopulations, organs of the body politic.

What Andrew McRae has dubbed 'the discourse of agrarian complaint'
exploded in the mid-Tudor period and centred on the complex antag-
onism that More and others had sketched between covetous landlords
and impoverished husbandmen.[18] That scholars have not usually read this
discourse as demographic thought may reflect its explicit embedding of

social processes in a moral vision, and its reliance on religious and political invective rather than quantitative argument. (It may also reflect the intensely local nature of the relationships involved.) Yet if one decouples the history of demographic thought from the progress of statistics, another view emerges. If, as current historians of economic thought have argued, the metaphor of the body politic and an Aristotelian emphasis on balance oriented early modern commentary on society, then it is only to be expected that sixteenth-century demographic discussions should dwell on matters of relative proportion within a closed system rather than the challenges of absolute and unbounded growth.[19] In this context, accurate numbers of people were not only unavailable; in themselves, they would have been meaningless. Such figures as did appear in this literature were not merely conjectural – such as the anonymous calculation made in 1552 that England had lost 50,000 'ploughs', each supporting six people, since Henry VII's time – but also powerfully symbolic.[20] Yet for all its quantitative imprecision, this was a discourse about population and its dependence on social, economic and physical arrangements, as well as on policy and morals. It was, after all, the landlords' passion for profit that depopulated the countryside and, indirectly, overstocked towns and cities; the solution most authors posited was a combination of positive intervention from above and Christian self-restraint from below.

This Tudor literature of rural depopulation fed into later writing on poverty and vagrancy – what one might call a Tudor-Stuart literature of urban overpopulation. Well-studied by both social historians and literary scholars, portrayals of the mobile poor as a teeming horde of masterless men that threatened private property and political stability dwelt, as did those of greedy landlords and decayed ploughmen, on the qualitative and the moral.[21] Vagrants represented a sort of anti-type to ploughmen; produced by the latter's decay, they threatened the commonwealth the latter sustained. Indeed, 'rogue literature' credited the purportedly idle and undeserving poor with a social structure that inverted the natural social hierarchy, institutions and scale of values, including its mechanisms of social and biological reproduction, namely apprenticeship and the monogamous household.[22] Yet moralistic and sensationalist as such tours through the underworld were, they were also about a subpopulation, its distribution, and its actual and potential regulation. Perhaps most famously, vagrants supplied Elizabethan and Jacobean colonial promoters with a ready-made case for plantation in Ireland and across the Atlantic as an outlet for overcrowded cities at home: 'Our multitudes,' wrote one such pamphleteer in 1609, 'like too much blood in the body, do infect our country with plague and poverty.'[23] More directly, the discourse around vagrancy spurred efforts to surveil, classify and enumerate the poor, the better to control their mobility and access to relief: in James Scott's terms, to render them legible, sedentary and, hence, governable.[24]

The conceptual pairing of vagrants and ploughmen illustrates the organic and moralistic nature of early English demographic discourse, but these were not the only multitudes to attract attention. Growing rivalry with the United Provinces over the North Sea fishery, Southeast Asian spices and the carrying trade, together with the rising importance of naval power in the context of counter-Reformation political and imperial competition, made seamen the heroes of many a Stuart economic tract, from John Keymor's *Observation ... upon the Dutch Fishing* (1601) through Tobias Gentleman's 1660 call 'for the increasing of Mariners against all forraign Invasions; and also for the bettering of Trades and Occupations, and setting of thousands of poor and idle people on work'.[25] In this connection, long-distance trades and monopolies such as the East India Company were both attacked and defended in part on the basis of their perceived effect on the multitude of English seamen – critics citing losses to disaster, disease and vice, apologists emphasizing trade's role in recruiting and maintaining mariners.[26] If different multitudes were important to the preservation of the kingdom, others besides the idle might threaten it. Perhaps the best-known seventeenth-century essay in population measurement was the 1676 'Compton Census', initiated by the earl of Danby, then lord treasurer, to establish 'what proportion or disproportion of number there is betwixt Papists and not Papists, as likewise betwixt other Non-Conformists and Conformists'.[27] Here, again, what was at issue was the relative strength of qualitatively distinct subpopulations subject to proportional augmentation or diminution by means of careful policy.

Yet by the later seventeenth century, the terms of English demographic thought had begun to change. Despite its seemingly archaic purpose, the Compton Census stood out from earlier discussions of ploughmen, seamen and vagrants in at least two obvious ways. First, it was an enumeration driven by a set of quantitative queries emanating from the centre of civil and ecclesiastical government; assessing the relative strength of conformity, recusancy and dissent was a matter of comparing numbers from above rather than tracing (imaginatively or empirically) physical or moral journeys on the ground level. Second, the census, although conducted by clergymen, was read by a new breed of demographic commentator, the 'political arithmetician', for whom the multiplicity of multitudes subject to government were all in principle mutually convertible and thus ultimately equivalent, reducible to a single, national population.[28] This tendency is clearest in the works of John Graunt and William Petty, which appeared between the early 1660s and the early 1690s. But the origins of this outlook, and of eighteenth-century political arithmetic's approach to population as a governable totality limited by natural as well as political circumstances, lie in the prior application of Baconian natural philosophy to programmes of social and political reformation and transformation in the era of the Civil War and Interregnum. The key thinkers here, the young Graunt and Petty among them, had as their common denominator an association with the German émigré and philosophical 'intelligencer' Samuel Hartlib.[29]

If early modern English population thought began with Tudor complaint about improvement, neo-Baconian proponents of improvement gave the discourse of multitude a crucial twist. Or, rather, two twists. First, in seeking a wholesale reformation of society and polity, the Hartlibians linked both specific improvement projects and the conditions of production and reproduction of the specific multitudes these touched to the welfare of the kingdom (or the Three Kingdoms) as a whole. Second, they championed an empirical methodology that ultimately encouraged more epistemologically ambitious use of quantification than before. In none of this, however, did they depart from an essentially providential, moral framework of population thought; nor did they cast doubt on the capacity of policy, per se, to shape population. What they did instead – both in their own comments, and even more in the mature works of the first political arithmeticians they taught – was to articulate both the mutual interrelationships and the governability of subpopulations with new reference not just to land use but to the environment in a more complex, geographically expansive, and state-oriented sense, and to nature writ large. Out of multitudes, they constructed an idea of the total subject population as governable within the constraints of this environment, or 'situation'. In their conceptual vocabulary, if not in their positive views or their projects, they suggested an approach to population whose traces would still be discernible in Malthus's *Essay* 150 years later.

One of the more stunning assertions about the links between population, nature and human intervention – and indeed about the history of human development – came from Gabriel Plattes. Plattes is perhaps best known as the author of the utopian tract *Macaria*, which claimed, among other things, that with proper improvement England could support double its then-current population.[30] He was especially interested in improvements to agriculture and mining, in each of which he claimed significant hands-on experience and to each of which he devoted a substantial book.[31] Yet beyond these realms, and beyond even the effects of their cultivation on food supply and employment in the English nation of his day, he saw a global demographic-historical context for his projects. At least 'three severall times' in the past, he wrote, God had given humankind the knowledge 'to improve the earth, in such a wonderfull manner, that it was able to maintaine double the number'. Each of these moments came as population pressed upon resources, and each resulted in a doubling of what later demographers would call carrying capacity:

> for when there were but few, they were maintained by Fish, Fowle, Venison, and Fruits ... but when they grew too numerous for that food, they found out the Spade and used industry to augment their food ... then they growing too numerous againe, were compelled to use the plough ... but when they grew too numerous for the food gotten that way, they were compelled to find out the fallowing and manuring of Land[.]

Now, again, 'people are growne numerous' and a crisis loomed: 'barrennesse doth by little and little encrease, and the fertilitie decrease every year ... which in regard that the people doe increase wonderfully, must needs at length produce an horrible mischiefe.' Moreover, while America might 'for the present' maintain a 'surplusage of people', this was obviously a short-term solution, 'in regard that the finding of new worlds, is not like to be a perpetuall trade'.[32] Just as the discovery of agriculture and later of the plough, crop rotation and fertilizer had relieved population pressure in the past, so a new round of improvement must do so now.

This would not, of course, be Malthus's view; Plattes's confident expectation of providential discovery was rather closer in expression to the schemes of equality and perfectibility Malthus mocked. And yet Malthus was far from rejecting providentialism either in the *Essay* of 1798, which concluded with two lengthy chapters on the subject, or (as we shall see) in the revised and expanded editions of 1803–26.[33] Further, the dynamic interrelationship Plattes posited between land, labour, technology (abetted by government) and multiplication – his vision of human population as periodically oscillating between near-disaster and new prospects of growth, and of the global history of humanity as conditioned by successive transformations of agricultural production at moments of crisis – was more than blind optimism. It was predicated on an economic understanding of history that, albeit sketchily, foreshadowed the stage theories of development that Malthus himself followed. Unlike radical eighteenth-century utopians, further, Plattes assumed no future transformation of *human* nature, and although he invoked God, the divine intervention he spoke of would come, as it had in the past, in the form of familiar human ingenuity purposefully applied to the consistent workings of the physical world. The picture Plattes drew was of a world population whose tendency to grow regularly inevitably pressed against the limits of the earth's fertility – limits that, as Plattes knew from experience, could be overcome only with difficulty, by methods that worked *with* nature rather than assuming its constraints away. If we are looking for pre-Malthusians, then this picture was closer to Malthus's than it was to those of Condorcet, Godwin or Price.

It was also far removed from the straightforward constructions of population as a military resource or labour pool associated with both reason-of-state discourse and with 'mercantilist' literature as usually read. Among Hartlib's associates, however, William Petty provides a clearer link between the early Stuart discourse of multitudes and the political-arithmetical approach that would become synonymous with the discussion of population in the eighteenth century.[34] In fact, a very particular set of discordant multitudes first set Petty thinking about population: the confessional and national subpopulations of Cromwellian Ireland. For Petty, the persistent failure of Gaelic Irish, Old English Catholic settlers, New English Protestant colonists and Ulster Scots to cohere into a single and governable subject population had historical and natural as well as institutional causes, ranging from the inherent tendency of people to disagree in matters beyond rational determination to linguistic difference and the memory of past injustices to environmental differences (which sustained different diets and ways of life, making the Irish reluctant to emulate English economic behaviour).[35] By the 1670s, he thought a policy of transplantation and intermarriage might solve these problems by reconstructing the Irish population from the household up. But a single national population that could function as a resource was the aim of policy and of political arithmetic, rather than the starting point; both as a concept and as an object, it would be achieved by reordering the links between pre-existing multitudes.

Following Baconian strictures, however, it would also require subjecting multitude to more careful empirical attention. In Cromwellian Ireland, motivations for demographic quantification were unusually forceful. Among the charges levelled at the defeated Irish rebels – and justifying the project of 'transplanting' large segments of the Irish Catholic population into Connacht – was the massacre of as many as 150,000 English Protestants in late 1641.[36] A more pressing concern for Petty was the

'Down Survey' of confiscated Irish land; from measuring the land, it was a short step to measuring the people.[37] Petty took this step by compiling a so-called '1659 Census' of Ireland from poll tax returns, on the basis of which he estimated both the total population and, more saliently for his projects, the relative proportions of Catholics and Protestants, Irish and 'British'.[38] In England after the Restoration, meanwhile, Petty similarly sought to calibrate the relationships between the kingdom's constituent subpopulations. Here the salient groupings, in the first instance, were the functional sort familiar from early Stuart writing. Thus the 1662 *Treatise of Taxes* proposed maximizing the number of artisans and husbandmen by maintaining fixed proportions between the professions and population as a whole, using annual bills of mortality to adjust recruitment as population grew.[39] Yet as the very idea of managing their proportions systematically suggests, these multitudes were increasingly seen not as essentially distinct organs of the body politic but as contingent groupings of radically malleable and potentially interchangeable human units. Population was now imaginable as the totality of these units, and the state, ideally, as the agent that maximized their numbers and rationalized their shape. (In later flights Petty imagined not just the fully peopled state, but also the maximal population of the globe itself as expressible in terms of a certain number of people per acre, a limit he located in the far future.)[40] Here was the conceptual basis for a kind of social engineering Malthus would openly despise.[41]

And yet if political arithmetic liberated government from the ideological straitjacket of the body politic, it arguably strengthened nature's role in limiting human policy. Fundamental to Petty's own programme was the distinction between 'natural, and perpetual impediments' to national greatness and those that were 'contingent, and removable'; policy could exacerbate or remove the latter, but could do nothing about the former.[42] The difference between the two hinged on the way a nation's 'situation' – an amalgam of location, territory, landscape, resources and history – impinged on its ability to produce certain kinds of people. Taking the example of seamen, Petty argued that the Dutch capacity to field large numbers reflected the country's coastal situation, access to inland waterways and limited arable land. England's situation should allow the Stuarts to emulate Dutch maritime success; France, on the other hand, lacked the natural harbours as well as the established seafaring population to train and sustain the seamen that Louis XIV's naval ambitions would require.[43] 'Full peopling' itself – the maximum ratio of hands to lands – varied from place to place, a function of land as well as trade. Environment, embracing the gifts of nature and the history of their cultivation, determined just how malleable subpopulations were in practice, and hence the effective scope of demographic manipulation. As Petty put it, in terms not unlike Malthus's, 'things will have their course, nor will nature be couzened'.[44]

'Number, weight and measure' was another catchphrase of Petty's, but the pioneering *Observations ... on the London Bills of Mortality* (1662) was the work of his friend John Graunt.[45] Graunt's *Observations* marked the most visible departure from older ways of talking about population: in place of scriptural invective were tables of figures, some reproduced from weekly parish or annual City bills, but many – like the 'Table of Casualties' for 1629–36 and 1647–60, which listed 81 causes of death – were concocted by Graunt himself. The book modelled a new style of argument, in which sometimes surprising or counterintuitive conclusions ('that few starve of the many that beg') were based on comparing aggregations of recorded observations, rather than imaginatively reconstructing the qualitative transformations of individuals; rather than agrarian laments inspiring a speculative or symbolic quantification of the damage done, informed speculation about social processes now flowed from the effects – the facts – that the numbers demonstrated.[46] In this regard perhaps more than any other, it has justly been regarded as the founding text not only of quantitative demography – Graunt launched a critique of sources that later fuelled the drive for a national census – but also of the self-consciously empirical and factual mode of demographic polemic that Malthus would make the trademark of the *Essay*'s later editions.

For all its innovations, Graunt's book reflected a wider set of changes. He himself framed his work as a repurposing of long-neglected sources rather than a discovery of demographic quantification *tout court*.[47] More to the point, he constructed the enterprise of demographic observation that these sources permitted in neo-Baconian terms as a natural and political reform, an advancement of learning that should improve the polity by shedding new light on the same kinds of connections other Hartlibian authors had indicated between providence, environment, policy and population. Much as Petty sought to show the environmental limits of national policy through his discussion of seamen, for example, Graunt's discussion of the sex ratio underpinned an argument about the providentially imposed natural link between monogamy and procreation, underlining the unnatural and hence counterproductive nature of both Catholic celibacy and Muslim polygamy.[48] Conversely, mortality rates showed that the growth of London was the product not of natural increase but of levies from the countryside. Human agency countermanded nature only at a cost: monogamy was most fruitful, rural life healthiest, idleness remediable. Policy was not impotent, but its effects depended on its working within a natural economy that statistics revealed and that bore the marks of divine craftsmanship. Quantifying these relations set a seal on the abstraction of population from specific multitudes and set the stage for eighteenth-century debates, but it did not mark a clean break with the past.

Eighteenth-century political arithmetic was a variegated enterprise.[49] Yet most of its manifestations retained more than vestigial traces of its Restoration origins. Best known is the overtly 'political' employment of political arithmetic, championed early on by Gregory King and Charles Davenant, as a data-gathering and policy-debating instrument of the fiscal-military state – and, eventually, the wider political nation.[50] Typified in the mid-eighteenth century by attempts to judge the nation's government, policies and general health by gauging the size and growth of the British population, this tradition had an ambiguous relationship to Malthus. On the one hand, it furnished him with much of the statistical material for his arguments, particularly in the second and subsequent editions of the *Essay*. On the other hand, it often seemed to imply a simplistic equation between numbers and strength, and the equally simplistic assumption that government could and should encourage numbers of itself.[51] Whether these latter impressions were fair or not, they were held both widely and by such influential writers as Adam Smith, who claimed to put little trust in political arithmetic even as he quoted its findings.[52] Malthus's own attitude towards the mid-century 'population debate' suggested a similar lack of faith: neither those who thought population had declined (either in post-Revolutionary Britain or globally and over the long term) nor those who trumpeted its increase argued from solid facts or sound axioms.[53] None had grasped the principle of population.

But if state-oriented political arithmetic was neither attitudinally nor doctrinally Malthusian, alternative uses of the approach suggest other bases for comparison. What initially seems an archaic adoption of quantification for religious polemic, for instance, turns out on closer examination to illuminate the structural assumptions of demographic discourse already sketched, and to show their capacity to contribute to disparate areas of intellectual endeavour. Sacred historians had in fact a long tradition of speculating about the history of human multiplication; establishing that Adam and Eve, or Noah's sons might have filled the earth with people in a small number of generations helped obviate objections to the short chronology (around 5,000 years) that scripture allowed from

Creation to the present. In the wake of Graunt and Petty, however, these discussions took on a new complexity, as mathematicians including John Arbuthnot, physico-theologians like William Derham, and theorists of the earth such as William Whiston emphasized not simply the mathematical possibility but the empirical and environmental probability of their demographic arguments. While Arbuthnot and others followed Graunt in citing the sex ratio as an empirical proof of providential demographic management, Whiston and more orthodox sacred historians debated both the climatic and institutional constraints operating on biblical lifespan and multiplication. In a tradition that kept up steam at least until mid-century, population emerged as a global phenomenon governed by God through a complex set of secondary causes, including human customs but also by a mixture of historically variable economies of nature and permanent, incontrovertible natural laws.[54]

These laws were adjusted, to be sure, for human happiness – but only in the aggregate, and only over the long haul. This was no Panglossian view of nature's bounty. Few voiced what it meant better or more influentially than William Derham, who noted in his *Physico-Theology* that 'extraordinary Expences of Mankind' not only punished sin but also kept 'the Balance of Mankind even; as one would be ready to conclude by considering the *Asiatick*, and other more fertile Countries, where prodigious Multitudes are yearly swept away with great Plagues ... and yet those Countries so far from being wasted, that they remain full of People'.[55] Divine design left ample room for human misery; indeed, insofar as it reflected both the moral weakness natural to human beings and the constant potential of the earth to be 'overstocked' with people, misery was a structural feature of the providential plan. The happiness this order of nature guaranteed was the essentially abstract, even otherworldly happiness of a species that persisted in spite of, or rather by means of, catastrophic suffering on earth – sojourning implacably through history from beginning to end, much as in *The Spectator*'s contemporaneous 'Vision of Mirzah'.[56] As anyone familiar either with the Bible or with England's history of epidemics knew, God's solicitude for human multiplication had little to do with the comfort, security or survival of individuals, families or communities. Nature was no respecter of persons.

This candid view coloured the emerging field of medical arithmetic, perhaps the most significant new development in eighteenth-century English demographic discourse prior to the *Essay*.[57] Malthus himself drew extensively on the works of Dr Thomas Short in particular – and not merely for their raw data, but at least sometimes for the sake of Short's interpretations and even his choice of words. Malthus approvingly, and repeatedly, quoted Short's characterization of recurring epidemics as 'terrible correctives of the redundance of mankind', and lauded the doctor's statistical demonstration of 'the constancy and universality of their operation'.[58] Short, for his part, would no doubt have approved the demographic import of Malthus's conclusion that 'Natural and moral evil seem to be the instruments employed by the Deity in admonishing us' to avoid imprudence and immorality; 'Not only do the Bills of Mortality discover the physical, civil, and commercial States of the City,' Short wrote in his 1750 *New Observations, Natural, Moral, Civil, Political, and Medical, on City, Town, and Country Bills of Mortality*, 'but the Decay of Virtue and Piety, and Prevalency of Vice and Impiety.'[59] Given his understanding of Poor Laws, Malthus dismissed as counterproductive Short's call for a bachelor tax to support poor families.[60] But in grasping population as a natural process subject to a combination of divine moral management through secondary causes and human influence through policies that were effectual in proportion as they respected natural law – and in privileging empirical, quantitative data as the common script and index of divine and human power – the two shared a framework.

Inasmuch as it revealed the salubrity or otherwise of particular sites and types of settlement and environment, medical arithmetic elaborated empirically on the seventeenth-century concept of situation as a source of differential constraints on both multiplication and policy. A simpler form of the same concept, however, lurked behind another set of arguments with which Malthus would engage, those touching the rapid doubling of populations in newly settled areas, and especially in the colonies that became the United States of America. Set against the slow or even negative growth held to characterize the 'old' world of Europe, the 25-year doubling period widely cited for the colonies seemed to colonials like Benjamin Franklin and Ezra Stiles to vindicate the enterprise of settlement – and, against the backdrop of Anglo-French imperial rivalry and displaced Native American populations, to imply the demographic necessity and hence the natural justice of annexing new territory.[61] To sympathetic correspondents in Britain such as Richard Price, on the other hand, American doubling and perceived stagnation in England underscored the moral and political corruption of Europe's *ancien régime*, and fuelled his and others' commitment to institutional reform and, in the last instance, revolution.[62] On the surface, this was simply an Atlantic inflection of the wider 'population controversy' that embroiled Hume, Wallace and others before them. Population figured as a measure of wealth and strength, its growth as a direct index of institutional, political and moral legitimacy. For Malthus, of course, this view was fatally mistaken.

Yet there was more to the contrast between old and new world demography than that. Juxtaposing the London mortality bills with his own observations of colonial fecundity and longevity, for example, the Puritan divine Cotton Mather seemed to suggest a similarity between New England and the biblical world that was, as Graunt would have put it, as much natural as political.[63] Still later, Franklin described multiplication as dependent on 'Room and Subsistence', with encouragement to marriage as the middle term; given this, he followed Mather in doubting the applicability of old world mortality tables to new world circumstances.[64] He also argued, more positively, that given sufficient land, the power of natural increase would soon fill 'any occasional Vacancy in a country' caused by war or emigration – an argument against metropolitan critics of colonial settlement as well as against German immigration to Pennsylvania. To be sure, Franklin conferred a great deal of demographic power on the prince or the legislator, who should promote population not only by punishing bachelors but more fundamentally by acquiring new territory for settlement and removing any 'Natives' who might stand in the way.[65] Malthus decried the former means as ineffectual and the latter as morally repugnant.[66] As Alan Houston has argued, however, Franklin's diagnosis of the material constraints limiting multiplication was close to Malthus's – even if the responses he proposed were not.[67]

A dynamic yet essentially coherent framework for population thought linked Tudor agrarians, Stuart improvers and Hanoverian (and colonial American) political arithmeticians. These were the 'pre-Malthusians' of English and Anglo-American demographic discourse. Further research might elucidate their relationship to other bodies of thought with which they interacted – the reason-of-state discourse of Bodin and Botero, the climatic-*cum*-institutional-*cum*-moral declension narrative of Montesquieu, or the providential political arithmetic of Süssmilch, to name three important ones. But the influence of this English discourse on Malthus, both directly and through the approaches and views he criticized, is beyond doubt. I have suggested, moreover, that Malthus's own thinking on population retained significant components of its framework, even as he drew very different practical conclusions than his predecessors. Where, then, did the similarities end and the differences begin? To answer this question, it may be helpful to return to the three characteristics of pre-Malthusian demographic thinking posited at the outset: the denial of more than hypothetical or temporally distant limits to growth, the cornucopian view of nature's bounty and the linkage between population and government. The foregoing suggests that the first two of these characteristics require significant qualification, and that from the pre-Malthusian perspective sketched here, Malthus's real departure pertains to the third. What fuelled this departure, it will be suggested in conclusion, was Malthus's engagement with political economy.

Plainly, the claim that Malthus ushered in the idea of real limits to population growth requires qualification. In part this is because it begs the question of what earlier commentators on population understood limits to signify: worldly disaster perhaps, but alternatively the end of history or the reign of Christ on earth – events that, for sixteenth- and seventeenth-century Protestants if not for eighteenth-century *philosophes*, were neither hypothetical nor necessarily distant. Nor were the earth's limited room or the dependence of its carrying capacity on the exploitation of land news: to Malthus's 'extreme practical limit of population', reached when 'the last employed labourers' could each support only four people, we might juxtapose Petty's description of 'full peopling', with three usable acres of land per person.[68] If Malthus did not pioneer the notion of limits, he certainly restricted its semantic and temporal application, redefining it in terms of an 'oscillation' between preventive and positive checks that operated throughout history rather than looming as a future apocalypse.[69] Even here, however, the case for his novelty is complicated. As we have seen, the notion that God governed population continuously – through secondary causes including climate and environment as well as periodic famine and disease, and for the sake of keeping numbers within limits the earth could support – was current a century before Malthus, in physico-theological applications of political arithmetic, and it marked the later medical arithmetic on which the *Essay* itself relied. From this perspective, the key development between William Derham's day and Malthus's was not the discovery of limits but their short-lived dismissal by the handful of philosophic revolutionaries Malthus took on. This should not surprise; Condorcet, not Malthus, was the radical.

The ascription to pre-Malthusian writers of a cornucopian view of nature needs similarly to be re-examined and the concepts involved, clarified. In particular, we must be wary of a modern critical elision – adumbrated in *Candide* and other eighteenth-century expressions of Enlightened irreverence – between providential and anthropocentric views of nature, on one hand, and arbitrarily optimistic expectations of natural bounty, or even of anthropogenic transformations of the natural order, on the other. The idea that Creation was a moral drama did not imply that it was a comedy. Malthus attacked the latter suggestion with Voltairean wit; but he shared the former belief in full measure.[70] This is most obvious in the closing chapters of the 1798 *Essay*, which explicitly set out the divine economy behind the principle of population.[71] But it is no less present – and is indeed more carefully and empirically integrated – in the later editions, which quoted medical arithmeticians such as Short and John Aikin to the effect that epidemics were providential instruments, and recommended the evangelical (later archbishop of Canterbury and fellow of the Royal Society) John Bird Sumner's comments on the 'calculated' link between the people's need to compete for resources and the 'improvement of human virtue'.[72] Malthus explicitly related both the imbalance between human multiplication and the production of food that constituted the 'principle of population', and the oscillation between positive and preventive checks that its operation entailed, to the divine purposes of replenishing the earth, 'improving the human faculties', and furnishing first 'admonitions' and ultimately 'penalties' for human 'disobedience'.[73] This was a much more systematic expression of divine demographic justice and its mechanisms than Derham's or Short's works could furnish. But it was not very different in its assessment of nature's indifference to human feeling or the suitability of nature's laws for human improvement.

Where Malthus differed strikingly from such predecessors, and increasingly so between the first edition of the *Essay* and the sixth, was in his articulation of the role of individual self-restraint in shaping population and in navigating the providential economy of checks and limits in which it was embedded. This brings us to the question of government. I have argued above that an emphasis on the natural limits of policy – typically expressed in terms of nature and human nature in general, on one hand, and of the particular constraints of specific 'situations', on the other – was part of demographic discussion more than a century before Malthus wrote. That good policy, like any art, respected nature's dictates, and that unnatural policy was doomed to fail (or to succeed only at an unacceptable cost), was widely agreed throughout the period.[74] It needed neither Adam Smith nor political economy to establish the impossibility of altering 'by a *fiat* the whole circumstances of the country'; indeed, establishing a relationship between population, policy, and circumstances was a large part of political arithmetic's purpose.[75] Yet the distinction between art and nature, policy and circumstance, was both movable and porous. Past policies, for one thing, were a component of present situation. More importantly, the Baconian empiricism Graunt and Petty embraced promised a science that studied nature's processes in order to redirect them to human – and chiefly, in Petty's rendering, political – ends. While seventeenth-century natural philosophy armed critiques of policy that anticipated Malthus's, it also bred a confidence about the human power to harness natural forces that Malthus did not share.[76]

For both intellectual and political reasons, Malthus spent a great deal of effort deflating the claims his targets made for the power of social institutions to change circumstances whose roots lay rather in human nature.[77] No human power could reverse nature's laws or augment *by fiat* its products; scarcity was a fact to be reckoned with, not assumed away.[78] But that institutions and laws had effects, good and ill, was certain – even if these were 'light and superficial in comparison with ... the laws of nature and the passions of mankind'.[79] Taxation and warmongering could do real damage to society, although not so much as revolutionaries suggested; the Poor Laws, foundling hospitals, bachelor taxes and bounties on births that political arithmeticians and 'projectors' championed, meanwhile, were all examples of unnatural policies that did varying degrees of harm.[80] Yet positive as well as natural laws protecting property rights and institutions fostering education and propagating prudential habits were not merely useful but in fact necessary for nature's order and the human propensity for self-improvement to interact as God intended.[81] Population growth was not an index of good government any more than gold was the source of wealth.[82] But depopulation was a sure mark of bad government: the product not of nature unaided but rather, at least proximately, of human ignorance, corruption, oppression or tyranny.[83] The link between policy and population was not broken. Rather, the boundary between politics and nature had moved. With this shift, a new figure came to the fore.

For political arithmeticians, the state had been the chief agent of human power. For Malthus, the principal intermediary between policy and natural law was, instead, the rational and moral individual. This shift of emphasis requires more elucidation than can be offered here, but Malthus's immediate source for it would seem to have been the political economy of Adam Smith. On one hand, this furnished an idea of 'effective demand' for labour that streamlined Malthus's discussion of the 'moral possibility' of population growth.[84] Since different levels of effective demand characterized different types of economy, Malthus could move from particular observations to general principles by reducing the vagaries of national experience described in Books I and II of the *Essay* to differences between economic 'systems' – agriculture, commerce and a mixture of the two – in Book III.[85] He thus traded the messy language of situation, an amalgam of natural and human inputs, for the elegance of systems whose consequences no government could contest. This redrew the lines between the immutable and accidental aspects of circumstance and shifted the balance between natural and unnatural policies such that legitimate and efficacious interventions in population processes became few, broad and indirect – furnishing individuals with protections, incentives and knowledge of their own interests – in comparison to the social engineering projects that characterized earlier demographic discourse.

On the other hand, Smithian political economy also furnished a model of individual agency that underwrote Malthus's continuing attachment to a moral and providential view of population. If the state could not legitimately or effectively direct human demographic behaviour, responsibility fell to individuals themselves, whose fundamental freedom to marry and procreate constituted them as the true subjects of multiplication. The front line of conflict between possibility and constraint accordingly shifted from the national stage to the individual struggle for balance between the satisfaction of providentially instilled natural drives and the calculated restraint of those drives in the service of an equally providential propensity for self-improvement. Here Malthus departed most dramatically from earlier discourse on population; here, too, he seems to have mirrored what historians have identified as a real shift in behaviour, an assertion of control over the size and shape of families that arguably amounts to the emergence of a new demographic subjectivity.[86] Yet if this represented a liberalization of demographic discourse, there is a certain irony in Malthus's hope that the diffusion of political-economic knowledge would foster habits of prudence in the poor and allow the preventive check to hold the fort against the positive. In identifying the advancement of human happiness with the deliberate expansion of 'the relative proportions of the middle parts' of the population, he offered a vision of demographic engineering more distinct from Petty's in expression than in aim.[87]

A final irony is that the providentialist optimism so often attributed to demographic thinking before the *Essay* characterizes Malthus's immediate antagonists – the rational Dissenter Price and the atheists Godwin and Condorcet – far better than it does the avowedly Christian medical and political arithmeticians, physico-theologians, utopian schemers and agrarian Jeremiahs who preceded them. Focusing on the structural framework of demographic thinking rather than on economic doctrines or attitudes towards growth enables us to see these latter as 'pre-Malthusians' not only in the usual negative sense, but also in a deeper positive one. For at least in some respects – notably his uncompromising inclusion of misery in God's plan; his attentiveness, particularly in Books I and

II, to the complex constraints of situation; and his running critique of policies that flouted nature or tempted providence – Malthus's response to the revolutionaries of his day returned to fundamental features of earlier English demographic discourse. It is impossible to grasp this without stepping beyond both the categorical boundaries of disciplinary history and the temporal boundaries of the late Enlightenment and the Age of Revolutions, to the history of moral, religious and scientific ideas from the Reformation onward. At the same time, this wider frame also clarifies what it was that distinguished Malthus. He did not introduce the idea of limits to growth, to nature's bounty or to the capacity of policy. But by assimilating the conceptual vocabulary of the new political economy into an older framework of demographic providentialism, he rendered these limits in simpler, more spare and more general terms – as theoretical principles alongside the principle of population.

Notes

1 Charles Emil Strangeland, *Pre-Malthusian Doctrines of Population: A Study in the History of Economic Theory* (1904; reprinted New York: Augustus M. Kelley, 1966). Other classic disciplinary histories include James Bonar, *Theories of Population from Raleigh to Arthur Young* (1931; reprinted London: George Allen & Unwin, 1992) and J.J. Spengler, *French Predecessors of Malthus: A Study in Eighteenth-Century Wage and Population Theory* (Durham, NC: Duke University Press, 1942). The first edition of the *Essay* was printed anonymously: *An Essay on the Principle of Population, as It Affects the Future Improvement of Society* (London: J. Johnson, 1798). Except where otherwise indicated, subsequent citations refer to the sixth edition, 2 vols. (1826; reprinted, New York: Cosimo Classics, 2007). Malthus's development of the *Essay*, successive editions of which refined arguments and added statistical evidence, has been the subject of exhaustive study; as the present chapter is concerned with setting his work in a much longer-term context these changes cannot be dealt with here.

2 See, for example, Michael S. Teitelbaum and Jay M. Winter, 'Bye-Bye, Baby', *The New York Times*, 6 April 2014. For a study of how twentieth-century attitudes toward population shaped political programmes, see Matthew Connelly, *Fatal Misconception: The Struggle to Control World Population* (Cambridge, MA: Harvard University Press, 2008).

3 The *locus classicus* for this view of mercantilist demography is Edgar S. Furniss, *The Position of the Laborer in a System of Nationalism: A Study in the Labor Theories of the Later English Mercantilists* (1918; reprinted New York: Augustus M. Kelley, 1965). Its persistence is evident in such recent works as Myron Weiner and Michael S. Teitelbaum, *Political Demography, Demographic Engineering* (New York: Berghahn Books, 2001), pp. 13–14.

4 See Jacqueline Hecht, 'Malthus avant Malthus: Concepts et comportement prémalthusiens dans la France d'Ancien Régime', *Dix-huitième siècle*, 26 (1994), 69–78. Hecht suggests that elements of Malthusianism are evident in a shift in emphasis among Enlightenment writers from maximal to optimal population; full-blown Malthusian pessimism, however, required the *Essay*.

5 See Robert J. Mayhew, *Malthus: The Life and Legacies of an Untimely Prophet* (Cambridge, MA: Harvard University Press, 2014), pp. 228–9. Murray Milgate and Shannon C. Stimson, *After Adam Smith: A Century of Transformation in Politics and Political Economy* (Princeton: Princeton University Press, 2009), pp. 121–2, credits Malthus with transforming political economy into the 'dismal science'.

6 See, for example, Mildred Campbell, '"Of People Either Too Few or Too Many": The Conflict of Opinion on Population and Its Relation to Emigration', in William Appleton Aiken and Basil Duke Henning (eds.), *Conflict in Stuart England: Essays in Honour of Wallace Notestein* (London: Jonathan Cape, 1960), pp. 169–201; Teitelbaum and Winter, 'Bye-Bye, Baby'; Connelly, *Fatal Misconception*.

7 Which side is which is, of course, a matter of perennial debate.

8 Mayhew, *Malthus*, p. 26. On cornucopianism, see Fredrik Albritton Jonsson, 'The Origins of Cornucopianism: A Preliminary Genealogy', *Critical Historical Studies* 1 (2014), 151–68.

9 A.M.C. Waterman, *Revolution, Economics and Religion: Christian Political Economy 1798–1833* (Cambridge: Cambridge University Press, 1991).

10 Proverbs 14:28 and Genesis 1:28 (both cited from King James Version). On demographic growth in sacred history, see Jed Z. Buchwald and Mordechai Feingold, *Newton and the Origins of Civilization* (Princeton: Princeton University Press, 2013), pp. 164–94; Ted McCormick, 'Political Arithmetic and Sacred History: Population Thought in the English Enlightenment, 1660–1750', *Journal of British Studies*, 52 (2013), 829–57.

11 Peter Biller, *The Measure of Multitude: Population in Medieval Thought* (Oxford: Oxford University Press, 2001).

12 For Malthus as moralist see Donald Winch, *Riches and Poverty: An Intellectual History of Political Economy in Britain, 1750–1834* (Cambridge: Cambridge University Press, 1996), pp. 221–405, which argues (pp. 223–248) that Malthus was concerned to reconcile Anglican Christianity and science in a manner strongly reminiscent of the seventeenth- and early eighteenth-century physico-theological writers discussed below (but who fall well outside Winch's area of interest).

13 John Elliott, 'Imperial Assumptions and Colonial Realities'. Keynote address given at 'The "Political Arithmetick" of Empires in the Early Modern Atlantic World, 1500–1807', Omohundro Institute for Early American History and Culture conference, the University of Maryland, College Park, 12 March 2012.

14 On Botero, see the chapter by Alison Bashford and Joyce Chaplin in this volume.

15 Jean Bodin, *The Six Bookes of a Common-weale* (London: Adam Islip, 1606); Giovanni Botero, *A Treatise, Concerning the Causes of the Magnificencie and Greatnes of Cities* (London: Printed by T. Purfoot for R. Ockould and Henry Tomes, 1606).

16 See Ted McCormick, 'Population: Modes of Seventeenth-Century Demographic Thought', in Carl Wennerlind and Philip J. Stern (eds.), *Mercantilism Reimagined: Political Economy in Early Modern Britain and Its Empire* (New York: Oxford University Press, 2014), pp. 25–45.

17 Joan Thirsk long ago noted that 'depopulation' was linked as much to engrossing as to enclosure, and that contemporaries, including More, understood the relationships between these to work differently in different parts of the kingdom; see Joan Thirsk, 'Enclosing and Engrossing, 1500–1640', in Joan Thirsk (ed.), *Chapters from the Agrarian History of England and Wales, 1500–1750: Volume 3: Agricultural change: policy and practice, 1500–1750* (Cambridge: Cambridge University Press, 1990), pp. 54–109, especially pp. 92–3. This localism only underlines the qualitative specificity of particular multitudes as objects of political attention.

18 See Andrew McRae, *God Speed the Plough: The Representation of Agrarian England, 1500–1660* (Cambridge: Cambridge University Press, 1996), especially pp. 23–57.

19 See, for example, Andrea Finkelstein, *Harmony and the Balance: An Intellectual History of Seventeenth-Century English Economic Thought* (Ann Arbor: University of Michigan Press, 2000). More recently, Paul Slack has drawn attention to under- and overpopulation as extremes to be avoided within an Aristotelian framework of seeking the mean; see Paul Slack, *'Plenty of People': Perceptions of Population in Early Modern England* (Reading: University of Reading, 2011), p. 4.

20 *Certayne Causes Gathered Together, Wherin Is Shewed the Decaye of England* (London: Printed for Heugh Singleton, 1552), sig. B3r-B3v. Sir Thomas Smith's *Discourse of the Common Weal* calculated that each plough supported 40 people; see McRae, *God Speed the Plough*, p. 54.

21 See A.L. Beier, *Masterless Men: the Vagrancy Problem in England, 1550–1640* (London: Methuen, 1985); Paul Slack, *Poverty and Policy in Tudor and Stuart England* (Harlow: Longman, 1988); Steve Hindle, *On the Parish? The Micro-Politics of Poor Relief in Rural England, 1550–1750* (Oxford: Oxford University Press, 2004); Patricia Fumerton, *Unsettled: The Culture of Mobility and the Working Poor in Early Modern England* (Chicago: University of Chicago Press, 2006).

22 Two useful modern collections are Gamini Salgado (ed.), *Cony-Catchers and Bawdy Baskets* (New York: Penguin, 1973), and Arthur F. Kinney (ed.), *Rogues, Vagabonds, and Sturdy Beggars: A New Gallery of Tudor and Early Stuart Rogue Literature* (Amherst: University of Massachusetts Press, 1990).

23 Robert Gray, *A Good Speed to Virginia* (London, 1609), excerpted in Joan Thirsk and J.P. Cooper (eds.), *Seventeenth-Century Economic Documents* (Oxford: Oxford University Press, 1972), pp. 757–8. Gray acknowledges the

scriptural stress on populousness as an index of good government (Proverbs 14:28) even as he cites examples from ancient and biblical history as well as from animal husbandry of the pressure of numbers on territory and resources.

24 One manifestation of this was the *Ease for Overseers of the Poor* (London: Printed by John Legat, 1601), which included a blank printed table for classification and enumeration on a parish basis. See James C. Scott, *Seeing Like a State: How Certain Schemes to improve the Human Condition Have Failed* (New Haven: Yale University Press, 1998), especially pp. 1–8 and 53–83. See also Geoffrey C. Bowker and Susan Leigh Star, *Sorting Things Out: Classification and Its Consequences* (Cambridge, MA: MIT Press, 1999), pp. 1–32.

25 John Keymor, *John Keymor's Observation Made upon the Dutch Fishing, about the Year 1601* (London: Printed for Sir Edward Ford, 1664); Tobias Gentleman, *The Best Way to Make England the Richest and Wealthiest Kingdome in Europe, by Advancing the Fishing Trade and Imploying Ships and Mariners* (London: s.n., 1660), p. 11.

26 See, for example, Thomas Mun, *A Discovrse of Trade, from England unto the East Indies* (London: Printed by Nicholas Okes for John Pyper, 1621), pp. 33–45.

27 BL Egerton MS 3329, f. 119, quoted in Anne Whiteman, 'General Introduction', in Anne Whiteman (ed.), *The Compton Census of 1676: A Critical Edition* (Oxford: Oxford University Press, 1986), pp. xxiii–lxxxii at p. xxiv.

28 Ibid., pp. lxxx–lxxxi.

29 On the Hartlib Circle, the most comprehensive guide is still Charles Webster, *The Great Instauration: Science, Medicine and Reform, 1626–1660* (London: Gerald Duckworth & Co., 1975); for more recent views and some criticism see Mark Greengrass, Michael Leslie, and Timothy Raylor (eds.), *Samuel Hartlib and the Universal Reformation: Studies in Intellectual Communication* (Cambridge: Cambridge University Press, 1994), and still more recently Koji Yamamoto, 'Reformation and the Distrust of the Projector in the Hartlib Circle', *The Historical Journal*, 55 (2012), 375–97. On Hartlib in relation to political arithmetic, see Ted McCormick, *William Petty and the Ambitions of Political Arithmetic* (Oxford: Oxford University Press, 2009), pp. 119–67.

30 Gabriel Plattes, *A Description of the Famous Kingdome of Macaria* (London: Printed for Francis Constable, 1641), p. 11.

31 Gabriel Plattes, *A Discovery of Infinite Treasure, Hidden since the Worlds Beginning* (London: Printed by I.L., 1639); and Gabriel Plattes, *A Discovery of Subterraneall Treasure* (London: Printed by J. Okes for Jasper Emery, 1639).

32 Plattes, *Discovery of Infinite Treasvre*, sig. C3r–C3v.

33 Malthus, *Essay* (1798), pp. 348–96.

34 See McCormick, *William Petty*.

35 See William Petty, *Reflections on Some Persons and Things in Ireland* (London: Printed for John Martin, James Allestreye and Thomas Dicas, 1660), especially pp. 90–2 on religion; and William Petty, *The Political Anatomy of Ireland* (London: Printed by D. Brown and W. Rogers, 1691).

36 See John Cunningham, *Conquest and Land in Ireland: The Transplantation to Connacht, 1649–1680* (Woodbridge: Boydell Press, 2011).

48 TED MCCORMICK

37 William Petty, *History of the Cromwellian Survey of Ireland, A.D. 1655–6, Commonly Called 'The Down Survey'*, ed. Thomas Aiskew Larcom (Dublin: Irish Archaeological Society, 1851).

38 Séamus Pender (ed.), *A Census of Ireland, circa 1659: With Essential Materials from the Poll Money Ordinances, 1660–1661* (Dublin: Irish Manuscripts Commission, 2002).

39 William Petty, *A Treatise of Taxes and Contributions* (London: Printed for N. Brooke, 1662), especially pp. 7–12.

40 See Petty's exchange of letters on 'full peopling' with Robert Southwell, in Marquis of Lansdowne [H.W.E. Petty-Fitzmaurice] (ed.), *The Petty-Southwell Correspondence, 1676–1687* (London: Constable & Co., 1928), pp. 91–3, 114–15, 143–57 and 160–8.

41 This is not to say that Malthus opposed all forms of state intervention – far from it; see below.

42 William Petty, *Political Arithmetick* (London: Printed for Robert Clavel and Henry Mortlock, 1690), pp. 51 and 87.

43 Ibid., pp. 1–34, 51–63 and 87–95.

44 Petty, *Treatise of Taxes*, sig. A4v.

45 John Graunt, *Natural and Political Observations Mentioned in a Following Index, and Made upon the Bills of Mortality* (London: Printed by Tho. Roycroft for John Martyn, James Allestry, and Tho. Dicas, 1662).

46 Ibid., p. 19. On Graunt's method, compare A.M. Endres, 'The Functions of Numerical Data in the Writings of Graunt, Petty, and Davenant', *History of Political Economy*, 17:1 (1985), 245–64; William T. Lynch, *Solomon's Child: Method in the Early Royal Society* (Stanford: Stanford University Press, 2001), pp. 197–231; Andrea Rusnock, *Vital Accounts: Quantifying Health and Population in Eighteenth-Century England and France* (Cambridge: Cambridge University Press, 2002), pp. 15–39.

47 Graunt, *Natural and Political Observations*, pp. 1–2.

48 Ibid., pp. 47–52.

49 See Julian Hoppit, 'Political Arithmetic in Eighteenth-Century England', *Economic History Review*, 49:3 (1996), 516–40; Joanna Innes, *Inferior Politics: Social Problems and Social Policies in Eighteenth-Century England* (Oxford: Oxford University Press, 2009), pp. 109–75.

50 Peter Buck, 'People Who Counted: Political Arithmetic in the Eighteenth Century', *Isis*, 73 (1982), 28–45; William Peter Deringer, *Calculated Values: The Politics and Epistemology of Economic Numbers in Britain, 1688–1738*, unpublished PhD thesis, Princeton University (2012).

51 Malthus explicitly likened pro-natalism to bullionism; *Essay*, vol. 2, p. 142.

52 Adam Smith, *An Inquiry into the Nature and Causes of the Wealth of Nations*, 2 vols. (London: Printed for W. Strahan and T. Cadell, 1776), vol. 2, p. 121.

53 See Malthus, *Essay*, vol. 1, pp. 151–2. On the population debate in England, see D.V. Glass, *Numbering the People: The Eighteenth-Century Population Controversy and the Development of Census and Vital Statistics in Britain* (Farnborough: D.C. Heath, 1973).

54 Buchwald and Feingold, *Newton*, pp. 164–94; McCormick, 'Political Arithmetic and Sacred History'.

55 William Derham, *Physico-Theology: Or, a Demonstration of the Being and Attributes of God, from His Works of Creation*, 3rd edn (London: Printed for W. Innys, 1714), p. 178.

56 *The Spectator*, 1 September 1711.

57 See Rusnock, *Vital Accounts*.

58 Malthus, *Essay*, vol. 1, pp. 307–8. See Thomas Short, *New Observations, Natural, Moral, Civil, Political, and Medical on City, Town, and Country Bills of Mortality* (London: Printed for T. Longman and A. Millar, 1750), p. 96.

59 Malthus, *Essay*, vol. 2, p. 151; Short, *New Observations*, pp. 217–18.

60 Malthus, *Essay*, vol. 1, pp. 238–9. In an analogous fashion, Malthus (vol. 2, p. 171) embraced William Paley's providentialism while dismissing as 'criminal' the promotion of marriage among the poor that Paley proposed.

61 See, for example, Benjamin Franklin, *The Interest of Great Britain Considered, with Regard to Her Colonies, and the Acquisitions of Canada and Guadeloupe* (London: Printed by T. Becket, 1760); Ezra Stiles, *A Discourse on the Christian Union* (Boston: Edes and Gill, 1761). On Franklin, see Joyce Chaplin, *Benjamin Franklin's Political Arithmetic: A Materialist View of Humanity* (Washington: Smithsonian Institution, 2009); Alan Houston, *Benjamin Franklin and the Politics of Improvement* (New Haven: Yale University Press, 2008), pp. 106–46.

62 See, for example, Richard Price, *An Essay on the Population of England, from the Revolution to the Present Time* (London: Printed for T. Cadell, 1780). On Price, see D.O. Thomas, *The Honest Mind: The Thought and Work of Richard Price* (Oxford: Oxford University Press, 1977), pp. 127–50.

63 See Ted McCormick, 'Statistics in the Hands of an Angry God? John Graunt's Observations in Cotton Mather's New England', *The William and Mary Quarterly* 72 (2015), 563–86.

64 Benjamin Franklin, *Observations Concerning the Increase of Mankind, Peopling of Countries, &c.* [1751], in Alan Houston (ed.), *The Autobiography and Other Writings on Politics, Economics, and Virtue* (Cambridge: Cambridge University Press, 2004), pp. 215–21.

65 Ibid.

66 See, for instance, Malthus, *Essay*, vol. 1, pp. 8–9.

67 Houston, *Benjamin Franklin*, pp. 106–46. Houston seems to me to go beyond the evidence, however, in seeing Franklin as having 'helped define Malthus's framework' (p. 143); as argued here, much of this framework was current among a wider and older set of authors.

68 Malthus, *Essay*, vol. 2, p. 92; Lansdowne, *Petty-Southwell Correspondence*, pp. 153–7.

69 Malthus, *Essay*, vol. 1, pp. 5–6 and vol. 2, pp. 1–5 and 151–2.

70 See, for example, ibid., vol. 2, pp. 1–10. Malthus's providentialism is in turn a separate question from his views on scripture. With respect to the latter, his stress on the immutability of natural law (see, for example, *Essay*, vol. 2, p. 6)

may seem to put him at odds with sacred history, according to which human lifespan had been drastically shortened after the Flood. But his target was Condorcet's claim that lifespan had and would in future *increase*, and indeed Malthus here alleged 'the prejudices of all ages', apparently including sacred history, *against* this. (In the *Essay* of 1798, meanwhile, he had gone so far as to defend biblical accounts of miracles, pp. 384–5.) Earlier writers on biblical demography and the history of the earth had attempted to reconcile the idea of natural law with scripturally attested mutations in the human constitution by postulating various natural effects of providentially ordained catastrophes such as the Flood.

71 Malthus, *Essay* (1798), pp. 348–6. A thorough exposition of Malthus's views on providence is A.M.C. Waterman, *Revolution, Economics and Religion: Christian Political Economy 1798–1833* (Cambridge: Cambridge University Press, 1991); on the wider context see also Boyd Hilton, *The Age of Atonement: The Influence of Evangelicalism on Social and Economic Thought, 1785–1865* (Oxford: Oxford University Press, 1986), pp. 73–80. Both works illuminate the religious dimensions and implications of Malthus's thought at the turn of the nineteenth century, but neither considers the longer-term relationship between demographic thinking and providentialism.

72 Malthus, *Essay*, vol. 2, pp. 25 and 131–2.

73 Ibid., vol. 2, pp. 151–2 and 157–8.

74 See, for example, ibid., vol. 1, pp. 111–12, which discusses the possibility of maintaining 'artificially', through import restrictions on corn, a balance between agriculture and manufactures 'which would not take place naturally'; 'The object can certainly be accomplished, but it may be purchased too dear.'

75 Ibid., vol. 1, pp. 46–7.

76 See, for instance, his comments on the absurdity of decreeing 'that two ears of wheat should in future grow where one only had grown before' (ibid., vol. 2, p. 51). Malthus here mocks legislation, not science, but the image perhaps unwittingly recalls Baconian and Hartlibian ambitions for agricultural improvement.

77 For the political context, see ibid., vol. 2, pp. 186–99. The philosophical point recurs throughout the *Essay*; see, for example, vol. 2, pp. 204–5.

78 See, for example, Malthus's comments on scarcity, ibid., vol. 2, p. 40, and on employment vol. 2, pp. 190–1.

79 Ibid., vol. 1, p. 12.

80 On the Poor Laws, see ibid., vol. 2, pp. 38–69.

81 On property see ibid., vol. 2, p. 52; on education see vol. 2, pp. 214–15, 242 and 259; on 'the desire of bettering our condition' as the spring of human action, see vol. 2, p. 257.

82 Ibid., vol. 2, p. 142.

83 Ibid., vol. 2, pp. 140 and 143.

84 Ibid., vol. 2, p. 86.

85 Ibid., vol. 2, pp. 70–96.

86 See, for example, Susan Klepp, *Revolutionary Conceptions: Women, Fertility, and Family Limitation in America, 1760–1820* (Chapel Hill: University of North Carolina Press, 2009); Leslie Tuttle, *Conceiving the Old Regime: Pronatalism and the Politics of Reproduction in Early Modern France* (Oxford: Oxford University Press, 2010).
87 Malthus, *Essay*, vol. 2, p. 254.

CHAPTER 2

Malthus and Godwin: rights, utility and productivity

Gregory Claeys

Introduction

In its broad outlines one version of the Godwin-Malthus story will be familiar to most readers of this volume.[1] A former dissenting minister turned essayist, historian and novelist, William Godwin (1756–1836) published his great tome on the first principles of politics and society, the *Enquiry Concerning Political Justice*, in 1793, in the midst of a fierce debate over the principles of the French Revolution and their implications for Britain. The book was regarded as somewhat obtuse, and the government, which had prosecuted Paine's *Rights of Man* for seditious libel the previous year, deemed it too expensive to merit such treatment. Godwin was quickly recognized as the most intellectually astute as well as the most utopian of the sympathetic contributors to this debate. He rapidly made converts among the youthful prodigies of the period, including Wordsworth, Coleridge and Southey. But his apparently overt primitivism, his resolute opposition to marriage and other forms of intellectually suffocating cooperation, and his opposition to rights doctrines made him an alien figure in the more mainstream, largely Paine-centred debates about rights, suffrage and the British constitution in the mid-1790s. Godwin was also an iconoclast whose faith in the voice of calm reason led him to dislike even tumultuous assemblies, and he fell out with friends like the London Corresponding Society lecturer John Thelwall over the issue.

Two editions of *Political Justice* followed (1795, 1798), with some interesting amendments to Godwin's argument, mostly by way of moving away from the embrace of Rousseauist primitivism or neo-barbarism that accompanied the egalitarian claims that defined the first edition. These amendments were signalled in part in some of the essays in Godwin's *The Enquirer: Reflections on Education, Manners, and Literature* (1797).[2] Then a demolition of Godwin's central themes, along with the aspiration to 'perfectibility'[3] in those of the French radical philosopher Condorcet, was accomplished by the insistence upon the corrosive effects of sexual desire in any society, which was the central principle of Thomas Robert Malthus's *Essay on Population* of 1798.[4] This was not a particularly original proposition, Robert Wallace having already suggested in *Various Prospects of Mankind, Nature and Providence* (1761) that any society based upon community of goods might well collapse through overpopulation. But it was an extremely timely intervention given the failure of the debate over the French Revolution to subside in the late 1790s, and indeed its evident rejuvenation among a new generation of admirers. Godwin had suddenly once again become the man of the hour, and by friends and critics alike was taken to epitomize the most extremely optimistic wing of the radical Enlightenment, implicating Paine and his followers in turn, and tacitly revealing the most naïve assumptions about likely changes to human behaviour under a more democratic republic. In Malthus's eyes, this utopianism simply masked an incapacity to come to terms with the unalterable demands of sexual passion, and the tendency of population to grow to the limits of subsistence even faster in conditions of the kind of social equality that Godwin promoted than elsewhere. Godwin's reputation never recovered, although his status as the founder of philosophical anarchism was assured.

The more extreme form of Enlightenment optimism that Godwin represented thus suffered a grievous blow at Malthus's hands. Malthus, in his cursory pamphlet (some 50,000 words), crafted the dystopian response to the Godwinian utopia of 1,000 pages. In 1817, Malthus would shift his target to the founder of British socialism, Robert Owen (who took advice from Godwin on the population issue), after the former began to propound communitarian schemes vaguely reminiscent of the schemes for equality associated by some with Godwinism.[5] Privately Godwin seems initially to have conceded substantial parts of Malthus's arguments about population increase.[6] But he soon became a resolute opponent of Malthus's ever more hard-line stance. The final act in this drama occurred with Godwin's own response to Malthus, *On Population* (1820), about which he claimed that 'if I am right the system of Malthus can never rise again, and the world is delivered for ever from this accursed apology in favour of vice and misery, of hard-heartedness and oppression'.[7] But later generations largely ignored the book, and Godwin slid into obscurity until achieving a modest revival in the late Victorian period. Malthus meanwhile attained both notoriety and, eventually, a worldwide reputation for being the first to warn of the dangers of overpopulation. His theories were integrated into political economy by Ricardo, turning the subject into the 'dismal science'. They became a key inspiration for both of the discoverers of the theory of natural selection, Charles Darwin and Alfred Russel Wallace. Beyond becoming one of the more important thinkers of the nineteenth century, his reputation would extend, indeed gaining in importance, to the present day.

This familiar account of the Malthus-Godwin relationship generally stresses that a substantial part of Malthus's early success was owing to the choice of Godwin as a target in the *Essay*, which, in Poynter's words, now appears as little more than 'an unashamed polemic against Godwin'.[8] There is reasonable evidence for this view, although it does make the *Essay* appear more as a political intervention than is usually conceded. We might recall the judgement of Robert Southey, for instance, who wrote that 'the direct object of Mr. Malthus's essay in its original form, was to confute the opinions of Mr. Godwin in particular, and of all those persons in general, who believed that any, material improvement in human society might be effected'.[9] William Hazlitt, too, emphasized that 'it will be recollected by those who are familiar with the history of Mr. Malthus' writings, that his first and grand effort was directed against the modern philosophy'. This purpose was achieved by Malthus having 'by the rigid interpretation which he gave to his favourite principle, or by what he called the *iron law of necessity*' then 'succeeded in laying the bug-bear of modern philosophy, relaxed considerably in the second and following editions of his book, in which he introduced *moral restraint* as a third check upon the principle of population, in addition to the two only ones of vice and misery, with which he had before combated the Utopian philosophers'.[10] Similarly, the *Critical Review* wrote in 1808 that 'the popularity which the work of Mr. Malthus obtained on its first appearance, was not more owing to the glitter of paradox, which always attracts fugitive-admiration, than to the refutation which it seemed to furnish of the system of Mr. Godwin, which was then an objection of general reprobation and dislike'.[11] Another account tells us that Malthus 'merely takes up the idea of the policy of forcibly suppressing population, in order to the counteracting the popularity of Mr Godwin's Political Justice, hoping thereby to raise his fortune and fame'.[12] Additional evidence for seeing the confrontation in terms of Malthus's reaction to *Political Justice* includes some correspondence from the period, including a letter from Malthus to Godwin in which the former wrote that 'great improvements may take place in the state of society, but I do not see how the present form or system can be radically and essentially changed, without a danger of relapsing again into barbarism'.[13] The confrontation thus appears almost entirely to be on the ground of high theory, with the juxtaposition of the hard-nose empiricism of the social pessimist Malthus to the wild-eyed utopianism of Godwin at the centre of the picture.

Relatively few treatments of Malthus have, however, taken his engagement with Godwin beyond the stage of seeing the latter as a straw man embodying radical Enlightenment principles as such (although the variation among this purported group was considerable).[14] A few writers, like St Clair, concede that Malthus was attracted by some of Godwin's theory 'even if he could not believe it'.[15] Winch establishes that neither was very keen on the prospects suggested by the new manufacturing system, Malthus being a 'Country Whig' with a clear 'agrarian bias'.[16] What is crucial is the obvious distance between both authors' positions on a range of issues; what is not hinted at is what they shared in common. None of the major studies of Godwin or Malthus makes an attempt to scrutinize the exact starting-point of the *Essay* in a confrontation with Godwin's particular arguments, as opposed to his general optimism.[17] Part of the reason for this is that the original rationale for the *Essay*, the assault on Godwin, was gradually dropped, disappearing entirely by the fifth edition, as Malthus achieved an independent reputation respecting his population theory.

Yet Malthus made clear that it was a close reading of Godwin's texts – probably both the first and third editions of *Political Justice* and most obviously *The Enquirer* – which formed the point of departure for the *Essay*.[18] My contention here will be that a close scrutiny of Malthus's treatment of Godwin reveals that he certainly found in Godwin several doctrines – namely utilitarianism and an opposition to rights doctrines – which would help underpin the *Essay*. Most commentators have ignored the fact that Godwin's utility-based theory of justice – an essential element in *Political Justice* – can be understood as being modified by Malthus in the first edition of the *Essay*, and can also be conceived as preparing the ground for the famous attack on the right to subsistence in the second edition of 1803. Malthus's engagement, in other words, was at least as much with *Political Justice* as with *The Enquirer*.[19] Hence the association of Malthus's utilitarianism solely with the theological utilitarianism of William Paley stands in need of some revision. In order to unpack this argument, we need first briefly to consider Godwin's positions, then to see what use Malthus made of them.

Justice and rights in Godwin's *Enquiry Concerning Political Justice* (1793)

It is worth reiterating at this point that the commencement of the revolutionary debate in the early 1790s had involved a radical restatement of natural jurisprudential concepts of rights, chiefly through Thomas Paine's immensely popular *Rights of Man* (1791–2). This had proposed against Edmund Burke that natural rights were a gift to mankind at the Creation, as attested by Genesis, and that they could be conceived as inhering in each individual thereafter. At the end of *Rights of Man Part the Second* (1792), and as clearly in his *Agrarian Justice* (1797), Paine made it clear that he saw these rights claims as extending to the right to subsistence, which was, of course, acknowledged in the English Poor Law.[20] Godwin – who had met Paine and clearly had the first part of *Rights of Man* before him in composing *Political Justice*, which was begun in May 1791 – famously rejected natural rights arguments on utilitarian grounds, as Jeremy Bentham would do. In the first edition of *Political Justice* (Book I, Chapter 5, 'Rights of Man'), Godwin stated dramatically that given the fact that rights could not clash with each other, and that 'I have no right to omit what my duty prescribes', it 'inevitably follows that men have no rights' in the sense of having 'a full and complete power of either doing a thing or omitting it, without the person's becoming liable to animadversion or censure from another, that is, in other words, without his incurring any degree of turpitude or guilt. Now in this sense I affirm that man has no rights, no discretionary power whatever.'[21] Godwin here used the specific example of 'the miser, who accumulates to no end that which diffused would have conduced to the welfare of thousands' and 'the luxurious man, who wallows in indulgence and sees numerous families around him pining in beggary', as individuals who 'never fail to tell us of their rights', when in fact it was their duties that needed reiterating.[22]

Godwin's position here was thus unequivocal: we have no rights, but we have duties to assist others in distress when our own means were sufficient, all property in principle being at the disposal of the community, although accountable as such only by its holders voluntarily acknowledging their duties.[23] Possibly because he thought he had been wrongly accused of promoting the levelling of the existing property system, this doctrine was later altered by Godwin in such a way as to reinforce a right to property.[24] By 1798 it included a more positive discussion of the 'rights of man', and rights based upon utility and to forbearance, among others, were acknowledged, and Godwin now asserted that 'duty is the treatment I am bound to bestow upon others; right is the treatment I am entitled to expect from them'. His opposition to what he now termed 'active rights', however, or at least his assertion that any such rights were imperfect, remained undiminished, and he still insisted that all such rights were in any case 'superseded and rendered null by the superior claims of justice'.[25] This remained consistent with Godwin's general account of duty as stewardship, where we naturally by the standard of 'simple justice' owe others what they need when we can spare it.²⁶ 'If justice have any meaning,' he had written in 1793, 'nothing can be more iniquitous, than for one man to possess superfluities, while there is a human being in existence that is not adequately supplied with these.' Property thus belonged to 'him who most wants it, or to whom the possession of it will be most beneficial'.²⁷ Godwin acknowledged, however, that it could be objected 'that we find among different men very different degrees of labour and industry, and that it is not just they should receive an equal reward'. But he let the matter drop, commenting only that it could not 'indeed be denied that the attainments of men in virtue and usefulness ought by no means to be confounded'.²⁸ He remained insistent, however, about the voluntary nature of these duties. Thus, while each person had 'a sphere the limit and termination of which is marked out by the equal sphere of his neighbour', Godwin continued:

> Compulsion to be exercised by one human being over another, whether individually, or in the name of the community, if in any case to be resorted to, is at least to be resorted to only in cases of indispensable urgency. It is not therefore to be called in for the purpose of causing one individual to exert a little more, or another a little less, of productive industry. Neither is it to be called in for the purpose of causing the industrious individual to make the precise distribution of his produce which he ought to make.²⁹

This emphasis on voluntariness could of course be read as a movement away from compulsory taxes on landed property to support the poor, and towards a purely voluntary system of charity, which was the position, we will shortly see, that Malthus would adopt. For both, then, governmental intervention as such was an evil, all forms of government being for Godwin 'in all cases an evil'.³⁰

This assertion of the presumptive priority of duty over right did not of course solve the problem as to how to act to assist others; it only insisted that we do so. This was explored further, however, in Book 2, Chapter 2 of the first edition of *Political Justice*. Here Godwin considered the utility of the individual as one of the measures of the 'distribution' of justice, defined as 'a general appellation for all moral duty'. One of his main aims here was to refute the Christian maxim 'that we should love our neighbour as ourselves'. As people, we might be entitled to equal treatment. Yet it was, Godwin asserted, probable that 'one of us is a being of more worth and importance than the other'.³¹ Individuals might be conceived as having a relative value to society that merited some form of differential treatment according to their contribution to it. Thus in the famous 'fire case' example introduced in the first edition of *Political Justice*, Godwin asked whether in the event of a conflagration we should rescue the great French author of *The Adventures of Telemachus* (1699), the archbishop of Cambray, Fenelon, or his chambermaid, if we could not save both. His answer was unequivocal:

> A man is of more worth than a beast; because, being possessed of higher faculties, he is capable of a more refined and genuine happiness. In the same manner the illustrious archbishop of Cambray was of more worth than his chambermaid, and there are few of us that would hesitate to pronounce, if his palace were in flames, and the life of only one of them could be preserved, which of the two ought to be preferred.[32]

This passage, which was probably indebted to the American colonial theologian Jonathan Edwards, proved to be extremely controversial, not least because of the complex utilitarian calculations every moral crisis thus implied, although philosophers will recognize it as a not-unfamiliar variant on the lifeboat-case scenario.[33] Yet for Godwin this was the only criterion for extending benevolence that established a universal standard. He here considered a number of other rival accounts, including the view that all benefits given increased the aggregate mass of benevolence and hence the common good. But these were rejected as leading each person to have a different standard of moral judgement and preference, which he thought his own standard did not. By 1797, however, he had fixed on a formula by which we could assist the poor on the basis of their pressing needs, provided such assistance actually contributed to their greater independence.

Godwin's *The Enquirer: Reflections on Education, Manners, and Literature* (1797)

How far was the essay 'Of Avarice and Profusion' conceived as a restatement of the accounts of rights and justice just described?[34] Its starting-point was clearly the passage on the miser and the luxurious man from Book 1, Chapter 5 of the first edition of *Political Justice*, which not only remained in the third edition of 1798 but was reinforced by another addition on the same theme, doubtless in turn drawn from *The Enquirer*'s approach to this question. In 1797 Godwin thus returned to this theme in earnest, perhaps agitated by having left the matter so ill-explored, indicating only a duty but not the means of fulfilling it; doubtless, too, driven by the debate about the Poor Laws that intensified with the threat of famine in the winter of 1795–6 and that placed the entire question squarely before the public eye. The collection of essays he produced is now sometimes seen only as remarkable because 'it incited Thomas Robert Malthus to write his *Essay on Population*'.[35]

The 1797 essay poses the question as to which moral outlook and resultant behaviour most benefits society, that of the avaricious or that of the profuse man. Godwin's argument focuses on the proposition that neither giving the poor money nor employing them as such was satisfactory. 'If,' he suggested, 'the rich man would substantially relieve the burthens of the poor, exclusive of the improvement he may communicate to their understandings or their temper, it must be by taking upon himself a part of their labour, and not by setting them tasks. All other relief is partial and temporary.'[36] As a stern republican critic of aristocracy, Godwin clearly aligns himself to Adam Smith's position vis-à-vis the disutility of the unproductive labour employed by landowning classes.[37] In Book 2 of *Wealth of Nations*, Smith had contended that:

> There is one sort of labour which adds to the value of the subject upon which it is bestowed: there is another which has no such effect. The former, as it produces a value, may be called productive; the latter, unproductive labour. Thus the labour of a manufacturer adds, generally, to the value of the materials which he works upon, that of his own maintenance, and of his master's profit. The labour of a menial servant, on the contrary, adds to the value of nothing.; ... the labour of the manufacturer fixes and realises itself in some particular subject or vendible commodity, which lasts for some time at least after that labour is past ... The labour of the menial servant, on the contrary, does not fix or realise itself in any particular subject or vendible commodity. His services generally perish in the very instant of their performance, and seldom leave any trace or value behind them, for which an equal quantity of service could afterwards be procured.

Smith recognized, of course, that this position produced anomalies, and that:

> In the same class must be ranked, some both of the gravest and most important, and some of the most frivolous professions: churchmen, lawyers, physicians, men of letters of all kinds; players, buffoons, musicians, opera-singers, opera-dancers, &c. The labour of the meanest of these has a certain value, regulated by the very same principles which regulate that of every other sort of labour; and that of the noblest and most useful, produces nothing which could afterwards purchase or procure an equal quantity of labour. Like the declamation of the actor, the harangue of the orator, or the tune of the musician, the work of all of them perishes in the very instant of its production.[38]

Nonetheless, this established a clear distinction between idleness and disutility and socially valuable activity that produced purchasable commodities.

We see how Godwin thus adopts this argument, in contending that

> If a rich man employ the poor in breaking up land and cultivating its useful productions, he may be their benefactor. But, if he employ them in erecting palaces, in sinking canals, in laying out his parks, and modelling his pleasure-grounds, he will be found, when rightly considered, their enemy. He is adding to the weight of oppression, and the vast accumulation of labour, by which they are already sunk beneath the level of the brutes … Such is the real tendency of the conduct of that so frequently applauded character, the rich man who lives up to his fortune. His houses, his gardens, his equipages, his horses, the luxury of his table, and the number of his servants, are so many articles that may assume the name of munificence, but that in reality are but added expedients for grinding the poor, and filling up the measure of human calamity.[39]

By contrast, Godwin argues, the avaricious man did not lock up the real sources of wealth, such as corn, oxen, clothes or houses, only money, which was not wealth. His outlook was thus 'much less pernicious to mankind, and much more nearly conformable to the unalterable principles of justice, than that of the man who disburses his income in what has been termed, a liberal and spirited style'. Yet neither was the miser a 'pattern of benevolence'. Godwin conceded that 'money, though in itself destitute of any real value, is an engine enabling us to vest the actual commodities of life in such persons and objects, as our understandings may point out to us … This engine, which might be applied to most admirable purposes, the miser constantly refuses to employ.' And so a 'rich man, guided by the genuine principles of virtue, would be munificent, though not with that spurious munificence that has so often usurped the name'.[40] This leaves open the possibility of using wealth to some socially desirable or 'admirable' end, although clearly not to all forms of the employment of the poor, only those that contributed substantially to their subsistence and independence. In 1793 it was left open as to how far this might include charity for the necessitous poor. By the second edition, however, this had altered,[41] and in 1798 Godwin stated that 'it must previously be seen that the claims of one man are originally of the same extent as the claims of another; and that the only difference which can arise must relate to extraordinary infirmity, or the particular object of utility which any individual is engaged in promoting'.[42] In 1820 he would offer against Malthus a defence of the Poor Laws of England while lamenting the need for them, and coming surprisingly close to Malthus on the issue of the desirability of charity being voluntary.[43]

Enter Malthus

Malthus had probably become acquainted with the basic principles of *Political Justice* when it was first published, for while he was isolated in the rural parish of Okewood from 1788 until this period, there is no reason to presume that he did not follow closely the unfolding debate about the French Revolution. At any event, we know that he and Godwin had breakfast in mid-1798, evidently at the house of Malthus's publisher and Godwin's friend, the Unitarian Joseph Johnson, after Godwin had begun reading the *Essay* on 5 August.[44] It would have been an interesting and much anticipated event for Malthus for, as we know, he had been initially inspired to write the *Essay* following what Malthus himself called a conversation with a 'friend' about the essay entitled 'Of Avarice or Profusion' in *The Enquirer*. The 'friend', Bishop Otter later noted, was in fact Malthus's father Daniel Malthus, a disciple of Rousseau who probably took Godwin's side on some if not many issues in these discussions.[45] It is reasonable to assume thus that this entry point, which Malthus says, relative to this conversation, 'started the general question of the future improvement of society', probably regressed back in the course of this or other previous discussions to Godwin's *Enquiry Concerning Political Justice* (1793). Malthus had clearly already formed a view about what he presumed was the palpably absurd proposition that the future perfectibility of mankind suggested by Godwin would inhibit population growth because reason would restrain the passions. But Malthus's approach to Godwin was also through his reading of *The Enquirer*, and both *The Enquirer* and *Political Justice* were at issue in the composition of the *Essay*.

Initially the crucial question here appears to be Godwin's discussion as to how charity might be most usefully disbursed in the first edition of the *Essay*. Here Malthus contended:

> It may at first appear strange, but I believe it is true, that I cannot by means of money raise a poor man, and enable him to live much better than he did before, without proportionately depressing others in the same class. If I retrench the quantity of food consumed in my house, and give him what I have cut off, I then benefit him, without depressing any but myself and family, who, perhaps, may be well able to bear it. If I turn up a piece of uncultivated land, and give him the produce, I then benefit both him, and all the members of the society, because what he before consumed is thrown

into the common stock, and probably some of the new produce with it. But if I only give him money, supposing the produce of the country to remain the same, I give him a title to a larger share of that produce than formerly, which share he cannot receive without diminishing the shares of others. It is evident that this effect, in individual instances, must be so small as to be totally imperceptible; but still it must exist, as many other effects do, which like some of the insects that people the air, elude our grosser perceptions.[46]

We note here, then, that Malthus's starting-point is very close to Godwin's conclusion in *The Enquirer*: giving the poor money or food is not an option, but assisting them to cultivate their own land such that they could employ and feed themselves as (hopefully independent) cultivators might be. Malthus then introduced two key arguments against the Poor Laws:

> The poor-laws of England tend to depress the general condition of the poor in these two ways. Their first obvious tendency is to increase population without increasing the food for its support. A poor man may marry with little or no prospect of being able to support a family in independence. They may be said therefore in some measure to create the poor which they maintain; and as the provisions of the country must, in consequence of the increased population, be distributed to every man in smaller proportions, it is evident that the labour of those who are not supported by parish assistance, will purchase a smaller quantity of provisions than before, and consequently, more of them must be driven to ask for support.
>
> Secondly, the quantity of provisions consumed in workhouses upon a part of the society, that cannot in general be considered as the most valuable part, diminishes the shares that would otherwise belong to more industrious, and more worthy members; and thus in the same manner forces more to become dependent. If the poor in the workhouses were to live better than they now do, this new distribution of the money of the society would tend more conspicuously to depress the condition of those out of the workhouses, by occasioning a rise in the price of provisions.[47]

The latter argument in particular, which appears not to have been associated previously with Godwin's stance, clearly indicates in its description of 'more valuable' and 'more industrious, and more worthy members' an affinity with the utilitarian premises of *Political Justice* (and one that, incidentally, points precisely to A.R. Wallace's and Charles Darwin's starting-points in their accounts of natural selection and 'fitness'). Malthus hints at a distinction between those types of the poor who deserve our assistance and those who do not. Supporting those who cannot maintain their own family is not an option. Malthus makes it clear that:

> If men are induced to marry from a prospect of parish provision, with little or no chance of maintaining their families in independence, they are not

only unjustly tempted to bring unhappiness and dependence upon themselves and children; but they are tempted, without knowing it, to injure all in the same class with themselves. A labourer who marries without being able to support a family, may in some respects be considered as an enemy to all his fellow-labourers.[48]

This is not, apparently, an attack on the right to subsistence as such of the type that would be mounted in 1803. What it indicates is preferential treatment for the more industrious and worthy, and for the provision of employment rather than relief. Yet how was this to be accomplished? Malthus rejects the proposition, associated with Condorcet, that it might be possible for 'an inquisition ... to be established, to examine the claims of each individual, and to determine whether he had, or had not, exerted himself to the utmost, and to grant or refuse assistance accordingly', but that 'this would be little else than a repetition upon a larger scale of the English poor laws, and would be completely destructive of the true principles of liberty and equality'.[49] The principle of assistance itself as embodied in the Poor Laws is thus at issue here. But if public bodies could not determine who was 'worthy', the only recourse was to leave the matter to 'nature', which was exactly what Malthus opted for in 1803.

This implies that the 1798 edition of the *Essay* lays the groundwork for the rejection of rights in the 1803 edition. In 1803, Malthus, mentioning Thomas Paine for the first time, lamented the 'mischiefs' that *Rights of Man* had occasioned, which he attributed to Paine's total lack of acquaintance 'with the structure of society, and the different moral effects to be expected from the physical difference between this country and America'. Now, confronting rights claims as such, Malthus insisted that there was 'one right, which man has been generally thought to possess, which I am confident he neither does, nor can, possess, a right to subsistence when his labour will not fairly purchase it'. No person had 'any claim of right on society for subsistence, if his labour will not purchase it'. And thus followed the conclusion that 'if the society do not want his labour', no-one had any 'claim of *right* to the smallest portion of food'.[50] Charity might be forthcoming, but it could not be expected automatically by those in distress.

Malthus was thus chiefly concerned in the first edition of the *Essay* as well as subsequently to substitute claims based on productivity for those emanating from abstract right. But it does seem that Malthus thought at least partly that this was the ground that Godwin had already occupied. What the *Enquirer* piece revealed that, by and large, *Political Justice* did not, Malthus recognized, was a closer engagement with Adam Smith on the question of the moral tendency of different uses of wealth. But here, Malthus thought, Godwin had come to radically different conclusions from Smith. Godwin did not recognize capital accumulation as a useful or virtuous activity, whereas to Smith it was essential to the onward progress of commercial society. Malthus wrote that

> Dr. Adam Smith has very justly observed, that nations, as well as individuals, grow rich by parsimony, and poor by profusion; and that, therefore, every frugal man was a friend, and every spend-thrift an enemy to his country. The reason he gives is, that what is saved from revenue is always added to stock, and is therefore taken from the maintenance of labour that is generally unproductive, and employed in the maintenance of labour that realizes itself in valuable commodities. No observation can be more evidently just. The subject of Mr. Godwin's essay is a little similar in its first appearance, but in essence is as distinct as possible. He considers the mischief of profusion, as an acknowledged truth; and therefore makes his comparison between the avaricious man, and the man who spends his income.[51]

Thus, Malthus continued,

> the avaricious man of Mr. Godwin, is totally a distinct character, at least with regard to his effect upon the prosperity of the state, from the frugal man of Dr. Adam Smith. The frugal man in order to make more money, saves from his income, and adds to his capital; and this capital he either employs himself in the maintenance of productive labour, or he lends it to some other person, who will probably employ it in this way. He benefits the state, because he adds to its general capital; and because wealth employed as capital, not only sets in motion more labour, than when spent as income, but the labour is besides of a more valuable kind. But the avaricious man of Mr. Godwin locks up his wealth in a chest, and sets in motion no labour of any kind, either productive or unproductive. This is so essential a difference, that Mr. Godwin's decision in his essay, appears at once as evidently false, as Dr. Adam Smith's position is evidently true. It could not, indeed, but occur to Mr. Godwin, that some present inconvenience might arise to the poor, from thus locking up the funds destined for the maintenance of labour. The only way, therefore, he had of weakening this objection, was to compare the two characters chiefly with regard to their tendency to accelerate the approach of that happy state of cultivated equality, on which he says we ought always to fix our eyes as our polar star.[52]

The latter proposition was, of course, to Malthus, 'absolutely impracticable'. Godwin's scheme would 'degenerate into a class of proprietors, and a class of labourers; and that the substitution of benevolence, for self-love, as the moving principle of society, instead of producing the happy effects that might be expected from so fair a name, would cause the same pressure of want to be felt by the whole of society, which is now felt only by a part'. As Marshall, among others, acknowledges, Malthus thus here did agree with Godwin that the frugal man was to be preferred over the profligate.[53] He appears to meet Godwin in other ways, too, however:

> Mr. Godwin would perhaps say, that the whole system of barter and exchange, is a vile and iniquitous traffic. If you would essentially relieve the poor man, you should take a part of his labour upon yourself, or give him your money, without exacting so severe a return for it. In answer to the first method proposed, it may be observed, that even if the rich could be persuaded to assist the poor in this way, the value of the assistance would be comparatively trifling. The rich, though they think themselves of great importance, bear but a small proportion in point of numbers to the poor, and would, therefore, relieve them but of a small part of their burdens by taking a share. Were all those that are employed in the labours of luxuries, added to the number of those employed in producing necessaries; and could these necessary labours be amicably divided among all, each man's share might indeed be comparatively light; but desireable as such an amicable division would undoubtedly be, I cannot conceive any practical principle according to which it could take place. It has been strewn, that the spirit of benevolence, guided by the strict impartial justice that Mr. Godwin describes, would, if vigorously acted upon, depress in want and misery the whole human race. Let us examine what would be the consequence, if the proprietor were to retain a decent share for himself; but to give the rest away to the poor, without exacting a task from them in return. Not to mention the idleness and the vice that such a proceeding, if general, would probably create in the present state of society, and the great risk there would be, of diminishing the produce of land, as well as the labours of luxury, another objection yet remains.

And in any case, Malthus insisted, this would do nothing to dispel the pressure of population:

> It has appeared that from the principle of population, more will always be in want than can be adequately supplied. The surplus of the rich man might be sufficient for three, but four will be desirous to obtain it. He cannot make this selection of three out of the four, without conferring a great favour on those that are the objects of his choice. These persons must consider themselves as under a great obligation to him, and as dependent upon him for their support.
>
> The rich man would feel his power, and the poor man his dependence; and the evil effects of these two impressions on the human heart are well known. Though I perfectly agree with Mr. Godwin therefore in the evil of hard labour; yet I still think it a less evil, and less calculated to debase the human mind, than dependence.[54]

We see thus that (the Whiggish) Malthus agreed with Godwin both in abhorring dependence and in regarding hard labour as superior to that form of dependence that the extravagance or benevolence of the rich in employing the poor was certain to forge.

Malthus's engagement with both *Political Justice* and 'Of Avarice and Profusion' thus suggests a more complex and interesting confrontation with Godwin than is usually assumed. Not only is Adam Smith a key intermediary here. It seems likely that both *Political Justice* and *The Enquirer* formed part of the central argument of Malthus's *Essay*, specifically by suggesting a utilitarian account of individual social worth, and hinting that assistance to the worthy poor – but only by actually employing them – might be justified while that to the unworthy certainly was not, at least outside of cases of extreme necessity. Moreover, by proposing in *Political Justice* (1793) that rights as such were to be trumped by duties, Godwin may have provided some of the basis for Malthus's famous tirade against rights in the second edition of the *Essay*. Here we recall the famous passage, immediately following on Malthus's comments on Paine, describing 'Nature's mighty feast'. This was deleted in the next edition (1806) and thereafter because of the furore it created. In it Malthus stated:

> A man who is born into a world already possessed, if he cannot get subsistence from his parents on whom he has a just demand, and if the society do not want his labour, has no claim of *right* to the smallest portion of food, and, in fact, has no business to be where he is. At nature's mighty feast there is no vacant cover for him. She tells him to be gone, and will quickly execute her own orders, if he does not work upon the compassion of some of her guests. If these guests get up and make room for him, other intruders immediately appear demanding the same favour. The report of a provision for all that come, fills the hall with numerous claimants. The order and harmony of the feast is disturbed, the plenty that before reigned is changed into scarcity; and the happiness of the guests is destroyed by the spectacle of misery and dependence in every part of the hall, and by the clamorous importunity of those, who are justly enraged at not finding the provision which they had been taught to expect. The guests learn too late their error, in counteracting those strict orders to all intruders, issued by the great mistress of the feast, who, wishing that all her guests should have plenty, and knowing that she could not provide for unlimited numbers, humanely refused to admit fresh comers when her table was already full.[55]

The political message of this claim Malthus then spelled out clearly. Radicals in the 1790s and often later were prone to blaming poverty on the unjust system of taxation and its unfair burden on the poor, which were supported by a system of legislation that favoured the wealthy. But, wrote Malthus, the poor were themselves in fact chiefly responsible for their condition:

> If the great truths on these subjects were more generally circulated, and the lower classes of people could be convinced that, by the laws of nature, independently of any particular institutions, except the great one of property, which is absolutely necessary in order to attain any considerable produce, no person has any claim of right on society for subsistence, if his labour will not purchase it, the greatest part of the mischievous declamation on the unjust institutions of society would fall powerless to the ground. The poor are by no means inclined to be visionary. Their distresses are always real, though they are not attributed to the real causes. If these real causes were properly explained to them, and they were taught to know how small a part of their present distress was attributable to government, and how great a part to causes totally unconnected with it, discontent and irritation among the lower classes of people would show themselves much less frequently than at present; and when they did show themselves, would be much less to be dreaded.[56]

The outrage that these passages encountered hinged, of course, in part on Malthus's resolute determination to evaluate each individual's contribution to society according to the worth of their labour in the market, which generated a right to a place at the feast. Without such a contribution, individuals were, it is implied, effectively useless; this was a point upon which both left and right would converge in the coming century. The result would be, for those who had 'had no claim of right on society for the smallest portion of food, beyond that which his labour would fairly purchase', that:

> if he and his family were saved from suffering the utmost extremities of hunger, he would owe it to the pity of some kind benefactor, to whom, therefore, he ought to be bound by the strongest ties of gratitude.
>
> If this system were pursued, we need be under no apprehensions whatever that the number of persons in extreme want would be beyond the power and the will of the benevolent to supply. The sphere for the exercise of private charity would, I am confident, be less than it is at present; and the only difficulty would be, to restrain the hand of benevolence from assisting those in distress in so liberal a manner as to encourage indolence and want of foresight in others.[57]

This position is stated in an extremely bald and stark manner in the second edition of the *Essay*. Here, however, Adam Smith may again have played an intermediary role. For Malthus was also to some degree only restating Smith's position in the *Wealth of Nations* respecting the relative value of types of labour. But we need now to assess what light it sheds upon Malthus's confrontation with Godwin, who was keen to stress that in the future ideal society, all these forms of unproductive labour would disappear, and the chief occupation of each would be 'that of man, and in addition perhaps that of cultivator'.[58]

Productivity trumps rights

Malthus's position in 1798 vis-à-vis claims to charity can be read as a modification of Godwin's original theory of justice as presented in *Political Justice*. Some individuals had stronger claims upon us. These were of two types, those who provided most to society and those who were most necessitous. Those who laboured clearly contributed more than those who did not. Malthus took up the former part of this argument in 1798 and made it imply that charity should be extended chiefly if not entirely to those who were economically productive. Thus in 1803 he claimed that no person had 'any claim of right on society for subsistence, if his labour will not purchase it'.[59] No 'right to charity' consequently existed, separate from the ability and willingness of the poor to make a contribution to common produce. This they could do by employing these on the land. This was both a productive and a morally justifiable application of charity. So the distance between Malthus's position in 1798 and that of 1803 is actually much smaller than is often assumed. Malthus was simply restating the need to employ the poor productively, even if he now overstepped accepted lines of propriety in his denigration of rights claims.

But this, too, is partly a legacy of Book 2, Chapter 5 of *Political Justice* (1793), which dwelt upon the 'immoral consequences of the doctrine of rights' defined as 'discretionary powers', duties alone to the public good circumscribing the bounds of human action. Indeed Godwin, as we have seen, had precisely used the examples of the miser and luxurious man to attack the concept of rights in 1793. Godwin, it is true, had in Book 8 asserted that 'justice' allowed an entitlement of 'each man to the supply of his animal wants so far as the general stock will afford it'. But in Malthusian hands this allegation was sufficiently malleable to permit a redefinition, still within the constraints of 'justice', of what could be afforded from the 'general stock', particularly when famine threatened, as it did in 1795–6. In 1793, Godwin had asked directly to whom a loaf of bread belonged when six men were starving. He had answered both that those who most needed bread deserved it, but also that in most circumstances all had a duty to contribute to the common stock, if necessary by reaping the common harvest.[60] This implies a principle of no labour, no reward, in other words – which was precisely Malthus's point, although Godwin did not carry it to such an extreme conclusion. Godwin had also claimed that the first and simplest degree of property was that based upon the production of the greatest sum of benefit or pleasure.[61] His conception of entitlement was thus still geared towards those who furnished society with useful produce, and away from a right on the basis of humanity as such. This again makes Malthus's 1803 proposed abolition of rights appear less abrupt and extraordinary. It was in fact only a short step from alleging that society should assist only those who proved 'worthy' by their contribution of labour. This places Godwin and Malthus in much closer proximity than we usually assume.

Conclusion

Generations of commentators have stressed the distance and enmity between Malthus and Godwin. We have seen here, however, not only that Malthus took up Godwin's opposition to simply assisting the poor on benevolent motives, but also his theory of justice, which stressed that rights as such were inferior to considerations of utility. Both agreed that there were different ways of assisting the poor and that here too considerations of utility had to be weighed. Both insisted that employing them in cultivation rather than giving them money was to be preferred, and that independence, in turn, was preferable to dependence. This embrace of utilitarianism was somewhat different from that usually associated with Malthus. The case for seeing Malthus as a theological utilitarian with a clear debt to William Paley has been stated by A.M.C. Waterman, Donald Winch and Niall O' Flaherty.[62] Here, it appears, Malthus also shifted Godwinian utilitarianism towards a 'productivist' assessment of the type Adam Smith had suggested in the first instance (although the roots of the idea are, of course, much older). Here Malthus was much closer to Godwin in 1798 than is usually acknowledged. Godwin may have underestimated the power of population to multiply, and he was of course in Malthus's eyes, like Condorcet, woefully optimistic respecting the construction of any ideal society that did not acknowledge this fact. But what Godwin had established that Malthus built upon was an account of how to assist the poor in the present circumstances. It might also be suggested (as Robert Torrens would shortly point out) that the famous addition by Malthus in 1803 of 'moral restraint' as a means of inhibiting population growth was an acknowledgement of Godwin's claim that the sexual passions could indeed be at least partly tamed, which admission has been seen as fundamentally undermining the force of his main arguments.[63] Again then, despite their apparent differences, both shared more in common than either was probably willing to concede.

Notes

1 Among general accounts of the relationship, John Avery, *Progress, Poverty and Population: Re-reading Condorcet, Godwin and Malthus* (London: Frank Cass, 1997) does not even discuss *The Enquirer*.

2 On Godwin's changes see Gregory Claeys, 'From True Virtue to Benevolent Politeness: Godwin and Godwinism Revisited', in Gordon Schochet (ed.), *Empire and Revolutions: Papers Presented at the Folger Institute Seminar 'Political Thought in the English-Speaking Atlantic, 1760–1800'* (Washington, DC: The Folger Library, 1993), pp. 187–226.

3 Godwin used the term to mean 'the progressive nature of man, in knowledge, in virtuous propensities, and in social institutions' (quoted in William St Clair, *The Godwins and the Shelleys: The Biography of a Family* [London: Faber and Faber, 1989], p. 73).

4 Malthus had, however, treated the theme in an unpublished pamphlet entitled 'The Crisis: a View of the Present Interesting State of Great Britain, by a Friend to the Constitution', which is discussed by John Wilson Croker in the *Edinburgh Review* (64, 1837, pp. 468–506). This cast doubt upon the size of a nation's population being an index of its happiness.

5 Population was one of the topics Godwin and Owen discussed when they first met in 1813 (Godwin Diary, 24 January 1813, Abinger Collection, Bodleian Library, Oxford).

6 See in particular his letter to James Pratt of 28–30 August 1804, where he asserted that 'the principle of population has no bounds', in direct reference to Malthus: *The Letters of William Godwin*, ed. Pamela Clemit (Oxford: Oxford University Press, 2014), vol. 2, p. 314.

7 Quoted in C. Kegan Paul, *William Godwin. His Friends and Contemporaries*, 2 vols. (London: Henry S. King & Co., 1876), vol. 2, p. 260.

8 J.R. Poynter, *Society and Pauperism: English Ideas on Poor Relief, 1795–1834* (London: Routledge and Kegan Paul, 1969), p. 110. This is also a prominent theme in A.M.C. Waterman, *Revolution, Economics and Religion. Christian Political Economy, 1798–1833* (Cambridge: Cambridge University Press, 1991), pp. 15–18.

9 Robert Southey, *Essays, Moral and Political*, 2 vols. (London: John Murray, 1832), vol. 1, pp. 82–3.

10 William Hazlitt, *Political Essays* (London: William Hone, 1819), pp. 414–15, emphasis in original.

11 *Critical Review*, 15 (1808), 270.

12 Anonymous, *A Clear, Fair, and Candid Investigation of the Population, Commerce, and Agriculture of This Kingdom, With a Full Refutation of Mr. Malthus's Principles* (London: J. Mawman and J. Richardson, 1810), p. 3.

13 I here summarize the concluding arguments of my *The French Revolution Debate in Britain* (London: Palgrave Macmillan, 2007), pp. 155–8.

14 Donald Winch is an exception here: see his *Riches and Poverty: An Intellectual History of Political Economy in Britain, 1750–1834* (Cambridge: Cambridge University Press, 1996), pp. 256–7.

15 St Clair, *Godwins and Shelleys*, p. 456.

16 Winch, *Riches and Poverty*, pp. 267–9.

17 Patricia James confessed to 'finding Godwin's "system" uncongenial', which apparently served as an excuse for not probing further into these issues: Patricia James, *Population Malthus: His Life and Times* (London: Routledge, 1979), p. 59. But most other commentators have been similarly minded. The secondary literature on Godwin is similarly unsympathetic to his great antagonist.

18 Patricia James concludes that Malthus had both the first and third edition of *Political Justice* to work with: *Population Malthus*, p. 60. The third edition appeared at the end of 1797, although it is usually referred to as the 1798 edition. The preface of Malthus's *Essay* is dated 7 June 1798. It is often assumed that Malthus did not read Godwin until 1797: see, for example, Brian Dolan. 'Malthus's Political Economy of Health', in Brian Dolan (ed.), *Malthus, Medicine and Morality: 'Malthusianism' after 1798* (Amsterdam: Rodopi, 2000), p. 12.

19 Monro concedes as much, without detail: D.H. Monro. *Godwin's Moral Philosophy* (Oxford: Oxford University Press, 1953), p. 81.

20 A reassessment of the context of this argument is given in my 'Paine and the Religiosity of Rights', in Rachel Hammersley (ed.), *Revolutionary Moments: Reading Revolutionary Texts* (London: Bloomsbury, 2015). For the general context, see my *Thomas Paine: Social and Political Thought* (London: Unwin Hyman, 1989), pp. 75–84, 196–208.

21 William Godwin, *An Enquiry Concerning Political Justice* (London: G.G.J. and J. Robinson, 1793), vol. 1, pp. 109–20.

22 Godwin, *Political Justice* (1793), vol. 1, pp. 113–14.

23 This idea has often been linked to Godwin's Sandemanian Baptist upbringing, which stressed such obligations.

24 Gregory Claeys, 'The Effects of Property on Godwin's Theory of Justice', *Journal of the History of Philosophy*, 22 (1984), 81–101, p. 96.

25 William Godwin. *Enquiry Concerning Political Justice*, 1798 edition, ed. Isaac Kramnick (Harmondsworth: Penguin Books, 1976), pp. 710, 184–5, 191–9.

26 Godwin, *Political Justice* (1793), vol. 1, pp. 88–9.

27 Ibid., vol. 2, pp. 790–1.

28 Ibid., vol. 2, p. 794.

29 Godwin, *Political Justice* (1798), p. 715.

30 Godwin, *Political Justice* (1793), vol. 2, p. 583.

31 Ibid., vol. 1, p. 81.

32 Ibid., vol. 1, pp. 81–2.

33 The key text is the *Essay on the Nature of True Virtue* (1765), which emphasized a preference for 'benevolence to being in general' over any private or

personal affections. This is explored in my 'The Concept of "Political Justice" in Godwin's *Political Justice*: A Reconsideration', *Political Theory*, 11 (1983), 565–84.

34 I here take up the argument first proposed in my *French Revolution Debate*, pp. 156–7.

35 Ford K. Brown, *The Life of William Godwin* (London: J.M. Dent, 1926), p. 124.

36 William Godwin, *The Enquirer: Reflections On Education, Manners, And Literature: In A Series Of Essays* (London: G.G. and J. Robinson, 1797), p. 173.

37 Godwin quotes *Wealth of Nations* respecting the division of labour in *Political Justice* (1793), vol. 2, p. 859. He did, however, later acknowledge that he had 'never been more than an occasional student of what is called Political Economy, that is of calculations of revenue, resources, trade and the means of subsistence, and that only when I felt myself called upon by the connexion of those subjects with my more congenial speculations respecting the morals, the independence and happiness of man in society' (quoted in Rosalie Glenn Grylls, *William Godwin and His World* [London: Odham Press, 1953] p. 182). Nonetheless, the general model of the free circulation of opinion presented in *Political Justice* is explicitly indebted to Smith. See *Political Justice* (1793), vol. 2, pp. 589–90.

38 Adam Smith, *An Inquiry into the Nature and Causes of the Wealth of Nations*, 2 vols. (Oxford: Clarendon Press, 1869), vol. 1, pp. 332–3. See generally my 'The Reaction to Political Radicalism and the Popularization of Political Economy in Early 19th Century Britain: the Case of "Productive and Unproductive Labour"', in Terry Shinn and Richard Whitley (eds.), *Expository Science: Forms and Functions of Popularization* (Dordrecht: D. Reidel, 1985), pp. 119–36.

39 Godwin. *Enquirer*, p. 178.

40 Ibid., pp. 182–3.

41 William Godwin, *An Enquiry Concerning Political Justice*, 2nd edn (London: G.G.J. and J. Robinson, 1795), vol. 2, p. 472.

42 Godwin, *Political Justice* (1798), p. 743.

43 'Mr. Malthus has brought these laws into discussion, while illustrating his principle, that "the poor man has no right to support." This principle I deny; but upon the poor-laws I have no design of pronouncing judgment. In England, those who are supposed unable to maintain themselves are aided from a general assessment: in France and some other countries, they are provided for in a different way. In both however they are under the protection of the law: I should prefer being the citizen of a country, where the deserted and the helpless should be sufficiently taken care of without the intervention of the state. But in England at least we are not yet ripe for this.' William Godwin, *Of Population* (London: Longman, Hurst, Rees, Orme and Brown, 1820), p. 560.

44 Godwin, *Letters*, vol. 2, p. 54. They met on 15 August 1798. Peter Marshall's biography of Godwin has them not meeting until 1800 (*William Godwin* [New Haven: Yale University Press, 1984], p. 228). They met again at least half a dozen times in 1801–2.

45 James, *Population Malthus*, p. 61. Marshall terms Malthus *père* a 'Godwinite' (Marshall, *Godwin*, p. 170).

46 [T.R. Malthus], *An Essay on the Principle of Population, as it Affects the Future Improvement of Society* (London: J. Johnson, 1798), pp. 79–80.

47 Ibid., pp. 83–4.

48 Ibid., pp. 85–6.

49 Ibid., pp. 149–50.

50 T.R. Malthus, *An Essay on the Principle of Population*, ed. Patricia James, 2 vols. (Cambridge: Cambridge University Press, 1989), vol. 2, p. 127, emphasis in original.

51 Malthus, *Essay* (1798), pp. 282–3.

52 Ibid., pp. 283–5.

53 Marshall, *Godwin*, p. 228.

54 Malthus, *Essay* (1798), pp. 285–6, 289–92.

55 Malthus, *Essay*, ed. James, vol. 2, p. 127, emphasis in original.

56 Ibid., p. 128.

57 Ibid., p. 141.

58 Godwin, *Political Justice* (1793), vol. 2, p. 859.

59 Malthus, *Essay*, ed. James, vol. 2, p. 128.

60 Godwin, *Political Justice* (1793), vol. 2, p. 791.

61 William Godwin, *An Enquiry Concerning Political Justice*, 4th edn, 2 vols. (London: J. Watson, 1842), vol. 2, p. 207.

62 Waterman, *Revolution, Economics and Religion*, pp. 114–22 and Winch, *Malthus*, p. 19. Here the concentration is in particular upon the avoidance of pain as a stimulus to civilization. On this theme see Niall O'Flaherty's chapter in this volume. See further Winch. *Riches and Poverty*, pp. 221–87, which is now the best general introduction to the debate. Here Winch argues against the description of Malthus's position as one of 'implicit secular utilitarianism' by Samuel Hollander, 'Malthus and Utilitarianism with Special Reference to the *Essay on Population*', *Utilitas*, 1 (1989), 170–210.

63 For example, by Andrew Pyle (ed.), *Population: Contemporary Responses to Thomas Malthus* (Bristol: Thoemmes Press, 1994), p. xviii. See Hollander's discussion of this in 'Malthus and Utilitarianism', p. 193.

CHAPTER 3

Malthus and the 'end of poverty'

Niall O' Flaherty

The aim of this essay is to explore Malthus's magnum opus, the second *Essay on the Principle of Population* (1803) as an Enlightenment programme for the amelioration of poverty. Malthus's first *Essay* (1798) was a contribution to the ideological debates of the 1790s, and specifically an attack on the doctrine of perfectibility as advanced by William Godwin in his *Enquiry Concerning Political Justice* (1793).[1] Godwin's aim in the *Enquiry* was to show that social inequality and injustice could be eradicated by removing the pernicious institutions of property and marriage. His optimism was based on the assumption that, by the concerted employment of reason, benevolence could replace self-love as the mainspring of human action. Malthus wanted to show that this was impossible. By removing all fear of want and greatly liberalizing the commerce of the sexes, Godwin's paradise would soon trigger exponential population growth, leading, in turn, to internecine struggles for meagre resources, until ultimately the community was forced to reinstate the institutions of government and private property. According to Malthus, indeed, the tendency of population growth to outstrip man's ability to increase food supplies meant that no great improvement could be expected in the condition of mankind. Nature had only two ways of reducing population to the means of subsistence: preventative checks, the delaying of married from 'a foresight of the difficulties attending the rearing of a family'; and positive checks, 'the actual distresses of some of the lower classes, by which they are disabled from giving the proper food and attention to their children' – and these invariably produced vice and misery.[2]

The introduction of moral restraint – a third check to population that was not accompanied by misery and vice – dispelled the gloomiest conclusions of the first *Essay*, and, as Waterman observes, appeared to suggest that 'continuous improvement in the human condition' was possible after all.[3] By this stage, however, discrediting the egalitarian schemes of Godwin and Condorcet (his secondary target) had fallen down the list of Malthus's priorities. He recalled in the preface how 'in the course of the discussion' with Godwin it had gradually dawned on him that the principle of population accounted 'for much of that poverty and misery observable among the lower classes of people in every nation, and for those reiterated failures in the efforts of the higher classes to relieve them.' He was thus impelled to undertake 'an historical examination' of the effects of his principle on societies past and present.[4] Although Malthus described this enterprise in terms reminiscent of the earlier debate about perfectibility – declaring his intention to explore 'the causes that have hitherto impeded the progress of mankind towards happiness' with a view to examining 'the probability of the total or partial removal of these causes in future' – what it amounted to, as we shall see, was a scientific investigation of the nature and causes of poverty, which would form the basis of a radical scheme for its amelioration.[5] To argue that this was the main aim of the second *Essay* is not to suggest that such concerns were entirely divorced from his political aims. Despite their deep entwinement, however, it seems justifiable to explore the social agenda in abstraction from the political, in the first place because it was by no means reducible to it, and second, because the political argument of the book can only be properly understood in the light of Malthus's analysis of human want.

Boyd Hilton has greatly enriched our understanding of how Malthus's ideas shaped mainstream attitudes to poverty in the first half of the nineteenth century, as they were assimilated into the evangelical ethos that increasingly characterized the intellectual culture of the period.[6] The construction of his image as the evil genius of the 'dismal science' of political economy, sacrificing the welfare of the poor in the name of cost-benefit, by his radical and romantic enemies has also been well documented.[7] In order to recover the complex intentions behind the *Essay* of 1803, however, we need to look beyond its reception, by restoring the arguments to the precise social and intellectual contexts in which they were formulated. The second *Essay* was primarily a contribution to the debates about the causes of poverty and the effectiveness of existing systems of relief that had been ongoing throughout the eighteenth century but that were 'quickened and transformed' by recurrent scarcities beginning in 1795, as poor harvests sent wheat prices spiralling.[8] These crises prompted a plethora of proposals for providing a sturdier safety net for the labouring poor, from wage subsidies to schemes for providing each family with a cow; while on the ground, magistrates and Poor Law overseers employed a range of expedients for coping with the immediate fallout from dearth, including allowance systems like the one famously adopted by magistrates in

Speenhamland in 1795, which supplemented wages in accordance with food prices. Such proposals and practical measures were predicated on the belief that the rich were morally bound to relieve the poor in times of distress, as part of the divinely ordained scheme of reciprocal rights and obligations that bound all the levels of society together. For the main part, even those who questioned the wisdom of the Elizabethan Poor Laws – which, it was widely held, gave legal force to such obligations – upheld the principles underpinning them. An exception here was the uncompromising Joseph Townsend, who held that the parish laws aggravated distress by encouraging idleness among the lower orders and by removing the anxieties – hunger 'foreseen and feared for his immediate offspring' – that discouraged the labourer from having more children than he could afford to feed.[9] This explained the seemingly paradoxical coexistence of soaring poor rates with increasing hardship. It was Malthus's *Essay* of 1803, however, that really gave such arguments traction, by seeming to identify the law of nature that rendered compulsory schemes for relief self-defeating.

Despite having been published nearly half a century ago, J.R. Poynter's *Society and Pauperism* (1969) is still widely regarded as the definitive account of these debates and Malthus's contribution to them. Although his account did not share the undisguised hostility that characterised much of the historical literature on Malthus in the 1950s,[10] Poynter corroborated in one crucial respect the damning assessment of Marx, accepting that 'his reputation as a gloomy prophet was not undeserved'.[11] Although the second edition of the *Essay* was ostensibly more optimistic than the unequivocally despairing first edition, Malthus's 'positive suggestions were less prominent than his exceedingly severe criticisms of all other proposals for relief.' Nor, in any case, did his positive proposals offer much hope to the needy, according to Poynter, for Malthus was deeply pessimistic about the likelihood of moral restraint, 'the only true remedy to poverty', being widely adopted by the poor.[12] It clearly grates with Poynter, furthermore, that Malthus condemned present arrangements for relieving hardship and poured scorn on every proposal for its relief on the basis of arguments so riddled with inconsistencies. Particularly culpable in this respect was his failure to remove his calls for the gradual abolition of the Poor Laws, despite being forced to admit that they did not promote early marriage in England. With the argument based on the principle of population in tatters, 'the *Essay* became not a reasoned case against poor relief, but a farrago of all available abolitionist arguments'.[13] That he continued to prophesize doom in the face of the facts suggests either that it was all a cynical ideological manoeuvre (as Marx had alleged), or that he had fallen

prey to a baneful intellectual fanaticism. Partly in the light of later scholarship – which has superseded Poynter's account on a number of issues –
but mainly on the basis of a more comprehensive contextual reading of
the second *Essay*, this chapter offers an alternative to this characterization.

My point of departure is an account of the *Essay* that tries to do justice to the enormously ambitious 'scientific' agenda of the book, that of
inaugurating a new science of poverty and of providing, on the basis of
this, a new paradigm for thinking about the problem of hardship. Given
the importance that Malthus attaches to it, this theoretical enterprise
clearly deserves more scholarly attention in its own right than it has hitherto received. What is more, it is only in the light of a proper understanding of the 'empirical' analysis of the book that we can properly make
sense of its practical aims. One crucial tenet of the 'doom-monger' thesis upheld by Poynter and others has already been overturned. Hollander
and Levy have observed that Malthus's hopes for human improvement
rested not on the prospect of a significant increase in *moral* restraint, but
on the increasing tendency already manifest in old countries to engage in
prudential restraint; that is, in preventive checks that may or may not be
accompanied by 'irregular gratifications'.[14] Malthus concluded his extensive survey of population checks in the first two books of the *Essay* with
the crucial observation that preventive checks prevailed far more in the
modern European states examined in Book 2 than they had done among
the 'savage' and pastoral nations considered in Book 1. This explained why
modern Europe increasingly escaped the positive checks – war, disease,
severe hardship and famine – that kept population down to the means
of subsistence in the 'lower' stages of civilization. Malthus's primary aim,
then, from 1803 onwards, was to give further impetus to this trend, notwithstanding that later marriages might lead to an increase in sexual vice.
Although only 'perfect chastity' would enable the labourer who delayed
marriage for prudential reasons 'to avoid *all* the moral and physical evils
which depend upon his own conduct', it was by no means 'necessary
to the success of my plan'.[15] However much unhappiness was produced
by 'the vices relating to sex', the effects of 'squalid and hopeless poverty'
caused by redundant population – not least, moral degradation leading to
recidivism – were 'still more pernicious'.[16] Far from revealing the impossibility of progress then, Malthus's doctrine provided the basis for a substantive programme of 'social reform', as Hollander puts it. By providing a
more comprehensive account of the observations underpinning Malthus's
optimism regarding the spread of prudential restraint in modern Europe
than we currently possess, this chapter will offer a fresh perspective on the

practical intentions behind the book. Emphasizing the cultural dimensions of his solution to poverty, it shows how the campaign to promote the
increase of prudential restraint among the poor was framed by a broader
programme to raise their level of civilization. Such a reading raises severe
doubts, as we shall see, about Poynter's assertion that Malthus jettisoned
the critique of the Poor Laws based on the principle of population.

The science of poverty

It was clear from his critique of Smithian economic thought, carried over
from the first edition, that Malthus saw the *Essay* as inaugurating a new
sub-branch of political economy.

> The professed object of Adam Smith's *Inquiry* is the *Nature and Causes of the
> Wealth of Nations*. There is another, however, still more interesting, which
> he occasionally mixes with it – the causes that affect the happiness and
> comfort of the lower orders of society, which in every nation form the most
> numerous class. These two subjects are, no doubt, nearly connected; but
> the nature and extent of this connection, and the mode in which increasing
> wealth operates on the condition of the poor, have not been stated with
> sufficient correctness and precision.[17]

Smith's mistake, as Malthus saw it, was to view the condition of the
labouring classes as depending entirely upon the increase in national
wealth, when what really mattered was the quantity of food their labour
could command. As this was primarily determined by the ratio between
population and levels of subsistence, the science of poverty was first and
foremost a demographic science. The first two books of the *Essay* were
therefore dedicated to examining the checks to population that had operated since the origin of society; and since it was the poor who bore the
brunt of these checks, what this amounted to was a history of their lives
and sufferings, a subject entirely neglected in the history books, exclusively concerned, as they were, with the lives of the rich and powerful.[18]
This history served two purposes. In the first place, it enabled Malthus
to demonstrate the operation of the existence of the oscillations between
happiness and misery he had identified in the first *Essay*.[19] In times of
relative plenty, labourers produced more children, increasing the supply
of labour and thereby reducing its price. In the harder times that inevitably followed, they tended to have fewer children, reducing the supply of labour, increasing its price, and the cycle resumed.[20] One problem
Malthus faced in terms of convincing his audience that the problems
created by the principle of population were ever-present was that the

complexity of the economy in old states – most importantly the difference between the nominal and real price of labour – tended to obscure
such vibrations. Their effects were starkly revealed, however, among 'the
lower stages of society', where the slightest depletion of the food supply
triggered an instant upsurge in vice and misery. The second and most
important object of this history, however, was to examine the nature of
the checks that operated at different stages of society. It is 'a curious circumstance', observed Malthus, 'that a truth so important, which has been
stated and acknowledged by so many authors, should so rarely have been
pursued to its consequences.' Given that 'people are not every day dying
of famine', how was population kept down to the means of subsistence?[21]
Being a deeply practical thinker, Malthus's only interest in creating a typ-
ology of miseries, was to assess 'the probability' of their 'total or partial
removal'.[22] The account offered here suggests, indeed, that we have generally underestimated the degree to which Malthus's multilayered scheme
for the reduction of this suffering was derived from this history.[23]

But it is also vital to appreciate the significance of the enquiry itself. By
delineating the 'various forms of misery' arising from population pressure,
Malthus was presenting a new understanding of what it meant to suffer
from want. The effect of his explaining this variety of afflictions in terms
of a single material cause was that the idea of poverty came to represent a
greatly expanded taxonomy of suffering. Before reflecting on these findings, however, it is necessary to examine the methodology employed in
the investigation, since only in this light can we begin to comprehend
Malthus's belief that he was placing the study of poverty on new and sturdier foundations. While Hume's remark that 'of all the sciences, there
is none where first appearances are more deceitful than in politics' was
'undoubtedly very just', observed Malthus, it was 'most peculiarly applic-
able to that department of the science which relates to the modes of
improving the condition of the lower classes of society.'[24] On several occasions in the first two books, Malthus presents himself as penetrating below
the surface of such mirages. These revelations were the fruit of a symbi-
osis between theory and factual evidence; that is, between the principle of
population and the observations relating to the various checks to population. Believing the geometrical growth of population to have been proven
'the moment the American increase was related', and the arithmetical ratio
of food growth 'as soon as it was enunciated', Malthus considered the laws
of population 'as established in the first six pages' of the book.[25] His 'faithful history' of the 'manners and customs' of the poor relied on three types
of sources. For the operations of the principle 'in the less civilized Parts of

the World, and in Past Times', he was wholly dependent on the numerous travel writings and historical works that formed the bulk of his research between 1798 and 1803. For the checks to population in the different states of modern Europe, he was able to supplement travel writings, on the one hand, with observations gleaned on his travels to Scandinavia and Russia in 1799, France and Switzerland during the Peace of Amiens (1802–3); and, second, with a wealth of statistics for births, deaths and marriages that was now available for European countries.[26] Malthus may be considered as one of the chief instigators of the 'avalanche of printed numbers' that began to gain impetus in Europe in this period through the efforts of bureaucrats and scholars to measure the power of the state.[27] A 'satisfactory history' of how population oscillations affected the poor 'would require the constant and minute attention of many observing minds' over long periods to general and local patterns. Because they provided 'more information ... than we could receive from the most observing traveller', inferences from this kind of data enabled us to see the reality beneath the misleading appearances that so often deceived such observers.[28]

Malthus was not alone in recognizing the potential of statistical knowledge as a tool for understanding poverty. In *The State of the Poor* (1797), Frederic Eden assembled a compendium of facts and numerical tables that he hoped would provide 'the raw materials' for statesmen to improve the management of poor relief in England.[29] But, from Malthus's perspective, the facts themselves were of relatively little value, in terms of looking beyond the appearance of things, if the conclusions drawn from them were not informed by the principle of population. Whereas the apparent plenty that travellers witnessed in their fleeting visits to Tahiti had led them to conclude that 'want is seldom known' there, the different sojourns of Captain Cook revealed the 'variations in the state of the island'; in other words, the times of want and war that preceded and followed those of plenty.[30] Numerical data might help to reveal patterns of this nature, but only when framed by an understanding of the underlying laws of nature could such information be properly interpreted and rendered serviceable to the cause of human improvement. 'The marked oscillations' in the 'prosperity and population' of Tahiti were 'exactly what we should suppose from the theory', observed Malthus: prosperity encourages breeding, leading to distress, followed by positive checks that eventually reduce the population to a level at which it can live comfortably again; and so on *ad infinitum*.[31] It was this synergy between the new paradigm and the burgeoning stores of statistics that gave Malthus's principle its superior penetrative power relative to the numerous studies of hardship in this period, and that explains his sense that he was revolutionizing the subject.

For the main part, efforts to understand the sufferings of the poor in this period centred on identifying the causes of high food prices, low real wages and periodic unemployment;[32] which is to say that they focused almost exclusively on the causes of poverty rather than its effects and searched for these causes in the operations of the labour and food markets. In asserting that these economic phenomena were largely manifestations of deeper 'environmental' laws, Malthus was offering a radically new aetiology of poverty – and this engendered a new description of its symptoms. He identified two main ways that population pressure took its toll on the poor. Among nature's most potent 'instruments of destruction' were the diseases and epidemics caused by scarcity.[33] This assumption of a strong correlation between poverty and disease, a feature of the theory from its inception, raised the stakes even higher in the quest to mitigate the causes of want.[34] If, as the physician William Heberden candidly confessed, the medical world was at a loss to explain the many and complex changes in the history of diseases, this was because they failed to look beyond their 'proximate causes'. Where, in a country with a stable population, there was a given average of marriages and births, there must be a given average of deaths; and 'the channels through which the great stream of mortality is constantly flowing will always convey off a given quantity'; block one of these channels, and you only increase the current flowing through another: in other words, if you 'eradicate some diseases, others will become proportionally more fatal'; unless, that is, the stream of mortality is reduced in the first place by 'an increase in the preventive check'.[35] Malthus's phlegmatic tone belied the audaciousness of the suggestion. For he clearly wished it to be understood that his principle offered a means – the only means, indeed – of securing the gains arising from advances in medical science, including, of course, the very recent and widely celebrated discovery of the small-pox vaccine.[36]

Disease was one of nature's last resorts, however, in her ceaseless endeavour to bring population levels into line with subsistence. Dearth was just as likely to manifest itself 'in other more permanent forms of distress, and in generating customs which operate sometimes with greater force in the suppression of a rising population than in its subsequent destruction.'[37] Much of the first half of the *Essay* was thus taken up with describing the multifarious behaviours that inhibited human fecundity. Malthus illustrated the point through an explanation of the extremely low fertility of American women. It was highly likely that the widely observed lack of sexual ardour among Native Americans was 'generated by the hardships and dangers of savage life', observed Malthus, 'rather than any absolute constitutional defect'. Constant fear of famine, disease and annihilation by enemy tribes, coupled with the sheer physical strain of life on the brink of starvation, caused a shut-down of the sexual passions. Malthus believed that the same causes could account for the horrific 'condition and customs of the women in a savage state.' So degraded and despised were women among the American tribes, and so grievous was their servitude, that mothers sometimes killed their newborn female babies as a kindness. What demonstrated the improbability that such patterns of behaviour arose from some innate defect was that they diminished 'nearly in proportion to the degree in which these causes are mitigated or removed'.[38] Where there was an abundance of food, women were treated much more humanely and the sexual passions were restored to their usual vigour. Whereas the lack of sexual ardour and the degradation of women among 'savages' seemed to represent a largely instinctive endeavour to cut off the source of misery, other checks involved a more conscious grappling with population pressure. In the numerous travel books that he surveyed, Malthus discovered a wide range of customs that he believed were attributable to anxieties about the dire prospect of having extra mouths to feed in conditions of scarcity.[39]

Easily the most pervasive check to population in past times and among 'less civilized' peoples, however, was war. The ferocity of war among 'savages in general' was not owing to some 'malignant passion' but to the extreme scarcity of resources, which meant that survival depended on the complete destruction of the enemy. There was, moreover, a vicious cycle between exponential population growth and war that generated its own set of injurious customs. The scarcity arising from population pressure occasions a perpetual struggle between nations and tribes for resources, while the resulting decimations create a bounty on children. These 'fresh supplies' pour forth with 'overflowing rapidity', furnishing 'fresh incitements and fresh instruments for renewed hostilities.'[40] Malthus observed in Book 4 how, owing to this predicament, statesmen in past times had done everything in their power to promote fecundity, and were invariably supported in this by 'popular religions' who made multiplication a solemn religious duty.[41] Part of his reason for raising the point in a chapter dedicated to asserting the duty to practice moral restraint was to expose the barbarous origins of the prevailing opinions about early marriage in England, as well as the perverse reasoning that sustained them. This elucidation was emblematic of an historical narrative that underpinned many of the practical proposals of the book. Whereas, for the main part, the customs that arose to hold famine and disease at bay were self-defeating or merely substituted one misery for another, in Book 2 Malthus charted the emergence of more rational nuptial practices that he believed ought to serve as a blueprint for future efforts to combat poverty. As well as identifying the particular behaviours that mitigated the principle of population, moreover, he provided a precise description of the wider socio-cultural conditions that gave rise to these habits. It will be shown in the second part of this chapter that this cultural narrative was integral to his thinking about how best to improve the lives of the labouring poor in England, providing a crucial framework for his proposals to supplant the ideas and institutions that were dragging them down.

The war on poverty

Malthus's ultimate objective, if we take him at his word, was to reduce the sufferings of the poor by convincing them of the benefits of prudential and moral restraint. But as he was relying on his educated readers to disseminate the message, we can assume that the 'philosophical' account of want in the opening two books was for their benefit. If we are to interpret the *Essay* properly, then, a distinction must be drawn between the relatively simple take-home message that Malthus wanted to disseminate among the poor about the benefits of delaying marriage for prudential reasons, which required only a very basic understanding of the principle of population, and the more complex case he was attempting to make to the educated public, which required a deeper grasp of the implications of his theory.[42] His aims in relation to this audience were threefold: to convince them of the efficacy of his remedy for poverty, to instruct them on how to bring about the requisite shift in attitudes among the poor to make it work, and to assure them that the plan in its entirety was feasible. It is hard to exaggerate just how discordant Malthus's programme was with mainstream attitudes. While the theory itself repudiated the consensus, upheld by Adam Smith, William Paley and practically every other writer on the subject, that demographic increase was the only true metric of political and economic progress, his proposed solution to it seemed to contradict the command of the Almighty to 'Be fruitful, and multiply'. Given, finally, the widespread anxieties about national power (of which, once again, population was the accepted measure) vis-à-vis France, this was an inopportune time to be making the deeply counterintuitive claim that cutting the birth-rate was the best way forward.

By immersing his readers in the sufferings of the poor throughout the ages and across the globe, Malthus sought to instil an intuitive sense of how little happiness, military power and even population depended on the birth-rate relative to levels of subsistence and the political and environmental factors influencing food production. Tragic irony abounds as the reader is presented with copious instances in which the efforts of governments or families to increase population – usually for military or religious reasons – produce only surplice population, and thus misery and vice. Cancelling any gains from their commendable encouragements to agriculture, the forcing of population in China 'has not only been an addition of so much pure misery in itself', observed Malthus, 'but has completely interrupted the happiness which the rest might have enjoyed.'[43] Abundant evidence was presented from histories of the ancient pastoral peoples of northern Europe and travel accounts of Africa and Asia that high birth-rates gave rise to 'a rapid succession of human beings' rather than a permanent population. Nor did Malthus spare his readers the gruesome details of this circulation. An excerpt from James Bruce's description of a stay in the famine-ravaged African village of Garigana recalled how they 'encamped among the bones of the dead', there being 'no space … free from them'.[44]

Without question, the centrepiece of Malthus's case for the benefits of reducing the birth-rate – i.e. for the inverse proportion between preventive and positive checks – was the contrast between Norway and Sweden with which he opened the examination of the checks to population in modern Europe. He began by observing that the wealth of statistics relating to births, deaths and marriages available in Europe made it possible to calculate the relative levels of preventive and positive checks with much greater precision than had been possible in the case of 'less civilized' places and past times. Some political calculators had been fooled by the similarities that naturally occurred in the tables of countries so similarly circumstanced into thinking there was 'an invariable order of mortality', when, in fact, the order was 'extremely variable', such that it might even differ in different parts of the same country. The crucial point, however, was that this order was in some degree amenable to human control.[45] A case in point was Norway. Despite its having the lowest mortality relative to the whole population of any country in Europe, Norway had never experienced a rapid growth in population.[46] With positive checks so low, we should expect that preventive checks would be relatively high, observes Malthus, and this is precisely what the registers indicate; of the countries with reliable records, only Switzerland had fewer marriages in proportion to the whole population.[47] This state of affairs was owing largely to 'the peculiar state of Norway' that 'throws very strong obstacles in the way of early marriages.' Low mortality rates in the countryside and an absence of large manufacturers meant that there were few openings for labourers. Their opportunities were further constricted by the system of 'house-men', which forced many young men and women to remain with the farmer as unmarried servants until he was able to provide them with a house and sufficient land to raise a family. The scarcity of these vacancies, although frustrating for the peasant, brought a highly salutary clarity to his affairs. 'If a man can obtain one of these places, he marries, and is able to support a family; if he cannot obtain one, he remains single. A redundant population is thus prevented from taking place, instead of being destroyed after it has taken place.'[48] The real winners in all this were the children of house-men who grew stout and sturdy, and generally lived into old age.[49] The 'sallow looks and melancholy countenances' of the Swedes told a very different story, one in which the imprudent procreative habits of the people and 'the continual cry of the government for an increase of subjects' produced frequent malnutrition and sickly seasons.[50] This domestic economy accorded with the high birth and mortality rates recorded in the registers, naturally enough, but also with the statistical correlation between high population growth and good harvests. Whereas the behaviour of the Norwegian peasants had the effect of calibrating population growth with the average growth in the means of subsistence, that of the Swedish peasants caused population to a 'start forwards at every temporary and occasional increase of food'.[51]

It is worth reflecting for a moment on how profound this discovery must have seemed to Malthus. The matter-of-fact tone with which Adam Smith observed that the only means by which dearth could 'set limits to the further multiplication of the human species' was 'by destroying a great part of the children which their fruitful marriages produce' reflected his assumption that this was a natural and unalterable part of the mechanism by which the demand for labour regulated the supply in a civilized society, rather than any particular callousness on his part.[52] Of course, it was also symptomatic of a society that was far more attuned to high rates of infant mortality than we are today, each child being 50 times less likely to make it past the age of four.[53] Smith assumed that the increase of population was the 'most decisive mark of the prosperity of any country', being the surest measure of 'the increase of revenue and stock'; and it was thus implied that every increase of national wealth must eventually give rise to a hike in child mortality among the poor.[54] With this mentality in his sights, Malthus characterized his solution as a momentous redirection of the nation's energies. Since it was clear that in our efforts to raise the ratio of provisions to consumers by constantly endeavouring to increase the quantity of the former, we were 'setting the tortoise to catch the hare … our next attempt should naturally be to proportion the population to the food. If we can persuade the hare to go to sleep, the tortoise may have some chance of overtaking her.'[55] Now that the means of maintaining this favourable ratio had been identified, high levels of child mortality could no longer be considered as the acceptable collateral damage from growth. Henceforth, indeed, governments would be principally judged by how many infants survived into adulthood.[56] E.A. Wrigley has provided us with an admirable account of the economic dimensions of this bucking of 'classical' assumptions.[57] In terms of the modern disciplines, however, Malthus's proposed solution to poverty could as well be described as a discovery in cultural anthropology as in economics, given that it was founded on a historical analysis of the customs relating to population pressure. Only by reintegrating the economic theory into the broader cultural project of the *Essay* can we fully grasp its historical import.

The contrast between Norway and Sweden – mirrored in the contradistinction between Ireland and parts of Scotland that framed much of the discussion of the English poor – showed what the labouring classes needed to do, in terms of nuptial behaviour, to improve their condition; but this raised the further question of how to get them to do it. There were basically two ways in which the ruling classes could help the English poor to become more like their Norwegian counterparts: by displacing prevailing opinions about early marriage and population, and by removing the main institutional obstacle to the increase of prudential restraint, the Poor Laws. In terms of the first objective, Malthus emphasized the need for a complete overhaul of the deeply embedded mores that worked to promote early marriage. He does so by frequently placing the reader in the shoes of the labourer as he considers whether he ought to marry. He is already hampered in this, says Malthus, by the enormous scale and complexity of the domestic economy, which make it difficult to get a true sense of his prospects of being able to support a family in the long term; and he usually overestimates his chances.[58] Any doubts he might have on this score are readily cast aside, due to the strong sense of patriotic and religious duty he feels to leave descendants; having obeyed the injunctions of Providence, he trusts that it will not desert him.[59] While the main objective of Book 4 of the *Essay*, according to Malthus, was to convince men of liberal education of the duty to practice prudential (ideally moral) restraint, this was with a view to persuading them to inculcate the duty among the poor.[60] Explaining to the labourer the real causes of poverty would make him realize that it was his duty, and his alone, to support his offspring; while at the same time showing him the only means at his disposal of improving his condition.

The main impediment to these plans, according to Malthus, was the system of Poor Laws. The rapid hike in the poor rates in recent years pointed to the aberration of 'a great nation, flourishing in arts and arms and commerce, and with a government, which has generally been allowed to be the best', yet in which a large proportion of the people were 'reduced to the condition of paupers.'[61] The irony was, of course, that the Poor Laws themselves were partly responsible for creating this indigence. In the first place, they enabled the poor man to marry regardless of whether or not he had sufficient means to support his family through thick and thin, thereby raising food prices and depressing real wages.[62] To feed the less productive members of society, furthermore, it was necessary to reduce the share of provisions normally belonging to the 'more industrious and more worthy members', forcing more of them into dependence.[63] Indeed, the general effect of money contributions from the rich to the poor in times of dearth was to spread the burden in this way, because they increased the demand for food but not the supply; thus everyone paid more for it.[64] The most humane remedy for these ills, as Malthus saw it, was gradual abolition. Notice should be given to the poor that no child born after a year from the passing of the law would be eligible for assistance.[65] When the grace period was over, those who fell on hard times through no fault of their own were the proper objects of charity; and when they had been relieved, something might be done for those whom, ignoring the warnings, had produced mouths they could not feed; but on no account were they to be given more than could be earned from 'the worst-paid common labour.'[66]

While these initiatives are well known to scholars, it is less well appreciated how far these instructions and his ameliorative programme in general were shaped by a broader socio-cultural analysis developed in the historical books of the *Essay*. According to this account, the adoption of prudential restraint was bound up in complex ways with a more profound shift in the culture of the poor, being conditional upon the continued growth of so-called 'decent pride' among them. Decent pride was the elevated sense of self-worth that came with enjoying comfortable economic circumstances, arising in large part, we may assume, from a feeling of being esteemed by one's neighbours; although Malthus sometimes used the term, or variants of it, to encapsulate a cluster of habits and attitudes associated with such passions. As well as taking pride in their newly acquired status, a labouring family who had risen above the hand-to-mouth existence that was the usual lot of the poor would become accustomed to a level of comfort that they would be loath to relinquish. The nurturing of decent pride was at the heart of Malthus's solution to poverty because it provided strong motives for checking the natural impulse to marry early. It could be argued, indeed, that what occasioned Malthus's dramatic change of heart about the future prospects of the poor between 1798 and 1803 was his realization that this type of self-regard – to which he had ascribed the high levels of prudential restraint among men of liberal education in the first *Essay*, but that he had treated exclusively as a gentlemanly characteristic – could be nurtured in the labouring poor.[67] Malthus's case for this holistic remedy, and for his positive prognosis with regard to the poor in England, was framed by the global-historical analysis of the first two books, neatly synthesized in the following passage.

> In most countries, among the lower classes of people, there appears to be something like a standard of wretchedness, a point below which they will not continue to marry and propagate their species. This standard is different in different countries, and is formed by various concurring circumstances of soil, climate, government, degree of knowledge, and civilization, &c. The principal circumstances which contribute to raise it are liberty, security of property, the diffusion of knowledge, and a taste for the conveniences and the comforts of life. Those which contribute principally to lower it are despotism and ignorance.[68]

What distinguished modern nations from ancient and 'savage' ones was a set of cultural and economic circumstances that raised this 'standard of wretchedness' to an unprecedented high. In terms of the historical framework of the argument, this was a contrast between the more instinctive customs in relation to fecundity generated among 'savage' and ancient peoples in their struggles with extreme hardship examined above, and the more rational habits that had evolved in 'old states'. When by some fortunate change in conditions, the pressure of want is removed from Native Americans or South Sea Islanders, habits favourable to fertility gradually re-emerge; they breed without restraint until famine and disease stalk them once more, and vicious customs return. Reacting reflexively to environmental stimulae, they are trapped in a cycle of feast and famine. Although Malthus did not offer a blow-by-blow account of how modern European nations had, to various degrees, broken out of this malignant loop, he mapped out clearly the manner in which a particular country might come to exercise more forethought in its reproductive behaviour; and decent pride was the lynchpin of the process. It might be assumed, observed Malthus, that in a country where per capita levels of subsistence were increasing, either as a result of some previous decimation of the population – such as that caused by the plague in European countries – or from improvements in agriculture and trade, that the proportion of annual marriages must follow suit. But where a 'sudden improvement' in the condition of any people bred 'a decent and proper pride' among them, 'the consequence would be that the proportional number of marriages might remain nearly the same, but they would all rear more of their children'; and a country in which population was restored by a reduction in mortality would be happier and healthier than one peopled by an increased birth-rate.[69] This was precisely what had happened in England, in fact. For the improvement in 'cleanliness and ventilation' to which Heberden had ascribed the extinction of the plague in England could not have produced the observed result, insisted Malthus, unless accompanied by an increase in the preventive check brought about by the spread of 'a decent and useful pride'.[70]

His economic analysis of this development, provided in a crucial reworking of the chapter on 'increasing Wealth, as it affects the Condition of the Poor' in the 1817 edition, reveals the increasingly Smithian character of his prognosis for poverty in England.[71] According to this account, the growth of decent pride was one of the advantages that 'nearly, if not fully, counterbalance' the 'considerable disadvantages' of the 'progress of opulence'.[72] The initial economic impetus for it came from a combination of developments – an increase in the real price of corn, 'the accumulation and better distribution of capital', improvements in machinery and the expansion of global commerce – which enabled the labourer to buy better food and clothing and 'to command the conveniences and comforts of life.'[73] While Malthus saw the diffusion of luxury as a mixed blessing, he shared Hume's and Smith's belief in its ability to act as an engine of civilization by stimulating industry and ingenuity.[74] And as with so many of the benefits arising from the progress of opulence, as described by his Scottish predecessors, the improvement of the poor emanated from a fortunate train of unintended consequences. Whereas the labouring classes generally preferred 'the luxury of idleness to the luxury of improved lodging and clothing', the reduction in real wages brought about by diminishing returns in agriculture in England had generated industrious habits among the poor, such that they were willing to work a little longer for such conveniences. And the taste of luxury, once acquired

> may be such as even to prevent, after a certain period, a further fall in the corn price of labour. But if the corn price of labour continues tolerably high while the relative value of commodities compared with corn falls

very considerably, the labourer is placed in a most favourable situation. Owing to his decided taste for conveniences and comforts, the good corn wages of labour will not generally lead to early marriages; yet in individual cases, where large families occur, there will be the means of supporting them independently, by the sacrifice of the accustomed conveniences and comforts; and thus the poorest of the lower classes will rarely be stinted in food, while the great mass of them will not only have sufficient means of subsistence, but be able to command no inconsiderable quantity of those conveniences and comforts, which, at the same time that they gratify a natural or acquired want, tend unquestionably to improve the mind and elevate the character.[75]

A crucial condition for these developments, and for all England's advantages, had been the security of property provided by good government. But the progress of opulence and decent pride among the poor was still in its early stages, as Malthus's reflections on the battle against disease made clear. Because prudential restraint had not reached sufficient levels to check the numbers previously eliminated by plague and dysentery, other diseases such as palsy, gout and small pox had become more fatal.[76] Only by continuing to cultivate 'a spirit of independence, a decent pride and a taste for cleanliness and comfort among the poor' could such diseases and other checks of last resort, alongside the barbaric customs that had evolved to deal with them, be consigned to the past.[77]

A vital aim of the *Essay* then was to set out for the governing classes the most effective means of cultivating this useful self-regard and a taste for comforts among the poor. The chief political requisites for the growth of prudential habits were, first and foremost, the security of property and, second, the 'respectability and importance, which are given to the lower classes by equal laws, and the possession of some influence in the framing of them' – advantages promoted by gradual reform but destroyed by revolution.[78] Paramount to Malthus's programme for actively instilling these values was the establishment of a system parochial education on the plan of Adam Smith. In addition to the lessons in basic geometry and mechanics recommended by Smith, the poor ought to be educated in the principles on which their happiness chiefly depended and the duties arising from them, insisted Malthus.[79] As well as correcting prevalent notions about marriage, however, Malthus believed that parochial education might help train:

> the rising generation in habits of sobriety, industry, independence and prudence, and in a proper discharge of their religious duties; which would raise them from their present degraded state, and approximate them, in some

degree, to the middle classes of society, whose habits, generally speaking, are certainly superior.[80]

In doing so, it would, of course, nurture those attitudes and values that raised the standard of living below which the labourer would be unwilling to sink for the sake of having a family. It is hard to underestimate the radical cultural implications of this conviction. Whereas the education of the poor, as provided at Charity Schools and Sunday Schools, was primarily concerned with 'transforming them into pious and respectful members of their communities' – such that even instruction in writing and spelling was geared towards instilling subjection – Malthus envisaged that his scheme would enable the poor to partake in that enlargement of mind and character that had long been the sole preserve of liberal (i.e. gentlemanly) education, and by doing so ultimately raise their level of civilization.[81] Although, there was nothing new about the proposal, the idea of a national system of schooling had not as yet gained wide acceptance among the political classes, as the failure of Whitbread's education bill in 1807 shows, and Malthus was intent on easing some of the doubts that blocked its progress.[82] The 'very peculiar advantage' of education, observed Malthus, was that 'raising one person may actually contribute to the raising of others', for the conduct of one man infused with 'that decent kind of pride' that encouraged prudential restraint would improve the condition of his fellows.[83]

Having exploded the various 'Systems of Equality' on the grounds of their unfeasibility, it was imperative for Malthus to demonstrate the practicality of his own solution. In this regard, it is important to observe that in encouraging his readers to nurture useful pride in the 'labouring poor', Malthus believed that he was asking them merely to expedite a process of improvement that was already well underway. Although, from the reader's perspective, the history of poverty in the first half of the *Essay* does not seem to unfold according to any preordained logic, Malthus's analysis of this account in Books 3 and 4 consistently presents it this light. His main intention, as he made clear in the concluding chapter, was 'to inculcate the necessity of resting contented with the mode of improvement which is dictated by the course of nature, and not obstructing the advances which would otherwise be made in this way.'[84] Decent pride and a taste for comforts had already taken root among the poor of England, as we have seen, reducing their general susceptibility to want and disease. Given the right conditions, they would further blossom, increasing prudential checks, so that English farm boys grew as sturdy as those in Norway. Malthus's confidence that the prudential check would continue to increase in England and in Europe generally, despite its apparent incongruity with the ruling political, religious and economic assumptions, was based on his conviction that everywhere 'the practice of mankind on the subject of marriage has been much superior to their theories', a conclusion arising, once more, from the history of population checks.[85] The fact that notwithstanding the constant pressures from their political and religious leaders to marry early, people were always and everywhere induced by self-interest to disobey such injunctions proved:

> That great *viz medicatrix reipublicæ*, the desire of bettering our condition, and the fear of making it worse, has been constantly in action, and has been constantly directing people into the right road, in spite of all the declamations which tended to lead them aside.[86]

One crucial advantage of prudential restraint in this regard was that it did not require anyone to act from selfless or distant motives. The narrowing of the labour supply arose from each labourer pursuing, for private ends, the very tangible benefits of rearing a smaller family. With history moving ineluctably in a Malthusian direction, he could be certain that even a partial adoption of his plan would do much good. Should calls for the establishment of elementary education and the gradual abolition of the Poor Laws fall on deaf ears, for example, he was positive nonetheless that principles so important to human happiness could not fail to be widely circulated in time.[87] The only general argument against the *Essay* that he saw as having any real weight was that the facts it presented appeared to obviate the need to spread opinions that might 'alarm the prejudices of the poor' and lead to undesirable outcomes as yet unforeseen; it was only required to improve the government, extend education to the poor and generally increase their personal respectability, and the decrease in births must necessarily follow. He accepted the validity of the argument, but thought that progress would be quicker and more certain if the main causes of want were more generally known.[88]

It is against the backdrop of this directional history and the broader cultural programme of the *Essay* that we need to examine Malthus's intervention in the debates about poverty and its relief in the period. In this light, his position on the Poor Laws appears more nuanced and fluid than his critics gave him credit for. He frequently acknowledged, for example, the good the Poor Laws had done in relieving hardship in the short term. In a chapter added to the 1817 edition, he recognized that the efforts to alleviate distress in the years following the First Peace of Paris (1814) had 'fulfilled the great moral duty of assisting our fellow creatures in distress'.[89] Elsewhere in the same edition, he welcomed the gradual shift in public opinion towards a more enlightened (i.e. critical) view of the Poor Laws since the first publication of the Quarto with an air of self-satisfaction. But he showed characteristic willingness, at the same time, to sacrifice the ideal for the sake of achieving some partial good. If the consensus was 'that this country cannot entirely get rid of a system which has been so long interwoven in its frame,' consideration ought at least to be given to placing limits on the poor rate.[90] Given this willingness to adjust his aims in accordance with the evidence, and his repeated injunctions on the need to ensure that practical principles were consonant with experience, it seems anomalous that he did not remove his main objection to the Poor Laws from later editions of the *Essay* despite conceding that the census of 1801 appeared to show that they did not encourage marriage. In a note added in 1807, he promised that should the inference turn out to be true, he would, of course, remove the arguments in question, but emphasized that he would do so 'in strict conformity to the general principles of the work, and in a manner to confirm, rather than invalidate, the main positions which it has attempted to establish.'[91]

His failure to revise the chapters on the Poor Laws in a systematic fashion – which meant that all editions after the first included the assertion that the Poor Laws encouraged population alongside the confession that the evidence suggested otherwise – was a singular dereliction, which must have left many readers perplexed. But it seems a very narrow reading of the book to suggest, as Poynter does, that Malthus's retraction reduced the *Essay* to a stock anti-Poor Laws polemic. An obvious answer to this argument is that his attack on parish relief was only one part of his broader plan; and, as noted earlier, Malthus was sure the book would do much good even if his calls for institutional change failed to meet with public approval. By 1807, indeed, he had reached the firm conclusion that the plan for abolition ought to be put on the backburner until more progress had been made in convincing both the middle classes and the poor of its necessity. To try to introduce such legislation when the values enshrined in the Poor Laws remained so deeply engrained in the political culture would only add fuel to existing resentments.[92] In view of his concession, we must assume that the increasing ratio of paupers that so alarmed Malthus after 1803 was attributable to the tendency of the Poor Laws to spread want among the slightly more prosperous labourers, rather than any propensity to increase population. In this sense, his admission unquestionably raised the relative importance of mainstream anti-poor laws arguments in the broader scheme. But he was far from abandoning the argument against the Poor Laws from the principle of population. To illustrate the point, it is necessary to view his apparent about-turn in relation to his core methodological principles. 'I should be the last person,' observed Malthus at the beginning of the *Principles of Political Economy* (1820), 'to think that a consistent theory, which would account for the great mass of phenomena observable, was immediately invalidated by a few discordant appearances, the realty and bearings of which, there might not have been an opportunity of fully examining.' But he was no less emphatic that if any theory was shown to be 'inconsistent with general experience', this was 'a full and sufficient reason for its rejection.'[93] It is clear from the highly qualified character of his concession that Malthus placed the statistical evidence about marriage in England in the first of these categories; i.e. as revealing one of those isolated facts that did not invalidate the broader theory. The census showed that the Poor Laws did not encourage marriage 'so much as might be expected from theory', that they were not acting in accordance with their 'obvious tendency'.[94] No doubt intellectual pride, ideological orientation and the constraints imposed on his thinking by the paradigm of the theory itself all militated against his abandoning one of the main planks of his original plan. But there were also solid evidential reasons for Malthus to believe that the effects of the Poor Laws in England were atypical of the normal relationship between systematic relief and population growth.

That the Poor Laws encouraged early marriage was an obvious implication of the postulate that population grew rapidly wherever subsistence was assured. Several examples were given in the history of population checks of well-intentioned efforts to improve the welfare of the poor that, by removing the severest disincentives to reproduction – fear of starvation and the stigma attached to abandoning children – increased surplus population. He quoted at length Samuel Turner's description of the 'mass of indigence and idleness' that arose from the 'indiscriminate charity' provided by Lama in Tibet. According to first-hand accounts, furthermore, the establishment of foundling hospitals in Russia in the reign of Catherine the Great had produced similar results. On a visit to the *Maison des Enfant Trouvé* in St Petersburg in 1799, Malthus heard how in the previous year attendants had buried up to 18 children a day; a tragedy that he attributed to the sexual licence such institutions encouraged by creating a blasé attitude to the abandonment of children.[95] As well as suggesting good reasons for believing that something was happening in England to counteract the natural propensity of the Poor Laws, Malthus's history of poverty offered strong clues as to what it was that was checking early marriages. According to this analysis, as we have seen, the main cause of reduced fecundity and better health in England since the Middle Ages had been an increase in decent pride. His position in 1798 and throughout the 1803 edition was that the spirit of independence engendered by this pride subverted the pernicious tendencies of the Poor Law. He was certain, indeed, that the Poor Laws of England would have long ago ruined the country had 'a decided taste for the comforts and conveniences of life' and 'a strong desire of bettering their condition' not fostered 'a most laudable spirit of industry and foresight' 'throughout a very large class of the people'.[96]

Malthus was warranted on the grounds of this analysis in assuming that the unexpectedly low number of early marriages was testament to the cultural progress made by the poor, and not to the harmlessness of the Poor Laws. Nor, given his explanation of the rude health of the sons of Norwegian house-men, was it illogical for him to conclude that a shortage of suitable accommodation for labouring families in England – caused by the Poor Laws themselves – was acting as a further limiting factor. Because it had greatly deterred landlords from building cottages on their estates, the legal obligation of each parish to relieve its own poor was 'probably the principal reason why' the Poor Laws were still in existence, observed Malthus in 1806.[97] In this way, they put the unmarried labourer in a similar position to the Norwegian house-man, bringing into clear view the dangerous consequences attending early marriage. From 1806 onwards, Malthus's energies were increasingly directed towards ensuring that nothing was done to 'alter those parts' of the Poor Laws that negated their destructive tendencies (i.e. their propensity to encourage early marriages), reconciled, as he was, to the fact that abolition was not on the horizon. Hence his opposition to Arthur Young's plans to build more cottages for the poor in 1806 and his entreaty to Samuel Whitbread in 1807 to ensure that his Poor Law bill did not inadvertently encourage the same.[98] While lacking the polemical punch of the more straightforward attack on public relief in the 1798 *Essay*, the critique of later editions was no less singular, being anchored just as firmly in the principle of population.

Clearly Malthus saw England's position in relation to poverty at that time as precariously balanced. The useful pride of the English labourer and the preventive checks created by parish regulations were just about holding the line against the pauperizing tendencies of the Poor Laws and prevailing opinions about the rights and duties of the poor. Against this backdrop, it is easy to see why Malthus was so assiduous in scotching the many piecemeal remedies for hardship put forth in this period. By filling

their heads with 'fascinating visions', Arthur Young's well-meaning proposals to provide poor families with a cow and a plot of land would deflect
the unmarried labourer's attention away from 'the terrific forms of workhouses and parish officers' that had previously bolstered his resolution to
delay marriage, with disastrous consequences.[99] Other, seemingly innocu-
ous measures, like Young's plan to wean English labourers on to cheaper
food like potatoes, were potentially even more harmful. Although land
devoted to growing potatoes unquestionably yielded a higher quantity of
food than land used to grow wheat, the failure of the new crop would be
'beyond all comparison, more dreadful' than a scarcity of wheat. For when
the poor lived on the dearest grain, as they did in England, they had 'great
resources in a scarcity' such as potatoes, soups and oats; whereas those
whose 'habitual food is the lowest in this scale' were 'absolutely without
resource'.[100] Worse still, such a move would undermine the economic basis
of the culture of decent pride to which they owed their comparative comfort. Were the potato system introduced in England, the great increase in
the supply of labour relative to the demand and the cheapness of the food
that regulated the price of labour would cause real wages to plummet, and
the 'rags and wretched cabins of Ireland' would soon follow. As things
stood, the demand for labour sometimes rose above the supply and wages
were regulated by wheat prices, enabling labourers to purchase some of
the comforts of life including 'decent' housing and clothes.[101] To restore
such frugal tastes would be to return the English poor to the hand-to-
mouth existence that had left their medieval ancestors so exposed to disease and starvation.

There was nothing gratuitous, then, about Malthus's unrelenting
efforts to uncover 'the errors in different plans which have been proposed, to improve the condition of the poor.' Each proposal was to be
judged entirely on whether or not it had 'a tendency to increase the prudence and foresight of the labouring classes.'[102] One-by-one Malthus put
each type of scheme to this test with a view to shutting down avenues of
investigation that he believed could not possibly produce a permanent
remedy to poverty (however effective they were in the short term) and
redirecting energies towards those that might. Plans aimed at creating an
artificial demand for labour, for example, could be consigned to obliv-
ion, because they prevented the poor from calibrating the population to
the food supply (i.e. the actual demand for labour).[103] For Poynter, as we
have seen, the fact that Malthus's criticisms were (allegedly) more prominent than his positive proposals was indicative of his gloomy outlook on
the prospects of the poor. Not only does this greatly underestimate the

prominence of the positive programme, but it misses the crucial point that the negative critique was rooted in his assurance of the positive direction history was taking in respect of poverty and population, since it was intended to deter government from meddling with the means of improvement clearly prescribed by nature and from thus obstructing the progress that would inevitably occur if the poor were allowed to follow the dictates of self-interest.

Conclusion

Gareth Stedman Jones has identified the 1790s as the moment when political theorists first came to question the scriptural assumption that 'the poor are always with us', as thinkers like Paine, Condorcet and Godwin raised hopes that statistical analysis might provide a means of risk assessment that enabled commercial societies to design workable social insurance and pension schemes for the poor, thereby removing the fear of indigence.[104] While opponents saw Malthus as an ideologically driven naysayer to all such proposals, the account offered here suggests that he was no less determined than them to dispel the notion that 'squalid poverty' was part of the divine plan. Malthus attacked such projects precisely because he believed that they were rooted in the erroneous modes of thinking about poverty and population that continued to condemn the great mass of mankind to periodic hardship. This is obviously not to suggest that Malthus's thought developed in isolation from the increasingly bipartisan political struggles that emerged in the period. His proposals were clearly in tune, for example, with the growing chorus of opposition to interventionist modes of dealing with scarcity.[105] In his *Thoughts and Details on Scarcity* (1800), Edmund Burke attacked the growing penchant for 'meddling with the subsistence of the people' – as exhibited in calls for the fixing of wages in 1795 – as a despotic overriding of the implied contract between employer and worker.[106] It was folly for government to involve itself in settling 'the balance of wants', when this was carried on with the utmost equity and efficiency by the free market in labour, an efficacy that Burke attributed to the wisdom of the Almighty in disposing things so that the pursuit of 'selfish interests' conduced to the 'general good'.[107] Clearly, Malthus's plan for reducing poverty embodied similar attitudes; self-interest, directed by the free labour market, would release the poor from the population trap. This helps explain why he has sometimes been seen as helping to realize the 'market-fundamentalist' agenda initiated by Joseph Townsend.[108] In

calling for population to be regulated by the demand for labour alone –
which could be achieved by a severe limitation of parish relief – and
in his assertion that charity lost its salutary effects on the donor and
the recipient when compulsory, Townsend unquestionably anticipated
some of the themes of the *Essay*.[109] But if Malthus's agenda overlapped in
important ways with the strident anti-interventionism emerging in this
period, his belief in the potential of the labouring classes to climb the
ladder of civilization through the cultivation of useful pride represented
a significant departure from some of the core assumptions about poverty that underpinned these views. Because the labourer lacked pride
and ambition, according to Townsend, he would never acquire prudent
habits unless pressurized by the fear of hunger. While Malthus agreed
that the prospect of seeing his children starve ought to come into the
labourer's calculations when considering whether it was time to take the
leap, his long-term wish was that anxiety about falling down the social
ladder (born of decent pride) might replace the more primeval fear as
a goad to prudence and industry. Nor, obviously, was Malthus sympathetic, as Townsend was, to the complaint of manufacturers that the
poor were 'seldom diligent, except when labour is cheap, and corn is
dear'.[110] He accused those who objected to his plans on the grounds that
higher labour prices would disadvantage England in European markets
of being disingenuous in their professed desire to help the poor; for 'a
market overstocked with labour, and an ample remuneration to each
labourer, are objects perfectly incompatible with each other.'[111]

Furthermore, while Malthus believed, of course, that the free market in
labour was the fairest and most effective means of distributing the surplus
from agriculture and manufactures, he was far from viewing it through
rose-tinted spectacles. He acknowledged throughout his writings the operation of that tacit 'combinations of masters', which, according to Adam
Smith, gave them a massive advantage when bargaining with workers, who
were forbidden to combine, exerting a constant downward pressure on
wages.[112] Passages in the first *Essay* observing how 'the rich by unfair combinations, contribute frequently to prolong a season of distress among the
poor' were toned down somewhat in later editions to reduce their inflam-
matory potential; but the substance remained the same.[113] It said much,
also, about Malthus's estimation of the market (morally speaking) that one
of his principal fears about Samuel Whitbread's proposal to make all types
of property equally rateable was that it might create a situation in which it
was in the interest of 'the capitalist' to increase population and pauperism.[114]

The great virtue of prudential restraint was that it created the 'scarcity of hands' that, according to Smith, enabled the poor to 'break through the natural combination of masters not to raise wages.'[115] The growth of useful pride implied a more dynamic model of social and economic relations than that which Burke saw as constituting the 'the natural and just order'.[116] Rather than accepting periodic hardship as part of the providential plan – to be borne with Christian fortitude and forbearance – they were to strive to banish its spectre from their lives forever. This characterization provides yet another nail in the coffin of the view of Malthus as a prophet of doom. Promoting a relatively optimistic view about man's potential to overcome environmental constraints on his material wellbeing based on a progressive history of his endeavours to overcome them, the *Essay* clearly belongs to the moderate Enlightenment traditions of Smith, Hume and Paley.[117] Yet, as we have seen, the science of poverty was born partly of dissatisfaction with some of the methods of the science of man as practised by these pre-decessors, from a growing sense that empirical data (the more the better), synthesized in statistics, held the key to grasping the underlying realties of social and economic life. In this sense, it may also be seen as a precur-sor to the positivistic social sciences of the nineteenth century. The irony here is that his closest descendants in these have been particularly culpable in perpetuating the mythical versions of Malthus's doctrine that historians of ideas have been labouring to banish.[118] It is hard to be sanguine about dispelling such myths when Malthus the doom-mongering scourge of the poor remains such a convenient and evocative straw man.

Notes

1 A.M.C. Waterman, *Revolution, Economics and Religion: Christian Political Economy, 1798–1833* (Cambridge: Cambridge University Press, 1991), pp. 1–170. Gregory Claeys' essay in this volume explores an important aspect of this inter-change that has hitherto been neglected.
2 T.R. Malthus, *An Essay on the Principle of Population* (London: J. Johnson, 1798), pp. 62–3. Hereafter the first *Essay*.
3 Waterman, *Revolution, Economics and Religion*, p. 142.
4 T.R. Malthus, *An Essay on the Principle of Population; or, a View of its Past and Present Effects on Human Society* [1803], ed. P. James, 2 vols. (Cambridge: Cambridge University Press, 1989), vol. 1, p. 380. Hereafter the second *Essay*.
5 Ibid., vol. 1, p. 9.
6 See Boyd Hilton, *The Age of Atonement: The Influence of Evangelicalism on Social and Economic Thought 1795–1865* (Oxford: Clarendon, 1988).

7 See Donald Winch, *Riches and Poverty: An Intellectual History of Political Economy in Britain, 1750–1833* (Cambridge: Cambridge University Press, 1996), pp. 13–14, 290, 306–7; Robert J. Mayhew, *Malthus: The Life and Legacies of an Untimely Prophet* (Cambridge, MA: Harvard University Press, 2014), ch. 4.

8 J.R. Poynter, *Society and Pauperism: English Ideas on Poor Relief, 1795–1834* (London: Routledge and Kegan Paul, 1969), p. 45.

9 Joseph Townsend, *A Dissertation on the Poor Laws: By a Well-Wisher to Mankind* (London: C. Dilly, 1786), pp. 2, 51.

10 For example, Harold A. Boner, *Hungry Generations: The Nineteenth-Century Case Against Malthusianism* (New York: King's Crown Press, 1955); K. Smith, *The Malthusian Controversy* (London: Routledge, 1951).

11 Poynter, *Society and Pauperism*, p. 161. Marx saw Malthus as an apologist for both the aristocracy and industrial capitalists. See Ronald L. Meek (ed.), *Marx and Engels on Malthus* (London: Lawrence and Wishart, 1953).

12 Poynter, *Society and Pauperism*, pp. 163, 158.

13 Ibid., p. 155.

14 Samuel Hollander, 'On Malthus's Population Principle and Social Reform', *History of Political Economy*, 18 (1986), 209–15; D.M. Levy, 'Some Normative Aspects of the Malthusian Controversy', *History of Political Economy*, 10 (1978), 271–85. Like Poynter, Himmelfarb assumes that Malthus focused exclusively on promoting moral restraint: Gertrude Himmelfarb, *The Idea of Poverty: England in the Early Industrial Age* (London: Faber & Faber, 1984), pp. 122, 124.

15 T.R. Malthus, '1806 Appendix' to *An Essay on the Principle of Population* [1803], ed. P. James, 2 vols. (Cambridge: Cambridge University Press, 1989), vol. 2, pp. 221–2, emphasis in original. Hereafter, '1806 Appendix'.

16 Second *Essay*, vol. 2, p. 111.

17 Ibid., vol. 1, p. 380.

18 See ibid., preface and ch. 1.

19 See Niall O'Flaherty, 'Malthus and the History of Population', in Shannon Stimson (ed.), *An Essay on the Principle of Population*, by T. R. Malthus (Yale: Yale University Press, forthcoming).

20 First *Essay*, pp.. 30–1.

21 Second *Essay*, vol. 1, p. 80 n.

22 Ibid., vol. 1, p. 9. On the practical bent of Malthus's mind see Mayhew, *Malthus*, pp. 58–9, 126.

23 Himmelfarb hardly mentions it in her account of Malthus's ideas: *The Idea of Poverty*, ch. 4.

24 Second *Essay*, vol. 2, p. 185. David Hume, 'Of the Populousness of Ancient Nations' [1752], in *Essays Moral, Political and Literary*, ed. Eugene F. Miller, 2nd edn (Indianapolis: Liberty Fund, 1985), p. 400.

25 '1806 Appendix', vol. 2, p. 212 n.

26 On Malthus's sources and travels see Patricia James, *Population Malthus: His Life and Times* (London: Routledge, 1979), pp. 92–8; Patricia James (ed.), *The Travel Diaries of T. R. Malthus* (Cambridge: Cambridge University Press, 1966).

27 Ian Hacking, *The Taming of Chance* (Cambridge: Cambridge University Press, 1990), *passim*. See pp. 16–95.

28 Second *Essay*, vol. 1, pp. 21–2, 193.

29 Frederic Morton Eden, *The State of the Poor: Or, a History of the Labouring Classes in England, from the Conquest to the Present Period*, 3 vols. (London: B. & J. White, 1797), vol. 1, p. xxix.

30 Second *Essay*, vol. 1, p. 53.

31 Ibid., vol. 1, pp. 53–4.

32 See Poynter, *Society and Pauperism*, pp. 45–105.

33 Second *Essay*, vol. 1, p. 70.

34 See First *Essay*, ch. 7.

35 Second *Essay*, vol. 2, pp. 116–8. See William Heberden, *Observations on the Increase and Decrease of Different Diseases and Particularly the Plague* (London: T. Payne, 1801), p. 143.

36 Edward Jenner had successfully tested his vaccine in 1796. Malthus's source was John Haygarth, *A Sketch of a Plan to Exterminate the Casual Small-Pox from Great Britain and to Introduce General Inoculation*, 2 vols. (London: J. Johnson, 1793).

37 Second *Essay*, vol. 1, p. 31.

38 Ibid., vol. 1, pp. 31–2.

39 Ibid., vol. 1, p. 33.

40 Ibid., vol. 2, p. 101.

41 Ibid.

42 Ibid., vol. 2, pp. 200–1.

43 Ibid., vol. 1, p. 126.

44 Ibid., vol. 1, pp. 94–5. James Bruce, *Travels to Discover the Source of the Nile in the Years 1768, 1769, 1770, 1771, 1772 and 1773*, 5 vols. (Edinburgh: G.G.J and J Robinson, 1790), vol. 4, p. 349.

45 Second *Essay*, vol. 1, p. 148.

46 Apart from a spurt in the previous 15 years.

47 Second *Essay*, vol. 1, p. 149.

48 Ibid., vol. 1, pp. 150, 152.

49 Ibid., vol. 1, p. 153.

50 Ibid., vol. 1, pp. 166, 159.

51 Ibid., vol. 1, p. 161.

52 Adam Smith, *An Inquiry into the Nature and Causes of the Wealth of Nations*, 2 vols. (London: W. Strahan and T. Cadell, 1776), vol. 1, p. 97.

53 Mayhew, *Malthus*, p. 14.

54 Smith, *Wealth of Nations*, vol. 1, pp. 86, 85.

55 Second *Essay*, vol. 2, p. 108.

56 Ibid., vol. 1, p. 261.

57 E.A. Wrigley, 'Malthus on the Prospects of the Labouring Poor', in *Poverty, Progress and Population* (Cambridge: Cambridge University Press, 2004), pp. 229–48.

58 Second *Essay*, vol. 1, p. 152.

59 Ibid., vol. 2, p. 120

60 Ibid., vol. 1, p. 332.

61 Ibid., vol. 2, p. 137.

62 Ibid., vol. 1, p. 358.

63 Ibid., vol. 1, pp. 358–9.

64 Ibid., vol. 1, Book 3, ch. 5. This was assuming a rigidly inelastic food supply. See Donald Winch, *Malthus* (Oxford: Oxford University Press, 1987), p. 43.

65 Second *Essay*, vol. 2, p. 139.

66 Ibid., vol. 2, p. 162.

67 In 1798, he had questioned whether the poor would ever be 'sufficiently free from want and labour, to attain any high degree of intellectual improvement.' First *Essay*, pp. 64, 218.

68 Second *Essay*, vol. 2, p. 155.

69 Ibid., vol. 1, p. 197.

70 Ibid., vol. 2, p. 118. Heberden, *Observations*, p. 35.

71 Second *Essay*, vol. 2, pp. 85–6. This undermines Himmelfarb's thesis that Malthus 'subverted the whole of Smith's theory' (Himmelfarb, *The Idea of Poverty*, p. 100).

72 Second *Essay*, vol. 2, p. 84. Later in the chapter, however, he says that they may in fact 'fully counterbalance the disadvantages', p. 86. Malthus first outlined this explanation in a footnote added to the 1806 edition. Ibid., vol. 1, p. 388 n.

73 Ibid., vol. 2, p. 85.

74 See David Hume, 'Of Refinement in the Arts' [1752], in *Essays*, pp. 268–80.

75 Second *Essay*, vol. 2, pp. 85–6.

76 Ibid., vol. 2, p. 118.

77 Ibid., vol. 2, p. 155.

78 Ibid., vol. 2, p. 131.

79 Ibid., vol. 2, p. 154.

80 Ibid., vol. 2, p. 155.

81 M.G. Jones, *The Charity School Movement: A Study of Eighteenth-Century Puritanism in Action* (Cambridge: Cambridge University Press, 1938), pp. 73–84. On the aims and socio-cultural assumptions of liberal education see Mohammed Helmi Mohammed Sobri, *The Establishment of the London University and the Socio-Cultural Status of English Liberal Education, 1825–1836*, unpublished PhD thesis, King's College London (2015), pp. 8–47.

82 Whitbread wanted to make the provision of parish schools, run by the local clergy and officers, compulsory. Jones, *Charity School Movement*, pp. 329–30.

83 Second *Essay*, vol. 2, pp. 189–90.

84 Ibid., vol. 2, p. 199.

85 Ibid., vol. 2, p. 198.

86 Ibid., vol. 1, pp. 80, 119; vol. 2, p. 198. See Smith, *Wealth of Nations*, vol. 1. pp. 416–17.

87 Second *Essay*, vol. 2, pp. 200–1.

88 '1806 Appendix', pp. 226–7.

89 Second *Essay*, vol. 1, p. 368. The hardships arose from a bad harvest and a typhus epidemic in 1816, accompanied by a fall in demand for labour and commodities following the end of hostilities. This echoes his concession that parish allowances had helped to mitigate suffering in 1800. See T.R. Malthus, *An Investigation of the Cause of the Present High Prices of Provisions* (London: J. Johnson, 1800), pp. 19–20.

90 Second *Essay*, vol. 2, p. 184.

91 '1806 Appendix', p. 226 n.

92 T.R. Malthus, *A Letter to Samuel Whitbread, Esq. M.P. on his Proposed Bill for the Amendment of the Poor Laws* (London: J. Johnson, 1807), pp. 6–7.

93 T.R. Malthus, *Principles of Political Economy Considered with a View to Their Practical Application* (London: John Murray, 1820), p. 10.

94 Second *Essay*, vol. 2, p. 170; '1806 Appendix', p. 226.

95 Second *Essay*, vol. 1, pp. 120, 173, 175–6. Samuel Turner, *An Account of an Embassy to the Court of the Teshoo Lama in Tibet* (London: W. Bulmer and Co, 1800), pp. 330–1.

96 Second *Essay*, vol. 2, p. 145. See also first *Essay*, pp. 84–5.

97 Second *Essay*, vol. 1, p. 363.

98 '1806 Appendix', p. 225; Malthus, *Letter to Whitbread*, pp. 15–34.

99 Second *Essay*, vol. 2, p. 170.

100 Ibid., vol. 2, pp. 171–2.

101 Ibid., vol. 2, pp. 173, 172.

102 Ibid., vol. 2, pp. 181–2. The one plan that did pass the test was the proposal to establish savings banks, p. 182.

103 Ibid., vol. 2, pp. 180–1.

104 Gareth Stedman Jones, *An End to Poverty? A Historical Debate* (London: Profile Books, 2004), pp. 1–63.

105 Of course, much of their influence was owing to their perceived congruence with evangelical theology. See Hilton, *Age of Atonement*.

106 Edmund Burke, *Thoughts and Details on Scarcity* (London: F. and C. Rivington and J. Hatchard, 1800), pp. 48, 6–7.

107 Ibid., pp. 25, 11.

108 Philipp H. Lepenies, 'Of Goats and Dogs: Joseph Townsend and the Idealisation of Markets – a Decisive Episode in the History of Economics', *Cambridge Journal of Economics*, 38 (2014), p. 457.

109 Townsend, *Dissertation on the Poor Laws*, pp. 50–1, 95–9.

110 Ibid., pp. 13, 24.

111 Second *Essay*, vol. 2, p. 110.

112 Smith, *Wealth of Nations*, vol. 1, p. 81.

113 First *Essay*, pp. 35–6. Second *Essay*, vol. 1, p. 22.

114 *Letter to Whitbread*, pp. 19–24.

115 Smith, *Wealth of Nations*, vol. 1, p. 84.

116 Burke, *Thoughts and Details*, p. 10. Although Burke accepted, of course, that the development of commerce and improvements in agriculture had raised the incomes of the poor.

117 See Winch, *Riches and Poverty*, pp. 13–14 and *passim*; Mayhew, *Malthus*, chs. 2 and 3.

118 See Paul Dauvergne, 'Globalization and the Environment' in John Ravenhill (ed.), *Global Political Economy*, 4th edn (Oxford: Oxford University Press, 2014), p. 374; Jeffery D. Sachs, *Common Wealth: Economics for a Crowded Planet* (London: Penguin, 2008), p. 73; Thomas Piketty. *Capital in the Twenty-First Century* (Cambridge, MA: Harvard University Press, 2014), p. 5.

CHAPTER 4

Malthus and the new world

Alison Bashford and Joyce E. Chaplin

Thus in the beginning all the World was America (John Locke).

Our People must at least be doubled every 20 Years (Benjamin Franklin).

The happiness of a country does not depend, absolutely, upon its poverty, or its riches, upon its youth, or its age, upon its being thinly, or fully inhabited, but upon the rapidity with which it is increasing (Thomas Robert Malthus).

Thomas Robert Malthus wrote the most famous book on population ever written, or ever likely to be, and yet its intellectual foundations have for the most part been incorrectly understood. Even as 'Malthusianism' is today thought of overwhelmingly in relation to the developing, extra-European world, Malthus's *Essay on the Principle of Population* has been largely explicated within a European if not British context. But it was the new world, not the old, which fundamentally shaped Malthus's central claim that population always existed within natural limits. This chapter focuses on the new worlds that were at the heart of Malthus's *Essay*, including the Atlantic (stretching through North and South America) and the Pacific (Van Diemen's Land, New Holland, Tahiti, New Zealand). New world land and new world peoples, both native and colonial, were the key exemplars of Malthus's thesis about population, life, and death. Thus, we radically recast analysis of Malthus and his *Essay* away from the British and European history that have dominated its reputation, to the colonial and new world history that inspired its genesis. And, as we do so, we shift the focus away from the slim, easily read first edition of the essay and toward the dramatically expanded *Essay*, first produced in 1803 and running through four more editions in 1806, 1807, 1817 and 1826.

The distinguished population historian and geographer, E.A. Wrigley, once characterized Malthus as 'standing between two worlds'. Wrigley meant that Malthus stood between two temporally distinct economic systems: the pre-modern organic and agricultural economy from which and about which Malthus wrote, and the modern industrial and manufacturing economy just beginning to accelerate. But what if we were to cast these 'two worlds' not just chronologically, but also into the geography of Malthus's own life and times, the old world and the new?[1]

The presence of new worlds is apparent within Malthus's analysis in three important ways. First, new world places, starting with the Americas, as featured in the first edition of the *Essay*, constituted Malthus's primary example of just how rapidly population growth could occur, whenever land fit for agriculture was first exploited by Europeans. New world places and their native peoples remained analytically essential within editions of the *Essay* from 1803 onward, their presence constituting an antithesis of the old world within stadial theory, the contemporary historical schema that presented humanity as progressing from savagery to commercial sophistication, which Malthus significantly modified to place population at its centre. From selected studies of indigenous people in the new world, Malthus argued that population numbers were always kept within the limits of resources, his 'principle of population'. Second, in relation to new worlds, Malthus privileged the evidence given by settlers of those places, if not persons born there, allowing them authority on matters of new world population increase, as products of it, in a way he did not for other parts of the world. The prime example of this is the work of Benjamin Franklin, whose influence on Malthus is typically noted only in passing, but is worth careful scrutiny. Third, Malthus used his principle of population to conclude – against prevailing opinion – that for settler populations to extirpate or subsume indigenous ones was unjust. In this regard, Malthus, long vilified as the scourge of the English poor, has a rather unexpected persona: defender of native peoples, even in the face of proliferating plans to colonize new world places.

Beginning with descriptions of the Americas, Europeans had always interpreted new worlds in terms of population. Two tropes recurred, and each emphasized how new worlds defined fresh opportunities for humanity, or at least parts of humanity. One trope belonged to natural theology, the interpretation of the natural world as evidence of a divine Creator and his mandate for humanity; the second was first articulated by, and descended from, Renaissance reason-of-state traditions that proposed plans for good government.

The first trope focuses on a primordial breeding pair. In the Christian tradition, those two people bore the names Adam and Eve; their persistence within population theories, and that of the paradise they had lost, reveals the deep impress of natural theology. In the beginning, the story went, sometime after God had created the world, the two first humans had sinned badly. They were expelled from paradise and cursed with gender-specific tasks, the man to delve into the earth in order to get food, the woman to bring forth children, thus consigned, along with their descendants, to drudgery and pain. Scripture made clear the duty to breed: 'increase and multiply', the Book of Genesis states, 'fill the earth, and subdue it'. Adam and Eve submitted to that duty so faithfully that they were presumed to have sent progeny into all corners of the Earth. Their diligence was itself a further point in natural theology, the doctrine of plenitude, the idea that God had created a world of plentiful capacity for the continuous reproduction of human beings. But these elements of natural theology made the European discovery of the Americas – which had gone unmentioned in scripture – somewhat of a problem. Were the Americas a newfound paradise resembling that which Adam and Eve had forfeited, unmentioned because their people were not included in the curses placed on the primordial couple? Or were these new worlds the realm of the devil, where humans, along with their modes of subsistence and reproduction, were particularly damnable evidence of human depravity?[2]

The Americas could be represented either as another Eden, a newly revealed reminder of God's creative beneficence and possible repository of human innocence, or else as a demonic counterfactual, the newly revealed realm of the devil. There would be a long, complex tradition of associating Native Americans with the scriptural past, even with paradise – Christopher Columbus was not unique in believing that Eden could be located in the Atlantic lands he had first explored. His descriptions of native Caribs as 'guileless', moreover, set off a long tradition of regarding Native Americans as primordially innocent, living sweetly naked in free-giving natural worlds, as if released from Eve and Adam's original sin. But equally commonly, the natives of the new world were depicted as Satan's prey and pawns. Suspicion that the peoples of the new world were cannibals was one of the most powerful of prejudices about them. The presumed practice of anthropophagy indicated both an inversion of European social norms and an appetite unsated by any available American foodstuffs, whether due to natural want or social depravity or both.[3]

Theodor De Bry's massive and influential *Grands Voyages* (1590), for example, reinforced both the primordially positive and negative comprehensions of the Americas. The frontispiece to De Bry's volume on the Americas shows a Native American idol attended by a priest and a sorcerer, with an Indian man and woman below. That male–female pairing, visually related to a state of sin, is echoed in a portrayal of the Fall and expulsion from paradise. Adam and Eve are there in the foreground, sampling the fruit of the tree of knowledge, and their fallen selves are in the background, performing their divinely mandated tasks. Eve nurses an infant Cain in a primitive hut while Adam scores the ground with a primitive hoe. Through the visual twinning of the two illustrations, the peopling of the world after the expulsion is connected to the peoples of the new world, with Edenic and Satanic implications depicted in ironic juxtaposition, a new problem for the Christian faithful.[4]

All the same, from 1492 onward and through the seventeenth century at the least, a central principle of natural theology remained in place: God had created a world uniquely suited to its human inhabitants, no matter how many of them there might be. The discovery and description of the Americas was an important moment, therefore, in the globalization of that argument from design, a test of Christians' faith in the idea of plenitude, which scripture had promised. Although several landmasses were still missing from European globes and world maps, the still-expanding extent of South and North America already showed just how much land existed. That raised the question of how fully it might be populated. Were the inhabitants of the new world fulfilling the mandate to increase and multiply, to subdue the earth? If not, how many more people could fit into their territories, once they were supplied with dutifully procreating European migrants equipped with forms of agriculture that were more intensive and commercially oriented? Those questions, and the issues they raised about the material and social natures of new worlds, was apparent perhaps most famously in John Locke's formulation, echoing scripture, that 'in the beginning all the World was *America*'. Although an Edenic interpretation of the Americas would fade, it would be marshalled in order to interpret the later discovered new worlds of the Pacific, as with the paradisical reading of Polynesia.[5]

The second interpretive trope we might call the vegetable imaginary. This was first articulated by the Renaissance man of learning and Jesuit-trained scholar Giovanni Botero.

In his *Delle cause della grandezza delle città* ('On the Causes of the Greatness of Cities', 1588). Botero argued for the value of large and dense human populations. Human fecundity was the ultimate source of power: one ancient couple in Mesopotamia (presumed site of Eden) had produced all the world's people, even 'to the countries we call the New World'. Against the prevailing assumption that a great nation needed a large territory, Botero countered that 'the multitude and number of the inhabitants and their power' mattered far more. The larger the population, the greater the nation and its military and economic power – more people allowed intensive and extensive growth, the former being necessary for the latter, an important piece of advice for princes. This was very much an Italian perspective, a means by which someone from a small but densely populated territory questioned the easy assumption that Spain and France were becoming global powers because they had greater territory.[6]

A burgeoning population was an asset not only to a nation but to its empire, actual or potential. To visualize the productive export of citizens, Botero represented humans as equivalent to other living beings in their dependence on natural resources – the vegetable imaginary. Just 'as plants cannot prosper so well nor multiply so fast in a nursery where they are set and planted near together as where they are transplanted into an open ground', Botero observed, so too would people flourish if sent abroad. Thus, he claimed, had the ancient Greeks benefited from colonies, where the poor were sent to multiply and produce goods for the imperial core. But Botero's scenario of multiplying humans imagined land that was somehow clear of other inhabitants. This was an imperial fantasy, not a description of the historical reality of most instances of conquest in ancient empires let alone modern ones.[7]

In this way, Botero betrayed his own context, which understood empires in relation to new worlds, places that were not assumed to have the commercial centres the Greeks had sought, or the populations that the Romans had found in Germania, Gaul and Britain. Botero was typical in his assumption that the Americas were lightly populated (an assumption Malthus would repeat in his *Essay*). Beyond the Mexica and Inca empires in Central and South America, America was assumed to be peopled by hunter-gatherers who lived in small migratory clans. (This stereotype erased urban sites, population concentrations, significant agriculture and other important alterations in the land that actually existed in North America.) And everywhere European observers noted a devastating decline in Native American populations, and a parallel rise in their own numbers. We now know that the two trends were linked. Colonists brought communicable diseases to which America's indigenes had no resistance, even as they demanded food, land, and labour from the battered native populations, a toxic combination, with deadly consequences noted as early as the sixteenth century.[8]

By the end of the next century, in the late 1600s, pioneers of the new science of political arithmetic, an ancestor of demography, would be busy analysing both metropolitan and colonial populations; John Graunt and William Petty are the acknowledged founders of this new science. Meanwhile, in the English colonies, it had become a point of pride that colonists produced large families, in contrast both to Native Americans and to the English at home. The fecundity was proof, settlers thought, that they were physically suited to the new lands and therefore destined to command them.[9]

Over the course of the eighteenth century, colonial population growth became a politically significant fact, not least because it was packaged as such by one particularly influential colonist, Benjamin Franklin, who repurposed both the trope of the breeding pair and the vegetable imaginary to champion the rights of British Americans. Franklin had read extensively in political arithmetic, as well as political economy, and began to offer statements on the significance of colonial populations as underappreciated imperial assets. In 1751 he wrote his most important population analysis, 'Observations Concerning the Increase of Mankind', which was to provide Malthus with his own principle of population.[10]

Franklin wrote his essay in the wake of the Iron Act (1750), a measure to prevent American production of iron in order to protect British manufacturers. He countered that colonists were optimal producer-consumers if freed from such regulation. Mere population accumulation guaranteed a big market for British goods. In North America, Franklin claimed, the population 'must at least be doubled every 20 Years'. The rapid increase resulted from the accessibility of land to any young couple intent on marriage – the reproducing dyad, yet again. Compared to their counterparts in Europe, these young folks could gain economic independency and marry sooner, and thus produce and sustain larger families, significant additions to the consumer economy in the Atlantic world. Franklin represented this continental economic contribution as a contrast to the sugar islands, where black slaves – the Caribbean's population majority – lacked the means and the free will to function as consumers.[11]

Franklin drew similar conclusions about America's indigenous populations. His analysis shows some familiarity with stadial theory, the great eighteenth-century proposition that the history of humanity occurred in stages according to mode of subsistence, moving from migratory hunting, to pastoralism, to agriculture, and then to commerce, the final economic stage that could be imagined in this pre-industrial era. According to that logic, Franklin maintained that Native Americans, as migratory hunters and, at best, occasional gardeners, failed to utilize North American land fully. That was prejudicial. Hunting was not the sole mode of subsistence for most natives of North America. And in any case, might not Native Americans become farmers and consumers of manufactures, moving forward through the stages laid out in theory? No: Franklin concurred with the claims that Native Americans, compared to colonists, were in severe population decline. He declared that the dwindling of native populations was inevitable and beneficial, given that it would free up yet more land for settlers. In a simultaneous attack on slavery and on non-European peoples, he rejoiced that in the colonies 'we have so fair an Opportunity, by excluding all Blacks and Tawneys, of increasing the lovely White and Red' complexion of Europeans.[12]

To help his readers visualize the quick reproduction of British colonists, on land never put to the plough, Franklin compared humans to other natural things, above all plants:

> There is in short, no Bound to the prolific Nature of Plants or Animals, but what is made by their crowding and interfering with each others Means of Subsistence. Was the Face of the Earth vacant of other Plants, it might be gradually sowed and overspread with one Kind only; as, for Instance, with Fennel; and were it empty of other Inhabitants, it might in a few Ages be replenish'd from one Nation only; as, for Instance, with Englishmen.

The replenishment was well underway. Franklin estimated that an original 80,000 white migrants to North America had generated, by 1751, over 1 million white colonists. Should they double their numbers within twenty-five years (estimating conservatively), there would be 2 million of them by around 1776.[13]

By 1776, that claim would hearten the American patriots in their War for Independence, when Franklin's prediction was in vigorous circulation, and indeed republished in London in 1779, at the height of the war. Population concerns were thus linked to Atlantic revolutions. And it was precisely to debunk two optimists who, in the wake of the French Revolution had predicted the possibility of human perfection, that Thomas Robert Malthus summoned the American example, reusing the new world tropes of the breeding couple and the vegetable imaginary. The two optimists Malthus attacked were William Godwin and the Marquis de Condorcet, whose 'talents' and 'candour' Malthus professed to admire, a bit of politesse that presaged a fundamental disagreement with the named individuals, and disapproval of their use of speculation as bases for recommending a course for humanity. Rather than begin with a statement of faith or conjecture, which were accepted strategies within moral philosophy, he proposed instead to examine 'laws'.[14]

Malthus defined two 'fixed laws of our nature' that were relevant to the question of human happiness. First, 'food is necessary to the existence of man'; second, 'the passion between the sexes is necessary, and will remain nearly in its present state'. His qualification of the second law, using the word 'nearly', indicated some uncertainty as to whether it was as 'necessary' as the first. To address that doubt, Malthus firmly stated: 'Towards the extinction of the passion between the sexes, no progress whatever has hitherto been made.' So the two laws were invariable. Their trajectories were also unbalanced. 'Population, when unchecked, increases in a geometrical ratio', he argued, while 'subsistence increases only in an arithmetical ratio'. It took only 'a slight acquaintance with numbers', to 'shew the immensity of the first power in comparison of the second'. Given these two unbalanced trends, there would always tend to be more people than could adequately be fed: 'I say, that the power of population is indefinitely greater than the power in the earth to produce subsistence for man'. For this reason, misery was as likely to persist as happiness to overtake it. Because of 'a strong and constantly operating check on population from the difficulty of subsistence', Malthus proposed, 'this difficulty must fall some where; and must necessarily be severely felt by a large portion of mankind'. For that reason, 'the argument is conclusive against the perfectibility of the mass of mankind'. Two laws; one bitter conclusion.[15]

In this way, the *Essay on the Principle of Population* was an essay in natural theology, a point rarely acknowledged. Although Malthus did not use the words 'original sin' to explain why humanity would always be prone to lust and therefore to misery, his implication was obvious, and as such it rebuked Godwin and Condorcet's secular terms of analysis. The twinned natural laws of Malthus's population principle were the same, moreover, as the curses placed on Adam and Eve: to cultivate the earth and to bring forth children. Malthus explicitly echoed the language of divine mandate when he declared that 'to furnish the most unremitted excitements of this kind, and to urge man to further the gracious designs of Providence, by the full cultivation of the earth, it has been ordained, that population should increase much faster than food'. That statement connected the scriptural mandate to 'increase and multiply' with its partner, 'subdue the Earth' – and good luck trying to keep them in balance. Malthus would at the end of his 1798 *Essay* add a clearer reference to original sin when he said that his principle of population was a powerful reason for humans to try to overcome their fallen state: 'Evil exists in the world, not to create despair, but activity.'[16]

From the initial presentation of his principle of population, Malthus moved to a deeper exegesis of the problem on three geographic scales and in three qualitatively different places, beginning with North America. Thus he moved from the natural theology that referenced a lost Eden to the historical discovery of a new world that might have seemed to offer a new Eden. Indeed, Malthus's description of the new republic in North America entertained that possibility, quoting the optimism of the American patriots that they had created a new order of the ages. 'In the United States of America,' he began, 'where the means of subsistence have been more ample, the manners of the people more pure, and consequently the checks to early marriages fewer, than in any of the modern states of Europe, the population had been found to double itself in twenty-five years.' This was a statistic based on 'actual experience'. But Malthus used that empirical example, adorned with the positive words 'ample' and 'pure', to project the consequences of this population increase for places that lacked North America's material and cultural advantages, and where positive descriptions would be unlikely.[17]

'Let us now take any spot of earth,' he continued, 'this Island [of Great Britain] for instance, and see in what ratio the subsistence it affords can be supposed to increase.' In his seemingly offhand choice of a small scale of analysis, Malthus established an important contrast. If North America offered perfect evidence for the geometrical rapidity of population increase, Great Britain was perfect evidence that agricultural improvement would never keep up – that was the point of the contrast between new and old worlds. At best, and even if 'every acre of land in the Island [was cultivated] like a garden', the produce of Great Britain could only be doubled in an initial 25-year period, not quadrupled over a succeeding 25-year period. So the most optimal rate of agricultural growth in Britain would be only 'equal to what it at present produces', and 'this ratio of increase is evidently arithmetical', in contrast to the proven geometrical rates of population increase in the new world. Malthus then proceeded to take these contrasting rates, from new and old worlds, and project them over the entire globe, his third and final scale of analysis, in a vision of the future that combined American fecundity of population with British intensity of agriculture. If both trends proceeded to their natural limits, there would still be a gap: 'No limits whatever are placed on the productions of the earth ... yet still the power of population being a power of a superior order', it would take 'the constant operation of the strong law of necessity' acting as a check upon the greater power' to prevent hunger.[18]

Malthus turned next to consider 'this check', the mechanism that he thought must exist in order to adjust for the gap between human increase and the availability of food. Plants and animals had no 'reasoning' that interrupted their reproduction. They simply proliferated until they and their offspring either starved or became 'the prey of others'. That merciless struggle was the check on unlimited growth in the world of nature. But 'the effects of this check on man are more complicated', Malthus conceded, because humans had reason and therefore the ability to avoid starvation or to become the prey of others. Possession of reason did not always operate to fullest advantage, however. When foresight had failed, humans could only resort to 'vice', attempts to prevent conception or procure abortion, or else they sank into 'misery' as they and their children suffered from want. 'The superior power of population cannot be checked,' Malthus concluded, 'without producing misery or vice, the ample portion of these too bitter ingredients in the cup of human life.' Again, the embedded fatalism reflected belief in God's original curses on humanity, with vice related to Eve's burden and misery to Adam's.[19]

At this point, Malthus thought it necessary to 'examine the different states in which mankind have been known to exist', a bid, yet again, to avoid abstract speculation about the human condition, the error of the optimists. He proceeded historically, and according to stadial theory, by beginning with 'the rudest state of mankind, in which hunting is the principal occupation'. His prime example of this societal stage was 'the North American Indians', a choice that showed, yet again, the centrality of new worlds to his analysis. American Indians subsisted by hunting, Malthus claimed, which required them to be spread thin over a large extent of territory – the familiar stadial definition of savagery. A hunting mode of subsistence resulted in a small population, because of its constant toll on human energies without any compensating payoff. As proof of that hazard, Malthus stated that American Indians who lived near European settlements, according to a 'civilized mode of life', had larger families. But elsewhere, Malthus continued, 'misery is the check that represses the superior power of population', particularly when it fell on American Indian women, whose capacity to bear and rear children was thereby impeded. The physical toll was ingrained, it 'is constantly acting now upon all savage nations', and it would operate 'a thousand years hence', as if a savage state would exist somewhere on the globe into the distant future, whatever the spread of commercial societies through European imperialism.[20]

Having begun with aboriginal America, Malthus would return to the Americas toward the end of his *Essay*, believing that settler society in North America represented the most optimal circumstances for human increase. By tracing this contrast, Malthus made clear his opinion that it was not America's primal state which offered a glimpse of an Edenic condition, but instead its historical development in turning from an aboriginal to a pre-commercial stage by means of European colonization. 'There is not a truer criterion of the happiness and innocence of a people,' he concluded, 'than the rapidity of their increase.' Had Malthus relied only on the 'happiness' of a people as his criterion, he would have indicated agreement with Condorcet and Godwin's terms of analysis. Adding the element of 'innocence', however, hinted at a moral state that at least approximated that before the Fall. In this way, Malthus continued the tradition of associating the Americas with a pre-lapsarian condition while rejecting any sentiment that colonizing Europeans had ruined that happy state among the American Indians. He repeated that iteration of a partially moral rather than solely physical condition when he concluded that North America had its rapidly increasing settler population both because 'the manners of the people [were] more pure' (a widely repeated commonplace about the early Republic) and because they had more land than their counterparts in Europe.[21]

Malthus's information about rapid population growth in the Americas had a specific origin, Benjamin Franklin. Malthus reported that in North America, specifically, 'the population was found to double itself in 25 years'. Later in his essay, Malthus increased the rate to 'every 15 years'. He knew he had seen this estimate in a sermon by the American clergyman Ezra Stiles, *A Discourse on the Christian Union* (1761) but, having it not 'to hand' when he wrote his essay, he cited someone who had cited Stiles, Richard Price, in his *Observations on Reversionary Payments* (1773). Although Price's essay was in fact a letter to Franklin, and footnoted Franklin's essay, the citation did not include Franklin's name as author, understandably, because the essay had at that point been published anonymously. Perhaps for that reason, Malthus did not recognize the statistic as Franklin's.[22]

The lack of clear attribution had a serious consequence. Had Malthus read Franklin's essay, he could not have defined his principle of population in the way that he did, or at least not as easily. Only half of his own famous contribution to political arithmetic was based on the American's estimate, the half that referred to humans. In stating that American settlers doubled in number at least every two decades, Franklin had postulated that human population increased geometrically. But Franklin had not claimed that food sources increased merely arithmetically. Instead, he explicitly compared humans to plants when he said that the English could fill up territory cleared of other humans just as readily as fennel did on land weeded of competitors. It is also notable that Franklin used as his example a plant that humans could eat, which, had Malthus read it, would have queried his assertion that food supply must lag behind population increase. The scenario that Franklin laid out should have mattered to Malthus. Just as he relied on Franklin's estimate of the doubling of North American settler population – it was essential to his principle of population – Malthus doggedly emphasized the relentless functioning of nature's laws. 'Since the world began,' he lectured, 'the causes of population and depopulation have probably been as constant as any of the laws of nature.' But Malthus and his main source did not agree on that central assumption. In material terms, Franklin equated the power of a breeding couple with the speed of the vegetable imaginary; Malthus did not.[23]

Malthus maintained his central assumptions in the greatly enlarged edition of his essay, which appeared in 1803. In this, he examined population in a range of human societies, past and present, and over much of the globe as it was known to Europeans at the time. His global aspirations, and his particular attention to new world places, were the analytical frameworks by which he made his principle of population into a universal one for all of humanity. He considered this 'new work' to be 'a whole of itself' and not a mere expansion or emendation of the first edition. And he insisted that his own analysis was singular. Of central importance was 'the comparison between the increase of population and food', and so were 'the various modes' by which population must necessarily 'be kept down to the level of the means of subsistence'. Whereas the first edition had stated an 'abstract truth', that would not itself 'tend to promote any practical good', and the doing of benefit to all of humanity throughout the world was Malthus's stated, central concern.[24]

New worlds led Malthus's exposition literally, constituting in the first book of the new edition what were for him the societal forms most unlike those of modern Europe and, by implication, most useful in exposing what was natural to humans as physical creatures that might be concealed by culture elsewhere. By progressing, chapter by chapter, through New South Wales, the Americas and then the South Seas, Malthus indicated modes of human subsistence that succeeded each other by stages, themselves succeeded by societies that better resembled those of the Europe of his day: ancient Northern Europe, inhabited by savage and barbarian societies that nevertheless prefigured present-day Europe in ways that new worlds did not; contemporary pastoral societies; Africa, Siberia, Turkey and Persia, and then Asia. He next proceeded to the ancient Greeks and Romans, the nearest ancestors of modern Europeans, thus sweeping through people in the 'lowest stages and past times', drawing material and inspiration from classical authors on Greece and Rome, Scottish writers on European and Asian barbarians, travellers' accounts of China, India, Africa and America, and the great proliferation of voyagers' accounts of the Pacific Ocean. He inquired into comparative means of subsistence, detailing the varying customs and manners by which life, death, sex and food were managed in vastly different times, climates and cultures the world over, and in the different economies of exchange conceptually organized by the four stages.

Malthus began at the beginning, in stadial theory's terms, writing chapters on 'savage' societies. Savagery meant, first and foremost, a mode of subsistence, a pre- or non-pastoral economy, a gathering and a hunting society. The most important characteristic was the lack of land cultivation, often presumed when it came to actual societies. Scottish and French Enlightenment theorists conventionally discussed American Indians as archetypal and historical savages – part of the tradition of thought from which Franklin had written. Yet Malthus had a new set of voyagers' accounts with which to think through population in terms of stadial theory, including its links both to colonization and to civilization. For him, the 'lowest Stage of Human Society' dealt in passing with Andaman Islanders, Tierra del Fuegians and Van Diemen's Land Aborigines, before dwelling at some length with Aborigines in New South Wales. For Malthus, these Aborigines were exemplars of savage hunter-gatherers.

In this foundational chapter that began the process of substantiating his principle of population, his 'abstract truth', Malthus drew on a particular kind of evidence: first-hand voyagers' accounts, those who had witnessed these far-away people and places, and in some cases had engaged with them very closely. The volumes published from James Cook's three journeys were a corpus that Malthus mined fairly extensively, beginning with the first voyage account compiled by John Hawkesworth, what Malthus cited as 'Cook's First Voyage'. Of all the exotic tableaux, florid description and dashing adventure therein, it is entirely clear what most grabbed and held Malthus's attention. The critical sentence was this: 'By what means the inhabitants of this country are reduced to such a number as it can subsist, is not perhaps very easy to guess.' Malthus bothered to copy the passage from 'Cook's First Voyage', transfer it into his *Essay* as a direct quotation and retain it in all editions. Indeed in the *Summary View of the Principle of Population*, published in 1830, Malthus cast back over his life's major work, and himself characterized the entire project as one long response to Cook. He had endeavoured 'to answer the question, generally, which had been applied, particularly, to New Holland by Captain Cook'.[25]

If Franklin's settler population in North America was thriving, the thin population of Aborigines in New Holland intrigued Malthus. His principle was clearly in operation there, since the population was so demonstrably reduced from the possibility of doubling every 25 or so years. Any reader of Malthus's major work, in any edition, was told firmly at the outset that human societies had the *potential* to reproduce very rapidly (like Franklin's fennel), but the real point was that they rarely did so. In this chapter, Malthus was showing just why and how the vast continent of New Holland, far from being overrun with humans as this potential would imply, in fact had relatively few. The availability of food, the nature of diet, and the economy of exchange were each important for Malthus to demonstrate the relation between food scarcity and low population density. 'By what means?' was Malthus's key query. Precisely how did population oscillate? How was population density kept low? The chapter thus served to illustrate how the Aboriginal population was limited by various checks, those relating to birth, death and sustenance. This was the detail that was brought into the long new edition of the *Essay*.

Malthus was putting specific instances to his generic positive and negative 'checks'. He described the epidemic disease, for example, that checked the population of New South Wales, recounting the terrible epidemic of smallpox over 1789, a tragic instance of new world depopulation, perhaps 50 per cent of the local population dead. 'The desolation that it occasioned was almost incredible', Malthus stated correctly. When whole tribes disappeared, those who were left united with other tribes 'to prevent their utter extinction'. This, too, was correct, from all accounts.[26]

Importantly, however, Malthus did not link massive Aboriginal mortality in 1789 from smallpox to the arrival of the British in New South Wales the year before, or to the presence of French ships, which is what the British governor thought might be the case. Instead Malthus drew attention to Aboriginal habits of living: 'the smoke and filth of their miserable habitations' produced 'loathsome cutaneous disorders, and above all, a dreadful epidemic like the small-pox'. In assessing the epidemic thus, Malthus took liberties with his sources, and actively ignored the wide contemporary speculation about British responsibility in this episode. It was a 'positive check' – one of the epidemics that naturally (although just as tragically for Malthus), operated when population levels pressed against subsistence levels. If for later observers the smallpox epidemic served as evidence of the fatal impact of colonialism, just as surely, in Malthus's view, it served as evidence of the permanent oscillation and regulation of population vis-à-vis resources. For him, it was the principle of population, not the principle of colonialism that was in operation.[27]

Notwithstanding such material on (what were for him) naturally occurring epidemics, it is erroneous to read Malthus's principle as crudely determinist, as nature acting on human populations in an unmediated way. Malthus was as interested in the culture, as the nature, that resulted in thin populations, and this is what engaged him most in the chapters derived from stadial theory. Fertility and mortality were moderated by all kinds of human intervention, by all manner of reason and custom.

Culture, for Malthus, was invariably about gender. Many contemporary histories of humankind assessed the treatment of women as an index of savagery or civilization; gender was thus part of stadial theory's core business. For Malthus, however, there was an additional interest; how relations between men and women affected fertility and mortality in a direct and physical way. In his main source on Aboriginal people, David Collins's *Account of the English Colony in New South Wales*, he read of the violence to which women were subject, permanently scarred with the 'traces of the superiority of the males', Malthus repeated. He surmised that miscarriage must be common in this context, exacerbated by the difficulties of wandering and gathering. This, plus the abuse of very young girls likely resulted in Aboriginal women's low fertility, he thought. In many ways, Malthus selected the worst that Collins's book had to offer, and painted a far grimmer overall picture than the first-hand *Account.* He noted that men could and did have more than one wife, but found it 'extraordinary' that only the first wife, it seemed, bore children. 'A great part of the women are without children', Collins had claimed, and other women appeared to have only a singleton. Some of the local people had told Collins (relayed Malthus), that the first wife 'claimed an exclusive right to the conjugal embrace'. Malthus himself thought this unlikely, supposing that the second, rather, 'might not be allowed to rear her offspring', one of the many references to infanticide in these chapters of the *Essay.*[28] Exposing and thus killing infants was one clear means by which populations were kept low, according to Malthus, and he recounted Collins's description of the Aboriginal practice of burying infants with their dead mothers. The practice was one of the parallels Malthus was to draw in the following chapter between Aboriginal people in New Holland and Native

Americans. All of this ran counter to the scriptural injunction to multiply on the one hand, and not to kill on the other, but Malthus's intention was neither to condemn nor expose these practices as evidence of heathen savagery. They were instances of population management, albeit deeply problematic ones. He presented this material rather more as matters of fact. The accumulation of such habits of life and death, Malthus considered, 'forcibly repress the rising generation'. It all furnished empirical evidence of the principle of population in operation.[29]

Malthus also wrote a chapter on the South Sea, distilling information from the celebrated French and British journeys through Oceania, which had accelerated from the 1760s. These offered Malthus extremely useful cases through which to demonstrate to his readers the oscillation of population over time and in limited space, and the range of checks that affected this oscillation in different locations and societies. He redeployed for his purposes the journeys of Bougainville, La Pérouse, Vancouver and especially Cook. Each had recorded and supplied information on customs and manners to do with reproduction, sex, food production and consumption, and indeed on population in order to form part of the histories of humankind then being written in England, Scotland and France. Malthus thus received a double dose of stadial theory: directly from the Enlightenment historians, but also from the South Sea travel accounts, themselves not just shaped by, but self-consciously offering up material for that tradition.[30]

Part of the reason Malthus wrote about the South Sea islands at all was the already conventional commentary on their varied fertility, mortality and population density. 'Otaheite' had become the talk of Enlightenment Europe and featured strongly in Malthus's Pacific chapter, serving his thesis well, because it was routinely observed as populous, even crowded, unlike sparsely populated New Holland. Cook, Banks and Bougainville all made a point of noting the great number of Tahitians, but more precisely tied to the principle of population was Malthus's own extrapolation from their observations that there were cycles of population growth and decline, a response to changing prosperity. It is unlikely, he proposed, that Tahiti's population had always been the same – stationary – or that it had been constantly increasing, however slowly. Rather, it oscillated – overpopulation would lead to war; this would lead to depravation, and over time (after war had been forgotten), population increase. Then, unfavourable seasons would bring about a society 'pressing hard against the limits of its food', and that would prompt more war or more infanticide, a process of depopulation that would continue longer than the famine itself.

A 'change of habits' then produced by the availability of food, would 'restore the population'. And so on. It was the oscillation between scarcity and living just on or over subsistence that Malthus noted from the Tahitian case, empirical evidence of his principle, and he made a point of saying so: '[T]his is exactly what we should suppose from theory.' In such statements, it is clear that Malthus saw his work as extending conjectural history into a wholly new domain of evidence. On the basis of these chapters, Malthus explicated the world's least and most commercial societies together to substantiate a *principle* that was observable and demonstrable; from a new world, he delivered empirical material that illustrated a *law* of population universally at work.[31]

Malthus established the distinctiveness of new world populations in a second way, by citing settlers on population matters, meaning that he took the producers and products of settler population growth to be authorities on their generative power, a strategy he did not pursue for other parts of the world. Although the settler authorities included David Collins on New South Wales, Malthus's foremost new world expert was Benjamin Franklin, who occupied pride of place at the start of the expanded *Essay*'s first chapter. Malthus had discovered that Franklin was the original author of the 'doubling every 20 years' estimate of American populations that he had quoted from Richard Price. Malthus had doggedly followed the citations backward from Price, thus establishing that Franklin's thesis was the basis for his original assessment of the fastest known speed of human population growth, which he duly noted in the 1803 edition. He read Franklin's essay as confirmation of his own principle of population, although this required him to ignore some of what his source actually had said. 'It is observed by Dr. Franklin,' Malthus explained, in a quotation that altered only one word of the original:

> that there is no bound to the prolific nature of plants or animals, but what is made by their crowding and interfering with each other's means of subsistence. Were the face of the earth, he says, vacant of other plants, it might gradually be sowed and overspread with one kind only; as, for instance, with fennel: and were it empty of other inhabitants, it might in a few ages be replenished from one nation only; as, for instance, with Englishmen.

It was 'incontrovertibly true', Malthus stated, again affirming that the principle of population was most starkly apparent in new world sites where one population (settlers) appeared to be unimpeded by any other (meaning Native Americans). That scenario had raised British colonial spirits in the 1750s, when Franklin wrote, and had definitely encouraged the American patriots and their sympathizers in the 1770s, when his essay had been republished in London. It might have had a similar effect on Britons in the 1800s – to see themselves overspreading the face of the earth – had not Malthus followed its logic in a different direction. If nature's limits were finite, even the fennel-like Englishmen must eventually starve, and here Malthus explicitly rejected the possibility that plants (and other sources of food) might keep pace with humans; in the end, the fennel would not be sufficient to feed the Englishmen. For that reason, a 'strong check on population' must always operate, and its dire effects – 'misery, or the fear of misery' – be eventually felt by 'a large portion of mankind'. Malthus restated his claim to a geometrical rate of population increase, doubling every 25 years, rather than Franklin's 20, deliberately choosing the slower rate to stave off any criticism that he was exaggerating.[32]

But why were humans different from plants and, by extension, all other non-human parts of nature that they might eat? Whereas Franklin had comfortably compared humans to plants, his attitude reflected an early acceptance of radical Enlightenment materialism, a habit acquired in his youth. That position troubled clergy at the time, unless they themselves were radicals, as with the famous example of Joseph Priestley, who interpreted the soul as a physical entity, to the horror of the orthodox. There is no hint that Malthus entertained similar thoughts about humans as merely material objects and he surely knew that, as a minister in the Church of England, he could not have published such sentiments without renouncing his livelihood. His steadfast distinction between humans and the things they ate reflected his orthodoxy and made his insistence on arithmetic rates of increase for food and geometrical rates of increase for humans impossible to support with data. They remained articles of faith.[33]

As in the first edition of the *Essay*, Malthus specified that humans differed from other natural beings because they could exercise judgement. This 'preventive check', as he put it, 'is peculiar to man, and arises from that distinctive superiority in his reasoning faculties, which enables him to calculate distant consequences'. Malthus presented this, rather vividly for the time and place, as the doubts a married man (specifically) might entertain 'if he follow the bent of his inclinations' to have sexual intercourse with his wife, yet knowing it might lead to the impoverishment of his household. In a very real sense, Malthus presented his treatise as another reason to give an ardent man pause, unless the man in question were lucky enough not to have reason to worry about his family's subsistence.[34]

As a case in point, Malthus offered white North Americans as persons who had a dangerous lack of disincentive to delay their gratification, a direct challenge to any wholehearted conception of new worlds as reservoirs of Edenic innocence. He conceded there had never been any 'country' where 'manners were so pure and simple, and the means of subsistence so abundant, that no check whatever has existed to early marriages'. And yet, 'in the northern states of America, where the means of subsistence have been more ample, the manners of the people more pure, and the checks to marriage fewer, than in any of the modern states of Europe, the population was found to double itself for some successive periods every twenty-five years'. Malthus added qualifications; mortality in New England towns sometimes exceeded the birth-rate, and the populations of these urban sites were only sustained through migration from the countryside. But in frontier settlements, 'where the sole employment was agriculture, and vicious customs and unwholesome occupations were unknown, the population was found to double itself in fifteen years'. That example was the closest to a free state of marriage and reproduction that had ever been observed to exist, although 'even this extraordinary rate of increase is probably short of the utmost power of population'.[35]

By placing this material at the very start of his analysis, Malthus made new world examples, from urban and frontier parts of the United States, function as primary evidence of the capacity of population to increase at its fastest known rate, doubling as quickly as every 15 years, which was perhaps close to the theoretical extreme, if humans somehow needed no more reason than animals. This analytic conclusion was not necessarily flattering to the western settlers along the US frontier, who were implied to breed nearly as indiscriminately as rats. That implication constituted a potential point of criticism about all new world colonists that Malthus would develop later in the book. For the moment, in his introductory material, he moved to examples of places where food production increased least quickly, if at all, in order to give evidence of the other half of his principle of population, thus establishing the contrasting swiftness and slowness that together constrained humanity. He again laid out a hypothetical rate of agricultural growth, at its fastest, only to conclude that it would never keep up with population. 'In Europe,' he ventured, 'there is the fairest chance that human industry may receive its best direction.' But it would never advance agricultural production to a geometric rate.[36]

If agriculture could not supply food endlessly to keep up with its eaters, this raised an ethical problem about the very nature of European colonization in the new worlds of the Atlantic and Pacific, the third and final way in which new worlds were central to Malthus's analysis. If settlers in a new land kept reproducing in a nearly rat-like fashion, they would make people faster than their land could make food. 'Even where this might take place,' Malthus considered, 'as it does sometimes in new colonies, a geometrical ratio increases with such extraordinary rapidity, that the advantage could not last long.' The eventual scarcity would afflict the heedless settlers' descendants, a problem for the future. And even in the present, settler proliferation would torment any 'new' territory's indigenous inhabitants. 'There are many parts of the globe, indeed, hitherto uncultivated, and almost unoccupied', Malthus reminded his readers, at this point looking beyond the Americas and into the new worlds of the Pacific. 'But the right of exterminating, or driving into a corner where they must starve, even the inhabitants of these thinly-peopled regions, will be questioned in a moral view.' In short, not only was this usurpation of indigenous peoples immoral, but it would let the settler population live on borrowed time only. This was the last important lesson about population that Malthus derived from new worlds.[37]

Malthus's concern about extermination, about 'driving' new world people 'into a corner', was far from abstract. Settler colonialism was, after all, a process of new world clearances of both land and people, and much of it took place in Malthus's lifetime. The great agricultural ventures in Upper Canada, in the western United States, and in the Australian colonies were key parts of the global environmental shift over the eighteenth and nineteenth centuries, from forest to farm, and from grassland to grainland. To be sure, Malthus was interested in the effect of 'new land' on the emigrant population, those neo-Britons who were busy replenishing the earth. But it turns out that he also recognized the cost of all this replenishment in the new worlds. The displacement of indigenous people that Malthus noted was sometimes organized, sometimes haphazard; sometimes actively violent, at other times passively so. Occasionally unwitting, the 'driving into a corner' was more often a deliberate and formal policy. Two such deliberations took place in 1830 – the Indian Removal Act in the United States and the so-called Black Line in Van Diemen's Land. In that year, Malthus published his *Summary View on the Principle of Population* (reprinting a piece originally published in 1824), again identifying the local impact when emigrants from the 'improved parts of the world' moved to those unimproved: '[I]t is obvious that it must involve much war and extermination.'[38]

What Malthus himself called an 'age of emigration' was one where the old world and the new clashed violently. The new world, for Thomas Robert Malthus, had revealed, as no other part of the world could do so well, that human population expanded, struggled and collapsed within limits set out by nature, moderated to some degree by human reason and custom. The new world had suggested the possibility of that notorious principle of population in the first place. Malthus has been thoroughly assessed as to his statement about the moral hazard of the possible increase in the numbers of British poor, yet his parallel claim about the moral hazard of colonial populations increasing in new world environments is equally arresting.[39]

Notes

1 E.A. Wrigley, 'Standing between Two Worlds', *Malthus and his Legacy: The Population Debate after 200 years*, Australian Academy of the Humanities, www.naf.org.au/papers.htm; Joyce E. Chaplin, *Benjamin Franklin's Political Arithmetic: A Materialist View of Humanity* (Washington, DC: Smithsonian Institution, 2009), pp. 41–3; Alison Bashford, 'Malthus and Colonial History', *Journal of Australian Studies*, 36 (2012), 99–110.

2 KJV Genesis 1:28, 3:16–19, 9:1; Jeremy Cohen, *Be Fertile and Increase, Fill the Earth and Master It: The Ancient and Medieval Career of a Biblical Text* (Ithaca: Cornell University Press, 1989).

3 Jean Delumeau, *History of Paradise: The Garden of Eden in Myth and Tradition*, trans. Matthew O'Connell (Urbana: University of Illinois Press, 2000), pp. 109–15; Michael Householder, 'Eden's Translations: Women and Temptation in Early America', *Huntington Library Quarterly*, 70 (2007), 11–36.

4 Theodor De Bry, *Grands Voyages* (Frankfurt, 1590).

5 John Locke, *Two Treatises of Government* (London: Awnsham Churchill, 1689), ch. 5 § 49; Richard H. Grove, *Green Imperialism: Colonial Expansion, Tropical Island Edens, and the Origins of Environmentalism, 1600–1800* (Cambridge: Cambridge University Press, 1995).

6 Giovanni Botero, *The Reason of State*, trans. P.J. Waley and D.P. Waley, and *The Greatness of Cities*, trans. Robert Peterson (New Haven: Yale University Press, 1956), pp. 227, 276, 278.

7 Ibid., p. 246.

8 Joyce E. Chaplin, *Subject Matter: Technology, the Body, and Science on the Anglo-American Frontier, 1500–1676* (Cambridge, MA: Harvard University Press, 2001), pp. 124–30.

9 Ibid., pp. 118–20, 124–30, 154–6, 318–20.

10 Joyce E. Chaplin, *The First Scientific American: Benjamin Franklin and the Pursuit of Genius* (New York: Basic Books, 2006), pp. 79–83, 141–3.

11 Benjamin Franklin, 'Observations Concerning the Increase of Mankind' [1751], in Leonard W. Labaree, *et al.* (ed.) *The Papers of Benjamin Franklin*, 40 vols. to date (New Haven: Yale University Press, 1959–), vol. 4, pp. 225–31.

12 Ibid., p. 228, p. 234. On stadial theory, see Ronald L. Meek, *Social Science and the Ignoble Savage* (Cambridge: Cambridge University Press, 1976), esp. pp.

37–67; J.G.A. Pocock, 'Gibbon and the Shepherds: The States of Society in the *Decline and Fall*', *History of European Ideas*, 2 (1981), 193–202; Christian Marouby, 'Adam Smith and the Anthropology of the Enlightenment: The "Ethnographic" Sources of Economic Progress', in Larry Wolff and Marco Cipolloni (eds.), *The Anthropology of the Enlightenment* (Stanford: Stanford University Press, 2007), pp. 85–102; P.J. Marshall and Glyndwr Williams, *The Great Map of Mankind: Perceptions of New Worlds in the Age of Enlightenment* (Cambridge, MA: Harvard University Press, 1982); Silvia Sebastiani, *The Scottish Enlightenment: Race, Gender, and the Limits of Progress* (New York: Palgrave, 2013).

13 Franklin, 'Increase of Mankind', p. 233.

14 T.R. Malthus, *An Essay on the Principle of Population, as it Affects the Future Improvement of Society* (London: J. Johnson, 1798), pp. 2, 7. For Malthus's use of Franklin, see Chaplin, *First Scientific American*, pp. 351–2; Chaplin, *Franklin's Political Arithmetic*, pp. 41–2; Alison Bashford, *Global Population: History, Geopolitics, and Life on Earth* (New York: Columbia University Press, 2014), pp. 32–3, 37.

15 Malthus, *Essay* (1798), pp. 10, 11, 13, 14, 17.

16 Ibid., pp. 361, 393.

17 Ibid., pp. 20–1.

18 Ibid., pp. 21–3, 25–6.

19 Ibid., pp. 27, 37.

20 Ibid., pp. 38–44.

21 Ibid., pp. 20, 108.

22 Ibid., pp. 104–5, p. 185; Ezra Stiles, *A Discourse on a Christian Union* (Boston: Edes and Gill, 1761), pp. 108–09; Richard Price, *Observations on Reversionary Payments: On Schemes for Providing Annuities* (London: T. Cadell, 1773), pp. 203, 204, 206; Chaplin, *Franklin's Political Arithmetic*, p. 41.

23 Franklin, 'Increase of Mankind', p. 233; Malthus, *Essay* (1798), pp. 127–8.

24 T. Robert Malthus, *An Essay on the Principle of Population*, 2nd edn (London: J. Johnson, 1803), pp. iii–vi.

25 John Hawkesworth, *An Account of the Voyages Undertaken by the Order of His Present Majesty for Making Discoveries in the Southern Hemisphere*, 3 vols. (London: W. Strahan and T. Cadell, 1773), vol. 3, p. 240, cited in Malthus, *Essay* (1803), p. 18; T.R. Malthus, *A Summary View of the Principle of Population* (London: John Murray, 1830), p. 44.

26 Malthus, *Essay* (1803), p. 23. In February 1790, Governor Arthur Phillip quoted one Aboriginal man who thought 'one-half of those who inhabit this part of the country died'. Governor Phillip to Lord Sydney, 13 February 1790: Frederick Watson, *Historical Records of Australia: Series 1: Governors' Dispatches to and From England* ([Sydney]: The Library Committee of the Commonwealth Parliament, 1914), vol. 1, p. 159.

27 Governor Phillip to Lord Sydney, 12 February 1790, *Historical Records of Australia*, series 1, vol. 1, p. 145; Malthus, *Essay* (1803), p. 22; Alan Moorehead,

The Fatal Impact: The Invasion of the South Pacific, 1767–1840 (1966; New York: Harper and Row, 1987).

28 Malthus, *Essay* (1803), p. 21. See David Collins, *An Account of the English Colony in New South Wales, with Remarks on the Dispositions, Customs, Manners, &c of the Native Inhabitants of that Country* (London: T. Cadell and W. Davies, 1798).

29 Malthus, *Essay* (1803), p. 22.

30 Harriet Guest, *Empire, Barbarism, and Civilisation: James Cook, William Hodges, and the Return to the Pacific* (Cambridge: Cambridge University Press, 2007), p. 12; Kathleen Wilson, 'Thinking Back: Gender Misrecognition and Polynesian Subversion Aboard the Cook Voyages', in Kathleen Wilson (ed.), *A New Imperial History: Culture, Identity and Modernity in Britain, 1660–1840* (Cambridge: Cambridge University Press, 2004), pp. 346–8.

31 Malthus, *Essay* (1803); for Tahiti, see Vanessa Smith, 'Crowd Scenes: Pacific Collectivity and European Encounter', *Pacific Studies* 27 (2004), 1–21.

32 Malthus, *Essay* (1803), pp. 2, 3, 4, 5.

33 Chaplin, *Franklin's Political Arithmetic*, pp. 7–8, 12–19, 25–35; Robert E. Schofield, *The Enlightened Joseph Priestley: A Study of His Life and Work from 1773 to 1804* (University Park: Pennsylvania State University Press, 2004), pp. 59–76, 263–89.

34 Malthus, *Essay* (1803), pp. 7–12.

35 Ibid., pp. 2–4.

36 Ibid., pp. 5–8.

37 Ibid., p. 6.

38 Malthus, *Summary View*, p. 29.

39 Malthus to William Whewell, 28 February 1831, in N.B. de Marchi and R.P. Sturges, 'Malthus and Ricardo's Inductivist Critics: Four Letters to William Whewell', *Economica*, 40 (1973), 379–93, p. 389.

CHAPTER 5

Island, nation, planet: Malthus in the Enlightenment

Fredrik Albritton Jonsson

During his tour of northern Scotland in 1772, the Welsh gentleman naturalist Thomas Pennant paid a brief visit to Jura, an island at the centre of the Hebrides. He found Jura the most 'rugged' of the archipelago, 'composed chiefly of vast mountains, naked and without the possibility of cultivation'. Lacking in arable land, Jura sustained only a small population, thinned continually by 'epidemic emigration'. The natural historian arrived on the island just after midsummer. He observed that many of the poor inhabitants had been reduced to a wretched condition while waiting for the harvest and had to subsist on a fare of 'limpets and perriwinkles [sic]' gathered on the shore. Others had taken to the upland pastures to tend the cattle herds of the island while living in stone and turf huts. Pennant's account, published in a widely read tour guide in 1774 and 1776, included a striking engraving of these conical Shielings by the draftsman Moses Griffith. Life on Jura seemed a vestige of a different stage of history.[1]

Pennant's melancholy view of a primitive island population squeezed by unrelenting natural limits was confirmed by the report on Jura filed by its own clergyman Reverend Francis Stewart for *The Statistical Account of Scotland* in 1794. Stewart's entry began with a bleak survey of the topography and the soil in the island. Small patches of arable land lay in a waterlogged declivity at the foot of the hills. 'The water is constantly oozing down through it, and in many places, bursting out in little springs.' Upland pastures offered only poor and difficult grazing to local herds. In fact, the cattle farmers were overstocking the land with too much cattle while the farms devoted to tillage had too many families living on them. Tenant farmers took a 'contracted view' of their native land, concentrated only on the present harvest or sales of livestock. Social ambition was channelled outward. They dreamed of acquiring large farms in America rather than improving their lot at home. Yet the steady departure of people for the New World had failed to alter the demographic balance at home.

Despite frequent emigration, population had remained relatively constant over the last generation. Webster's 1755 census enumerated 1,097 inhabitants whereas a 1792 survey listed 929 souls. From this account of soil, husbandry and population trends, Stewart concluded that the poor people of Jura lacked the requisite will and reason to improve the condition of the island. He used the language of pests and parasites to describe his own parishioners. They were a useless 'swarm' of no value to the state and a 'very great load upon the proprietors'. Change had to come from above, through the benevolence and initiative of the landowners. Stewart recommended parish schools to introduce the English language. Boats and nets would induce the poor to become fishermen. An end to the coal duties could provide cheaper fuel. The hills should be stocked with fine wool sheep for local spinners. There was fine sand on the beaches to support a glass manufacture. Such measures would rouse the industry of the poor and make them wish to emulate their 'more enlightened neighbours'. It would also lift the population out of the trap of subsistence farming and 'extinguish' 'the spirit of emigration'. Stewart's call for landlord intervention was common in the Scottish Enlightenment. The Highlands and the Hebrides provided an outdoor laboratory for numerous schemes of internal improvement in the period, from wasteland colonization and peat moss reclamation to the establishment of larch plantations and fishing villages. Leading figures in the movement – including John Sinclair, the Caithness landowner and editor of *The Statistical Account of Scotland* (1791–9) – hoped to double or triple the population of the region. Some improvers even thought that it might be possible to ameliorate the climate itself, bringing the north of Scotland into the ambit of the Lowland climate. Limits of population, soil and climate were only apparent and could be overcome through human ingenuity.[2]

The world of Enlightenment improvement played a decisive role in shaping Malthus's political economy. He shared with Scottish savants an enthusiasm for mixed husbandry and wasteland cultivation. From Adam Smith, Malthus inherited a 'liberal ecology' of improvement, which celebrated the power of commerce and urban demand in driving environmental transformation. From John Sinclair and his ally Arthur Young, Malthus learnt a political arithmetic of limits and needs, probing how much land was needed to feed a population at multiple scales. But Malthus rejected the sanguine expectations of his contemporaries, developing instead an understanding of the natural order that was at odds with their models of progress. Taking issue with Smith's rosy account of agricultural improvement, he worried that urban taste for butcher's meat might actually undermine grain production and therefore national security. Malthus also turned Sinclair's optimism on its head, by stressing the danger of population growing faster than the rate of agricultural productivity.

When Malthus presented an empirical defence of his theory in the second edition of *An Essay on the Principle of Population* (1803), he singled out the Scottish Highlands and Hebrides as the region most burdened by overpopulation in Great Britain.[3] His argument drew heavily on Sinclair's *Statistical Account of Scotland*, but he read it selectively, rejecting the cornucopian forecasts of the improvers in favour of a darker strain of natural history. The reference to Stewart's Jura report is a telling case in point. Malthus stripped down Stewart's 17 pages to three sentences. In this abbreviated version, the detailed account of island life vanished from view, along with the plea for economic projects and social change. Jura appeared simply as an object lesson in the explosive force of population. The place was 'absolutely overflowing with inhabitants in spite of constant and numerous emigrations'. Malthus reiterated Stewart's comments about plebeian parasites nearly verbatim: '[S]uch a swarm of inhabitants, where manufactures and many other branches of industry are unknown, are a very great load upon the proprietors, and useless to the state.' On Jura, the common people had become redundant, depending on patrician largesse to subsist and emigration to avoid mass mortality. Malthus's use of the word 'swarm' was hardly a coincidence. The swell of human numbers on the island resembled the physical pressure of an animal herd on patchy pastureland or an insect infestation within a closed space.[4]

Much ink has been spilled investigating Malthus's place within the history of classical political economy. Most scholars agree that Malthus introduced a new conception of nature into economic thought, but for a variety of reasons, we lack a detailed understanding of how he viewed physical environment. At times, Malthus has been portrayed as a 'pre-industrial' thinker caught unawares by the Industrial Revolution, a savant out of sync with his own time. On this reading, Malthus's political economy can be treated as an extended meditation on the general demographic realities of the old biological regime. Other scholars have suggested that Malthus's understanding of nature was an ideological construction to cover up and justify his defence of social inequality. Malthus developed this pessimistic notion of human nature in his polemics against the enlightened radicals Godwin and Condorcet. It signalled a hardening view of the lower orders. The poor constituted a surplus population, unwanted at 'nature's mighty feast.' They were biologized or animalized as creatures without foresight and rational restraint.[5]

To assess Malthus's view of the natural world, we need to take seriously his basic intuition about the problem of runaway growth in a finite system. Malthus's idea of population mixed natural history and political economy, defining population both as a physical force in space and a supply of labour for exchange. Humans, animals and plants were all governed by the same 'law of nature' – which limited the multiplication of population by the availability of food. To demonstrate the universal reach of this law, Malthus imagined biological growth in an empty universe. With unlimited sustenance and no competitors, a species could expand prodigiously, filling 'millions of worlds in the course of a few thousand years'. This thought experiment followed an ascending scale from the local to the planetary level. Given sufficient resources, a population would quickly colonize available territories, flowing into all the empty corners of the nation and the planet. The contrast between American and British population growth drove home the same point. Under conditions of abundant land in the colonies, population seemed to double every 25 years. Yet in a long-settled country like Great Britain, growth must be slower. In Malthus's forecast, food production could be doubled in the course of a generation. But after that, population would outpace improvements. Even if 'every acre of land in the island' became 'a garden', the food supply would lag population by the third or fourth decade of the nineteenth century. When population approached the limits of subsistence, the 'positive check' of famine, disease and war culled surplus numbers and restored the balance of nature. The same iron law applied to the world as a whole. Malthus predicted that human population growth could overshoot the food production of the planet within a few generations. 'In two centuries the population would be to the means of subsistence as 256 to 9.' The forecast for Britain thus offered a lesson for the species, 'taking the whole earth instead of this island'.[6]

To this diagnosis of agricultural limits, Malthus added a lengthy analysis of the institutional and moral factors that encouraged excessive population growth. Famously, he launched a sweeping attack against the English Poor Laws, arguing that this parish-based system of poor relief encouraged early marriage and myopic attitudes toward the future among the poor. The comparative scope of the second edition of the *Essay* included a wide-ranging and complex account of the causes of overpopulation outside England. In Scotland where poor relief was far less generous than in England, population still increased rapidly in many parishes, thanks to the

growth of manufactures, the subdivision of land and the pattern of emigration. The Irish population in turn expanded thanks to the introduction of the potato and the degenerate state of plebeian morals. Malthus
included Ireland in a broader group of nations too morally degraded by
'ignorance and barbarism' to impose restraints on early marriage.[7]

Hardly by coincidence, Malthus formulated his forecast of island strain
and overpopulation at a moment when Great Britain seemed more isolated and vulnerable than it had been for centuries. Global warfare, the
threat of invasion and dearth all served to illuminate a fact easily forgotten
in more fortunate times: disruptions of trade showed how dependent the
nation was on resources that had to be grown at home on relatively scarce
arable land. This bleak sense of insular geography set Malthus apart from
his predecessors in liberal political economy. He shared with Adam Smith
and the French Physiocrats a commitment to mixed husbandry and agricultural improvement, but he diverged from them in stressing the feeble-
ness of technology and knowledge in the face of geographic restraints and
demographic forces. Malthus's pessimistic assessment echoed broader anxieties about resource management and island limits among improvers,
politicians and naturalists in the age of the Revolutionary and Napoleonic
Wars. From Enlightenment natural history, Malthus also inherited a fascination with thought experiments and imaginary journeys. The authority
and analytical reach of his model derived in great part from his claim that
natural limits operated at every geographic scale: local, national, imperial
and planetary.

This essay explores the environmental foundation of Malthus's political economy by scaling upward from soil husbandry to national economy and planetary history, linking together three themes – liberal ideas
of improvement, the political arithmetic of island autarky and thought
experiments about world-making.[8] Environmental history and the history
of science provide complementary approaches to investigating the genesis
and influence of Malthus's political economy. We need to take seriously
the ecological strains in late eighteenth-century Britain charted by economic and environmental historians. But we must also understand how
these strains were perceived by contemporaries through the lens of natural history and agricultural improvement. Intellectual historians rightly
remind us that the eighteenth century notion of the 'oeconomy' must be
carefully distinguished from later conceptions of the economic sphere.
The same historical specificity applies to the idea of the 'environment', a
word of quite recent construction. However, such caution should not be
allowed to obscure a number of important continuities across the early

modern and modern divide, including longstanding concerns about climate change, deforestation and other kinds of degradation. Worries about the ecological strain caused by economic development have roots as deep as empire and capitalism.[9]

Malthus composed the first edition of *An Essay on the Principle of Population* in the midst of a great transformation that would later come to be known as the Industrial Revolution. Yet this sea change was not always apparent to contemporaries, and its most dramatic expression – the large-scale switch to steam technology in factory production – came only at the very end of Malthus's life. Personal inclination may also have blinded Malthus to some of the signs of change. At the age of 20, he declared a fervent wish to take orders and find 'a retired living in the country.' Much of his life was spent in small towns and villages across rural England: the Rookery outside Dorking, the Dissenting Academy at Warrington, Jesus College in Cambridge, Okewood in Surrey and the East India College in Haileybury. His writings betray a barely concealed distaste for the world of manufacturing labour. One of the earliest surviving fragments of his writing is the 1794 travel journal to the Lake District, the crucible of romantic aesthetics and literature.[10]

Energy consumption offers a useful lens to understand the predicament of Britain around the turn of the century 1800. E.A. Wrigley argues that the pace of demographic growth put serious pressure on the productive capacity of the land between 1780 and 1840. Both agriculture and manufacturing required increasing resources. Coal provided crucial relief by tapping into underground stocks of energy. In Wrigley's account, Britain gradually moved from the organic economy of the early modern period centred on the produce of agriculture, constrained by the limits of photosynthesis and the finite supply of land towards what he calls the modern 'mineral energy economy' based on the abundant deposits of fossil fuel energy in the form of coal and later natural gas and petroleum. In practical terms, this transition saw the move of a growing portion of the population from work in the agricultural sector into manufacturing and urban occupations. The structure of aggregate demand also changed, no longer focused primarily on basic products of food, clothing and fuel, but expanded to include commodities such as sugar, tobacco and printed calicoes, many of them imported from the colonies or overseas producers. Market expansion and increasing division of labour fostered a new economic dynamism. Yet only fossil fuel could sustain such growth in the long run. Wrigley observes that England would have faced 'a catastrophic decline in living standards' if it had doubled its population without access to coal. To demonstrate the importance of fossil fuel, Wrigley also calculates the 'ghost acres' of British energy consumption. One million tons of coal was equivalent to one million acres of woodland. In 1800, coal consumption amounted to 11.2 million acres of forest, roughly 35 per cent of the land surface of England and Wales. Clearly, adopting this much land for wood fuel would have been extremely difficult. Fifty years later, the level of coal consumption took up the equivalent of 150 per cent of the total land area.[11]

Malthus's political economy recognized the constraints of population growth in a long-settled land without grasping how industrial technology would transform the nation in the long run. We might say that the *Essay* expressed a partial understanding of the forces at work in Britain's transition from the organic economy to the mineral energy economy. He realized that population growth was putting increasing strain on the agrarian economy, yet failed to forecast the arrival of mechanized agriculture and synthetic fertilizer. To reconstruct the environmental foundation of his political economy, we must see these processes through Malthus's own eyes. His theory of population and improvement combined elements of the liberal thought of the Scottish Enlightenment with the experience of ecological strain and wasteland colonization during the Revolutionary and Napoleonic Wars.

Adam Smith pioneered a powerful liberal interpretation of the essential harmony between markets and agriculture in *The Wealth of Nations* (1776). The notion of the natural world in Smith was a distillate of book learning and practical experience. The Scottish savant was well read in Enlightenment natural history. To construct his global history of European empires and commerce in *The Wealth of Nations*, he drew on a number of travel accounts, including works by Pehr Kalm, Antonio de Ulloa and Pierre Poivre. Such armchair science was refracted through Smith's personal experience of improvement. Lowland agriculture in Scotland underwent a dramatic transformation after 1760, doubling or even tripling output in some cases. This great leap forward was accompanied by a lively debate about central problems of agrarian reform, including such issues as the optimal size of farms, the need to abolish the feudal vestige of entail and the proper means of conserving soil fertility. Smith knew these debates first-hand, through his many connections with theorists and practitioners of agricultural improvement such as William Cullen, Henry Home (Lord Kames), James Hutton and the Duke of Buccleuch.[12]

Smith articulated his own views of these questions in Book III of *The Wealth of Nations*. He argued that investments when unimpeded by protectionism would flow naturally first to agriculture at home, then to national manufactures and finally to overseas trade. He called this ideal path the 'natural progress of opulence'. Smith also explained how European husbandry had been shaped in practice by the strictures of mercantilist legislation such that capital had flowed outward to the colonies first and only belatedly to agricultural improvements at home, leaving them underfunded and underdeveloped. Britain too was a product of the 'unnatural and retrograde order' of the Navigation Acts. But elsewhere in *The Wealth of Nations*, Smith made it clear that the formation of a unified livestock market in Great Britain with the Act of Union in 1707 between Scotland and England presented a crucial step towards the liberal order. The condition of internal trade was far more important to the nation than the smaller export and import trade. The Union boosted demand for Scottish beef among English consumers. A higher cattle price made it profitable to use cattle dung to replenish soil fertility on Lowland farms, giving tenant farmers and landlords an incentive to promote mixed husbandry north of the border. Market expansion, meat-eating and soil husbandry went hand in hand. Smith expected the same process to take place in North America, once demand for beef increased there. In fact, he suggested that the link between liberal trade and agricultural improvement held true not only for the wheat-growing belt around the world, but also rice-producing countries.[13]

These economic arguments presupposed a certain understanding of natural history. In Smith's 'liberal ecology' of commerce, the benign system of nature underwrote the promise of efficacious markets. There were no environmental disturbances so severe that they could not be countered by the prosperity of commercial agriculture in a regime of free exchange. Smith admitted that episodic dearth and scarcity were inevitable in every agrarian economy, but he rejected the notion that harvest failure could cause a famine in a wheat-growing liberal country. When a shortage escalated to large-scale suffering and mortality, the cause was always government meddling, not a failure of the soil or climate. This ecological warrant for liberal political economy competed with a distinctly different understanding of nature in mercantilist and cameralist circles during the Enlightenment. Natural historians frequently collaborated with state officials to manage perceived threats to the social and natural order. Linnaeus and his allies sought to secure national autarky in Sweden through ecological exchange and import substitution. Pierre Poivre established forest preserves to counter anthropogenic climate change in the French colony of Isle de France. William Roxburgh supported the construction of water tanks to combat drought and famine in Bengal. The British politician Henry Dundas led the first global survey of naval timber stands in an effort to safeguard the timber supply of the Royal Navy. The New World voyager Pehr Kalm raised alarm about threats of soil exhaustion, species extirpation and adverse climate change in American husbandry. In contrast with Smith, these observers stressed the fragility and complexity of the environment. They rejected liberal exchange as an insufficient means of managing natural systems, favouring instead expert rule, oriented towards self-sufficiency.[14]

Malthus's political economy bore an ambivalent relation to Smith's 'liberal ecology'. His theory recognized the self-regulating properties of social and natural systems, but it was also far more pessimistic than Smith about the relation between agricultural improvement, population and national wealth. This tension was apparent already in the first edition of Malthus's *Essay on the Principle of Population* from 1798. Like Smith, Malthus saw the rising price of butcher's meat as a 'natural and inevitable consequence of the general progress of cultivation'. A hundred years ago, beef was cheap and lean in England, from livestock raised chiefly on 'waste lands' and killed with 'but little ... fatting'. In Malthus's own day, cattle production had become big business. More and better butcher's meat meant improved fertilizer for exhausted land: 'The soil of England will not produce much without dressing, and cattle seem to be necessary to make that species of manure which best suits the land.' This new regime extended to North Britain. The common people in Scotland were eating more butcher's meat than ever before. Yet the fashion for fatty meat among contemporaries had led to a reduction in the grain production of the country. Too much livestock was a far more serious threat than soil exhaustion. Beef-eaters were willing to pay such a high price for meat that it had become profitable to graze cattle on land fit for tillage. The rich ate better than ever, the soil too was much improved, but the poor did not benefit from this kind of prosperity. Malthus compared the well-fed livestock of Britain with the 'unproductive labourers' of the 'French oeconomists'. They were parasites on the national wealth, diminishing the food supply for the common people. Malthus used this analysis of cattle breeding to launch an explicit critique of Smith's 'liberal ecology'. Not 'every increase of the stock or revenue of a nation' could increase the 'real funds for the maintenance of labour'. The push to a beef-eating diet among the wealthy had produced a serious imbalance within the national economy.[15]

Malthus's journey to Scandinavia in 1799 added a new comparative dimension to the analysis of agricultural improvement. Norway was a poor country at the margin of grain cultivation, still largely untouched by the kinds of husbandry Malthus knew from home. Denmark was better-off in terms of soil and climate but had been burdened until recently by an absolutist regime and a system of serfdom. Malthus kept a detailed diary throughout his trip, making observations about local flora, minerals and weather, and recording conversations with both rich and poor people about the state of agriculture. The Norwegian part of the diary paints a vivid picture of the basic steps of improvement in social and environmental terms. These impressions were summed up in the second edition of the *Essay on the Principle of Population*. Norway was a nation beset by severe disadvantages. 'The greatest part of the soil' was 'absolutely incapable of bearing corn'. The climate was 'subject to the most sudden and fatal changes', especially at the end of August, when a sequence of 'iron nights' could ruin the harvest of the poor. Inheritance rules also interfered with the security of property. The ancient law of 'Odel's right' made it possible for 'any lineal descendant' to 'repurchase an estate, which had been sold out of the family, by paying the original purchase money'. Yet still there was potential for some measure of improvement, especially if a sufficient number of 'gentleman farmers' would 'set examples of improved cultivation'. In the diary, Malthus described how settlement and forest clearance had transformed the climate around Drontheim. A merchant testified to a 'very marked change' that had rendered the 'winters ... much less cold & the summers less warm'. This case of anthropogenic climate amelioration appeared to follow a common pattern described by naturalists and improvers elsewhere in Europe and in North America. Malthus also recorded the spread of techniques of farming among 'intelligent merchants and well informed general officers'. This involved more systematic manure collection to improve soil fertility as well as a 'culture of artificial grasses' to boost fodder production for livestock. Malthus's account of basic agricultural improvement stressed supply-side factors rather than urban demand. Outside Oslo, he visited a model farm established by the Englishman John Collet to popularize the methods of mixed husbandry, including rotations of rye, turnips, carrots and clover. However, Malthus also recognized clear limits to the English model in Norway. The 'nature of the country' posed 'an insuperable obstacle to a cultivation and population in any respect proportioned to the surface of the soil'. The widespread reliance on dairy farming placed constraints on the use of arable land for grain cultivation, since these lands had to be reserved to grow winter fodder for the cattle. In this way, Norway still belonged to the second pastoral stage of history and seemed unlikely to advance much further. Britain and Norway thus represented opposite poles of agricultural improvement. While Britain possessed the soil and climate to produce great quantities of grain, a growing taste for meat was limiting the total food supply. In Norway, the bias towards dairy farms was dictated by natural disadvantages.[16]

Malthus raised the problem of English beef again in the 1803 edition of the *Essay*. A remarkable footnote at the end of the chapter on corn bounties suggested that livestock farming served at the same time as the origin of improvement and the Achilles' heel of the nation. Malthus quoted Arthur Young's dictum that the 'first and most obvious improvement in agriculture' was to make fallow land support livestock. A large population of cattle was crucial in regenerating soil fertility and growing a sufficient 'surplus produce' of grain to feed the working population. Yet the full advantage of a mixed husbandry required a stable balance between livestock and grain production. It would be disastrous to 'throw all the land that is fit for it into pasture'. The 'more lands' were 'laid down in grass', the greater the reliance of the nation on grain imports. Excessive taste for beef in the upper orders could swing the balance of agrarian production and distort the nature of the economy. In the long run, such dependence might even 'destroy the power and population' of Britain. Beef was for Malthus a luxury as pernicious as the wealth and refinement that had corrupted the republics of antiquity. He was well aware of the defence of 'trinkets and baubles' in Smith and accepted that consumer wants were vital to economic development. But the problem of beef revived the old problem of luxury in a new more vicious form since it encouraged a self-destructive tendency within the liberal regime. The liberty of the consumer to eat more and more meat combined with a policy of free trade in grain would pave the way for import dependence. Like a latter-day Polybius, Malthus predicted that roast beef might bring about the downfall of the nation.[17]

A conservative notion of balance and symmetry was central also to Malthus's understanding of breeding and plant economy. He used the example of Leicestershire sheep to attack Enlightenment arguments about perfectibility and progress. This was the famous 'Ditchley breed' associated with Robert Bakewell's new practice of renting out rams to raise the quality of local livestock. From Malthus's perspective, Bakewell and his supporters were espousing an absurd kind of utopianism. They boasted that it was possible to 'breed to any degree of nicety you please' because offspring inherited 'desirable qualities of the parents in a greater degree'.

Malthus heaped scorn on the notion of indefinite improvement of the breed. The characteristic properties of the Leicestershire sheep included 'small heads and small legs'. Was a sheep without head and legs really a measure of progress? Malthus agreed that the precise limit of breeding had not yet been discovered but insisted that improvers would sooner or later reach an organic limit beyond which they could not pass without destroying the vitality and function of a breed. The same lesson applied to the improvement of plants. Carnations and anemones could be enlarged through new gardening techniques. Yet it was impossible to grow them to the 'size of a large cabbage'. Experience suggested that animals and plants would 'fall by their own weight' if they grew too large. The stalk of the carnation could not support a flower the size of a cabbage. Crucially, the same principle applied also to the growth of timber and grain. 'No man can say that he has seen the largest ear of wheat or the largest oak that could ever grow ... [yet] he might easily and with perfect certainty, name a point of magnitude, at which they would not arrive.' In this way, Malthus rejected the prospect of perfectibility in natural history. The agrarian economy was governed by strict limits of symmetry and function beyond which no breeder could pass. Malthus's pessimism here stood in sharp contrast to the cornucopian natural history of his contemporary Erasmus Darwin. The latter proclaimed in his 1794 work *Zoonomia; or the Laws or Organic Life* 'that all nature exists in a state of perpetual improvement'. Darwin even argued that it was possible to create new species of plants and animals, an idea contrary to the teachings of the Church and conventional natural history, which assumed that the number of species had been fixed at Creation. The physician and inventor Darwin was closely associated with the manufacturers and natural philosophers in the Lunar Society of Birmingham. His notion of biological plasticity ran parallel with his Promethean view of technology.[18]

Malthus's argument against perfectibility was political and aesthetic as much as organic and functional. A 'florist' could improve the carnation in 'size, symmetry, and beauty of colour'. But modifications of 'one quality' might 'impair the beauty of another'. By applying a 'richer mould', it was possible to 'increase the size' of the plant, but such growth would 'probably burst the calyx, and destroy at once its symmetry'. The calyx was the cover of sepals that protected the buds of the flower. This was not just a warning to gardeners but also a lesson for republicans and radicals. The 'forcing manure used to bring about the French Revolution' had 'burst the calyx of humanity, the restraining bond of all society' and produced a 'loose, deformed, disjointed mass, without union, symmetry, or harmony of colouring'. Overly optimistic assessments about plant breeding went hand in hand with revolutionary radicalism in Malthus's argument. Too sanguine a notion of improvement threatened to explode the proper limits of the organic economy and the social order.[19]

The peculiar situation of Britain in the age of the French Revolution gave Malthus's political economy much of its social impetus and urgency. The first edition of the *Essay* explicitly targeted the work of British and French radicals. Yet it is important not to let Malthus's debate with Marquis de Condorcet and William Godwin obscure another important dimension of the text. In the opening of the *Essay*, Malthus made a startling forecast. The island of Britain could double its food production in the next quarter-century. By following the 'best possible policy', 'breaking up more land' and offering 'great encouragements to agriculture', the nation might accommodate twice the population without importing any food. Here, Malthus was indebted to the campaign led by Sir John Sinclair and his ally Arthur Young in favour of general enclosure and internal colonization. Christopher Bayly and Richard Drayton identify Sinclair and Young as prominent figures in a wave of 'agrarian patriotism' during the Revolutionary Wars. The movement was devoted to a British version of cameralist ideology, seeking national self-sufficiency in food and strategic raw materials such as hemp and naval timber. Reliance on overseas trade and colonial resources was a major liability in a period of growing French power and escalating warfare.[20]

The push for wasteland colonization made the limits of British food production a question of public debate. Statistical knowledge and agricultural surveys provided the foundation of the campaign. Sinclair's first efforts were directed at charting the transformation of the Scottish economy and suggesting further improvements. The 21-volume *Statistical Account of Scotland* 1791–9 presented a parish-by-parish description of Scottish natural history and political economy. Sinclair expanded the scope of his survey to Britain as a whole with the establishment of the Board of Agriculture in 1793, serving as its first president with Young as the secretary of the board. Sinclair also authored a series of Select Committee reports on wasteland improvement and general enclosure. At the heart of these many projects was the geography and arithmetic of food production. Sinclair and his allies sought to establish precise quantitative estimates of the proportion of arable to non-arable land in Great Britain. Two Select Committee reports in 1796 and 1797 offered estimates of grain imports along with the equivalent amount of land needed to remedy the shortfall. These calculations included projections of how large a population could be contained in the territories of reclaimed land. Sinclair's campaign thus appeared to reveal the upper bound of population growth in the island. Sinclair and Young also put forward calculations about the minimum unit of land needed to sustain a family of cottagers, employing the art of spade husbandry rather than plough-based farming. Such an interest in marginal land was commonplace in the last decade of the eighteenth century when rising rents and political pressure transformed wasteland colonization and upland farming into a broad public concern. Sinclair and his allies wanted to show just how much more room for population growth there was in the island, but their calculations could also be read the other way, as an indication that the nation was approaching the physical limits of development. The pace of growth was at the heart of the question. How far into the future could current trends of improvement and population be sustained?[21]

The push for general enclosure and wasteland colonization in the 1790s was more than an ideological response to revolution and warfare. Sinclair's campaign also reflected a certain awareness of underlying demographic pressure and ecological strain. E.A. Wrigley characterizes the whole period between 1780 and 1840 as one of narrowly averted demographic crisis. Kenneth Pomeranz and James Belich in turn argue that Britain became increasingly dependent on 'ghost acres' overseas in the same period. For Brinley Thomas, a crucial turning point came in the 1780s when Britain went from a net producer of grain to increasing reliance on Irish imports. The domestic stock of grain reached a critical low at the outbreak of war with France in 1793. Bad harvests and dearth in the period 1794–6 and again in 1799–1801 sharpened anxieties about food production. At the same time, Admiralty officials grew increasingly concerned about the state of naval timber reserves, culminating in a global search for alternative timber supply at the turn of the century. Sinclair's wasteland reclamation campaign envisioned a Britain wholly self-sufficient in grain, timber and naval stores. Britain was to 'become a world' unto itself, in the words of Sinclair's assistant James Headrick.[22]

By recovering this political and environmental context, we gain a better sense of how Malthus's thought developed between the first and second edition of the *Essay*. He shared with the agrarian patriots a strong interest in the prospect of internal improvement and the strategic priority of self-sufficiency in food production. Indeed, Malthus's political economy was arguably an expression of the same island consciousness that shaped the wasteland campaign. Despite fierce criticism from his friend David Ricardo and other liberals, Malthus placed national autarky above the principle of free trade and defended a renewal of the Corn Laws that protected domestic grain growers from foreign competition. But Malthus rejected the arithmetic of ghost acres championed by Sinclair in favour of a more abstract model of limits. This proved a shrewd gambit. By eschewing the empirical problem of classifying arable land and calculating the precise measure of food production, Malthus was able to construct a model of great simplicity and intuitive appeal, which could not be falsified in the short run.[23] The a priori contrast between arithmetic and geometric growth rates relied on the appearance of analytical rigour rather than exhaustive quantitative data. He strengthened the rhetorical force of the model by deriving from it the forecast of near-future crisis. Here he introduced another speculative notion: what would happen if the British population grew at the same rate as the American settler colonies? Benjamin Franklin had argued that the American settler population doubled every 25 years. Using this estimate for British agriculture, Malthus suggested that improvers who followed 'the best possible policy, by breaking up more land and by great encouragements to agriculture' could keep up with a ballooning population the first 25 years (1798–1823). But he found it impossible to believe that the improvers might double the produce once more in the next stage of demographic growth between 1823 and 1848. There would be no more waste to break up and no fertilizers capable of raising productivity at this rate. Such growth was 'contrary to all our knowledge of the qualities of land'. For Malthus, the notion of quadrupling the produce of agriculture by mid-century was the equivalent of feeding too much dressing to a carnation. It could not be done without bursting the calyx (although he did not explicitly associate this future crisis with the threat of radical revolution).[24]

Malthus made his critique of the agrarian patriots explicit in the second edition of the *Essay* (1803). The question of bounties on corn exports gave him an occasion to address the movement for wasteland reclamation and a general enclosure bill. He expressed support for Sinclair's campaign but also downplayed its long-term significance. He did not doubt that it was possible to 'raise substantially more corn than at present' 'by cultivating all our commons'. Indeed, his support for corn bounties was intended to boost domestic production by encouraging sale of surplus grain abroad. But the pace of improvement would always lag behind the rate of population growth. Even if the produce of the earth was 'absolutely unlimited', population would always win the race. This critique of wasteland colonization did not deter Malthus from relying on Sinclair's empirical work. The chapter on the Scottish population in the second edition rested to a very great degree on the parish reports of Sinclair's *Statistical Account of Scotland*, which he praised as 'an extraordinary monument to the learning' of the Scottish clergy. These accounts provided Malthus with a great deal more detailed information about local condition than he had mustered for the preceding chapter on demographic conditions in England. Indeed, he emphasized that the small scale of the parish unit was ideal for the analysis of population. The trends of births, deaths, marriages and subsistence were all easier to grasp at this level, especially if there was 'no power of emigrating' from the locality. But 'when a great number of parishes were added together in a populous kingdom', the observer lost the ability to track these patterns. The aggregate scale of analysis and the confounding factor of mobility between parishes 'served to obscure and confuse' the obvious fact that population was limited by subsistence, tempting observers to overstate the capacity for demographic growth.[25]

The parish reports in *The Statistical Account of Scotland* also suggested to Malthus that the relationship between population and subsistence was particularly precarious in the north and west of Scotland. The region seemed to be experiencing the condition of demographic strain that Malthus forecast for the future of Great Britain as a whole. He painted a gloomy portrait of exceptionally high birth-rates, primitive husbandry and high rates of emigration. A number of factors conspired to promote early marriage in the Highlands, including the introduction of potatoes, the use of the spade instead of the plough and the great subdivision of land. These pressures were felt across the north, from the mainland to the Outer Hebrides. The village of Callander in Perthshire was filled with 'naked and starving crowds of people who are pouring down for shelter or for bread'. In Malthus's view, the Scottish Highlands represented the most striking case of a 'redundant population' in Great Britain. The difficult climate and soil of the region imposed severe constraints on the subsistence of the common people. In effect, the Highland population had reached the natural limits of the productive capacity of the land. By 'redundant', Malthus meant a population without sure employment and subsistence, forced to live on charity and public assistance. His discussion of the Highland problem was conspicuously lacking in social and political analysis. There was little attempt to engage with the potential for development in the region, including the schemes suggested in *The Statistical Account of Scotland*. By the time of the third edition of the *Essay* (1806), Malthus endorsed the position of Thomas Douglas (Lord Selkirk) in favour of assisted emigration to relieve population pressure in the region. Selkirk described the soil and climate of the Highlands as fit only for livestock grazing. In effect, he conflated natural advantage with the social interest of the landlord class, reducing the economic function of the region to the profits from sheep and cattle farms. Malthus turned a blind eye on the social basis of Highland immiseration.[26]

At the end of the Napoleonic Wars, the protectionist legislation of the Corn Laws came under debate. Some observers saw the coming of peace as an opportunity to strengthen liberal bonds of trade between former enemy nations. Yet Malthus remained committed to the norm of national autarky in the food supply. He rested his argument on the investigations of the agrarian patriots. There was 'ample testimony' about the 'resources of Great Britain and Ireland for the further growth of corn'. Part of the boost would come from extending the Norfolk method to light soils around the nation, but even more important was the Scottish way of cultivating clay soil with lime. This could open up 'vast tracts' and increase crops 'prodigiously'. Malthus relied here on John Sinclair's surveys and Arthur Young's testimony in the 1814 Select Committee on the Corn Laws (chaired by the Elgin MP Patrick Milne). As long as the price of domestic wheat was protected from foreign competition, improvement could continue. However, Malthus at same time retained his original pessimism about the balancing act between the forces of food production and demography. He reiterated in the 1817 edition of the *Essay* the claim that population growth could quickly outpace agricultural gains.[27]

The appeal of Malthus's analytical model derived in great part from his multi-scalar understanding of demography. All the editions of the *Essay* shared the same premise: population growth was everywhere subject to the limit of the food supply. This trend of population was most evident in miniature, at the level of parishes, islands and other bounded units. But the same law applied also to large communities. The comparison of the geometric and arithmetic ratios of growth demonstrated how quickly population could mushroom in a nation, moving closer and closer to the ceiling of agrarian production. At this level, Malthus's analysis amounted to a conjectural and hypothetical forecast about unchecked population growth rather than the collection of aggregate statistics based on local data. The forecast hinged on a judgement about carrying capacity. How much land was needed to sustain a given population? Such reasoning about the margins of cultivation would have been quite familiar to readers in the 1790s, as we have seen.[28]

However, Malthus was not content to make predictions only about the nation. He insisted on the universality of his forecast. The case of Great

Britain offered a way to think about the planet; 'taking the whole earth instead of this island'. Demographic growth at a geometric rate must lead to crisis at every level, from the parish to the nation to the globe. To follow Malthus's argument to its conclusion was to move upward in scale. In this sense, his political economy was a form of planetary thinking. It inscribed the central questions of enlightened economic analysis into a biophysical context, which was at the same time local and global. The movement between different scales of analysis encouraged readers to think of geographic scale as a form of activity. Scaling presented a powerful way to grasp the force of population across space, distinct from the other Enlightenment idiom of conjectural history, which had imagined social processes as a movement between four stages of history.[29]

One important element of Malthus's forecast can be traced back to Benjamin Franklin's 1751 estimate of the rate of population growth in the American colonies. Franklin used natural history to imagine a hypothetical case of unconstrained growth. What if the 'face of the earth' had been left 'vacant of other plants' and harboured just one single species? In such a world without natural predators and abundant land, any kind of plant could fill every space available in a few generations. Curiously, Franklin chose the fennel – a perennial herb with both culinary and medicinal uses – as his exemplary species. Of Mediterranean origin, fennel had been widely dispersed from its original habitat and seems to have been cultivated in at least some colonial kitchen gardens.[30]

Franklin's meditation on fennel took the form of a thought experiment. This intellectual device was commonplace in early modern natural philosophy and political economy. It presented a hypothetical condition that stripped away confounding variables to highlight the effects of a specific social or natural change. Pierre Bayle imagined what moral order might obtain in a society of atheists. Bernard Mandeville's *Fable of the Bees* explored what would happen to commerce in a society governed by virtue. Locke defended the supremacy of sensory knowledge by contemplating the acquisition of sight in a man who had been blind from birth ('Molyneux's problem'). Harro Maas argues that the authority of such virtual experiments stemmed from their power to disrupt arguments that had passed for common sense. They demonstrated that widely held assumptions generated deep contradictions, which, when followed to their conclusion, might produce a 'fundamental paradox'.[31]

Frequently, thought experiments encouraged a play with scales. A long tradition in natural philosophy and natural history sought to imagine the fundamental forces that had shaped the physical world. In its most audacious form, it involved taking the place of God, and re-enacting the process of Creation. Descartes invited his readers to witness a second beginning of the universe in his posthumous treatise *Le Monde*: 'Allow your thought to wander beyond this world, to view another, wholly new world, which I call forth in imaginary spaces before it.' Thought experiments in world-making permitted natural philosophers to peer into the realm of invisible corpuscles, which they thought comprised the fundamental substrate of reality. Virtual journeys into the macrocosm and microcosm also let sceptics like David Hume speculate about the structure of the universe. In *Dialogues Concerning Natural Religion*, Hume's mouthpiece Philo imagined the world first as an animal organism and then as a kind of plant, only to suggest that full knowledge of the heterogeneous structure of reality might require an interstellar perspective. '[C]ould we travel from planet to planet and from system to system' – we might discover the diversity of principles that shaped the 'immense extent and variety of the universe'. While Hume made his recommendation tongue-in-cheek, the challenge to scale upward to the planetary level was heeded by many of Hume's contemporaries and successors.[32]

Malthus's forecast about runaway population combined elements of natural history and political economy into a novel type of thought experiment. By comparing the arithmetic and geometric rates of growth, Malthus demonstrated that population was as much a physical as an economic force, eating away at resources, overwhelming the finite supply of land. The idea of geometric growth provided a bridge between the national and the planetary level. '[T]aking the whole earth instead of this island', he invited his reader to ascend upward to probe the material limits of the economy. Such island thinking has been one of the most enduring features of Malthus's political economy. In particular, it has shaped those forms of environmentalist science and politics that concern themselves with the limits to economic growth. The forecast of an overpopulated planet led John Stuart Mill to recommend a pre-emptive version of the stationary state. Meanwhile, William Stanley Jevons introduced fossil fuel scarcity into Malthusian political economy. Increasing population growth and consumer demand threatened to deplete the finite stock of fossil fuel on which Britain's industrial economy rested. In the twentieth century, environmentalist worries about population and consumption have given rise to a broad range of influential concepts, including the tragedy of commons, the ecological footprint and, most recently, the notion of planetary boundaries and the Anthropocene. Despite a number of crucial differences, these varieties of Malthusian and Neo-Malthusian thought all share a common preoccupation with forecasts of the future and nested scales of exponential growth.[33]

What Malthus himself might have made of this legacy is an intriguing if unanswerable question. As we have seen, his views of the natural world reflected the 'liberal ecology' of the Scottish Enlightenment, modified by the anxieties of the French Revolutionary wars. Malthus's concern with environmental limits focused on the finite supply of land rather than specific forms of degradation like deforestation, soil exhaustion or adverse climate change. While some contemporaries pressed for government intervention to husband natural resources and provide relief, Malthus confined his interest in agrarian legislation to a defence of the Corn Laws. Notoriously, he defined the positive check – famine, war and pestilence – as the necessary operation of the laws of nature. In this sense, Malthus's theory of population retained and reinforced Smith's liberal view of the natural order as a self-regulating system. But in his eagerness to give the theory of population universal validity, he introduced a new conception of scale into liberal political economy, framing the project of improvement within the closed system of the planet. This, in the end, was perhaps Malthus's most important gift to posterity.

Notes

1   Thomas Pennant, *A Tour in Scotland and a Voyage to the Hebrides, MDCCLXXII* (Chester: B. White, 1774), p. 243; see also Elizabeth Bray, *The Discovery of the Hebrides: Voyages to the Western Isles 1745–1883* (Edinburgh: Birlinn, 1998), p. 75.
2   John Sinclair, ed. *The Statistical Account of Scotland: Volume 12* (Edinburgh: William Creech, 1794), pp. 320, 324, 332–3; Fredrik Albritton Jonsson, *Enlightenment's Frontier: The Scottish Highlands and the Origins of Environmentalism* (New Haven: Yale University Press, 2013).
3   For more on Malthus's engagement with a wider range of sources in the 1803 edition, see the chapter by Bashford and Chaplin in this volume.
4   T.R. Malthus, *An Essay on the Principle of Population*, 2nd edn (London: J. Johnson, 1803), p. 326.
5   E.A. Wrigley, *Energy and the English Industrial Revolution* (Cambridge: Cambridge University Press, 2010), p. 3; Karl Polanyi, *The Great Transformation: The Political and Economic Origins of Our Time* (New York: Beacon Press, 2001); Malthus, *Essay* (1803), p. 531. The paragraph including the phrase 'nature's mighty feast' was removed from subsequent editions of the *Essay*, see Donald Winch, *Riches and Poverty: An Intellectual History of Political Economy in Britain, 1750–1834* (Cambridge: Cambridge University Press 1996), p. 223.
6   [T.R. Malthus], *An Essay on the Principle of Population* (London: J. Johnson, 1798), pp. 15, 20, 22, 25, 71, 101, 346; Malthus, *Essay* (1803), pp. 2–4, 7–8,

12–13. See also Margaret Schabas, *The Natural Origins of Economics* (Chicago: University of Chicago Press, 2005), pp. 106–8.

7 Malthus, *Essay* (1803), pp. 14, 324–5, 327, 329, 548.

8 This chapter will be preoccupied with Malthus's early writings rather than the refinements and modifications elaborated in the later editions of the *Essay*, the correspondence with David Ricardo, and the *Principles of Political Economy*. For an eminent guide to the full arc of Malthus's thought, see Winch, *Riches and Poverty*. For popular Malthusianism, see Boyd Hilton, *The Age of Atonement: The Influence of Evangelicalism on Social and Economic Thought, 1795–1865* (Oxford: Oxford University Press, 1988); A.M.C. Waterman, *Revolution, Economics and Religion: Christian Political Economy, 1798–1833* (Cambridge: Cambridge University Press, 1988).

9 Lissa Roberts, 'Practicing Oeconomy During the Second Half of the Long Eighteenth Century: An Introduction', *History and Technology*, 30 (2014), 133–48; Ralph Jessop, 'Coinage of the Term Environment: A Word Without Authority and Carlyle's Displacement of the Mechanical Metaphor', *Literature Compass*, 9 (2012), 708–20; Jean-Baptiste Fressoz and Fabien Locher, 'Modernity's Frail Climate: A Climate History of Environmental Reflexivity', *Critical Inquiry*, 38 (2012), 579–98; James W. Moore, '"Amsterdam Is Standing on Norway": Part II: The Global North Atlantic in the Ecological Revolution of the Long Seventeenth Century', *Journal of Agrarian Change*, 10 (2010), 188–227; Karl Appuhn, *A Forest on the Sea: Environmental Expertise in Renaissance Venice* (Baltimore: Johns Hopkins University Press, 2009); Richard Grove, *Green Imperialism: Colonial Expansion, Tropical Island Edens and the Origins of Environmentalism, 1600–1860* (Cambridge: Cambridge University Press, 1995).

10 Wrigley, *Energy and the English Industrial Revolution*, p. 48; Patricia James, *Population Malthus: His Life and Times* (London: Routledge, 1979), p. 30; 'Malthus Diary of a Tour of the Lake District' in J.M. Pullen and Trevor Hughes Parry (eds.), *T.R. Malthus: The Unpublished Papers in the Collection of Kanto Gakuen University*, 2 vols. (Cambridge: Cambridge University Press, 1997–2004), vol. 2, pp. 25–55.

11 Wrigley, *Energy and the English Industrial Revolution*, pp. 99, 174, 208. Alternative accounts of British growth include, for example, Kenneth Pomeranz, *The Great Divergence: China, Europe, and the Making of the Modern World Economy* (Princeton: Princeton University Press, 2000); Maxine Berg, 'The Pursuit of Luxury: Global History and British Consumer Goods in the Eighteenth Century', *Past & Present*, 182 (2004), 85–142; Joel Mokyr, *The Enlightened Economy: An Economic History of Britain 1700–1850* (New Haven: Yale University Press, 2009); Prasannan Parthasasarathi, *Why Europe Grew Rich and Asia Did Not: Global Economic Divergence 1600–1800* (Cambridge: Cambridge University Press, 2011).

12 Jonsson, *Enlightenment's Frontier*, pp. 121–46; T.M. Devine, *The Transformation of Rural Scotland: Social Change and the Agrarian Economy, 1660–1815* (Edinburgh: Edinburgh University Press, 1994); Brian Bonnyman, *The Third*

Duke of Buccleuch and Adam Smith: Estate Management and Improvement in Enlightenment Scotland (Edinburgh: Edinburgh University Press, 2014).

13 Adam Smith, *An Inquiry into the Nature and Causes of the Wealth of Nations*, 2 vols., ed. R.H Campbell, A.S. Skinner and W.B. Todd (Oxford: Oxford University Press, 1976), vol. 1, pp. 165, 380; Istvan Hont, *The Jealousy of Trade: International Competition and the Nation-State in Historical Perspective* (Cambridge, MA: Harvard University Press, 2005), pp. 354–88; Jonsson, *Enlightenment's Frontier*, pp. 129–34; Winch, *Riches and Poverty*, p. 205.

14 My use of the modern term 'ecology' is intended as shorthand for eighteenth-century concepts such as the 'oeconomy of nature' and the 'balance of nature', see Jonsson, *Enlightenment's Frontier*, pp. 135–41, 156–61. For further explorations of the place of natural history in Enlightenment thought, see Donald Worster, *Nature's Economy: A History of Ecological Ideas*, 2nd edn (Cambridge: Cambridge University Press, 1994); Emma Spary, 'Political, Natural and Bodily Economies', in Nicholas Jardine, James A. Secord and E.C. Spary (eds.), *Cultures of Natural History* (Cambridge: Cambridge University Press, 1996), pp. 178–96; Lisbet Koerner, *Linnaeus: Nature and Nation* (Cambridge, MA: Harvard University Press, 1999); Grove, *Green Imperialism*; Fredrik Albritton Jonsson, 'Climate Change and the Retreat of the Atlantic: The Cameralist Context of Pehr Kalm's Voyage to North America 1748–51', *William and Mary Quarterly*, 72 (2015), 99–126.

15 Malthus, *Essay* (1798), pp. 76, 316–18; Malthus, *Essay* (1803), pp. 323, 397–400; Malthus was aware of the problem of soil exhaustion but did not refer to it frequently, see Malthus, *Essay* (1798), pp. 106–7; Malthus, *Essay* (1803), p. 120; T.R. Malthus, *An Inquiry into the Progress and Nature of Rent* (London: John Murray, 1815), p. 37; T.R. Malthus, *An Essay on the Principle of Population*, 5th edn, 3 vols. (London: John Murray, 1817), vol. 2, pp. 491–2.

16 Malthus, *Essay* (1803), pp. 189, 191, 193; Patricia James (ed.), *The Travel Diaries of Thomas Robert Malthus* (Cambridge: Cambridge University Press, 1966), pp. 101–2, 158. See also Robert Mayhew, *Malthus: The Life and Legacies of an Untimely Prophet* (Cambridge, MA: Harvard University Press, 2014), pp. 105–9. For climate change, see Jonsson, *Enlightenment's Frontier*, p. 71; Jonsson, 'Climate Change and the Retreat of the Atlantic'; Jan Golinski, *British Weather and the Climate of Enlightenment* (Chicago: University of Chicago Press, 2007), pp. 196–200.

17 Malthus, *Essay* (1803), p. 467. E.A. Wrigley charts a dramatic increase in animal fodder production in the period, *Energy and the English Industrial Revolution*, pp. 83–5.

18 Malthus, *Essay* (1798), pp. 164–7. See also Harriet Ritvo, 'Possessing Mother Nature: Genetic Capital in Eighteenth Century Britain,' in John Brewer and Susan Staves (eds.), *Early Modern Conceptions of Property*, (London: Routledge, 1995), pp. 413–27; Maureen McNeil, *Under the Banner of Science: Erasmus Darwin and His Age* (Manchester: Manchester University Press, 1987), p. 103; Erasmus Darwin, *Zoonomia: Or the Laws of Organic Life*, 3rd edn, 4 vols. (London: J. Johnson, 1801), vol. 2, p. 318; The Malthus collection in

Jesus College, Cambridge, contains an annotated copy of Erasmus Darwin's treatise in the 1794 edition (which also speaks of indefinite improvement in the animal kingdom). For Darwin's Prometheanism, see Fredrik Albritton Jonsson, 'The Origins of Cornucopianism: A Preliminary Genealogy', *Critical Historical Studies*, 1 (2014), 151–68.

19 Malthus, *Essay* (1798), p. 274. There is some tension between this organic conception of the limits to improvement and the critique of improvement in the discussion of arithmetic and geometric growth that emphasizes relative divergence rather than absolute limits.

20 Malthus, *Essay* (1798), p. 21; Christopher A. Bayly, *Imperial Meridian: The British Empire and the World, 1780–1830* (London: Longman, 1989); Richard Drayton, *Nature's Government: Science, Imperial Britain, and the 'Improvement of the World'* (New Haven: Yale University Press, 2000); Jonsson, *Enlightenment's Frontier*, pp. 55–7. There is good circumstantial evidence that Malthus was familiar with the work of the improvers well before writing the *Essay*. The text from Malthus's tour of the Lake District in 1794 combined aesthetic judgements with a series of observations about the local economy. These remarks were inspired in part by Arthur Young's *Six Months' Tour Through the North of England* (1770). During the trip he visited the estate of Richard Watson (the Bishop of Llandaff), another wasteland improver of the period, see Pullen and Perry, *Malthus: Unpublished Papers*, vol. 2, pp. 34–5. Watson wrote an essay on wasteland improvement for Andrew Pringle's *General View of the Agriculture of the County of Westmoreland, with Observations on the Means of its Improvement* (London: J. Chapman, 1794), pp. 5–15. The Westmoreland survey was drawn up for Sinclair's Board of Agriculture. On Watson, see Colin Russell, 'Richard Watson: Gaiters and Gunpowder', in Mary D. Archer and Christopher D. Haley (eds.), *The 1702 Chair of Chemistry at Cambridge: Transformation and Change* (Cambridge: Cambridge University Press, 2005), pp. 57–83.

21 Anonymous, *The First Report from the Select Committee … Appointed to Take into Consideration the Means of Promoting the Cultivation and Improvement of the Waste, Uninclosed, and Unproductive Lands* (London: House of Commons, 1796); Arthur Young, *The Question of Scarcity Plainly Stated and Remedies Considered* (London: B. M'Millan, 1800); John Sinclair, *Observations on the Means of a Cottager to Keep a Cow* (London: W. Bulmer, 1801); Jonsson, *Enlightenment's Frontier*, pp. 54, 223–7, 256.

22 Wrigley, *Energy and the English Industrial Revolution*, pp. 39, 87, 208; Pomeranz, *The Great Divergence*, pp. 26, 216–17, 220–1; James Belich, *Replenishing the Earth: The Settler Revolution and the Rise of Anglo-World, 1783–1939* (Oxford: Oxford University Press, 2010), pp. 443–6; Brinley Thomas, *The Industrial Revolution and the Atlantic Economy: Selected Essays* (London: Routledge, 1993), pp. 60, 78, 86–7; Jonsson, *Enlightenment's Frontier*, pp. 156–61, 229–31.

23 Malthus, *Essay* (1803), p. 457. On Malthus and the 1815 renewal of the Laws, see below, and Winch, *Riches and Poverty*, pp. 332–5. Malthus's decision to

craft a simple and general model of population trends should be seen as part of the broader trend towards formalization in political economy between Smith and Ricardo.

24 Malthus, *Essay* (1798), pp. 21–2. Malthus seems to have been indebted to Robert Wallace for his understanding of these ratios, see John M. Hartwick, 'Robert Wallace and Malthus and the Ratios', *Journal of the History of Political Economy*, 20 (1988), 357–79. For Wallace's place in the Scottish Enlightenment, see Jonsson, *Enlightenment's Frontier*, pp. 18–26.

25 Malthus, *Essay* (1803), pp. 13, 194–5, 321–35, 457, 482. Malthus also engaged Young on the question of allotments and spade husbandry in the second edition of the *Essay*, pp. 573–7.

26 Malthus, *Essay* (1803), pp. 188, 326, 349; Malthus, *Essay* (1806), p. 513. See also Jonsson, *Enlightenment's Frontier*, pp. 248–52; Schabas, *Natural Origins of Economics*, p. 108.

27 T.R. Malthus, *The Grounds of an Opinion on the Policy of Restricting the Important of Foreign Corn* (London: John Murray and John Johnson, 1815), pp. 20–2, see also note on p. 21; *Report of the Select Committee on Petitions Relating to the Corn Laws of this Kingdom* (London: James Ridgway, 1814), pp. 85–6; Malthus, *Essay* (1817), p. 14; Boyd Hilton, *A Mad, Bad and Dangerous People?: England 1783–1846* (Oxford: Oxford University Press, 2006), pp. 264–66. For the increasing reliance of Britain on Irish grain, see Thomas, *Industrial Revolution and Atlantic Economy*. Another debt of Malthus to the Scottish Enlightenment came by way of his reading of James Anderson's works, see Renee Prendergast, 'James Anderson's Political Economy – His Influence on Smith and Malthus', *Scottish Journal of Political Economy*, 34 (1987), 388–409, p. 400.

28 Malthus, *Essay* (1803), p. 194. Malthus also argued in the same chapter that demographic trends were easier to detect in small kingdoms like Norway. I use the concept of 'carrying capacity' in the broad sense of calculating the limits of population set by food production. On the history of predicting the maximum population of the world, see Joel E. Cohen, *How Many People Can the Earth Support?* (New York: W.W. Norton, 1996). For the history of scale and scaling, see Deborah R. Coen, 'What is the Big Idea? The History of Ideas Confronts Climate Change,' *European Journal for the History of Ideas*, forthcoming; Julia Adeney Thomas, 'History and Biology in the Anthropocene: Problems of Scale, Problems of Value,' *The American Historical Review*, 119 (2014), 1587–607.

29 Malthus, *Essay* (1803), pp. 7–8. The first edition of the essay also moved from the island case to the earth as a whole, *Essay* (1798), pp. 25, 143. On planetary history, see Joyce Chaplin, *Round About the Earth: Circumnavigation from Magellan to Orbit* (New York: Simon & Schuster, 2012); Alison Bashford, *Global Population: History, Geopolitics, Life on Earth* (New York: Columbia University Press, 2014).

30 Benjamin Franklin, *Political, Miscellaneous, and Philosophical Pieces* (London: J. Johnson, 1779), pp. 9–10; Joyce Chaplin, *Benjamin Franklin's Political*

Arithmetic: A Materialist View of Humanity (Washington, DC: Smithsonian Institution, 2006), pp. 25–7; Rudy Favretti and Gordon P. DeWolf Jr., 'Colonial Garden Plants', *Arnoldia*, 31 (1971), 172–249, p. 200. Another notion of population explosion was suggested to Malthus by the natural history of ungulate irruptions, see Jonsson, *Enlightenment's Frontier*, pp. 190–5.

31 Pierre Bayle, *Political Writings*, ed. Sally Jenkinson (Cambridge: Cambridge University Press, 2000), p. xxxiii; Harro Maas, *Economic Methodology: A Historical Introduction* (London: Routledge, 2014), pp. 105–8; Jessica Riskin, *Science in the Age of Sensibility* (Chicago: University of Chicago Press, 2002), pp. 20–4.

32 Descartes quoted in William McAllister, 'Thought Experiments and the Exercise of Imagination in Science', in Melanie Frappiér *et al.*, *Thought Experiments in Philosophy, Science, and the Arts* (London: Routledge, 2013), pp. 11–29; David Hume, *Dialogues Concerning Natural Religion*, ed. Dorothy Coleman (Cambridge: Cambridge University Press, 2007), p. 54; Stephen Dick, *Plurality of Worlds: the Extraterrestrial Life Debate from Democritus to Kant* (Cambridge: Cambridge University Press, 1984). This is not to suggest that all planetary thinking took the form of thought experiments. For the perspective from travel literature and natural history, see Chaplin, *Round About the Earth*.

33 For the development of Malthusian and Neo-Malthusian thought in the nineteenth and twentieth centuries, see Murray Milgate and Shannon C. Stimson, *After Adam Smith: A Century of Transformation in Politics and Political Economy* (Princeton: Princeton University Press, 2009), pp. 191–210; Graham Macdonald, 'The Politics of the Golden River: John Ruskin and the Stationary State', *Environment and History*, 18 (2012), 125–50; Donald Winch, *Wealth and Life: Essays on the Intellectual History of Political Economy in Britain, 1848–1914* (Cambridge: Cambridge University Press, 2009); Bashford, *Global Population*; Thomas Robertson, *The Malthusian Moment: Global Population Growth and the Birth of American Environmentalism* (New Brunswick: Rutgers University Press, 2012); Fabien Locher, 'Les pâturages de la guerre froide: Garrett Hardin et la Tragédie des communs', *Revue d'Histoire Moderne et Contemporaine*, 60 (2013), 7–36; Johan Rockström, Will Steffen, Paul Crutzen, *et al.*, 'Planetary Boundaries: Exploring the Safe Operating Space for Humanity', *Nature*, 461 (2009), 472–5; Will Steffen, Jacques Grinevald, Paul Crutzen and John McNeill, 'The Anthropocene: Conceptual and Historical Perspectives', *Philosophical Transactions of the Royal Society A*, 369 (2011), 842–67; Libby Robin, Sverker Sörlin and Paul Warde, *The Future of Nature: Documents of Global Change* (New Haven: Yale University Press, 2013).

PART II

The reception of Malthus

CHAPTER 6

Malthus, women and fiction

Ella Dzelzainis

Reviewing the first five instalments of Harriet Martineau's *Illustrations of Political Economy* (1834) in June 1832, Josiah Conder was one of the earliest to praise her innovative splicing of fiction with political economy. As with so many of Martineau's reviewers – both hostile and approving – Conder measured her achievement in gendered terms, hailing 'Professor' Martineau's rare union of 'masculine faculty of abstraction' and 'feminine power of illustration'.[1] She was 'a phenomenon' who had 'succeeded in making her principles talk and act, and in exhibiting abstract truths in the tangible shape of living experiments'.[2] Martineau's aim in the *Illustrations* was to teach political economy to men, women and children of all classes. The 25-part monthly series followed the structural organization of James Mill's *Elements of Political Economy* (1821) and each story was followed by a simple summary of the economic principles that had just been illustrated through the narrative devices of character, setting and plot.[3] It became a publishing sensation, estimated at its peak to have sold more than 10,000 copies a month and reaching more than 144,000 readers.[4] But in his October review of the next three instalments, Conder's former enthusiasm for his 'fair *Dotteressa*' had congealed into disappointment: Martineau had since revealed herself to be 'a female Malthus'.[5] Two of these latest stories raised Malthusian questions – how to control population growth in 'Weal and Woe in Garveloch' and how to reform the Poor Laws in 'Cousin Marshall' – and supplied Malthusian answers by advocating moral restraint to halt proliferating numbers among the poor and the complete withdrawal of charitable relief. In this second review, Conder offered a detailed rebuttal of the pro-Malthusian arguments in each tale, before finally declaring that Martineau (now demoted to 'Miss') ought not 'to bear the blame of the miserable philosophizing into which she has been initiated'.[6] She should, instead, be thanked for demystifying 'the jargon of the school'.[7] In other words, Martineau's literary success had done the public an ironic favour: the abhorrent truth of Malthusian philosophy had been exposed – 'displayed in all its native ugliness' to the people – through her innovative use of fiction.[8]

Conder was being patronizingly over-courteous in his decision not to blame Martineau for her Malthusianism. But later reviewers showed no such restraint, particularly those in Tory journals such as the *Quarterly Review* and *Fraser's Magazine*, who used the idea of her as 'a *female Malthusian*' as a point of attack.[9] Martineau's sexual unattractiveness, her single status and her virgin ignorance were all savagely mocked. John Wilson Croker, for example, boasted about 'tomahawking' her in the *Quarterly*, while *Fraser's* illustrated William Maginn's review with a picture of her as a witch-like spinster, holding a pot over the fire while being nuzzled by a lubricious-looking cat.[10] Recent scholars have wondered why Martineau was singled out by the Tory quarterlies in this way, especially when Jane Marcet, another openly pro-Malthusian woman writer of the time, was not.[11] Their answer to this question has, in brief, been to read the reviews as a sign of reactionary disquiet at the idea of a radical woman openly meddling in politics. For Tory writers opposed to Malthusian political economy and her reforming brand of liberalism, Martineau's gender presented an easy target: as a woman, she had stepped outside her proper sphere by writing about the masculine discourse of political economy; and as a spinster (Marcet was married), she should not be writing about the sexual topics that were fundamental to Malthusianism.[12] When writing her *Autobiography* two decades later, Martineau reflected on these public assaults on her character with relative equanimity: in composing the series, it was her duty 'to exemplify Malthus's doctrines among the rest' and it was merely 'that doctrine "pure and simple," as it came from his virtuous and benevolent mind' that she had presented.[13] Malthus himself, she claimed, had told her she had 'represented his views as precisely as he could have wished'.[14]

However, one of my aims in this chapter is to question the character of Martineau's advocacy of Malthusianism in the *Illustrations*. To what extent was it *really* Malthus's doctrine 'pure and simple' that she presented and to which her critics responded? Malthus's *Essay on the Principle of Population* was written to counter the perfectibilism and egalitarianism of Nicholas de Condorcet and William Godwin.[15] In consequence, critics have read the *Essay* as also conducting an implicit critique of the gender politics of the men's wives, Sophie de Grouchy and Mary Wollstonecraft, both of whom were controversial early feminists in their advocacy of equal rights.[16] Noting that the preface to Malthus's quickly written treatise was dated 9 June 1798, both Henk W. Plasmeijer and Gail Bederman position

Malthus's work as partly an immediate response to the scandal created by the revelation of Wollstonecraft's unorthodox sexual history in Godwin's *Memoirs of Mary Wollstonecraft* in January 1798 – an event widely seen as ensuring the marginalization of discussion of women's rights in Britain till the 1850s.[17] As Deborah Valenze has argued, Malthus's *Essay* did much to reinforce the notion of separate gender spheres in that it assumed women's dependency on men.[18] It also construed the sexual double standard (whereby women who had children out of wedlock were more disgraced than men) as an unfortunate social necessity that was 'natural, though not perhaps perfectly justifiable'.[19] Yet examination of the *Illustrations of Political Economy* suggests that its more astute reviewers – not just the anti-Malthusian Tories, Croker and Maginn, but also the pro-Malthusian Whig, William Empson, in the *Edinburgh Review* – had spotted that, incrementally and over the course of the series, the Unitarian Martineau was co-opting Malthusian thinking for millennialist purposes, weaving it into a breezily optimistic and necessarian account of political economy that imagined a feminist and utopian future effected through the progress of human reason. In essence, she was writing the Enlightenment optimism of Godwin and Condorcet back into a popular, theodicial account of Malthusian political economy that was reaching thousands of readers. It is no wonder that Croker reached for the hatchet.

In what follows, I seek to substantiate this claim through an examination of Martineau's literary method in her series, as well as a more detailed discussion of the critical response to it, not only in periodical reviews but also in the realm of fiction. Literary scholars often position the *Illustrations of Political Economy*, with its blend of fact and fiction, as a precursor to the canonical Condition-of-England novel of the 1840s and 1850s.[20] I wish to push this idea further by examining the anti-Malthusian (and anti-Martineauian) writings of another early industrial novelist, the Tory pre-Millenarian Evangelical Charlotte Elizabeth Tonna, to suggest that the *Illustrations* and the literary reaction to it established the parameters of a significant debate over the nature and treatment of women that took place in Condition-of-England fiction.

Martineau, feminism and Malthusian fiction

In the *Illustrations* Martineau draws on the work of a number of economists, but her greatest debt is to Adam Smith's *Wealth of Nations* (1776) and Malthus's *Essay*.[21] To both Smith and Malthus, political economy was not the science it has since become, but a system of moral philosophy: a conception with which Martineau agreed.[22] As Gareth Stedman Jones has argued, the hope of eliminating poverty that was made available by an optimist reading of Smith in the early 1790s was dampened by the publication of Malthus's *Essay*, with its pessimistic, conservative and anti-utopian arguments.[23] One aspect that united Smith and Malthus, however, was that they each drew on a stadial or four-staged account of civilized progress in their theorization of political economy – a paradigm Martineau imported directly into her series and proceeded to embellish.[24] Four-stages theory was predicated on the assumption that in order to achieve civilization, societies had to work through a series of stages: hunting and fishing; pasturage; agriculture; and commerce or manufacturing.[25] A society's position on the civilized scale could be deduced from its primary means of subsistence, and its social and political institutions would correspond. The third, agricultural stage, for example, was identified with the politics of feudalism, paternalism and the codes of chivalry. This freighting of political economy with a stadial account of civilized progress persisted well into the nineteenth century, perhaps most notably for the purposes of this discussion in the economic work of one of the leading liberal and feminist thinkers of the period, *Principles of Political Economy* (1848) by John Stuart Mill.[26] At the time that Martineau was writing, England was understood to be in a state of transition, moving unevenly from the third into the fourth, commercial stage, which was associated with the increasing spread of liberty, citizenship and equality of rights.[27]

Axiomatic within four-stages theory was the assumption that the civilized stage reached by any given society could be inferred from its treatment of women. As William Alexander put it in *The History of Women* (1779), this civilized status could be ascertained even in the absence of any other evidence:

> the rank ... and condition in which we find women in any country, mark out to us with the greatest precision, the exact point in the scale of civil society, to which the people of such country have arrived; and were their history entirely silent on every other subject, and only mentioned the manner in which they treated their women, we would, from thence be enabled to form a tolerable judgment of the barbarity, or culture of their manners.[28]

Implicit in this axiom – which, in her work on Mary Wollstonecraft, Barbara Taylor has described as 'a veritable *idée fixe*' – is a requirement that women's social and political condition be read inferentially and symbolically for socio-political purposes.[29] In the eighteenth century and beyond, the theory was predominantly used by 'complacently Whiggish' writers like Alexander to justify separate spheres for men and women on the basis that such a gendered demarcation between public and private was in itself evidence of civilized achievement.[30] From the very first edition of his *Essay*, Malthus also took this position: among savage nations such as the North American Indians, women were drudges living 'completely in a state of slavery to the men'; but in advanced civilizations such as England, a labourer would expect to work hard 'for the sake of living with the woman that he loves'.[31] Yet the theory's emphasis on contingency in gender relations rendered it amenable to more radical and subversive readings. After all, if a society's position on the civilized scale could be construed from its treatment of women, then it followed that any changes in women's behaviour should be read as a symbol of change in the entire social and political body.

As Taylor has shown, Mary Wollstonecraft was early in seeing stadial theory's radical potential for women and used it to advance her argument for gender equality in *The Vindication of the Rights of Woman* (1791).[32] Accordingly, the theory had become an established favourite in early nineteenth-century feminist circles.[33] It was seized on by Martineau. Exploring the radical, feminist potential of political economy's structuring rhetoric of four-stages theory in her *Illustrations*, she pushed the idea of historical contingency in gender relations to the heart of public debate. In her *Autobiography*, Martineau fully acknowledged the critical insight of Empson, who in a nervously favourable review had shown a 'perfect understanding of [her] view and purpose' in the series.[34] Her literary method was, primarily, a blending of the realistic and the allegorical enacted through what Empson described as the use of 'miniature models of select portions of society' in which each 'model works out its own specific fact and lesson'.[35] As a pro-Malthusian, Empson had nothing to say about her views on population and charity, but he noted with alarm the feminist and utopian strain in Martineau's thinking in his comments on 'For Each and For All', a story in which she uncouples feminism from socialism: 'if she is looking forward to ... a millennium of her own, in which our ladies will have taken out of our monopolising hands the cares of Parliament and public life, – there is no knowing whither a mind, which has already got so high into the visionary empyrean, may ultimately soar'.[36] He also expressed fear that Martineau might subsequently 'reduce her powers and reputation to the mere circulating-library glory of being the most gifted novelist of the Godwin school'.[37] His consternation was justified when, toward the end of the series, Martineau imagined a further utopian fifth stage 'when society shall be *wisely* arranged, so that all may become intellectual, virtuous and happy' – that egalitarian 'all' comprising men and women of all classes – and imagined a society in which the harnessing of nature by advances in human intellect meant that there were six philosophers to every labourer.[38] Turning now to perform the kind of metonymic reading of the *Illustrations* that Empson had done and Martineau hoped for, it will become evident that, however patriarchal Malthusianism and political economy may appear in retrospect, the progressive potential inherent in its stadial framing meant that for Martineau it was replete with possibilities for women.[39]

Martineau made short work of advancing her feminist interpretation of stadial theory by introducing it in the first number of the *Illustrations*, 'Life in the Wilds'. The story focuses on a settlement of English emigrants in the Cape of South Africa, attacked by Bushmen. All the goods that signify the four stages of civilized progress are either removed or destroyed in the raid: the fishing tackle and weapons that symbolized hunting; the flocks associated with pasturage; the harvested crops of the agricultural stage; and the tools denoting entry into the fourth stage of commerce and manufacturing. Under the goad of necessity, the community rebuilds itself, taking this 'cancellation of history' as an opportunity to re-evaluate its social and political constitution.[40] In the story, Martineau introduces her utopian vision of the ideal arrangement of a society in the advanced stages of civilized progress. It consists of a meritocratic democracy, working in harmony with the natural laws of political economy and equal in its treatment of the sexes. The tale ends with the symbolically named Captain Adams as chief magistrate – head of a new Eden in which he derives his governing powers from the consent of the 'whole society' (that is, from *all* the adult men and women of the community).[41] As Conder's first favourable review suggests, there is no explicit reference to Malthusianism in this opening work, although its presence can be detected in a concluding discussion about whether the fledgling meritocracy should endorse a young couple's wish to marry. Mrs Stone, the 'strong-minded' wife of the community's chaplain, decides that in an 'infant settlement' such as theirs, 'there was more than work enough for every body' (unlike England) and so there could be no objection.[42]

The *Illustrations* is strewn with women like Mrs Stone, demonstrated as manifestly worthy of being considered rational actors and who accrue to make the case for women's entitlement to full legal, economic and political personhood. In 'For Each and For All', for example, Martineau not only uncouples feminism from socialism in order to attach the former to political economy, but also subverts the laws of coverture by having the 'enlightened' husband, Lord Henry, tell his newly wed and former actress wife,

Letitia, that a key motive behind his wish to become minister of the crown is so 'that you might espouse another kind of public service in espousing me'.[43] A further critique of the denial of women's autonomy appears in the two-part story, 'Berkeley the Banker', where Martineau dismantles James Mill's claim in his 1820 'Essay on Government' that women did not require the vote because there was an identity of interest between them and their menfolk.[44] There is also the heroine of 'Cousin Marshall', through whom Martineau – going further than Malthus himself – proposes scrapping the Poor Law altogether and positions the paternalism of alms-giving as a remnant of feudalism.[45] We learn how Mrs Marshall's opposition to charitable relief places her in the vanguard of civilized progress; her neighbours' hostility indicating that she has 'lived too early' for her wisdom to be recognized by the society in transition around her.[46] This Malthusian story caused consternation enough among Martineau's hostile critics – the *Quarterly* frothed italics at the idea of Martineau as 'a *young woman* who deprecates charity and a provision for the *poor*!!!' – but that was nothing to the opprobrium heaped upon her for 'Weal and Woe in Garveloch'.[47]

The story tells how a thriving fishing industry in a set of remote Scottish islands has produced a thriving population: the isle of Garveloch resounds to 'the shouts and laughter of innumerable children at play among the rocks'.[48] It is the starvation that ensues from the unthinking conception of these 'innumerable children' once the herring harvest fails and the population outstrips food supply that forms the subject of the tale. One of Martineau's 'miniature models', Garveloch is England writ small. The explanations of Malthusian population theory take place in conversations between Ella, her husband Angus, her friends Katie and Mr Mackenzie, the local magistrate. Between them, they situate the problem of surplus population within a framework informed by four-stages theory, just as Malthus himself did.[49] The dilemma is understood to be typical of older, advanced nations like England, where capitalism has led to significant population growth, but the means of subsistence is restricted. Their analysis is accompanied by a perfect illustration of how Martineau's understanding of the social and historical contingency inherent in stadial theory could combine with her Unitarian hermeneutics. Mackenzie explains that God's injunction to Noah – 'Be fruitful, and multiply, and replenish the earth' – was not valid for all time, but should be applied only to its specific moment, a position highly provocative to those who founded their anti-Malthusianism on the literal truth of scripture.[50]

But it is the female characters who advance the theory's more sexually intimate applications by separately discussing the desire of Ella's brother,

Ronald, to marry Katie, a widow with young children. As the supply of food dwindles, Katie recognizes the need to check the population, as does Ronald, who refrains from proposing to her. Talking together, Ella and Katie hold up such self-restraint as a social duty, concluding that a marriage is not a contract between two consenting parties, but rather between three. Society itself should be consulted, as the right to a family life is contingent upon social circumstances. 'If Ronald were in a new colony, where labour was more in request than anything else, he would be honoured for having ten children, and doubly honoured for having twenty.'[51] For Katie, to grasp this was to understand the necessarian doctrine of causation: 'Since Providence has not made food increase as men increase ... it is plain that Providence wills restraint here as in the case of other passions.'[52] Starvation and distress would continue until the people learned to 'understand those natural laws by which and under which they subsist'.[53] It is in statements like these, where Malthus's theories are interwoven with Martineau's necessarianism, that one can see most clearly the grounds on which her optimistic view of Malthusianism is based: Malthus's *Essay* had made known one of the natural laws governing the universe and such knowledge was a source of power. By putting this discussion in the mouths of two female characters, Martineau places the concept of sexual restraint – the assertion of reason over passion – in the feminine domain, underscoring her point about women's rational capacities. At the same time, she insists that such rationality is wholly consistent with maternal feeling: 'Ella and Katie, sensible and unprejudiced, and rendered quick-sighted by anxiety for their children, were peculiarly qualified for seeing the truth when fairly placed before them.'[54] If women, like men, were required to subordinate their sexual and reproductive desires in deference to the demands of Providence, then they too needed to understand the reasons why.

As already noted, Martineau's positioning of the family's right to exist as subordinate to the providential laws of political economy caused outrage in anti-Malthusian quarters. But I would suggest, too, that Martineau's narrative exemplifications of women's capacity for reason – a reason that could override the demands of the sexually or maternally desiring body – added to the conflagration. It is not merely that she herself has transgressed conventional gender boundaries, but also that, instalment by instalment, the *Illustrations* was arguing that all women potentially could and should do the same. Malthus might have agreed that Martineau had represented his views accurately in individual stories such as 'Weal and Woe', but across the series, Martineau was serving up Malthusianism with a feminist twist.

Recognizing this sheds a different light on the ridicule to which she was subjected in the more reactionary quarters of the press – portraying her as undesirable and, therefore, sexually naïve undermines her case for gender equality. The *Quarterly*, for example, mockingly claimed that she had confused the reproduction rates of fisherwomen with those of herring, implicitly basing her argument on the presumption that 'every female should marry at three months old, and have twenty children at a birth! ... Poor innocent! She has been puzzling over Mr. Malthus's arithmetical and geometrical ratios, for knowledge which she should have obtained by a simple question or two of her mamma.'[55] They also implied that she has been manipulated into advocating the use of contraception by 'certain gentlemen of her sect', although in fact neither she nor Malthus did.[56] She was thus scandalously unwomanly in writing about Malthusianism and only too feebly womanly in failing to understand its implications.

In *Fraser's Magazine*, however, Maginn was more explicit, showing he fully understood the feminist implications of Martineau's advocacy of Malthusianism. After disparaging her personal charms, he compares Martineau to 'Mother Woolstonecroft [sic]', who had argued in her *Vindication* that women should be taught anatomy as part of their education as rational beings:

> Disgusting this, no doubt; but far less disgusting than when we find the more mystical topics of generation, its impulses and consequences – which the common consent of society, even the ordinary practice of language ... has veiled with the decent covering of silence, or left to be examined only with philosophical abstraction – brought daily, weekly, monthly before the public eye, as the leading subjects, the very foundation-thoughts, of essays, articles, treatises, novels! tales! romances! ... to lie on the breakfast-tables of the young and the fair, and to afford them matter of meditation.[57]

Martineau is worse than Wollstonecraft because by reifying the abstractions of Malthusian theory in her fiction – embodying its principles – she has lifted the veil on 'the mystical topics of generation' and is corrupting the nation's daughters. Yet, having complained at her fictional exposure of the procreative body, with 'its impulses and consequences', Maginn advises Martineau to contemplate the body a little more. As a bluestocking spinster who will only ever give birth to 'chubby duodecimos', she has failed to connect signifier and signified.[58] In view of this, he proposes she 'sit down in her study' and:

> depict to herself what is the precise and physical meaning of the words used by her school – what is preventive check – what is moral check – what it is they are intended to check – and then ask herself, if she is or is not

properly qualified to write a commentary on the most celebrated numbers
of Mr. Carlile's *Republican*; or to refute the arguments addressed by the
learned Panurge to the Dame de Paris, as founded upon false notions of
philosophy.[59]

Martineau is instructed here to imagine the desiring body and the mechanics of sex in order to grasp fully what the abstractions of Malthusian terms
such as 'preventive check' signify in practice. The reference to Carlile
joins the *Quarterly* in an innuendo about birth control, but the allusion
to Panurge, a character from François Rabelais' *Pantagruel* (1532), evokes
images that are at least as sexually graphic and certainly more coarse
than any in Carlile's article advocating the contraceptive sponge.[60] In the
notorious scene referred to here, Panurge makes a blunt and unsolicited
proposition to the haughty Lady of Paris: 'Madam, it would be a very
great benefit to the commonwealth, delightful to you, honourable to your
progeny, and necessary for me, that I cover you for the propagating of my
race' and then points to his 'long codpiece', inside which is:

> Master John Thursday, who will play you such an antic that you shall feel
> the sweetness thereof even to the very marrow of your bones. He is a gal-
> lant, and doth so well know how to find out all the corners, creeks and
> ingrained inmates of your carnal trap, that after him there needs no broom
> to follow, he'll sweep so well before, and leave nothing to his followers to
> work upon.[61]

This allusion to a scabrous French novel flatters an elite male readership,
of course, and it is certainly intended as an affront to Martineau. But
the pungent references to male and female genitalia and the rhythms of
copulation have meaning beyond that of using sexual innuendo for the
purposes of *ad feminam* attack. In his vivid interposition of the body
and its reproductive needs through the use of literary allusion, Maginn is
following a much better-known critic of Malthus, Robert Southey, who
persistently asserted the primacy of the body in his sustained campaign
to counter what he saw as the specious abstractions of Malthusian political economy. But what is new about the *Illustrations*, and thus what is so
disconcerting for Maginn, is that resting on Martineau's prioritization of
the reasoning mind over the feeling body is a claim for equality of rights
for women. As reviewers such as Empson and Maginn have so astutely
spotted, standing behind Malthus in her series is Godwin and behind
him, Wollstonecraft – and the heterodox ideas on women's rights of all
three of them are infiltrating the domestic realm through the medium of
popular fiction.

Throughout his writing, it is habitually a male body that Southey interposes in his critique of Malthus. In his 1803 review of the second edition of the *Essay*, Southey laid out with Swiftian irony an imagined 'perfect system of policy' to implement Malthusianism.[62] The first step would be to ensure that fear of starvation had made celibate slaves of the poor. Having thus achieved the despotic Oriental monarchy, the next move would be to adopt 'Oriental manners; and introduce into England the wise invention of Semiramis for counteracting the principle of population'; that is, turn the poor into eunuchs.[63] The benefits to England of mass castration would be that 'we should rear our own opera-singers' and the government would be better able to control the people: 'for John Bull has been at times a refractory animal, but John Ox would certainly be tractable'.[64] In a letter to John Rickman written after sending the piece to the *Annual Review*, Southey was explicit about his polemical aims, which had been to show that the logical consequence of Malthusian theory was the regulation of population 'by the knife of the sowgelder'.[65] Historically, sowgelders neutered both sows and boars and, although in the public article Southey is clearly referring to male castration, the imagery in his private note does double duty by also invoking the spaying of women. Celibacy would affect both sexes and in a later letter to Rickman his description of the impact of Malthusianism on women was no less graphic: those who supported Malthus were 'voiders of menstrual pollution'.[66] As already mentioned, Malthus's *Essay* had relatively little to say about women in advanced civilizations such as England beyond the assumption of separate gender spheres, and the public row in the press prompted by Malthus's theories in the early part of the nineteenth century was enacted largely as an argument about, by and among men. However, in his personal correspondence, Southey is able to move beyond irony and say the publicly unsayable. Prevented by Malthusian social policy (rather than the metaphorical gelder's blade) from being mothers, women would remain unmarried and barren – and thus menstruate more often.

Charlotte Elizabeth Tonna, anti-Malthusianism and the menstrual economy

Southey's frank but private acknowledgement of the bodily consequences of Malthusianism for women (both for their fertility and their sexual and maternal fulfilment) suggests that, by having her female characters talk so openly about moral restraint, Martineau's offence was not merely that she was announcing a case for women's rights in her series. By writing tales that were read by 'the young and the fair' in prosperous homes, she had also infringed the rules of polite discourse regarding public discussion of the *Essay*'s implications for women's sexuality (although the furore over the 1834 New Poor Law's Bastardy Clause was shortly to tear them up completely).[67] As we have seen, her male Tory reviewers tried to meet the challenge through sexual innuendo and the liberal use of exclamation marks, but it was to be a woman – the ultra-Tory Charlotte Elizabeth Tonna – who engaged most closely and fiercely in ideological combat with Martineau on her chosen ground of fiction. Her anti-Malthusian stories include her pro-Ten Hours factory novel *Helen Fleetwood* (serialized in *Christian Lady's Magazine*, 1839–41) and *The Wrongs of Woman* (1843–4), a separately published novella comprised of four short stories written in response to the findings of the 1842 Children's Employment Commission. Both works assume a female readership. That her opposition was toward Malthusianism of a specifically Martineauian kind is signalled by her chosen titles, which invoke the radical feminist politics of Godwin (whose *Fleetwood; or the New Man of Feeling* appeared in 1805) and Wollstonecraft (whose *Maria: or, the Wrongs of Woman*, was published posthumously by Godwin in 1798, the same year as his infamous *Memoir*). My primary focus here will be on an Empsonian reading of the first part of *The Wrongs of Woman*, 'Milliners and Dressmakers', in order to examine the way in which Tonna positioned women's reproductive bodies and immortal souls as counters to Martineau's valorization of human reason.

Tonna was part of a tight-knit circle of pre-Millenarian Evangelical Tories who campaigned for legislation to raise the condition of the labouring classes in the 1830s and 1840s (in particular a Ten Hours Factory Bill).[68] Boyd Hilton has situated pre-Millenarianism as an extreme minority strand of Evangelicalism in this period, identified with a fiercely paternalist opposition to the laissez-faire ethos.[69] Along with other members of her sect, Tonna believed that the failure of the rich to fulfil their duty to the poor meant that, although seemingly at the height of her commercial glory, England in fact stood on the precipice of an 'awakening volcano'.[70] As she sets out in her anonymously published polemic, *The Perils of the Nation* (1843), Malthusian political economy was the work of Satan, as demonstrated through its disregard for the biblical injunction to go forth and multiply, its encouragement of 'unmitigated selfishness' through the focus on profit and the advocacy of extreme self-interest that was fracturing social ties between rich and poor.[71] Unless brought to recognize where their paternalistic obligations lay, the wealthy would ensure England's destruction in the apocalypse sent to inaugurate the Second Coming. In her attempt to avert God's wrath, Tonna used her roles as editor of the *Christian Lady's Magazine* (1834–46) and writer of didactic fiction as a platform from which to mobilize the philanthropic sympathy of her lady readers and turn it into an active care for the working classes.

As an avowedly Pauline advocate of separate gender spheres, Tonna negotiated her own campaigning career with tact and (dis)ingenuity – and showed other women how to do the same. For example, in 'Politics', a regular magazine feature framed as conversations between Uncle and Niece (with Tonna performing both feminine and masculine roles), she deployed the part of Uncle to urge her readers to use their influence with their menfolk and persuade them to vote only for parliamentary candidates supporting the Ten Hours Factory Bill. The voice of Niece is then used to articulate the fear that women might be setting themselves up as 'agitators', allowing Uncle to reassure her and the reader that such 'modest perseverance in so sacred a cause' was not 'overstepping the boundary'.[72] Like Martineau, Tonna accepted a stadial account of civilized progress, as well as its axioms about the treatment of women as an index of civilization. But her commitment to separate gender spheres meant that she subscribed to the majority conservative interpretation of the theory. Describing the role of Christianity in enabling man's progress from savagery to civilization in another 'Politics' column, Uncle locates the Christian woman in her role as domestic paragon as the true motor of commerce:

> It is when man has recovered, under the mild beam of gospel truth, somewhat of the original blessing which constituted woman 'an help meet for him,' – it is when his home becomes the abode of gentle sympathy and intellectual companionship, and spiritual communion, that man begins to feel he has somewhat worth fencing around, with more stable and enduring bulwarks than shield and spear. And thus in its most secret, most unconscious exercise, does the talent of female influence form the basis of even all commercial intercourse among the nations of the earth.[73]

This understanding of home as the rightful place for women formed one strand of Tonna's critique of Martineau who, 'in the fashion of the age' was one of those women who had left 'their assigned sphere, setting themselves up for political agitators, political economists and what not'.[74] In her anti-Malthusian jeremiad, *The Perils of the Nation*, she identifies Martineau as a writer of 'pernicious little books' that were popularizing a system in which 'the bright lamp of truth [was] wilfully hidden, and man's shallow reasonings substituted for the infinite wisdom of God'.[75]

In the introductory chapters to 'Milliners and Dressmakers', Tonna sets out her Pauline understanding of women's rights. Repudiating 'all pretensions to equality with man, save on the grounds specified by the Apostle, that "in Christ Jesus there is neither male nor female"', she claims nothing but 'the capacity assigned to her in Scripture, "the weaker vessel"'.[76] It is on this weakness (it being Eve who committed the first transgression in the Garden of Eden) that she grounds her notion of both the rights and wrongs of women. As 'the sex who were lost by giving heed to the deceivableness of Satan', women would be 'saved in childbearing' as long as they exercised faith in the Saviour who would redeem the world.[77] But Eve's 'extreme instability' – the extent to which she had allowed 'the pride of carnal reason' to 'conquer faith' and then allowed 'presumptuous folly' to override both – confirmed the rightness of her designation by God as a '*help* meet' for Adam.[78] While neither Martineau nor Wollstonecraft is referred to explicitly here, their claims for equal rights are. Part of Tonna's aim in setting out Eve's disobedient subordination of faith to reason and her foolish overreaching is to criticize those 'aspiring individuals of the female sex' who claim more than spiritual equality with men and protest at being debarred from 'joining in the intellectual pursuits of their academic friends; and figuring in halls of science, or in the senatorial chamber'.[79] Martineau's feminist new millennium is implicitly dismissed with the assertion that 'all we know of the paradisiacal state is comprised in so brief an outline' in Scripture that such conjecture is futile.[80]

Like many radical Tories in this period, Tonna was profoundly influenced by Robert Southey.[81] As Donald Winch has noted, Southey was 'one of the first, though by no means the last, to counterpose *moral* economy against *political* economy' and in *The Wrongs of Woman*, Tonna proves herself his follower.[82] But she explicitly places the experience of women in critical relation to Malthusian thinking as the stories are a protest against the exploitation of female labour. Southey often reached for metaphors of disease in his writing when protesting at the breakdown of paternalistic relations between rich and poor. In his *Letters from England* (1807), for example, he had figured wealth as blood failing to circulate 'equally and healthfully through the whole system' of the body politic and instead sprouting 'into wens and tumours' and collecting 'into aneurisms which starve and palsy the extremities'.[83] However, as his private reference to the Malthusian 'voiders of menstrual pollution' shows, the figurative could give way to the literal – and in the first part of Tonna's novella, metaphor similarly yields to pathology. Throughout *The Wrongs of Woman*, one of Tonna's chief claims for working-class women is that, in their weakness, they are entitled to paternalistic protection and, where possible, their labour should take place in the domestic realm. In doing so, the novella provides narrative exemplification of her arguments in *Perils of the Nation*, where she also draws attention to Malthusianism's impact on poor women's relation to their maternal role. This includes 'the sterility consequent on universal prostitution' ensuing from delayed marriage and also infanticide, as the babies of abandoned single mothers (who now 'thanks to the New Poor-law, must rise from childbed to earn by their labour ... the morsel that shall enable them to give suck') starve to death or, it is implied, are strangled out of necessity.[84] As part of her polemic, she counters Malthusian reasoning through reference to God's covenant with the Israelites in Deuteronomy: '[o]ne of the main blessings promised to their obedience was, that there should be *neither male nor female barren* among them'.[85] Having identified female fecundity as a sign of God's blessing in *Perils*, she develops this anti-Malthusianism point in 'Milliners and Dressmakers'. Here she draws on parliamentary testimony from the medical profession to tell a story illustrating the injury done to the gynaecological health of apprentice seamstresses by having to labour for up to 18 hours a day. In the process, pre-Millenarian Evangelical bibliolatry fuses with medical evidence to predicate national wellbeing on the establishment of the childbearing capacity of the adolescent seamstress's womb. Where Southey privately invoked the idea of too much menstruation to condemn Malthusianism, Tonna publicly wielded gynaecological catastrophe. Central to her analysis of a fit moral economy is a properly ordered 'female economy' – that is, a balanced relationship between body and mind, as evidenced by regular menstruation – which she counterposes not only against Malthusian political economy but also against the claim for the rational, egalitarian feminism that Martineau had woven into it in the *Illustrations*.[86]

In 'Milliners and Dressmakers', Tonna draws substantially (to the extent of direct quotation and paraphrase) on R.D. Grainger's 1842 'Report on Millinery and Dress-Making', written as part of his work as one of the sub-commissioners for the Children's Employment Commission.[87] The report focused on a class of young working women who had paid up to £60 for a two- or three-year apprenticeship, mostly as boarders in London fashion houses. The majority of them were between 14 and 16 years old and therefore, importantly, at the average age of puberty for girls in the nineteenth century. As an anatomist and physiologist, Grainger's interpretation of their health was informed by his medical understanding of the impact of hours of stitching on their constitution and in the supporting

evidence to his report, Grainger includes the testimony of ten other medical men. As one would expect, among the many ailments attributed to
the seamstresses' excessive hours of sedentary close stitching in confined
rooms were blindness, dyspepsia and deformities of the spine and shoulder. But, beyond these, each and every medical witness made reference
to diseases and symptoms that they understood to be the result of damage
done specifically to what they variously termed the 'female constitution',
the 'female functions' or the 'uterine system'.[88] Each of these descriptors
indicates an assumption that the seamstress's health could be diagnosed
using orderly menstruation as a measure of wellbeing. Amenorrhea, leu-
corrhea and anaemia were mentioned by name, while chlorisis was indicated through the repeated descriptions of an abnormal pallor denoting
loss of blood, fainting fits, emaciation and loss of appetite.[89] Hysteria,
understood at the time to be a gynaecological disorder (the traditional
cure was marriage), was also frequently mentioned.[90] As Dr G. Hamilton
Roe observed, because 'these young persons commence this laborious
occupation at the age of 14 or 16, when the great change occurs in the
female constitution, the most serious interruption to the functions of
the uterus is likely to be produced; and daily experience shows that this
is the result'.[91] He was typical of his medical colleagues in declaring the
prognosis to be that 'the action of the uterus is frequently *permanently*
deranged'.[92] In other words (and in an alarming paradox), long hours
engaged in sewing – the archetypal signifier of the feminine – was damaging young women's childbearing capacity.

In these early nineteenth-century medical conceptions of the female
economy or system, the uterus was central. As one doctor expressed it, 'all
[women's] organs partake, more or less, in the condition of the uterus'.[93]
There was, for example, a 'well-known sympathy' between the womb and
the bladder, in addition to the 'intimate consent' that existed between
the uterus and the stomach.[94] However, the apparent emphasis in the
report on the physical did not prelude consideration of the moral. Just as
the uterus could influence the other organs, so could the other organs –
including the mind – influence the uterus. Any 'mental or moral agitation'
could lead to uterine derangement and, similarly, the failure to establish
normal menstruation could lead to a downward spiral of hysteria, mad-
ness and melancholy.[95] Thus women's moral health could be deduced from
their physical condition – and vice versa. Intrinsically volatile, the female
economy was at the mercy of the uterus, which accounted for the 'natural
affectability' or 'susceptibility of woman, and her less mental and muscu-
lar power' when compared to the male.[96] It also went some way to explain

why young seamstresses, who worked so hard during the 'most important epoch of life' for women, were notoriously prone to seduction.[97] As
pubescent working girls, they were in need of constant physical and moral
monitoring by their largely female employers if they were to stand any
chance of controlling their 'extreme instability' (to repeat Tonna's description of Eve) and going on to become fit wives and mothers.

Unsurprisingly, Grainger's report caused a public panic and inspired a
number of stories to protest at the plight of the seamstress. While these
medico-moral beliefs about the repercussions of disordered menstruation for women's nubility and procreativity had popular currency in
the 1840s, the difficulty for authors was how to allude to the gynaecological consequences of the girls' labour with literary decorum. Almost
invariably, the writers elected to split the mind/body circularity of
the female economy into its component parts by featuring two seamstresses, one of whom dies a physical death, the other a moral one.[98]
Tonna uses exactly this method in 'Milliners and Dressmakers', which
tells the story of the King sisters: apprenticed to different employers in
London, Ann rapidly succumbs to consumption, while Frances ends
her days not long after as a drink-raddled prostitute. Even so, Tonna
implies the connection between the physical and the moral. Ann herself offers a spiritual diagnosis of her condition by suggesting to her
doctor (who does not disagree) that she has sickened because fatigue
from overwork meant she no longer went to church on Sundays, even
though she knew religious observance 'did [her] good, *body and mind*'.[99]
In contrast, Frances's descent into the 'abyss of wretchedness and guilt'
is inscribed on her face: prematurely aged, her immorality 'has bloated
her cheek and wrinkled her brow'.[100] Scattered throughout the story are
descriptions of young seamstresses whose physical symptoms were commonly understood as denoting menstrual disorder. For example, Ann
initially mistakes 'that universal air of languor, that absence of healthy
glow, that reed-like attenuation of figure' among her fellow apprentices
for 'London polish' rather than what it would actually have signified
to Grainger's medical witnesses and Tonna's middle- and upper-class
female readership: the failure to establish secondary sexual characteristics at puberty that denoted gynaecological disorder.[101] Ann herself
rapidly becomes 'wan and sunken' and suffers from a long list of complaints: pain in her shoulder blades, palpitations, a mist over her eyes, a
choking in the throat, sickness and loss of appetite, pains in her limbs,
headaches and fainting fits.[102] All these symptoms link the origin of her
consumption to menstrual irregularity, as does the doctor's impossible

prescription of fresh air, exercise and food at regular hours, which was the standard treatment for uterine derangement at the time.[103]

Having set out her diagnosis of the seamstress's moral and physical condition, Tonna locates its etiology and cure within a larger female economy: the relationship between employee, employer and client. Lying behind the employers' failure to limit the girls' hours of labour and also to attend to their spiritual needs on Sundays, was the 'root of evil ... filthy lucre'.[104] Their wealthy clientele were equally selfish, although motivated by vanity rather than greed. Tonna urges her female readers to act forthwith, giving their patronage only to those houses that guaranteed a ten- or 12-hour maximum day for their apprentices. If moral pressure was insufficient to make the avaricious employer recognize her duties towards her charges, then the commercial pressure of a boycott would force her to. The actively devout Christian woman is figured as a key line of defence against the second deluge in which the Malthusian sins of the rich would be visited upon the poor. In Tonna's pre-Millenarian analysis, only the Christian moral economy can serve as a 'breakwater' against the 'ocean of ... selfishness' among female employers and 'curb its force and prevent its bursting in, to bring ruin, destitution and death to the hearths of English cottages'.[105] To ram this message home in the closing lines of her story, she holds up the figure of Salome, 'who went forth to the dance, as one of courtly splendour, and elicited even royal applause, while captivating a throng of nobles by her external appearance; yet who, in that very act, brought upon her soul the guilt of innocent blood'.[106] Tonna thus asks her female reader to help stem the tide – not of metaphorical, but of pathological and apocalyptic blood – by subduing her vanity and participating in a movement to restore paternalistic (or, perhaps more fittingly, maternalistic) principles to the marketplace. This would enable young apprentices later to fulfil the biblical and biological destinies as help-meets and mothers that Malthusian laissez-faire was denying them.

Before she died in 1846, Tonna was to rebuke Martineau publicly once more: the latter's enthusiasm for the mesmerism – a 'branch of sorcery', according to Tonna – indicated she was being 'led captive' by the Antichrist.[107] But it is notable that, for all their ideological warfare over Malthusianism (whether as a lever for Satan or merely for liberal feminism), what the two of them shared was a powerful concern with the position and future of women in a commercial economy. In this controversy in fiction, they each held fast to the stadial axiom that the treatment of women was an index of civilization, even as they differed over what denoted civilized progress for the subordinate sex. Where Martineau foresaw a rationalist new millennium in which pro-Malthusianism had secured women's equal rights through the development of human reason, Tonna prioritized women's bodies and souls to ensure their temporal and spiritual salvation and stop England from being blotted off the face of the earth before the Second Coming. What also emerges from this analysis of the standoff between the two authors, however, is just how much Malthusianism has shifted in popular meaning in the 40 or so years since the *Essay*'s original publication. It had become shorthand, in the literary arena and beyond, for an emphasis on reason and a denial of the needs of the body.

Malthusianism and the Condition-of-England novel

As I have indicated, both Martineau and Tonna have been seen as antecedents of the canonical Condition-of-England novelists on account of their didactic blending of fact and fiction. But I want to conclude by suggesting that one of their key contributions to the genre (at its peak from 1845 to 1855) also lies in the way in which their overtly pro- and anti-Malthusian fictions pushed a set of notations regarding the right relation between women's minds, bodies and souls to the heart of literary debate over the future of industrial society. This can readily be seen in Charles Dickens's *Hard Times* (1854) and Elizabeth Gaskell's *North and South* (1854–5), serialized consecutively in Dickens's periodical, *Household Words*. Known for his anti-Malthusianism since the publication of *Oliver Twist* (1838), Dickens's primary target in his industrial novel is excessively utilitarian thinking, with its emphasis on the rational over subjective (or embodied) feeling. His conflation of it with Malthusian political economy can be located in the brief reference to the utilitarian Mr Gradgrind's youngest sons, Adam Smith and Malthus – characters named only to vanish from the text – and a sardonic reference to charity pauperizing the poor.[108] But the distorting effects of utilitarian and economic rationalizations that prioritize the mind over the body and soul are most visibly inscribed on the female characters in the novel. The spectral Mrs Gradgrind, chosen as a bride by her husband because in his view she is 'most satisfactory as a question of figures' and has 'no nonsense' (or 'fancy') about her, ends her days reduced to a 'faint transparency' of a woman and dies declaring 'I think there's a pain in the somewhere in the room ... but I couldn't positively say that I have got it'.[109] Similarly taught only to reason and not to feel, Gradgrind's daughter Louisa ('the pride of his heart and the triumph of his system') flees the implications of her adulterous desire for James

Harthouse and collapses in 'an insensible heap' at her father's feet after asking him where to find 'the graces of [her] soul' and 'the sentiments of [her] heart'.[110] If the condition of women was truly the index of civilization, then the depictions of one woman so self-alienated that she cannot feel her own pain and another whose inability to locate the consolations of the spirit causes her to disintegrate tell the reader all they need to know about Dickens's dim view of a regressive society founded on utilitarianism, Malthusian political economy, and the various 'Ologies' to which Mrs Gradgrind alludes.[111]

In contrast, Margaret Hale, the 'strong-minded' heroine of *North and South* learns to embrace and understand both political economy and its representative, the northern manufacturer John Thornton. Throughout her writings, Gaskell makes plain her belief that manufacturing and commerce were the signs of social and political advancement and, like Martineau, she was a Unitarian. But where she parts company with Martineau's analysis in the *Illustrations* is in the centrality that she gives to subjective emotions and bodily feeling, especially those of her women characters. In a personal letter discussing Harriet Taylor Mill's *Westminster Review* essay on 'The Enfranchisement of Women', Charlotte Brontë tells Gaskell: 'You are right when you say that there is a large margin in human nature over which the logicians have no dominion'.[112] This scepticism toward the experiential adequacy of human reason alone appears throughout *North and South*. Gaskell persistently emphasizes Margaret's bodily experiences – her tears, blushings and tremblings – and the final betrothal scene of the novel is one that tries to incorporate female sexual desire into its understanding of gender relations in a commercial economy. Indicating the couple's first kiss by describing a period of 'delicious silence', Gaskell has their clasp end with Margaret looking up at Thornton and 'glowing with beautiful shame'.[113] Taking 'shame' to be a post-lapsarian response to sexual feeling, Margaret's blushing glow thus gives her erotic desires an open and central role in her marriage. And, importantly, this visible expression of female sexual desire (the gradual acknowledgement of which has been the motor of the novel's romance plot) is described as 'beautiful'. Critics have read this final tableau as symbolizing a marriage of north and south, of the masculine public and private feminine spheres, of commerce and philanthropy, and so on.[114] But by placing the novel against Martineau's account of Malthusianism in her series and Tonna's response to it, the scene can be taken as an attempt by Gaskell to imagine a further and very different kind of marriage – a wholly internal one in which

Margaret integrates her desiring body with her reasoning mind and thus attains a recognizably feminist and liberal autonomy.

Martineau assuredly did not present Malthus 'pure and simple' in the *Illustrations*. Instead, through her feminist appropriation of Malthusian thinking she initiated a debate over the nature of women while putting the *Essay*'s terms and arguments into discursive play in industrial fiction. As a subgenre, the Condition-of-England novel tailed off after the mid-1850s. But the literary engagement with Malthus was later recalibrated by canonical writers such as George Eliot and Thomas Hardy, once the ideas in his *Essay on Population* were acknowledged by Charles Darwin as influencing the conceptualization of the 'struggle for existence' in *The Origin of Species* (1859).[115] Thereafter the fictional response to Malthus was continued by a cadre of *fin de siècle* New Woman writers, most notably Sarah Grand and George Egerton (the pen name for Mary Chavelita Dunne), whose stories engaged with the eugenicist policies inspired – if not endorsed – by Darwin. Underpinning works that include Grand's bestselling *The Heavenly Twins* (1893) and *The Beth Book* (1897) and Egerton's 'Virgin Soil' (1894) and *Rosa Amorosa* (1901) is a eugenic feminism that places women's rational reproductive choices at the heart of national and imperial regeneration.[116] Through the turn to eugenics, this strand of New Woman fiction asserts a different but no less polemical account of the nature, needs and rights of women than that advocated by either Martineau or Tonna and, in doing so, carries the traces of Malthusian thinking controversially into the late nineteenth century and beyond.

Notes

1 Josiah Conder, '*Illustrations of Political Economy*. By Harriet Martineau. Nos I–V [and One Other Work]', *Eclectic Review*, 8 (1832), 44–72, p. 60.

2 Ibid., pp. 60 and 67.

3 R.K. Webb, *Harriet Martineau: A Radical Victorian* (London: Heinemann, 1960), p. 116.

4 Ibid., p. 113.

5 Conder, '*Illustrations*. Nos I–V', p. 60; Josiah Conder, '*Illustrations of Political Economy*. By Harriet Martineau. Nos VI–VIII [and Two Other Works]', *Eclectic Review*, 8 (1832), 328–49, p. 329.

6 Conder, '*Illustrations*. Nos VI–VIII', p. 340.

7 Ibid.

8 Ibid., p. 329.

9 [John Wilson Croker, John Gibson Lockhart and George Poulett Scrope], '*Illustrations of Political Economy*. Nos. 1–12. By Harriet Martineau', *Quarterly Review*, 49 (1833), 136–52, p. 151, emphasis in original.

10　Harriet Martineau, *Autobiography*, ed. Linda H. Peterson (Peterborough, Ontario: Broadview, 2007), p. 167; [William Maginn], 'Gallery of Literary Characters. No. XLII. Miss Harriet Martineau', *Fraser's Magazine*, 8 (1833), p. 576. The illustration is by Daniel Maclise.

11　On the comparison with Marcet, see James P. Huzel, *The Popularization of Malthus in Early Nineteenth-Century England: Martineau, Cobbett and the Pauper Press* (Aldershot: Ashgate, 2006), pp. 78–89.

12　See, for example, Valerie Sanders, '"Meteor Wreaths": Harriet Martineau, "L.E.L", Fame and *Frazer's* [sic] *Magazine*', *Critical Survey*, 13 (2001), 42–60, pp. 48–50; and Alexis Easley, 'Victorian Women Writers and the Periodical Press', *Nineteenth-Century Prose*, 24 (1997), 39–50, pp. 40–1.

13　Martineau, *Autobiography*, p. 170.

14　Ibid., p. 251.

15　Donald Winch, *Malthus* (Oxford: Oxford University Press, 1987), pp. 16–18.

16　See, for example, Chris Nyland, 'Women's Progress and "the End of History"', in Robert Dimand and Chris Nyland (eds.), *The Status of Women in Classical Economic Thought* (Cheltenham: Edward Elgar, 2003), pp. 108–26, pp. 122–5.

17　Henk W. Plasmeijer, 'The Talk of the Town in 1798', in Nora Fuhrmann, Eva Schmoly and Ravinder Stephan Singh Sud (eds.), *Gegen den Strich: Ökonomische Theorie und politische Regulierung* (Munich: Rainer Hampp, 2003), pp. 41–8; Gail Bederman, 'Sex, Scandal, Satire, and Population in 1798: Revisiting Malthus's First *Essay*', *Journal of British Studies*, 47 (2008), 768–95.

18　Deborah Valenze, *The First Industrial Woman* (New York: Oxford University Press, 1995), pp. 136–7.

19　T.R. Malthus, *An Essay on the Principle of Population*, ed. Geoffrey Gilbert (Oxford: Oxford University Press, 1993), p. 84; Nyland, 'Women's Progress', p. 124.

20　As one example, see Monica Correa Fryckstedt, 'The Early Industrial Novel: *Mary Barton* and Its Predecessors', *Bulletin of the John Rylands University Library of Manchester*, 63 (1980), 11–30, pp. 12–16.

21　Webb, *Harriet Martineau*, pp. 116–17. See also Harriet Martineau, 'The Moral of Many Fables', *Illustrations of Political Economy*, 9 vols. (London: Charles Fox, 1834), vol. 9, p. vi.

22　Donald Winch, *Riches and Poverty: An Intellectual History of Political Economy in Britain, 1750–1834* (Cambridge: Cambridge University Press, 1996), pp. 3, 287.

23　Gareth Stedman Jones, *An End to Poverty? A Historical Debate* (London: Profile Books, 2004).

24　Smith and Malthus differed from Ricardo, who figured political economy as a science. See Winch, *Riches and Poverty*, pp. 3, 285–7. On the pressure later placed on Martineau's stadial thinking by racial encounter, see Cora Kaplan, 'Slavery, Race, History: Martineau's Ethnographic Imagination', in Ella Dzelzainis and Cora Kaplan (eds.), *Harriet Martineau: Authorship, Society and Empire* (Manchester: Manchester University Press, 2010), pp. 180–96.

25 Ronald L. Meek, *Social Science and the Ignoble Savage* (Cambridge: Cambridge University Press, 1976). On Smith as the founder of four-stages theory, see Chapter 4; on Malthus, p. 223. Given Martineau's deployment of stadial theory in the series, Webb, *Harriet Martineau*, p. 116, understates the influence of Smith.

26 On Mill, see William C. Lehmann, *John Millar of Glasgow, 1735–1801: His Life and Thought and his Contributions to Sociological Analysis* (Cambridge: Cambridge University Press, 1960), pp. 152–3. But note its later use by Marx: see Meek, *Social Science and the Ignoble Savage*, pp. 220–1, 229.

27 Meek, *Social Science and the Ignoble Savage*, pp. 160–2 identifies Smith's pupil John Millar as the pre-eminent proponent of four-states theory. For correspondences between modes of subsistence, political institutions and social phenomena, see Millar's *Origin of the Distinction of Ranks* (1771).

28 William Alexander, *The History of Women, from the Earliest Antiquity, to the Present Time*, 2 vols. (London: Strahan and Cadell, 1779), vol. 1, p. 103.

29 Barbara Taylor, *Mary Wollstonecraft and the Feminist Imagination* (Cambridge: Cambridge University Press, 2003), p. 156.

30 Jane Rendall, *The Origins of Modern Feminism: Women in Britain, France and the United States, 1780–1860* (Basingstoke: Macmillan, 1985), p. 30.

31 Malthus, *Essay*, pp. 22–3, 33. But see Chapters 3 and 4 *passim*.

32 For key examples, see Mary Wollstonecraft, *A Vindication of the Rights of Men and A Vindication of the Rights of Woman and Hints*, ed. Sylvana Tomaselli (Cambridge: Cambridge University Press, 1995), pp. 85–6, 235–6. On Wollstonecraft's use of civilization theory, see Taylor, *Mary Wollstonecraft*, pp. 154–75.

33 Kathryn Gleadle, *The Early Feminists: Radical Unitarians and the Emergence of the Women's Rights Movement, 1831–1851* (Basingstoke: Macmillan, 1995), pp. 64–70; Barbara Taylor, *Eve and the New Jerusalem: Socialism and Feminism in the Nineteenth Century* (London: Virago, 1983), pp. 28–30.

34 Martineau, *Autobiography*, p. 124.

35 [William Empson], 'Mrs Marcet – Miss Martineau', *Edinburgh Review*, 57 (1833), 3–39, p. 7.

36 Ibid., p. 11.

37 Ibid.

38 Martineau, 'Moral of Many Fables', *Illustrations*, vol. 9, p. 141. On the ratio of philosophers to manual workers, see Martineau, 'Briery Creek', *Illustrations*, vol. 8, p. 81, emphasis in original.

39 On political economy's patriarchalism see Peter Groenewegen, 'Introduction: Women in Political Economy and Women as Political Economists in Victorian England', in Peter Groenewegen (ed.), *Feminism and Political Economy in Victorian England* (Aldershot: Elgar, 1994), pp. 11–15; Michèle A. Pujol, *Feminism and Anti-Feminism in Early Economic Thought* (Aldershot: Elgar, 1992), p. 4.

40 Simon Dentith, 'Political Economy, Fiction and the Language of Practical Ideology in Nineteenth-Century England', *Social History*, 8 (1983), 183–99, p. 191.

41 Martineau, 'Life in the Wilds', *Illustrations*, vol. 1, p. 96.

42 Ibid., pp. 6, 121.

43 Martineau, 'For Each and For All', *Illustrations*, vol. 4, pp. 19, 12.

44 For further discussion, see Ella Dzelzainis, 'Feminism, Speculation and Agency in Harriet Martineau's *Illustrations of Political Economy*', in Ella Dzelzainis and Cora Kaplan, *Harriet Martineau: Authorship, Society and Empire* (Manchester: Manchester University Press, 2010), pp. 118–37.

45 On Martineau's zealotry compared to Malthus's doubts, see Patricia James, *Population Malthus: His Life and Times* (London: Routledge, 1979), pp. 449–52.

46 Martineau, 'Cousin Marshall', *Illustrations*, vol. 3, p. 129.

47 [Croker *et al.*], '*Illustrations*', p. 151.

48 Martineau, 'Weal and Woe in Garveloch', *Illustrations*, vol. 2, p. 2.

49 Meek, *Social Science and the Ignoble Savage*, p. 223.

50 Genesis 9:1. Martineau's critical approach to Old Testament verities continues a well-established Unitarian tradition: see John Rogerson, *Old Testament Criticism in the Nineteenth Century: England and Germany* (London: SPCK, 1984), pp. 158–9.

51 Martineau, 'Weal and Woe', p. 99.

52 Ibid., p. 96. For more on Martineau's necessarianism, see Webb, *Harriet Martineau*, p. 79–88.

53 Ibid., p. 103.

54 Ibid., p. 104.

55 [Croker *et al.*], '*Illustrations*', p. 141.

56 Ibid., 151. On contraception: for Martineau, see Valerie Kossew Pichanick, *Harriet Martineau: The Woman and Her Work, 1802–76* (Ann Arbor: University of Michigan Press, 1980), p. 64; for Malthus, see Winch, *Riches and Poverty*, pp. 13, 242. The 'gentlemen' are probably J.S. Mill and Francis Place.

57 [William Maginn,], 'Gallery of Literary Characters. No. XLII. Miss Harriet Martineau', *Fraser's Magazine*, 8 (1833), p. 576. On women acquiring anatomical knowledge, see Wollstonecraft, *Vindications and Hints*, p. 209.

58 [Maginn], 'Gallery', p. 576. The snippets of poetry are from Thomas Moore's skit on Martineau, 'Love Song. To Miss –' (1832).

59 [Maginn], 'Gallery', p. 576.

60 [Richard Carlile], 'What is Love?', *Republican*, 11 (1825), 545–69.

61 François Rabelais, *Gargantua and Pantagruel*, trans. Sir Thomas Urquhart and Peter Motteux (New York: Digireads.com, 2009), p. 153. Urquhart's 1653 translation of the relevant chapter (Book II, Chapter XII) is the version most likely to have been read by Maginn's audience.

62 Robert Southey, 'Malthus's *Essay on Population*', *Annual Review and History of Literature*, 2 (1803), 292–301, p. 301.

63 Ibid. The reference to Semiramis is probably a literary echo of Samuel Butler's *Hudibras* (1663–78), Part II, lines 705–18.

64 Ibid.

65 Southey to Rickman, 8 February 1804, Kenneth Curry (ed.), *New Letters of Robert Southey*, 2 vols. (New York: Columbia University Press, 1965), vol. 1, p. 351.

66 Southey to Rickman, 9 March 1804, Curry, *New Letters*, vol. 1, p. 357.

67 On the Bastardy Clause controversy, see Lisa Forman Cody, 'The Politics of Illegitimacy in the Age of Reform: Women, Reproduction, and Political Economy in England's New Poor Law of 1834', *Journal of Women's History*, 11 (2000), 131–56.

68 For Tonna's involvement, see Ella Dzelzains, 'Charlotte Elizabeth Tonna, Pre-Millenarianism and the Formation of Gender Ideology in the Ten Hours Campaign', *Victoria Literature and Culture*, 31 (2003), 181–91.

69 See Boyd Hilton, *The Age of Atonement: The Influence of Evangelicalism on Social and Economic Thought, 1785–1865* (Oxford: Clarendon Press, 1986), pp. 14–19, 94–98.

70 Charlotte Elizabeth Tonna, 'The Lace-Runners', in *The Wrongs of Woman* (London: Dalton, 1844), p. 138.

71 [Charlotte Elizabeth Tonna], *The Perils of the Nation: An Appeal to the Legislature, the Clergy, and the Higher and Middle Classes* (London: Seeley, Burnside and Seeley, 1843), p. 149, and see Chapter 9 *passim*.

72 [Charlotte Elizabeth Tonna], 'Politics', *Christian Lady's Magazine*, 1 (1834), p. 160

73 Ibid., p. 250.

74 Ibid., p. 74.

75 [Tonna], *Perils*, p. 155.

76 Charlotte Elizabeth Tonna, 'Milliners and Dressmakers', in *Wrongs of Woman* (New York: Taylor, 1844; first published London: Dalton, 1843) pp. 3 and 6.

77 Ibid., p. 4.

78 Ibid., p. 5, emphasis in original.

79 Ibid., pp. 4, 8.

80 Ibid., p. 6.

81 See David Eastwood, 'Robert Southey and the Intellectual Origins of Romantic Conservatism', *English Historical Review*, 104 (1989), 308–31.

82 Winch, *Riches and Poverty*, p. 5, emphasis in original.

83 Robert Southey, *Letters from England*, ed. Jack Simmons (London: Cresset, 1951), p. 210. See also David Eastwood, 'Ruinous Prosperity: Robert Southey's Critique of the Commercial System', *Wordsworth Circle*, 25 (1994), 72–6; and Philip Connell, *Romanticism, Economics and the Question of 'Culture'* (Oxford: Oxford University Press, 2001), pp. 247–54.

84 [Tonna], *Perils*, p. 147.

85 Ibid., p. 160, emphasis in original. Compare Deuteronomy 7:14.

86 The phrase 'female economy' was ubiquitous, for example, M[ichael] Ryan, *A Manual of Midwifery, and Diseases of Women and Children*, 4th edn (London, 1841), p. 73.

87 See R.D. Grainger, 'Report to the Commissioners on the Employment of Children and Young Persons', in *Children's Employment Commission: Appendix to the Second Report of the Commissioners. Trades and Manufactures*, Part I (London: House of Commons, 1842), ff. 1–42. The 'Report on Millinery and Dress-Making' is a sub-section on ff. 29–33; the corresponding evidence is supplied in 'Evidence Collected by R.D. Grainger, Esq.', on ff. 204–37.

88 Grainger, 'Evidence', ff. 234, 232, 235.

89 On chlorosis, see Helen King, *The Disease of Virgins: Green Sickness, Chlorosis and the Problems of Puberty* (London: Routledge, 2004).

90 Unsurprising, given that 'hysteria' was derived from the Greek for 'womb'; see Julie-Marie Strange, 'Menstrual Fictions: Languages of Medicine and Menstruation, *c.* 1850–1931', *Women's History Review*, 9 (2000), 607–28, p. 616. On marriage as cure, see Rachel P. Maines, *The Technology of Orgasm: 'Hysteria,' the Vibrator, and Women's Sexual Satisfaction* (Baltimore: John Hopkins University Press, 1999), pp. 2, 27, 32.

91 Grainger, 'Evidence', f. 233.

92 Ibid., emphasis added.

93 Ryan, *Manual of Midwifery*, p. 73.

94 Charles Waller, 'Lectures on the Function and Diseases of the Womb', *Lancet*, 25 January 1840, p. 640.

95 Walter Johnson, *The Morbid Emotions of Women: Their Origins, Tendencies and Treatment* (London: Simpkin, Marshall, 1850), p. 24.

96 Thomas Laycock, *A Treatise on the Nervous Diseases of Women* (London: Orme, Brown, Green and Longmans, 1840), pp. 76, 83.

97 Grainger, 'Evidence', f. 206.

98 For example, Camilla Toulmin, 'The Orphan Milliners: A Story of the West End', *Illuminated Magazine*, 2 (1844), 279–85; F.D., 'The Dressmaker's Apprentices; A Tale of Woman's Oppression', *Lloyd's Penny Weekly Miscellany*, 3 (1844), pp. 433–4.

99 Tonna, 'Milliners', p. 29, emphasis added.

100 Ibid., pp. 53, 51.

101 Ibid., p, 18.

102 Ibid., p. 27.

103 See also Laycock, *Treatise*, p. 210.

104 Tonna, 'Milliners', p. 52.

105 Ibid., p. 62.

106 Ibid., p. 63.

107 [Charlotte Elizabeth Tonna], *Mesmerism: A Letter to Miss Harriet Martineau* (London: Seeley, Burnside, and Seeley, 1844), p. 5.

108 Charles Dickens, *Hard Times*, ed. Grahame Smith (London: Dent, 1994), p. 109.

109 Ibid., pp. 96, 185.

110 Ibid., p. 201.

111 Ibid., p. 116.

112 Letter from Brontë to Gaskell, 20 September 1851, cited in Elizabeth Gaskell, *The Life of Charlotte Brontë*, ed. Angus Easson (Oxford: Oxford University Press, 1996), p. 390.

113 Elizabeth Gaskell, *North and South* ed. Angus Easson and intro. Sally Shuttleworth (Oxford: Oxford University Press, 1998), p. 436.

114 For a critical summary, see Bonnie Gerard, 'Victorian Things, Victorian Words: Representation and Redemption in Gaskell's *North and South*', *Victorian Newsletter*, 92 (1997), 21–4, p. 21.

115 See Charles Darwin, *The Origin of Species*, ed. Gillian Beer (Oxford: Oxford University Press, 1996), pp. 6, 53–4, and Malthus's use of the same phrase in his *Essay*, p. 26.

116 See Angelique Richardson, *Love and Eugenics in the Late Nineteenth Century: Rational Reproduction and the New Woman* (Oxford: Oxford University Press, 2008).

CHAPTER 7

Finding a place for the anti-Malthusian tradition in the Victorian evolution debates

Piers J. Hale

Thomas Robert Malthus holds a prominent place in the history of science primarily because his famous *Essay on the Principle of Population* inspired Charles Darwin to develop his theory of natural selection as the origin of new species.[1] Historians have long debated the precise nature of Malthus's contribution to Darwin's thinking about speciation, and as a result they have also been led to ponder the broader historical and philosophical connections between science and society.[2] Both Darwin's own contemporaries and present-day scholars have commented on the connections between the Malthusian struggle for existence that Darwin presented as being central to natural selection and the competitive individualism of nineteenth-century capitalism, and I shall recapitulate the main insights of that literature here. Building on this, however, I want to argue that we have much to gain from broadening our view of contemporary reactions to the Malthusian elements of Darwin's work. While historians have noted the anti-Malthusian evolutionary ideas of the Russian naturalist Peter Kropotkin, and a number of scholars have written on the connections between socialism and evolutionary thought, the existence of a rich, sizable and sustained English tradition of anti-Malthusian evolutionism has not yet been fully appreciated.[3] I want to suggest that if we acknowledge this counter-tradition, which ran throughout the nineteenth and into the twentieth century, we reveal a contest over the moral meaning of evolution that demands a revision of our understanding of the politics of evolution in the period. Throughout the long nineteenth century there was little doubt that the mechanisms of evolution, and thus our evolutionary history, spoke to the kinds of creatures that humans had become and, in consequence, to how best to organize society. Historians have long emphasized the links between evolutionary theory and capitalism, but Kropotkin was only one of a significant number of people who contended that, rightly understood, the mechanisms of evolutionary progress were grounded in the cooperative behaviours of mutual aid and that a scientifically informed politics should be built upon and foster those qualities. As the historian Adrian Desmond has pointed out, anti-Malthusian evolutionism predated Darwin's work, and thus, when Darwin allied evolutionism with Malthusian political economy, he was writing very much against the grain, and by doing so he made the idea palatable to middle-class men of science.[4] What I particularly want to point out here, however, is that this anti-Malthusian tradition persisted despite Darwin's publication. Indeed, rather than reject Darwin's contribution to evolutionary science, many of Darwin's contemporaries embraced Darwin's name and evolutionary message, but rejected the Malthusian individualism that Darwin had made central to natural selection in *On the Origin of Species*. Acknowledging this reveals that the political implications – and thus the moral meaning – of evolution were much more aggressively contested than we have hitherto recognized.

The significance of Darwin's Malthusian moment

In 1876 Darwin turned 67. That summer, looking back on a long and successful career, he recorded in his autobiography what many historians have come to regard as the signal moment in the history of Western science:

> In October 1838,[5] that is, fifteen months after I had begun my systematic enquiry, I happened to read for amusement Malthus on Population, and being well prepared to appreciate the struggle for existence which everywhere goes on from long-continued observation of the habits of animals and plants, it at once struck me that under these circumstances favourable variations would tend to be preserved, and unfavourable ones to be destroyed. The result of this would be the formation of new species. Here, then, I had at last got a theory by which to work.[6]

Yet, as Sandra Herbert noted back in 1971, prior to the discovery of key missing pages from Darwin's notebooks in which he recorded his developing thoughts on evolution, it was far from clear exactly why Darwin gave Malthus so much credence, either in his autobiography or in *Origin*. Indeed, a number of scholars argued that there was evidence that Darwin's reading of Malthus was much less significant. In a letter he had written to fellow naturalist Alfred Russel Wallace in April 1859, Darwin had given a quite different account of the development of his thinking on the origin of new species. Here he clearly emphasized the significance of the information he had derived from his study of animal breeding – apparently over and above anything he might have taken from Malthus. Wallace had only recently told Darwin of his own very similar ideas about speciation,

which prompted Darwin to recount the origins of his own thoughts on
the matter: 'I came to the conclusion that selection was the principle of
change from the study of domesticated productions; and then, reading
Malthus, I saw at once how to apply this principle.'[7] Here the implication
appeared to be that Darwin had developed the theory of natural selection prior to reading Malthus; Malthus had only been useful in so far
as it helped him to see how his theory might be applied to the natural
world. The difference might appear to be a small one, but for Darwin
scholars (and, I trust, for scholars of Malthus), its significance is far from
trivial: was Malthus Darwin's inspiration for natural selection or not?

Among those historians who saw the role of Malthus's influence as
less than other influences were some of the most notable Darwin scholars of the day; not only Gertrude Himmelfarb and Loren Eiseley, whose
Darwin and the Darwinian Revolution, and *Darwin's Century* had respectively secured their reputations within what was becoming known as 'the
Darwin industry', but the experimental embryologist and Darwin scholar,
Sir Gavin de Beer.[8] Himmelfarb acknowledged that it was Malthus who
had set Darwin on the path to thinking about the mechanisms of evolution, but had provided no more than an awareness of the struggle for
existence. In this respect, she believed, Malthus's influence concerned
'not how the struggle for existence affected the quality of the population,
but simply how it limited its numbers'.[9] Eiseley, while equally sceptical
of Malthus's role in the development of Darwin's thought, allowed even
less. It was from Lyell, who had cited the Swiss naturalist Augustin de
Candolle, that Darwin had obtained his ideas of the struggle for existence, and not from Malthus at all, later citing them both in this respect
in *Origin*.[10] Further, from what Darwin had recorded in his notebooks
in 1837, Eiseley was convinced that 'Darwin had grasped what was to
become the essential principle of his theory before reading Malthus',
Malthus giving him only an 'increased growth of confidence in his previously perceived idea'. Eiseley cited the opinion of Darwin's son, Francis,
to substantiate this claim. Francis Darwin argued that there was evidence
in his father's notebooks that Darwin had arrived at the idea of natural
selection prior to reading Malthus. This opinion was echoed by Gavin de
Beer, who had recently edited the manuscript pages of Darwin's notebook
for publication and based his conclusions on a detailed study of their contents. He too believed that Darwin had described selection prior to his
first mention of Malthus.[11]

This seemed conclusive, but as Herbert pointed out in her 1971 reflection on this period of scholarship, the discovery of new information can

unsettle even the most decided judgements, and this is exactly what had happened in 1967 when previously lost notebook pages came to light. Among them were the crucial pages in which Darwin recorded his reading of Malthus and the insights that struck him as he did so.[12]

> 28th. We ought to be far from wondering of changes in numbers of species, from small changes in nature of locality. Even the energetic language of ~~Malthus~~ <Decandolle> does not convey the warring of the species as inference from Malthus ... population in increase at geometrical ratio in FAR SHORTER time than 25 year – yet until the one sentence of Malthus no one clearly perceived the great check amongst men ... – One may say there is a force like a hundred thousand wedges trying force into every kind of adapted structure into the gaps of in the oeconomy of Nature, or rather forming gaps by thrusting out weaker ones. <The final cause of all this wedgings, must be to sort out proper structure, & adapt it to change.>[13]

This turned what was becoming conventional wisdom on its head; Darwin had started reading Malthus on 28 September 1838, putting it down five days later. The clarification of this date placed his reading of Malthus prior to any direct mention of selection and, importantly, we can see that it was Malthus that led Darwin to formulate the 'wedgings' metaphor – which, as Darwin here articulated it, was quite clearly a selective process.

From her own detailed consideration of the now-expanded notebook archive, Herbert conceded that Darwin had certainly given some attention to the artificial selection practiced by animal breeders prior to reading Malthus, but this had been in relation to his study of variation and heredity, not, at this point in his thinking, as an analogy for a selective process in nature – as he had indicated had been the case in his letter to Wallace. Darwin's autobiographical recollections, Herbert argued, now trumped the letter to Wallace, in which Darwin had, she believed, misspoken.[14]

Historians should always be wary of thinking that matters can be settled conclusively, either by the weight of the available evidence, or by any other means. Subsequent to Herbert claiming to have closed the book on Malthus and Darwin, the historian and philosopher Michael Ruse drew our attention to the fact that there was much more in the archive pertinent to this question than Darwin's notebooks, letters and autobiography. Darwin both owned and had annotated a number of pamphlets on animal breeding prior to his September–October reading of Malthus; most notable among them being Sir John Sebright's *The Art of Improving the Breeds of Domestic Animals* and John Wilkinson's *Remarks on the Improvement of Cattle*. Both Sebright and Wilkinson had acknowledged the power of artificial selection in creating new breeds and Darwin had marked up his copies of these works in such a way as to demonstrate that he understood this point and, crucially, that he had done so some six months prior to his reading of Malthus.[15] Ruse's contribution fills out our picture of events in a manner that subsequent historians have found compelling, for Ruse acknowledges that despite recognizing the power of artificial selection in these breeders' works, Darwin's notes show that he could not see how this observation could be applied to nature. It was only through reading Malthus that Darwin appreciated both the intensity of the struggle for existence in nature and recognized that it would act as a selective force. Thus, Ruse's account reconciles both Darwin's recollection in his auto-biography, in which he attributed such significance to Malthus, with his letter to Wallace, in which he had claimed that Malthus had led him to see how the breeders' power of selection could be applied to nature.

Ruse did not dispute that Malthus was 'of absolutely crucial import-ance' to Darwin's development of natural selection, however, for even if Darwin had recognized artificial selection as a potential model for the natural world, it was Malthus that prompted him to see how it might actually operate as such.[16] Thus, even though Herbert misread the signifi-cance of Darwin's appreciation of artificial selection, she did recognize two related points regarding what Darwin had taken from Malthus, and they are arguably far and away the most important. The first was regarding the nature of the struggle for existence; the second related to its consequences.

As Eiseley pointed out, prior to his reading of Malthus Darwin had taken his conception of the struggle for existence from Charles Lyell's *Principles of Geology*, and he, in turn, had taken it from the Swiss nat-uralist Augustin de Candolle.[17] Rather than seeing the 'warring of spe-cies' as a dynamic force for change, however, as Herbert pointed out, both Lyell and de Candolle had seen it as the mechanism that ensured stability in the natural economy.[18] A Lyellian conception of the struggle for exist-ence would therefore undermine, rather than underpin, a mechanism for the formation of new species. As Herbert put it: 'Lyell's concentration on competition at the species level could well have numbed – and I believe did – Darwin to the evolutionary potential of the struggle for existence at the individual level.'[19] In light of reading Malthus, however, the struggle for existence took on a wholly new tenor. 'Even the energetic language of de Candolle does not convey the warring of the species as inference from Malthus.' The war of nature was much more intense than Darwin had hitherto recognized and – and this is the second point – the consequence was that in such a vicious struggle for life, even the smallest difference between one organism and another would make a difference. The war of nature was a war between individuals, not between species. Herbert again:

> Malthus, by showing what terrible pruning was exercised on the individuals of one species, impelled Darwin to apply what he knew about the struggle at the species level to the individual level, seeing that survival at the species level was the record of evolution, and survival at the individual level its propulsion.[20]

Without this recognition, Darwin could by no means have conceived of a natural selection that echoed the selective process he had read so much about in the breeders' manuals. The selective power of this competition would be such that, focused on weeding out all but the best-adapted organisms, it could change the character of entire populations – a shift to what the systematist, ornithologist and some-time historian of science Ernst Mayr has called 'population thinking'.[21] Darwin recognized that given enough time, such a theory of natural selection could indeed explain the origin of new species.

Biology and society

While historians and historically inclined biologists debated the significance of Malthus's work for the development of Darwin's theory, it was only following the publication of Robert M. Young's signal essay 'Malthus and the Evolutionists' in 1969 that debate about Darwin's 'Malthusian moment' took a more sociological turn. Rather than limit his investigation of the Darwin–Malthus connection to an inquiry regarding what Darwin might have taken from his reading of Malthus, Young constructed an altogether more far-reaching thesis; namely, that science was a much more social enterprise than historians of science had hitherto acknowledged. Malthus's work was accepted as speaking to natural history as well as political economy. The fact of Darwin's having read Malthus was therefore not only relevant for reconstructing how Darwin developed his theory (and for asking questions about the relationship between prevailing ideas about political economy and those of biology), it was also relevant for its reception.[22] Young, a Marxist scholar, argued that theories of political economy, natural history and natural biology were intimately and inextricably linked; these were not the exclusive categories that biology, theology and economics were later to become.[23] Young compared the impact that reading Malthus had had upon a number of contemporary thinkers, including the Scottish theologian and political economist Thomas Chalmers, Charles Lyell and Wallace, among others. It is clear that the meaning of Malthus was very much contested.[24]

Young's article signalled a move among historians of science, and among historians of biology in particular, to look much more closely at the connections between science and society. In their impressive biography, *Darwin: The Life of a Tormented Evolutionist* (1991), Adrian Desmond and James Moore made exactly these kinds of connections their focus, arguing that Darwin's science was very much the product of the society in which it was formed. As Desmond and Moore noted, 'Darwin's biological initiative matched advanced Whig social thinking'; by emphasizing the relative merits of each individual organism, natural selection was 'a mechanism that was compatible with the competitive free-trading ideas of the ultra-Whigs'.[25] The political connotations of Malthusian selection coloured not only Darwin's theorizing, but how his readers would read *Origin* when it was eventually published some 20 years later.

The connection between natural selection and Whig political economy did not go unnoticed by Darwin's contemporaries. Significantly, in the immediate aftermath of the publication of *Origin*, Thomas Huxley, the young comparative anatomist who would go on to adopt the title of 'Darwin's Bulldog', embraced Darwin's work not only as a notable contribution to natural history, but as 'a veritable Whitworth gun in the armoury of liberalism' – the hexagonal rifling of the Whitworth barrel gave it a superior range over conventional firearms, making it, quite literally, unanswerable.[26] Huxley was not alone in reading *Origin* as a tool in the service of liberal ideology. In the immediate aftermath of publication, Darwin had written to Lyell with some amusement that he had 'received in a Manchester Newspaper rather a good squib, showing that I have proved "might is right," & therefore that Napoleon is right & every cheating Tradesman is also right'.[27] The paper in question was the *Manchester Guardian*, the article, 'National and Individual Rapacity Vindicated by the Law of Nature'. The *Manchester Guardian* had been founded in 1821 by a group of nonconformist mill owners. Uncompromising in its editorial policy, the paper spoke for the interests of what in 1846 Benjamin Disraeli had christened the 'Manchester School' of Cobden, Bright, and the Free Trade Hall.[28]

Others who recognized the connection between Darwin's work and the prevailing political economy of liberal capitalism were less enthusiastic, however. Having recently read *Origin* for a second time, Karl Marx wrote to his comrade and friend Friedrich Engels, that 'it is remarkable how Darwin rediscovered, among the beasts and plants, the society of England with its division of labour, competition, opening up of new markets, "inventions," and Malthusian "struggle for existence." It is Hobbes' *bellum omniun contra omnes.*'[29] These few voices were representative of broader opinion; indeed, those who did not read political implications into *Origin* were few and far between. Given the social and political circumstances in which Darwin published, his repeated citation of Malthus in *Origin* made it unsurprising that his work was read in this way. This assessment was seemingly validated by the fact that in the fifth edition, which was published in 1869, Darwin adopted Herbert Spencer's phrase 'the survival of the fittest' to describe his theory of natural selection.[30]

Huxley ensured that this view of the *Origin* persisted throughout the nineteenth century. As Adrian Desmond has shown, Huxley was deeply committed to advancing a liberal Whig agenda in which merit rather than birth was rewarded.[31] In 1888, Huxley published the article 'The Struggle for Existence: A Programme' in the journal *Nineteenth Century*, in which he portrayed humans as not only at odds with nature, but at odds with each other. It was a piece of writing that reflected Huxley's attempt to make sense of a changing world; a world coloured not only by the rise of organized labour and the rise of a new collectivist liberalism, but also by personal tragedy.

The essay was written-up from a speech he had delivered to the Technical Education Association at Manchester at the end of November 1887; the city was raising taxes to fund local technical education, an act that was not without controversy, and Huxley had been eager to lend his support. Yet, just as he was preparing to travel to Manchester, his daughter Mady was taken ill, and despite Huxley's best efforts to get her the help she needed, she died after only a few days. This was not the first time that Huxley and his wife Henrietta had had to grapple with the death of a child, but it was clearly no easier to deal with a second time around. Back in 1860, his first-born son, Noel, had died of scarlet fever and despite his medical training, Huxley had been helpless to stop him from slipping away. Now Mady too was lost at only 28 years of age. In shock and in grief, Huxley scribbled lecture notes and caught the train to Manchester, refusing to break his appointment to speak on the 29th.

In his lecture, Huxley was a loose cannon, firing off shot in all directions. He lashed out at former allies like Herbert Spencer, who maintained that laissez-faire was the true liberal ideology. Those who would emulate the overwhelming carelessness of nature and attempt to replicate its amoral war of each against all were woefully misguided, Huxley argued. Another broadside once again blasted natural theologians – Huxley's old enemy – and a third was aimed at the romantic notions of radials and socialists who shared the propensity to see nature as a place of beneficence and harmony.[32] Anyone who saw nature as a beneficent guide to human action was in his sights, and he was determined in his belief that they could not be more wrong.

The lecture, although revised for publication, was still raw. Huxley, who had always been ambivalent about the ability of natural selection alone to form new species, brought the full force of a Malthusian natural world down upon the ambitions and aspirations of mankind. Life was a ruthless and relentless struggle for existence and even man's best efforts to sue for peace would ultimately prove futile. Again, it was Malthus who had convinced him that this was so: 'One of the most essential conditions, if not the chief cause, of the struggle for existence, is the tendency to multiply without limit, which man shares with all living things,' he wrote.[33] Even if society might temporarily suspend the full implications of the Malthusian law of the struggle for existence through the growth of ethical feeling, the expansion of social welfare, of education and the application of science and technology to industry, ultimately he believed, the natural tendency of mankind to reproduce would undermine even the best organized society. This was a thesis he expanded upon most famously in his 1893 Romanes Lecture 'Evolution and Ethics'.[34]

Of course, while Huxley attacked his opponents for attempting to look to nature for guidance on how to best organize society, despite his claims to the contrary, he was guilty of the same offence. Huxley was adamant that nature beset society on all sides, and that the only way to counter this was to organize society to resist the challenge. The state of Huxley's mind was such that even though he saw this struggle against nature as the lot of mankind, he was also convinced that it was ultimately futile. Nevertheless, he delivered his address in Manchester, arguing the necessity of a technical education and the means to pay for it. In doing so he sought a middle road for liberalism, in between the laissez-faire ideology of the 'let-alone' school and the state socialism being pedalled by the growing number of revolutionary organizations that had been fostered by the economic hardship and vicious social policies of the previous decade. Huxley, who had long considered himself the workingman's friend, now found himself arguing the necessity of curbing wages in order to keep English industry at the cutting edge. There was no hope to be gained from 'fiddle-faddling with the distribution of wealth' as the socialists proposed; 'a moderate price for labour, is essential to our success as competitors in the markets of the world', he argued.[35] Huxley marshalled Darwinian ideas in the service of what Michael Freeden has termed the 'new liberalism', a collectivist political economy, which Huxley promoted as being in the national interest.[36]

Here I would like to ask that we pause. It is clear from the account I have given so far that the general consensus among historians is that Darwin's reading of Malthus was crucial to the development of his theory of natural selection. It is also clear that both historians and Darwin's contemporaries recognized that the incorporation and explicit acknowledgement of Malthus into his theory made natural selection, to use Desmond and Moore's words, 'a mechanism that was compatible with the competitive free-trading ideas of the ultra-Whigs'. As Huxley exemplifies, from at least the late 1880s (and, in fact, Huxley was arguing this point against Herbert Spencer in the early 1870s), it also served reformist liberals well, as they sought a justification for a role of government in advancing science, education and other social policies in what they perceived to be the nation's interest.[37] In the context of a historiography that gives so much emphasis to the Malthusian nature of Darwin's work (and despite Young's contention that the meaning of terms like 'Malthusian' are far from fixed and uncontested), the claim made by the Russian anarchist naturalist and geographer Peter Kropotkin, that a correct understanding of Darwin's work was much less Malthusian – by which he meant much less competitive and individualistic – seems anomalous, at best. After all, Darwin had clearly stated that he had not only been inspired by Malthus, but that natural selection (and not just the struggle for existence) was 'the doctrine of Malthus applied with manifold force to the whole animal and vegetable kingdoms'.[38] Indeed, in the vast majority of the extant scholarship on the history of evolutionary thought Kropotkin stands alone as the foreign revolutionary who argued that mutual aid was the most significant factor in evolution.

Kropotkin's anti-Malthusian Darwinism

Kropotkin was an anarchist-socialist, best known for his work *Mutual Aid: A Factor in Evolution*, published in 1902. *Mutual Aid* was a collection of essays that had begun as a response to Huxley's 1888 essay 'The Struggle for Existence', and which appeared in the same journal as Huxley's essay had, *Nineteenth Century*. Kropotkin thought Huxley's essay an 'atrocious article', and he rejected the presumptions that Huxley had made not only about the state of nature, but about human nature and the history and significance of the dominant factors in evolution as well.[39]

Kropotkin had first read *Origin* while in Siberia and had eagerly sought to test Darwin's insights in the field. However, as he reported in his introduction to *Mutual Aid*, the war between each and every individual was nowhere in evidence; rather, his observations led him to conclude that those organisms that practised mutual aid were much more likely to survive and reproduce than were those that were out-and-out individualists.

> I recollect myself the impression produced upon me by the animal world of Siberia when I explored the Vitim regions in the company of so accomplished a zoologist as my friend Polyakoff was. We both were under the fresh impression of the *Origin of Species*, but we vainly looked for the keen competition between animals of the same species which the reading of Darwin's work had prepared us to expect.[40]

Certainly organisms of one species occasionally came into competition with those of another species, but far more often the struggle he witnessed was the struggle to exist in the face of a harsh and unforgiving environment. Indeed, and as Kropotkin went on to document, the more social species were by far the fittest, in Darwinian terms, and humankind was perhaps foremost among them.

With this evidence in hand, Kropotkin was therefore surprised to find that the majority of the scientific community shared Huxley's view of life. 'I found the interpretation of the "struggle for life" in the sense of a war-cry of "Woe to the Weak," raised to the height of a commandment in nature revealed by science, almost a matter of religion,' he lamented. The only exceptions among his English scientific friends were the editor of the journal *Nineteenth Century*, James Knowles (who had encouraged Kropotkin to write his riposte to Huxley), and the entomologist who was at that time also secretary to the Royal Geographical Society, Henry Walter Bates.[41] Bates agreed that Kropotkin's interpretation of nature was 'True Darwinism', and that that of Huxley and his followers was wrong. He confessed to Kropotkin it was 'a shame to think of what they have made of Darwin's ideas'.[42]

Kropotkin blamed Huxley for popularizing an association between Darwinism and capitalist individualism. After all, and as Kropotkin was well-aware, aside from the one sentence in which he had noted that 'Light will be thrown on the origin of man and his history', Darwin had said practically nothing about the implications of evolution for mankind in *Origin*.[43] Huxley had missed the significance of Darwin's insistence that his appeal to Malthus had been but a metaphor that he had intended also include 'dependence of one being on another'.[44] Indeed, Kropotkin went on to point out that in *Descent of Man*, in which Darwin actually had given his views on human evolution, he had clearly pointed out that mankind was a deeply social species and highlighted the importance of mutual aid throughout the natural history of mankind.[45]

Kropotkin did not absolve Darwin of all responsibility for the way in which Huxley and his like had misread the implications of his theory, however. While Darwin had stated clearly that he had intended Malthus only as a metaphor, Kropotkin suggested that on a number of occasions Darwin had also taken his own metaphor too literally. Further, when it came to the 'Theory of Divergence', which was the central element of Darwin's theory of speciation, Kropotkin pointed out that Darwin had asserted the relentless extermination of one species by another as a fact, whereas he should have also recognized that to talk in terms of 'extermination' was at best another metaphor for what was actually taking place in nature, and not a particularly good one at that. Kropotkin argued that it was much more often the case that the replacement of one species by another occurred by mechanisms other than conflict and extermination. Rather, he observed the migration of ill-adapted organisms to regions where they might exploit less competitive niches, suggesting this was a means to avoid a struggle for scarce resources. He also suggested that it was quite likely that the less fit organisms might adapt directly to their environment so as to be able to subsist better from different resources, rather than engage in a fight they were ill-equipped to win.[46]

As I have noted above, in the past, scholars have dismissed Kropotkin as having either missed the point – Darwin had, after all, insisted that his theory was grounded in Malthus's work – or been misled by his own political convictions – Kropotkin saw in nature what he wanted to see. However, not only has recent scholarship gone a long way to recover the full weight of Kropotkin's scientific credentials, but so too should we be mindful of the sociologist of science David Bloor's observations about being even-handed in our historical analysis.[47] If we are going to analyse the merit of Kropotkin's science in light of his political commitments, then we should do likewise for Darwin, Huxley and others who embraced evolution. In so doing, it is no longer legitimate to reject Kropotkin's perception that mutual aid was a significant factor in evolution simply because this fit well with his politics any more than we should reject the views of Huxley in light of the fact that his conception of nature matched his own political convictions.

In one of his many popular essays on evolution and its history, Stephen Jay Gould once argued that 'Kropotkin was no crackpot', but even Gould thought that Kropotkin was an outlier in the range of responses to Darwin. He admitted that he too had long seen Kropotkin as 'daftly idiosyncratic, if undeniably well meaning', until he read Dan Todes's work putting Kropotkin in the context of the response of Russian biologists to Darwin.[48] While it is certainly the case that Todes has done a lot to explain the contextual origins of Kropotkin's views – an emphasis upon mutualism in evolution was common among Russian naturalists[49] – where he has not been overlooked all together, the tendency has still been to put him in a minority of one when viewed in the context of English biology – as Kropotkin's own comments about the views of all but two of his English associates in the scientific community appear to illustrate. Indeed, this view of Kropotkin as an isolated figure is repeated even in the very best of more recent scholarly consideration of Kropotkin. Mark Borrello and Oren Harmen have each done a lot to rehabilitate Kropotkin's scientific credentials, Borrello noting that he had travelled extensively on scientific expeditions supported by the Imperial Russian Geographic Society, and wrote a number of scholarly articles about his discoveries and co-authored the prestigious Olekmin-Vitim expedition's scientific report. Further, Kropotkin was elected a member of the Imperial Geographic Society and was awarded the 1868 gold medal for his work, and in 1870, was appointed secretary of the society's section of mathematical and physical sciences. He published articles both while imprisoned for his political views and upon his escape to London, these including articles in the journal *Nature* as well as *Nineteenth Century*. As Borrello notes, in 1893 he became a member of the British Association for the Advancement of Science, reported to the Royal Geographic Society of London, and in 1896 was offered a chair in geology at Cambridge University (although he declined the position as it was contingent upon his giving up activist politics).[50] However, while it is clearly no longer tenable to assert that Kropotkin was purely an amateur naturalist, both Harman and Borrello still characterize Kropotkin as an anomalous figure; a lone advocate of group selection adrift in a sea of individualists.[51] What I want to contend is that this does not give an accurate reflection of just how contested the politics of evolution were throughout the nineteenth and into the twentieth century.[52] It is not enough merely to take Kropotkin's science seriously – Borrello, Harman and Lee Dugatkin have made this point well – rather, we need to recognize that he was but one figure in a long tradition of British anti-Malthusian evolutionism.

If we pay attention to those whom Huxley attacked in his 1888 essay 'The Struggle for Existence', it is clear that he was rejecting influential contemporary views of nature, human nature and of the relationship between nature and society. As I have pointed out above, he was eager to undermine not only the natural theologians who argued that the beneficence that they saw in nature was indicative of the goodness of a benevolent God, but to undermine the radicals and socialists who also saw nature through romantic eyes. When we look to both radical and socialist newspapers and journals of the period (the British socialist movement had its origins in the London radical clubs), we find that the embrace of evolutionary ideas was widespread among both radicals and socialists, and so too was a rejection of the politics that had become associated with Malthus's name and ideas.

The anti-Malthusian evolutionary tradition in England

As Adrian Desmond has shown, both the idea of evolution and the recognition that it had significant political implications predated the publication of *Origin*. This is something that is easily overlooked in a story of the discovery of evolution that begins with Darwin, as many accounts of the history of evolution do. Further, those unfamiliar with this earlier period might be surprised to discover that prior to the 1860s, the politics of evolution were Francophile, radical, mutualist and used to advance a much more egalitarian politics than the competitive Whig ideals with which evolution became associated after 1859. While the respectable gentlemen of science at Oxford and Cambridge universities did not acknowledge evolution as good science (in large part, because they did not think it good politics), it was rife in both the London medical schools as well as in radical clubs across the nation.[53]

As not only Desmond, but also Paul Elliott have shown, evolutionary views were deeply engrained in British radicalism.[54] Not only were the works of the French evolutionists, Jean Baptiste Lamarck, Étienne Geoffroy Saint-Hilaire and Étienne Serres well known, but so too were those of Erasmus Darwin. Erasmus Darwin, Charles Darwin's grandfather, had long embraced an evolutionary natural history that he interwove with his radical politics – inspiring William Paley's *Natural Theology* (1802) in critical response.[55] When Malthus published his essay in 1798, he did so as a response to the radical views of both the Englishman William Godwin and the Frenchman Nicolas de Condorcet. Godwin and Condorcet had argued that as a result of the expansion of the role and place of reasoned discussion in society, both the individual and society would undergo a continual progressive development. Malthus's work was thus read by radicals as a direct attack upon their most fundamental beliefs about the nature and future of mankind, and, as a result as Malthus's biographer Patricia James has pointed out, the radical press was populated with refutations of Malthus for the next 30 years.[56]

Radicals of all stripes lined up to castigate Malthus for his opinions from the outset; however, it was the debate leading up to the passage of the Poor Law Amendment Act of 1834, the year in which Malthus died, that provoked the most concerted and most vitriolic attacks on his ideas. The one-time radical poet, Robert Southey called Malthus 'an apostle of the rich'; he was both amazed and appalled by the 'stupid ignorance of the man'; the essay, he wrote, was typical of the trend towards 'mediocrity in literature', it's 'insipidity' was 'well suited to a weak intellect' and had thus appealed to 'the shallow, the selfish, the sensual, and the vain'. It was, he concluded, 'rubbish'.[57] The journalist William Hazlitt, who by the 1830s had little else to say in agreement with Southey, attacked Malthus's 'shameless and cruel sophisms'; the book, he said, was no more than 'a miserable reptile performance' of an 'ice-cold adder-like selfishness which he elevated into a virtue and employed for the soul purpose of torturing the poor with the pretence of reforming their morals'.[58] To William Cobbett, who was arguably England's most famous radical, Malthus was 'a monster in human shape', further expressing his less-than-charitable opinion of Malthus in the following extract from an open letter ostensibly addressed to him: 'I have, during my life, detested many men; but never anyone so much as you. Your book on Population contains matter more offensive to my feelings, even than that of the Dungeon Bill.'[59]

In addition to the ready access to the writings of Lamarck and Erasmus Darwin in the libraries of the Derbyshire Philosophical Society and other similar radical organizations, as Desmond acknowledges, authors of penny pamphlets 'cannibalized fragments of Lamarck's evolutionary biology' to support their ideals, 'radical artisans abhorred Malthus's doctrines and the callous anti-working class legislation passed in their name. By contrast they envisaged society progressing through cooperation, education, emancipation, technological advance, and democratic participation.'[60] Desmond has documented the extent to which the medical schools in Edinburgh and in London were a hotbed of radical anti-Malthusian evolutionary politics from the 1820s. Among only the more notable were Thomas Wakley, Robert Knox, Patrick Matthew and Robert Grant – the last of whom was tutor to the young Charles Darwin while he was enrolled at the medical school in Edinburgh, and whom, as Darwin later recalled, had 'burst forth in high admiration of Lamarck and his views on evolution'.[61]

It was in the wake of the 1832 Reform Act, a development that effectively split the radical movement along class lines, that Malthus was embraced by Whig reformers. However, as John Stuart Mill, a self-styled 'philosophical radical', attested, in doing so they turned Malthus's work to suit their own agenda. Mill recorded in his autobiography that during this period of his life, 'Malthus' population principle was quite as much a banner, and point of union among us as any ... This great doctrine, originally brought forward as an argument against the indefinite improvability of human affairs, we took up with ardent zeal in the contrary sense.'[62] Where Malthus had intended to undermine the extremes of Enlightenment faith in progress, the Whigs saw in Malthus a mechanism that would ensure progressive development: one that would not come by nature alone, but by dedication to industry and moral restraint.

The Whig parliamentarian Henry, Lord Brougham, took up Malthusian ideas to this same end, arguing for reform of the Poor Laws that taxed local communities to provide relief to those who were unable to fend for themselves, and had enlisted the aspiring and outspoken author and journalist Harriet Martineau to popularize his politics, which she had done through a series of successful pamphlets.[63] William Cobbett, who could always be relied upon for a cutting turn-of-phrase turned his anti-Malthusian wrath upon Brougham: 'He is the weasel, he is the indigestion, he is the nightmare, he is the deadly malady of the ministry', he ranted, castigating Brougham for giving representation to the 'scotch monsters of the school of Parson MALTHUS', and, as such, for being among 'the most cowardly, the very basest and most scandalously base, reptiles that were ever warmed into life by the rays of the sun'.[64] Cobbett could write and had a long association with the Francophile radical evolutionists, having been a crucial supporter of Thomas Wakley, the founding editor of the radical medical journal *The Lancet*, since its inception in 1823. Wakley modelled his campaign against corruption, nepotism and Anglican privilege in the Royal College of Physicians on Cobbett's style of journalism, and Cobbett joined the materialist evolutionist and convicted blasphemer William Thompson in giving Wakley his support.[65]

Thus by the mid-1830s, Malthus's very name was deeply wedded to Whig politics, and this was the Malthus that Charles Darwin embraced as he looked for a mechanism for the progressive competition he saw going on around him throughout the natural world. By 1859, the Whigs had secured their place at the centre of English politics and parliament, but even then the citing of Malthus's name and doctrine could not be read as being innocent of anti-radical associations. Whereas in the 1820s the very idea of evolution had deeply radical and even socialist connotations, Darwin's appeal to Malthus not only attempted, but ultimately succeeded, in casting the evolutionary process in a very different light, but this transformation in the politics of evolution was not uncontested.

Historians have thus been in error when they have portrayed Kropotkin as a lone figure advancing a mutualist theory of evolution. Evolution had deeply mutualist associations long before the younger Darwin ever encountered the idea – and indeed, when he did, it was through the works of his grandfather and his own working partnership with Robert Grant, as they studied *flustra* or sea matts, a species of bryozoan dredged off the Leith coast in the Firth of Forth.[66] Erasmus Darwin had speculated about an oceanic origin of life, and Darwin was well-aware that Lamarck had written on *flustra* in the same vein and thus, as the historian Rebecca Stott has noted of this period in young Darwin's life, 'evolutionary riddles were to be pursued in the dark crevices of rock pools and on the seabed'.[67] Grant was a part of a later generation of evolutionary radicals, a tradition anti-Malthusian evolutionist politics that ran through into British socialism, which was rejuvenated in the London radical clubs in the 1880s.

From radicalism to socialism

It was in this context that we need to view Kropotkin, for although he was an immigrant to Britain, like many other European revolutionaries who were fleeing oppression in their own countries in the last decades of the nineteenth century, Kropotkin found an intellectual home in the growing socialist movement in England and he was influential. The socialist, artist and craftsman William Morris, who was the author of the utopian novel *News from Nowhere*, was just one of many people who came to share many of Kropotkin's views; the two men became acquainted in the late 1880s, and Kropotkin became an occasional visitor to the Morris household.[68] Set in 2102, in *News from Nowhere* Morris wrote of a socialist future. As the historian Stephen Yeo has pointed out, the book quickly became 'a central text in this period of British Socialism'; and it continues to be admired.[69] However, what has largely been overlooked is that the means by which Morris envisaged social change to be effected was through Darwinian evolutionary means – the kind of anti-Malthusian Darwinism advanced by Kropotkin, that is.[70] Morris, who was particularly outspoken in his opposition to Malthus, considered him to be little more than an apologist for capitalism. Morris rejected what he called 'this foolish Malthusian craze' that was being adopted not only by scientists, but by some of his social-ist associates too (many of the leading lights of the Fabian Society were particularly impressed by Malthus, for instance).[71] Morris responded that if labour was the source of value, as Marx had maintained, then it was impossible that a high birth-rate among the working population could be an explanation of poverty. Poverty was a product of social injustice, he argued, not a fixed law of nature. The vast wealth that stood cheek-by-jowl with such poverty in the growing industrial cities was testament to as much.[72]

Morris hoped to see a world in which everyone had sufficient, in which there were no idle rich, and no one was kept out of work to keep the price of labour artificially low. In *Nowhere*, people produced only what was needed, and had time enough for leisure once their working day was done. The book was subtitled 'an epoch of rest', under socialism Morris foresaw an end to the mindless struggle for existence perpetrated, not by nature, but by capitalism. Once the artificial social arrangements of capitalism had been overthrown, humanity would return to their natural propensity for cooperation and mutualism; there would be no place for the mean-spirited ideological creed of individualism. For Morris, social-ism was not only about social and economic change, but was also a mat-ter of effecting evolutionary change. The means by which socialism was to be brought about and his focus on the quality of life and of labour under socialism, were fundamental in bringing about the evolution of a much more physically and mentally healthy race of people, and, echoing Kropotkin, this was about environment, as well as heredity.[73]

Ambivalence about the Malthusian elements of Darwin's theory were rife throughout the socialist movement. While members of the Fabian Society – a reformist rather than revolutionary organization that sought to bring about socialism by encouraging the ruling political party to enact ever-more social legislation – embraced Malthus as having described the true and natural laws of population growth, many more socialists could not accept that Malthus's work was anything other than apologetics for the status quo. Embracing the idea that Darwin made more sense without the Malthusian elements, J. Willis Harris could write without contradic-tion in *Justice*, the paper of the Social Democratic Federation:

> Every Discovery of Science, every invention of mankind, has been seized upon by the bourgeoisie to delude and exploit the proletariat ... In a like manner the bourgeoisie accept the teachings of Malthus and pervert those of Darwin to bolster up the tottering fabric of society today, and they steal from the armoury of the evolutionist weapons which they use in their own defence.[74]

Clearly, and despite the fact that Darwin had acknowledged Malthus by name, many socialists made the argument that to accept a Malthusian interpretation of evolution was to pervert it. Socialists followed Kropotkin's view that Darwin had intended his reference to Malthus only as a meta-phor, and – as Kropotkin had later pointed out – it was not a particularly good one. Willis Harris here again asserts that evolution had long been a part of socialist ideology, which was illegitimately being appropriated by capitalists in defence of their own worldview.

Of course, not all socialists rejected the Malthusian view of nature. Alfred Russel Wallace, who was particularly appreciative of Morris, Kropotkin and George Bernard Shaw, and who had become a socialist in 1889, had, after all, been inspired by his own reading of Malthus as he worked towards very similar conclusions to Darwin.[75] However, what is clear is that none of them believed that Malthusian struggle should be read in terms of the competition between one individual and another, or that the struggle for existence should be left to play out in human society unhindered; to believe as much, Wallace wrote, was 'the greatest of all delusions'.[76] Humanity, he and many other socialists believed, could raise itself out of the necessity of struggle through the application of technol-ogy to labour, through cooperative work and the fair and equitable dis-tribution of goods to those that needed them. Of course, resources were only half of the Malthusian conundrum, and while many socialists, like Morris and Hyndman, argued that population was no problem, as more labour power could only mean more produce, Wallace was less dismissive of the issue, arguing that the so-called 'law of population' was a product of social conditions rather than an immutable dictate of nature; and that female emancipation would mitigate fertility rates. Basing his arguments on his experience of the many diverse cultures he had encountered on his travels, Wallace argued that female education would discourage early mar-riage and its consequences; indeed, he was among the first to point out the correlation between female education and fertility rates.[77]

Anti-Malthusian ideas continued to dominate socialist understand-ings of the evolutionary process throughout the nineteenth and into the twentieth century. Across the socialist movement the emphasis upon cooperation rather than competition, and the direct adaptation of organisms to their environment won out over arguments about the nat-ural selection of the most competitive individuals. Where natural selec-tion was invoked, it was in the context of group selection. Social groups of organisms – whether of ants, wolves, apes or humans – had won out in competition with other groups that were less successful. Even in these instances, however, the authors were usually keen to remind their readers that the most bitter competition a social group might face was with its environment, and that in these circumstances, cooperative strategies were likely to be more successful than individualistic competitive ones. This kind of argument only increased in socialist discourse to counter the use of group-selectionist interpretations of evolution to justify the international rivalries that would eventually spill out into the First World War.

There is much more that could be said about the range of different ways in which Darwin's theory of evolution was interpreted as having implications for human political organization. Central to understanding Darwinian evolution were interpretations of the moral meaning and political importance of Malthus, and the range of views that passed under cover of his name. However, at the very least, what I hope is clear from what I have said here is that there was a strong and persistent tradition of anti-Malthusian thought in Britain throughout the nineteenth century that had its roots in English radicalism and thrived in the socialist movement that grew out of it.

Conclusion

Recognizing the existence and the strength of this anti-Malthusian tradition in evolutionary thought leads us to a number of conclusions. First, it undermines the historical emphasis upon the connection between evolution and the politics of individualism. There were Darwinian individualists, who argued that nature substantiated the claims of capitalism and laissez-faire, but this is not the whole story. The moral meaning of Darwinism was – and remains – hotly contested. Second, it supports the view that a large part of Darwin's anxiety about publishing *Origin* was not merely to do with the theological implications of evolution, but was about the dangerously Francophile political associations of transmutationism. His repeated assertion that his views were 'the doctrine of Malthus applied with manifold force to the whole animal and vegetable kingdoms', can, I believe, be legitimately read as an attempt to woo a middle-class readership to accept evolution as thoroughly compatible with their own ideological views.[78] Finally, and something that paying close attention to Kropotkin's assessment of the moral meaning of Darwinism reveals, is that there is some merit to his contention that Huxley misrepresented Darwin's views on the matter. Certainly, Darwin was explicit in his acknowledgement of Malthus in his theorizing of natural selection and, again, in *Origin* this was presented as a mechanism that did indeed fit well with the competitive individualism of the industrial economy of the day. However, when Darwin discussed social species, as he did briefly in *Origin* regarding the social insects, and more fully in *Descent of Man* regarding humanity, he described the evolution of humankind not only as a social species, but as a moral species; a species that had evolved moral sensibilities that had been selected on the basis of what was good for society, rather than good for any one individual. While Darwin was no socialist, it is clear that he thought that human evolution was moving towards an ever-more social future, describing his vision of the future evolution of mankind in *Descent of Man* thus:

> As man advances in civilisation, and small tribes are united into larger communities, the simplest reason would tell each individual that he ought to extend his social instincts and sympathies to all the members of the same nation, though personally unknown to him. This point being once reached, there is only an artificial barrier to prevent his sympathies extending to the men of all nations and races.[79]

Further, Darwin looked forward to a day when the moral community was expanded to more fully include all sentient creatures. He continued:

> Sympathy beyond the confines of man, that is humanity to the lower animals, seems to be one of the latest moral acquisitions ... This virtue, one of the noblest with which man is endowed, seems to arise incidentally from our sympathies becoming more tender and more widely diffused, until they are extended to all sentient beings.[80]

While this is not the main point I wish to make in this essay, it gives us a very different understanding of what might be meant by the term 'Darwinian ethics' than we have hitherto been led to expect.

Notes

1 Malthus's influence upon Alfred Russel Wallace has been much less thoroughly attended to, although see James Moore, 'Wallace's Malthusian Moment: The Common Context Revisited', in Bernard Lightman (ed.), *Victorian Science in Context* (Chicago: University of Chicago Press, 1990), pp. 290–311.
2 Robert M. Young pioneered this line of inquiry in his 'Malthus and the Evolutionists: The Common Context of Biological and Social Theory', *Past and Present*, 43 (1969), 109–45.
3 For the breadth of Victorian responses to Malthus, see Robert J. Mayhew, *Malthus: The Life and Legacies of an Untimely Prophet* (Cambridge, MA: Harvard University Press. 2014), pp. 128–55.

4 Adrian Desmond. *The Politics of Evolution: Morphology, Medicine and Reform in Radical London* (Chicago: University of Chicago Press, 1989). As James Secord has pointed out, the anonymous publication of Robert Chambers's *Vestiges of the Natural History of Creation* in 1844 did a lot to make the ideas of evolution acceptable to mid-nineteenth-century middle-class sensibilities. James Secord, *Victorian Sensation: The Extraordinary Publication, Reception, and Secret Authorship of Vestiges of the Natural History of Creation* (Chicago: University of Chicago Press, 2000).

5 According to Darwin's notebooks he actually began reading Malthus's essay on 28 September, finishing it some five days later. See Paul H. Barrett, Peter J. Gautrey, Sandra Herbert, David Kohn and Sydney Smith (eds.), *Charles Darwin's Notebooks, 1836–1844*, (Cambridge: Cambridge University Press, 1987), pp. 374–6; see also Darwin's reading notebooks, included as Appendix IV to Frederick Burkhardt and Sydney Smith (eds.) *The Correspondence of Charles Darwin: Volume 4, 1847–1850* (Cambridge: Cambridge University Press, 1988), pp. 434–573.

6 Nora Barlow (ed.), *The Autobiography of Charles Darwin, 1809–1882* (New York and London: W.W. Norton & Co., 1993), p. 120.

7 Charles Darwin to Alfred Russel Wallace, 6 April 1859, in Frederick Burkhardt and Sydney Smith (eds.), *Correspondence of Charles Darwin: Volume 7, 1858–1859* (Cambridge: Cambridge University Press, 1992), pp. 279–80.

8 Gertrude Himmelfarb, *Darwin and the Darwinian Revolution* (Chicago: Elephant, 1996); Loren Eiseley, *Darwin's Century: Evolution and the Men Who Discovered It* (New York: Double Day, 1958); Gavin de Beer, (ed.), 'Darwin's Notebooks on Transmutation of Species. Part I. First Notebook [B] (July 1837–February 1838)', *Bulletin of the British Museum (Natural History). Historical Series*, 2 (1960), 23–73.

9 Himmelfarb, *Darwin and the Darwinian Revolution*, p. 161.

10 Eiseley, *Darwin's Century*, p. 180.

11 Ibid., pp. 180–1. De Beer cites Francis Darwin, Charles Darwin's son, who referred to evidence from Darwin's notebooks to substantiate this point. De Beer, 'Darwin's Notebooks'.

12 Sandra Herbert, 'Darwin, Malthus and Selection', *Journal of the History of Biology*, 4 (1971), 209–17.

13 Barrett *et al.*, *Charles Darwin's Notebooks*, pp. 374–6, passages indicated by <brackets> indicate Darwin's insertions.

14 Herbert, 'Darwin, Malthus and Selection', p. 212.

15 See Michael Ruse, 'Charles Darwin and Artificial Selection', *Journal of the History of Ideas*, 36 (1975), 339–50, p. 344.

16 Ibid., p. 350.

17 Eiseley, *Darwin's Century*, pp. 101–2.

18 Herbert, 'Darwin, Malthus and Selection', pp. 215–16.

19 Ibid., p. 217.

20 Ibid.

21 Ernst Mayr, *What Evolution Is* (New York: Basic Books, 2001), p.75.

22 Young, 'Malthus and the Evolutionists'.

23 See also Donald Winch, *Riches and Poverty: An Intellectual History of Political Economy in Britain, 1750–1834* (Cambridge: Cambridge University Press, 1996), and Margaret Schabas, *The Natural Origins of Economics* (Chicago: University of Chicago Press, 2005) on this point.

24 Young, 'Malthus and the Evolutionists'.

25 Adrian Desmond and James Moore. *Darwin: The Life of a Tormented Evolutionist* (New York: W.W. Norton, 1992), p. 267.

26 Thomas Huxley, 'The Origin of Species', *Westminster Review*, April 1860.

27 Charles Darwin to Charles Lyell, 4 May 1860, Frederick Burkhardt, Janet Browne, Duncan M. Porter and Marsha Richmond (eds.), *Correspondence of Charles Darwin: Volume 8, 1860* (Cambridge: Cambridge University Press, 1993), pp. 188–9.

28 Asa Briggs, *Victorian Cities* (London: Odhams Press, 1963), p. 125.

29 Karl Marx to Friedrich Engels, 18th June 1862, *Collected Works of Karl Marx and Friedrich Engels: Volume 41* (New York: International Publishers, 1975–2004), 381.

30 Alfred Russel Wallace had urged Darwin to adopt Spencer's phrase to avoid the theistic and teleological associations that many readers of *Origin* were reading into the phrase 'natural selection'.

31 Adrian Desmond, *Huxley: From Devil's Disciple to Evolution's High Priest* (London: Penguin, 1997).

32 Thomas Henry Huxley, 'The Struggle for Existence: A Programme', *Nineteenth Century*, 23:132 (1888), 161–80. This essay was later reprinted as 'The Struggle for Existence in Human Society', in *Collected Essays of T.H. Huxley: Volume 9: Essays in Science*, (London: MacMillan, 1894), pp. 193–236. Further references are to this edition.

33 Huxley, 'The Struggle for Existence in Human Society', pp. 205–6.

34 Thomas Huxley, 'Evolution and Ethics', reprinted in James Paradis (ed.), *Evolution and Ethics: T.H. Huxley's Evolution and Ethics with New Essays on Its Victorian Context and Sociobiological Context* (New Jersey: Princeton University Press, 1989).

35 Huxley, 'The Struggle for Existence in Human Society', pp. 212–13.

36 Michael Freeden, *The New Liberalism: An Ideology of Social Reform* (Oxford: Clarendon, 1978).

37 Desmond and Moore, *Darwin*, p. 267. Huxley had in fact marshalled evolutionary arguments against laissez-faire from as early as 1871 in his essay 'Administrative Nihilism' discussed in Piers J. Hale, *Political Descent: Malthus, Mutualism and the Politics of Evolution in Victorian England*, (Chicago: University of Chicago Press, 2014), pp. 155–205.

38 Charles Darwin, *On the Origin of Species by means of Natural Selection, or the Preservation of Favoured Races in the Struggle for Life* (London: John Murray, 1859), p. 63.

39 Peter Kropotkin, *Memoir of a Revolutionist*, (New York: Grove Press, 1968), p. 499.

40 Peter Kropotkin, *Mutual Aid: A Factor in Evolution*, (London: Freedom Press, 1993), p. 26.
41 Kropotkin, *Memoir of a Revolutionist*, p. 499.
42 Ibid.
43 Darwin, *Origin*, p. 488.
44 Kropotkin, *Mutual Aid*, p. 21, quoting Darwin, *Origin*, p. 62.
45 Kropotkin, *Mutual Aid*, pp. 63–4.
46 Ibid., pp. 65–6.
47 David Bloor, 'The Strong Programme in the Sociology of Science', in *Knowledge and Social Imagery* (Chicago: University of Chicago Press, 1992).
48 Stephen Jay Gould, 'Kropotkin Was No Crackpot', reprinted in *Bully for Brontosaurus: Reflections in Natural History* (New York and London: W.W. Norton & Co., 1992), p. 331.
49 Daniel P. Todes, *Darwin without Malthus: The Struggle for Existence in Russian Evolutionary Thought* (New York: Oxford University Press, 1989).
50 Mark Borrello, *Evolutionary Restraints: The Contested History of Group Selection* (Chicago: University of Chicago Press, 2010), especially pp. 30–1; Oren Harmen, *The Price of Altruism, George Price and the Search for the Origins of Kindness* (New York: Norton, 2010).
51 See Joel Schwartz in 'Robert Chambers and Thomas Henry Huxley, Science Correspondents: The Popularisation and Dissemination of Nineteenth-Century Natural Science', *Journal of the History of Biology*, 32 (1999), 343–83, p. 366.
52 Lee Alan Dugatkin, *The Prince of Evolution: Peter Kropotkin's Adventures in Science and Politics*, (Amazon.com, 2011). Dugatkin notes Kropotkin's popularity among the Jewish community in London, but does little to flesh out the extent to which they shared his biological views as well as his political views.
53 Desmond, *Politics of Evolution*.
54 Paul Elliot, *The Derby Philosophers: Science and Culture in British Urban Society, 1700–1850* (Manchester: Manchester University Press, 2009).
55 Maureen McNeil, *Under the Banner of Science, Erasmus Darwin and his Age* (Manchester: Manchester University Press, 1987), pp. 89–90; David Burbridge, 'William Paley Confronts Erasmus Darwin: Natural Theology and Evolutionism in the Eighteenth Century', *Science and Christian Belief*, 10 (1998), 49–71.
56 Patricia James, *Population Malthus: His Life and Times* (London: Routledge, 1979), as cited in Young, 'Malthus and the Evolutionists'.
57 Robert Southey, 'On the State of the Poor: The Principle of Mr. Malthus's Essay on Population, and the Manufacturing System,' in *Essays Moral and Political*, 2 vols. (London: John Murray, 1832), vol. 1, pp. 75–158, quotations on pp. 78–9.
58 William Hazlitt, quoted in C.M. Maclean, *Hazlitt Painted by Himself* (London: Temple, 1948).
59 William Cobbett to Thomas Robert Malthus, 8 May 1819, quoted in James P. Huzel, *The Popularization of Malthus in Early Nineteenth Century*

England: Martineau, Cobbett and the Pauper Press (Aldershot: Ashgate, 2006), p. 105.

60 Desmond, *Politics of Evolution*, p. 4.

61 Ibid., p. 5; Barlow, *Autobiography of Charles Darwin*, p. 49.

62 John Stuart Mill, *Autobiography of John Stuart Mill* (New York: Signet, 1964), p. xii.

63 Desmond and Moore, *Darwin*, pp. 153–4.

64 Cobbett, quoted in Huzel, *Popularization of Malthus*, p. 106.

65 Cobbett's relationship with the radicals in the London medical establishment has been documented in Desmond, *Politics of Evolution*. Cobbett had supported the foundation of Thomas Wakley's *Lancet* (pp. 15, 375–7), which Desmond describes as the 'medical mirror' of Cobbett's *Political Register* (p. 15). The radical Lamarckian anatomist Robert Grant, incorporated Cobbett's environmentalist concerns into his own articulations of evolutionism.

66 Desmond and Moore, *Darwin*, pp. 31–44.

67 Rebecca Stott, *Darwin and the Barnacle: The History of One Tiny Creature and History's Most Spectacular Breakthrough* (London: Faber & Faber, 2003), p. 5; Paul H. Barrett (ed.), *The Collected Papers of Charles Darwin*, 2 vols. (Chicago: University of Chicago Press, 1977), vol. 2, pp. 285–91. Darwin notes that his own observations are an advance of those 'hitherto observed by Lamarck[,] Cuvier[,] Lamouroux[,] or any other', p. 288.

68 J.W. Hulse, *Revolutionists in London: A Study of Five Unorthodox Socialists* (London: Clarendon Press, 1970), pp. 90–9; Ruth Kinna, 'Morris, Anti-Statism and Anarchy', in Peter Faulkner and Peter Preston (eds.), *William Morris Centenary Essays* (Exeter: University of Exeter Press, 1999), pp. 215–28; Piers J. Hale, 'William Morris, Human Nature and the Biology of Utopia', in P. Bennett and R. Miles (eds.), *William Morris in the Twenty-First Century* (Oxford: Peter Lang, 2010), pp. 107–28.

69 Stephen Yeo, 'A New Life: The Religion of Socialism in Britain, 1883–1896', *History Workshop Journal*, 4 (1977), 5–56.

70 See Patrick Parrinder, 'Eugenics and Utopia: Sexual Selection from Galton to Morris', *Utopian Studies*, 8 (1997), 1–12. I have made this case elsewhere, see Piers J. Hale, 'Of Mice and Men: Evolution and the Socialist Utopia. William Morris, H.G. Wells, and George Bernard Shaw', *Journal of the History of Biology*, 43 (2010), 17–66 and in Chapter 6 of Hale, *Political Descent*.

71 Henry Meyers Hyndman and William Morris, *A Summary of the Principles of Socialism: Written for the Democratic Federation.* (London: Modern Press, 1884), pp. 46–7.

72 Ibid.

73 See, for example, William Morris, *News from Nowhere and Other Writings*, (London: Penguin, 1993), pp. 134, 63, 118. For more on Morris's evolutionary socialism, see Hale, *Political Descent*, pp. 252–300.

74 H. Willis-Harris, 'The Survival of the Fittest', *Justice*, 28 April 1888, p. 2.

75 For Wallace's appreciation of Morris, Kropotkin and Shaw, see Peter Raby, *Alfred Russel Wallace: A Life* (Princeton: Princeton University Press, 2001), p. 273. Malthus led Wallace to emphasize the importance of the 'positive checks to increase' in a species numbers – including 'disease, accidents, war, and famine', rather than competition between individuals for scarce resources (see Raby, *Wallace*, p. 131). See also Greta Jones, 'Alfred Russel Wallace, Robert Owen, and the Theory of Natural Selection', *British Journal of the History of Science*, 35 (2002), 73–96.

76 Frederick Rockell, 'The Last of the Great Victorians: Special Interview with Dr. Alfred Russel Wallace', *The Millgate Monthly*, 7:83 (1912), 657–63, quotation on p. 662.

77 Raby, *Wallace*, pp. 256–7.

78 Darwin, *Origin*, p. 63. Of course, in the context of nineteenth-century England, politics and religious identity cannot be taken as separate entitles. As Dov Ospovat has shown, however, the Malthusian elements of natural selection were quite compatible with the theodicy of natural theology.

79 Charles Darwin, *The Descent of Man, and Selection in Relation to Sex*, 2 vols. (London: John Murray, 1871), vol. 1, pp. 100–1.

80 Ibid., p. 101.

CHAPTER 8

Imagine all the people: Rockefeller philanthropy, Malthusian thinking and the 'peasant problem' in Asia

David Nally

Imagine no possessions
I wonder if you can
No need for greed or hunger
A brotherhood of man
Imagine all the people
Sharing all the world.

– John Lennon, 'Imagine', 1971

As the snow flies
On a cold and grey Chicago mornin'
A poor little baby child is born
In the ghetto

And his mama cries
'Cause if there's one thing that she don't need
It's another hungry mouth to feed
In the ghetto

People, don't you understand
The child needs a helping hand
Or he'll grow to be an angry young man some day.

– Scott 'Mac' Davis, 'In the Ghetto', 1969

Antecedents, antagonists and unlikely alliances

The year before Mac Davis wrote 'In the Ghetto', connecting excess births ('another hungry mouth to feed') to future threats (the 'angry young man' in the ghetto), Stanford biologist Paul Ehrlich published his best-selling book, *The Population Bomb*.[1] Ehrlich opened with a well-known and dire warning: 'The battle to feed all of humanity is over.' According to Ehrlich, mass famines and social upheavals were imminent because of the widespread failure to control human reproduction.[2] Indeed the only imponderable was just how bad things would get: how many millions must perish, Ehrlich asked, before drastic measures are introduced to control unbound human fertility? Whereas Mac Davis's spatial imaginary fixes on the American 'ghetto' – where, significantly, the (white) 'helping hand' is juxtaposed with the angry (black) man – Ehrlich identifies the 'underdeveloped countries' as the source of the problem, a menacing 'global ghetto' that threatens planetary ruin. In a revealing description, Ehrlich makes the Indian city of Delhi a model for the holocaust-to-come, for it is there, in the city's environs amidst the hostile atmosphere of the amorphous crowd, that the population problem reveals itself. The passage is worth citing in full:

> My wife and daughter and I were returning to our hotel in an ancient taxi. The seats were hopping with fleas. The only functional gear was third. As we crawled through the city, we entered a crowded slum area. The temperature was well over 100, and the air was a haze of dust and smoke. The streets seemed alive with people. People eating, people washing, people sleeping. People visiting, arguing, and screaming. People thrusting their hands through the taxi window, begging. People defecating and urinating. People clinging to buses. People herding animals. People, people, people, people. As we moved slowly through the mob, hand horn squawking, the dust, noise, heat, and cooking fires gave the scene a hellish aspect. Would we ever get to our hotel? All three of us were, frankly, frightened ... [S]ince that night I have known the *feel* of overpopulation.[3]

Significantly, Ehrlich claimed that he was first prompted to write about overpopulation after hearing the Indian statesmen, Chidambaram Subramaniam (1910–2000), address an audience at Stanford.[4] In his lecture, Subramaniam singled out a series of important breakthroughs in genetic science, which he saw as the first step toward the massive expansion of farm yields in the global South. He was, of course, describing the scientific breakthroughs later known as the 'Green Revolution', a movement he played no small part in advancing in India. In fact, in the same year Ehrlich published *The Population Bomb*, Subramaniam was a keynote speaker at an international symposium sponsored by the Rockefeller Foundation titled, 'Strategy for the Conquest of Hunger.'[5] The Rockefeller Foundation was the key driver behind the Green Revolution and buoyed by its successes in Mexico – where it had supervised a fourfold increase in wheat production in just 25 years – the philanthropic foundation would soon decide to 'scale up' its programmes to address the problem of global hunger.

Unsurprisingly, in Subramaniam Ehrlich found everything he thought injurious with respect to Western development. For Ehrlich, it was foolish to hope to modernize the 'underdeveloped countries' since more calories would only lead to more births and more famines. Whereas the Rockefeller Foundation and Subramaniam stood for 'seeds of plenty', Ehrlich saw only 'seeds of want'.[6] The reason for the former's optimism seemed to be the self-same reason for the latter's pessimism. Was this a case of two irreconcilable views locked together – Ehrlich playing Mac Davis to Subramaniam's John Lennon?

Perhaps that is how the protagonists saw things – certainly it was Ehrlich's view – but as is often the case, the simple answer is not always the correct one. Part of the argument in this chapter is that the two 'opposing' views converge in important ways that can only be fully understood when filtered through the ideas of a third protagonist: the eighteenth-century scholar, political economist and Church of England cleric, Thomas Robert Malthus.

I shall argue that it is possible to interpret the apparent conflict between Subramaniam/Rockefeller, on the one hand, and Paul Ehrlich, on the other hand, as a twentieth-century version of the arguments involving Malthus and his contemporaries. Those arguments originate in Enlightenment ideas about the self-improvement of humanity and the perfectibility of social order, but by the eighteenth and nineteenth century those beliefs had fractured into a multiplicity of perspectives about the pathway to a better world. Greg Grandin calls this the 'age of competitive redemptions' in which socialists, nationalists, capitalists, millenarians and religious fundamentalists vied with each other to impose their vision of Progress.[7] Malthus's writings on the population question were penned from *within* this tradition of utopian planning. Indeed, it is important to recall that he was writing in a period gripped by social, political and economic convulsions, an age when 'government of the people, by the people, for the people' made 'the people' the focus of alarm. 'Man is born into a world already possessed', Malthus warned, and although he later excised this paragraph (which also contains the oft-quoted line, 'At nature's mighty feast there is no vacant cover for him' ['him' meaning the poor person who could no longer support themselves]), it is clear from the remainder of the *Essay* that 'the people' – particularly the indigent, uprooted and dispossessed – haunt Malthus's thoughts.[8] They are the fear that finds expression in the 'excess' of population, the supernumerary hands that if left to themselves might soon find devil's work.[9] Malthus poses an important and abiding question regarding the future: *in a world of limits, what should those with possessions do about those without?* His *Essay* evokes a circumscribed moment of danger, one located in the swelling ranks of the precarious poor – and he does this, I want to argue, to legitimize a politics of protection against the incursion and threat of competing others.[10]

Of course, the context for Ehrlich's text is quite different, but the sense of danger is no less apparent. The biologist had read the alarmist writings of American eugenicist Fairfield Osborn (1857–1935), who in 1948 published *Our Plundered Planet*, and ecologist William Vogt (1902–68) who published *Road to Survival* the following year. Both books did much to revive Malthusian thinking in the twentieth century.[11] As ever, the timing of Vogt and Osborn's publications is important. Coming at the tail of two murderous world wars, both authors gave expression to fears linking population growth to Armageddon.[12] The invention and use of thermonuclear weapons only heightened anxieties with many – including Ehrlich – describing technologies of mass destruction as the ultimate 'population controlling device'.[13] A pall of fear seemed to envelope global politics. Population growth, future food production, environmental degradation, techno-warfare, the 'loss' of China and the rise of communism – these were the issues that dominated public discussion. In hindsight we might say that postwar society seemed uniquely aware of its own capacity for self-annihilation.

Inside the Rockefeller Foundation, few doubted the seriousness of the population challenge (in fact several were in sympathy with Ehrlich's view that population growth was the *original* cause of human misery), but this realization tended to prompt forward-thinking, pre-emptive action; after all, as one Rockefeller-led report ran, 'To do nothing is to invite despair. To act is to hope.'[14] Notwithstanding such guarded optimism, there was quite a bit of disagreement about what proleptic actions were required: some within the Foundation felt that philanthropy should concentrate its efforts on boosting farm yields, while others demurred favouring instead actions, both technical and socio-psychological, to stymy global birth-rates. These two groups are often separated by scholars into neat divisions – the so-called Cornucopians (who listened to John Lennon) and the (neo-)Malthusian doomsayers (who played Mac Davis) – whereas, in reality, both groups acted from a shared sense of dread about the exponential power of population and its potential to wreak havoc on the world. It is this sense of an incipient menace that galvanized postwar development efforts and, in particular, the decision of philanthropists to turn their attention to the problems of the so-called 'underdeveloped world'. We turn now to Malthus who gave the spectre of population fierce and tangible form.

Malthus and the menace of population

Malthus's famous essay is best known today as a statement about the effects of 'overpopulation' – a word Malthus never actually used – but the first thing to note is that the essay began as a response to the Marquis de Condorcet's (1743–94) views on the 'perfectibility of man', and William Godwin's (1756–1836) writings on political justice and equality. In short, Malthus thought that these progressive ideas were baseless, pernicious and dangerous.

The principal difference between Godwin and Malthus lay in their understanding of the origins of poverty. For Godwin, vice and misery was the outcome of human actions and institutions. Like Giambattista Vico before him, Godwin insisted that people make history and he passionately argued that social progress and moral improvement were attainable goals, but only if society could be freed of the institutions that degrade the population. Chief among those vice-making conventions was private property. In Godwin's view, property is a social institution that aggregates wealth to a few, keeping the many property-less and wracked in poverty. Godwin determined that things need not be so and, like John Lennon, he invited his readers to 'imagine' a very different social arrangement: 'There will be no war, no crimes, no administration of justice, as it is called, and no government. Beside this, there will be neither disease, anguish, melancholy, nor resentment. Every man will seek, with ineffable ardour, the good of all.'[15]

Malthus countered strongly. He begins by attacking the view that human agency creates and perpetuates poverty:

> The great error which Mr. Godwin labours through his whole work is the attributing of almost all the vices and misery that prevail in civil society to human institutions ... [T]he truth is, that though human institutions appear to be the obvious and obtrusive causes of much mischief to mankind, they are, in reality, light and superficial in comparison with those deeper-seated causes of evil which result from the laws of nature.[16]

The order of nature referred to by Malthus is, of course, the tendency for population growth to exceed agricultural productivity. It was the operation of powerful 'checks' on population growth and not the advance of improved civil governance that restored order to society.

However, Malthus does not stop there; Godwin's attack on the evils of private property arguably earns Malthus's sternest rebuke. It was, Malthus argued, 'merely an imaginary picture' to see social salvation in the extirpation of private property, for '[m]an cannot live in the midst of plenty. All cannot share alike in the bounties of nature.'[17] In a powerful passage, Malthus provides a counter-image of society constituted among Godwin's lines, in which 'all men are equal', property is abolished and the fruits of labour are distributed evenly and in accordance with the 'spirit of benevolence'. For Malthus, no system could be contrived that is *more* conducive to the expansion of population and *more* amenable to the removal of the checks that limit human fertility than the one imagined by Godwin. This is so because the 'equalization of property', which Godwin's plan presupposes, destroys not only the landed wealth of the country; more perniciously, it eradicates the powerful principle of self-interest (Malthus's term is 'self-love'), the true source of human industry and social wellbeing.[18] 'The substitution of benevolence, as the masterspring and moving principle of society, instead of self-love', Malthus warned, would lead only to 'violence, oppression, falsehood, misery, every hateful vice and every form of distress'.[19]

In drawing attention to this discussion, we become aware of two further arguments that structure Malthus's thought. For Malthus, 'property' is both a *material* and *psychological* state. It marks the politico-legal basis for possession – that is, property in its conventional sense – but it also, crucially, marks a mode of subjectification – self-love – that he regards as fundamental to the reign of order in society. The point here, as Isabell Lorey perspicaciously notes, is how the very concept of human worth is ineluctably tied to the conditions that support the accumulation of property.[20] In Malthus's view, property, as one of 'two fundamental laws of society' – the other, tellingly, is the bourgeois 'institution of marriage' – has twin instrumental functions. First, it guards against the 'fatal effects' of equality of the kind that Condorcet and Godwin advocated; and, second, by making a world where it is a normative convention that 'everything [is] appropriated' and nothing remains in common, property obliges each and all to labour to support themselves and their offspring or else face permanent destitution. 'A state, in which an inequality of conditions offers the natural rewards of good conduct, and inspires widely and generally the hopes of rising and the fears of falling in society,' cautions Malthus, 'is unquestionably the best calculated to develop the energies and faculties of man, and the best suited to the exercise and improvement of virtue.'[21] Thus, not only do capitalist relations reduce the 'quantity' of the population, they achieve this while also *increasing the population's 'quality'*, making it more virtuous, judicious, industrious and prudential. Malthus's outline of the

normative conditions 'calculated to develop' useful human subjects is, as
we shall see, an issue that continues to inflect population debates.

This leads us to our final point to be discussed regarding Malthus's
Essay. If inequality, as manifest in wage and property relations, is an essential feature of the liberal social order, it stands to reason that almost every
effort to lessen social disadvantage will induce further immiseration.
Hence charity, although it possesses 'moral merit', is ultimately retro-
gressive. In Malthus's view, good intentions do not excuse bad outcomes.
'Hard as it may appear in individual instances,' he wrote, 'dependent
poverty ought to be held disgraceful.'[22] Yet it is important to add here
that while Malthus spoke out against charity – especially the so-called
Speenhamland system of poor relief – he did not in principle oppose the
idea of social improvement. What matters for Malthus is that ameliorative
acts accord with 'natural laws', and that such acts are made concordant
with a liberal understanding of personal freedom wherein the goal is 'to
make every person depend more upon himself and less upon others'.[23]

It seems important to stress that before the success of Malthus's *Essay*,
both market forces and 'misery and vice' were widely understood as elements that the poor and vulnerable ought to be protected against; indeed
this was part of the 'old paternalism' that bound rich and poor together.
Arguably Malthus's lasting achievement was to reconfigure public attitudes so that these formerly nefarious elements were now seen as precon-
ditions for securing the wellbeing of all. In short, one of Malthus's lasting
achievements was to rebrand the age-old cry 'give us our daily bread' as an
assault on private ownership.[24] The poor, then, are recast as a dangerous
residuum to be constrained and held in check in the name of social order.
We miss much of the force of Malthus's arguments if we fail to appreciate the fear that underwrites his unique ontology of poverty as well as the
hope he placed in the corrective powers of capitalism.[25]

Governing through philanthropy

At first blush, Malthusian philosophy seems a strange bedfellow for modern philanthropy. After all, the latter's *raison d'être* is to intervene in the
social in order to improve![26] Yet the two ideas intersect in important ways.
First and most obviously, philanthropy shares with Malthusianism a profound abhorrence of charity. We see this clearly in Andrew Carnegie's
pioneering essay 'Wealth' first published in the *North American Review*
in 1889. Beginning with the assumption that the 'laws of competition' are
natural and overwhelmingly beneficial to society (a view that Malthus

shared), Carnegie nonetheless claims that capitalist societies must undertake some redistribution of wealth if they are to avoid polarizing inequality and destabilizing upheavals. For Carnegie, the great challenge lay in the fact that 'most of the forms in vogue to-day for benefiting mankind only tend to spread among the poor a spirit of dependence upon alms, when what is essential for progress is that *they should be inspired to depend upon their own exertions*'. Like Malthus the concern here is *dependent* poverty. Faced with such problems, Carnegie concluded, 'the best means of benefiting the community is to place within its reach the ladders upon which the aspiring can rise'. In other words, the goal is to help the poor help themselves; self-correction over and above charitable assistance.[27]

The Standard Oil magnate John D. Rockefeller Sr. (1839–1937) certainly agreed with this view. 'The best philanthropy,' he wrote, 'is constantly in search of the finalities – a search for cause, an attempt to cure evils at their source.'[28] This quest for 'the finalities' went hand-in-hand with a hardened belief that 'lasting gains come not from help but from self-help', as Will M. Myers, vice-president of the Rockefeller Foundation, observed.[29] Similarly, Henry Ford extolled the virtues of 'self-reliance' and believed it was his personal duty to mould free-thinking independent citizens.[30] As 'self-made men', Carnegie, Ford and Rockefeller understood success as the outcome of personal qualities – skill, graft, application and resilience. It was therefore of paramount importance that philanthropic acts stoke feelings of self-actualization and personal fulfilment.

The great American philanthropists shared Malthus's faith in the catalysing power of markets. While the philanthropic actions of the 'big three' – Carnegie, Ford and Rockefeller Foundations – were intended to retool free-market capitalism, at all times the aim was to save capitalism from itself, rather than substitute it for another socio-economic system. 'No one, except the most extreme and disaffected elements of our society, is foolish enough to talk about replacing it [capitalism],' wrote John D. Rockefeller III, 'since all other systems have been less successful. If we can preserve the successes and yet change the system to resolve its problems, the revolution in our society will remain nonviolent in nature and our prospects for attaining a desirable future will be immeasurably improved.'[31] Moreover, in answer to the rhetorical question – one that Malthus also posed – why not have complete economic equality among all members of society? Rockefeller responded: 'The answer simply is that it will not work. It would do violence to our ideas of democracy, freedom, free enterprise, and it would destroy incentives.'[32] A better solution was for capitalism to embrace the practice of strategic gift-giving. This suturing of help and markets has encouraged several critics to herald the advent of 'philanthrocapitalism'. It is an awkward neologism, but useful nonetheless in singling out the gradual incorporation of market norms in practices of salvation.[33]

Third and finally, philanthropy draws on Malthusian thinking in so far as it saw the population problem always in relation to a broader set of geopolitical anxieties about mass poverty and its corrosive effects. Writing in 1954, for example, Warren Weaver, leader of the natural sciences division at the Rockefeller Foundation, warned: 'Since the birth of Christ, the population of our planet has ... doubled three successive times. It took 1750 years in all for the first doubling but only 200 years for the next, and only 100 years for the most recent. Population not only increases; it grows like a snowball faster and faster.'[34] Weaver enrolled another metaphor – that of the crowded table – to conjure the threat as real and immediate:

> I assume that you had breakfast this morning at about 7:30 and that you will dine this evening about 12 hours after breakfast. As you sit down to the table tonight, stop for a moment. Ask your wife and children to crowd over and make room, for there will be 35,000 more persons at the world's dinner table tonight than were there this morning for breakfast.[35]

Of course, the metaphor had been used before. In a speech in 1949, the director general of the FAO, Norris E. Dodd, warned that 'tomorrow morning there will be 55,000 more persons for breakfast than there were in the world this morning ... But we are not producing 55,000 more cups of milk a day for the new children ... nor 55,000 more bowls of rice (the image of the 'bowls of rice' is significant, as we shall see).'[36] Malthus also famously warned against admitting the dependent poor to 'nature's mighty feast' (as we noted above, this passage was later excised), and in the 1970s ecologist Garrett Hardin would swap the 'table' for the 'life boat' claiming that 'crowding over' to make room for others would ultimately imperil the security of all.[37] The recycling and updating of the metaphor is certainly revealing, but so too is the fact that a formidable scientist like Weaver (firmly in the 'Cornucopian' corner of the population–food debate), felt it necessary to situate his arguments within a well-established geopolitics of fear. In its early years, American philanthropy had concentrated on discrete problems – the building of public libraries, support for religious institutions, tackling plant viruses and curing human diseases – but now it seemed the world had become more interconnected, unsettled and complex. As Raymond Fosdick, one-time president of the Rockefeller Foundation, warned in his important address, *A Philosophy for a Foundation*, to continue 'serving the welfare of mankind', philanthropists must confront head-on a frightening present marked by 'turbulent and explosive change'. A 'planetary consciousness' was forming, one that imagined the future as fraught with uncertainty. 'A new era had dawned, black and ominous,' reflected Fosdick, and few problems appeared more bleakly imminent than the 'population bomb'.[38]

Philanthropy and the geopolitics of need

A conventional reading of American philanthropy's engagement with the population question would begin with the onset of the Cold War period and John D. Rockefeller III's establishment of the Population Council in 1952. 'JDR', as he was known to colleagues and friends, would oversee the rise of the Population Council into a vanguard organization of the global population movement, but the operation of the Council, particularly as it developed new lines of interest and policy, drew from, and indeed was validated by, historically constituted patterns of thought on the nature of poverty and the best means for its redress.[39] In particular, two early Rockefeller-led organizations, well known to JDR, played an important part in his thinking on population matters and how they intersected with a wider politics of underdevelopment.

The first of these organizations was the General Education Board (GEB), a subsidiary philanthropy of the Rockefeller Foundation incorporated in 1903.[40] The GEB was founded to promote the cause of public education in the United States but it soon struck those involved that the moral uplift of the population would not be possible without a corresponding elevation in the people's material conditions. This led to incorporation of new medical and agricultural programmes, the latter proving pivotal to the Foundation's appreciation of rural poverty and underdevelopment. Conditions in the US South were particularly worrisome when Wallace Buttrick, secretary of the GEB, was asked to find a bold reformer able to align the immediate problem of assisting the poor with the Foundation's emphasis on tackling the 'root cause' of social problems. Buttrick was fortunate to meet Seaman Ashel Knapp, a writer, preacher and farmer who was then working for the United States Department of Agriculture (USDA).[41] Knapp had made a name for himself as an early pioneer of 'scientific farming', but it was his methods of instruction that attracted the GEB's interest. Knapp had been employing farm demonstrations to teach and familiarize poor farmers with new agricultural techniques and products.[42] His 'teaching by doing' approach proved extraordinarily successful. Illiterate farmers could easily use the new methods and soon began to experiment and innovate on their holdings. Knapp also used Girls' and Boys' Clubs to encourage *inter alia* corn-growing, poultry-rearing, bread-making, canning, the cultivation of vegetable gardens and 'home economics', reasoning that children are likely to be more receptive to new ideas, more disposed to follow instruction and 'on the whole, better demonstrators than their parents'.[43] Targeted campaigns ('clean-up week', 'drink more milk' promotions etc.), pilot programmes (testing new seed varieties, for example) and growing competitions also proved highly effective tools for instilling a spirit of change and reform. Self-study and continuous appraisal were also encouraged and gradually new media technologies, including popular motion pictures, supplemented the use of radio, print and 'mobile schools' as a means of radiating change through the countryside. The work of the GEB convinced leaders at the Rockefeller Foundation that for development programmes to be successful they must embrace programmes of *socio-cultural adjustment*. The poor had to be roused from their stupor and inspired to try new seeds, fertilizers, technologies and growing practices.

Dr James 'Jimmy' Yen [Yan Yangchu] was yet another source of inspiration for JDR. Educated in Yale and Princeton, Yen returned to China after World War I where he assisted the YMCA on a national literacy programme and later went on to found the National Association of Mass Education Movements (MEM). Like the agents at the GEB, Yen quickly grasped that his educational programmes would founder unless they were also linked to efforts to better the economic position of peasants in the countryside. Through his contacts in the YMCA, Yen met with John D. Rockefeller Jr – JDR's father – and from 1934 he secured Rockefeller support for an integrative programme of rural reconstruction in China, including sanitation, marketing, rural economics and preventative medicine.[44] Like Knapp, Yen employed 'model farms' to encourage 'receptivity' among Chinese peasants and he urged reformers to take seriously the local pattern of village life as well as the attitudinal 'make-up' of the peasant. With the rise of communism and the descent into violence, Dr Yen left for Taiwan where he re-established his remarkable rural programmes and gained further acclaim. However, the 'loss' of China spoke to another lesson that the Rockefeller Foundation took from its early engagement with rural problems; namely reformers learnt to see the countryside as a political battleground wherein the 'hearts and minds' of peasants are won or lost.[45] In the US South, the GEB had worried that its failure to address rural poverty and outmigration could lead to large-scale urban unrest as deracinated peasants entered cities in search of better prospects.[46] In China – and indeed Asia more generally – the spread of communism gave serious impetus to rural reconstruction efforts. By shaping the peasant's disposition and outlook reformers felt they could exert control over the countryside, a realization that converted 'modernization' into a relatively inexpensive form of counterinsurgency.

JDR was no hawkish Cold Warrior but neither was he immune to the political currents of the period. Like other Americans he watched the communists take North Korea and China, invade South Korea and foment insurrections in Burma (Myanmar), French Indo-China (comprising Cambodia, Laos, Vietnam), Indonesia, Malaysia and the Philippines.[47] For Malthus, as we saw, the population problem was similarly tied to the threat of revolution. In the twentieth century, overpopulation and rural malaise – often abridged as the 'peasant problem' – was now being linked to the new Cold War policy of 'containment'.[48] To tackle these interlaced problems and prevent instability required new and ambitious programmes of reform.

The 'breeders' versus the 'feeders'

While it is fair to say that JDR was the arch promoter of the population problem at the Rockefeller Foundation, others within the organization were also beginning to see population as a cardinal issue. In particular those who cut their teeth in the medical and agrarian programmes later observed a negative side to their collective success. 'The ease with which death rates can be changed, and particular diseases drastically reduced or eliminated,' commented one report, 'brings public health face to face with its inevitable consequences, the population problem.'[49] Thanks in no small part to the Foundation's accomplishments in poor countries – notably through the operations of its International Health Division – people around the world were living longer, if not always 'better' lives. Gains in longevity, of course, meant that population numbers were steadily increasing. Life, which Hobbes once characterized as 'nasty, brutish and short', now appeared to be 'nasty, brutish and *long*'. The gradual medicalization of the population was now forcing a stern reassessment of development priorities and goals.

No less of a concern were the profound changes wrought by 'globalization' (although it would be some decades before the term itself was used). Sovereign borders appeared worryingly porous as food, peoples, weapons and deadly viruses travelled rapidly across continents. For many commentators it seemed as though the traditional distinction between domestic and international spheres no longer applied. As early as 1924, Raymond Fosdick wrote to the president of the Rockefeller Foundation to draw his attention to arguments made by Winston Churchill. In a bleak pamphlet titled *Shall We Commit Suicide?* Churchill pointed to the 'tremendous mechanical strides' that had knitted the 'world into a compact unit'. This process, he said, fostered new forms of interdependency, but also heightened levels of collective vulnerability. This struck a chord with Fosdick, who commented on the 'menace of this new propinquity' and openly speculated as to whether these developments warranted a full-scale reassessment of the Foundation's strategic goals, which up to this point had been 'predicated on a world of peace'.[50] By the end of World War II, the concerns Fosdick expressed were commonly vocalized by staff at the Foundation. A 1944 report on the Foundation's 'Plans for the Future' is fairly indicative:

> We are going to live, in the future, on and near the surface of a pretty small sphere. Our existence will be three dimensional to an extent never before practicable; and we shall be led by a generation of men and women to whom Iraq and Iceland and Indo-China are familiar places, hours away ... Is not geography, in the modern and scholarly sense that [Isaiah] Bowman uses this word, something we should look into?[51]

The new 'three-dimensional' space-time of globalization meant that 'the international' was no longer something remote – something 'over there' – but something intimate and indeed immanent; something that was always already 'over here'.

It appeared the world was getting smaller while the threats were getting larger. As a consequence, managing both the pace and direction of global social change became a Foundation priority. The first great stride in this direction was the establishment of a programme of agricultural research and education in Mexico. The Mexican Agricultural Programme (MAP) – led by the able scientist J. George Harrar – is sometimes styled as the beginning of the 'Green Revolution', whereas in fact the programme was a logical extension of the work carried out by the GEB in the US South. Beginning in 1943, MAP concentrated on improvements to wheat and corn varieties, the training of scientists and the dissemination of improved agronomic practices.[52] Before the end of the decade, programme leaders were reporting astonishing successes. A 20–50 per cent increase in corn yields meant that Mexico could suspend its corn imports and concentrate on exporting its newly created surplus. The success of its wheat programme was equally emphatic: 12 new varieties with inbuilt resistance to stem and leaf rust were developed and within a decade Mexico, previously an importer of international wheat, was claiming self-sufficiency.[53] The new varieties of wheat and corn were later exported to Pakistan, Peru, Columbia, East and West Africa, Chile, Ecuador, Peru, Venezuela and the Philippines. In addition, the Foundation established formal programmes of agricultural assistance in Colombia (1950), Chile (1955) and India (1956), as well as a network of international agricultural research centres, including the International Rice Research Institute (1960) and International Maize and Wheat Improvement Center (1966) established in the Philippines and Mexico respectively. The 'peasant problem' was now being addressed at a global scale through the advancement of agricultural production.

However, the focus was never exclusively on food. In a letter to Warren Weaver, Paul Mangelsdorf, a botanist at Harvard and member of the original survey party sent to Mexico, expressed his concern that despite – or rather *because of* – the huge leaps in food production, the next 25 to 50 years were crucial in terms of 'stabilizing' global population:

> There is very great danger that world population will outrun its food supply before man has mastered the new techniques which he must invest in order to allow him to make more efficient use of the abundant supply of energy at his command. Should this happen, a state of chaos will develop which would preclude the research so desperately needed to solve the problem. Indeed, this very situation already exists in parts of the world. Vast populations in India and China are barely existing on a near-starvation diet and are making no contributions toward the solution of the very problem which they represent.[54]

Around the time that Mangelsdorf voiced his concerns, JDR was becoming sensitized to the magnitude of the population problem and the necessity of doing something about it. He had travelled to the Far East in the early 1940s and those in-country experiences helped to confirm his initial impression that population pressures were both real and pressing.

Although the Rockefeller Foundation had been funding the work of well-known demographic experts – including Frank Notestein and his research group at Princeton – JDR now pressed the board of trustees to launch a separate and distinct programme on population.[55] Sceptical at first, Raymond Fosdick nevertheless agreed to dispatch a survey team in 1948. The group, ably led by public health expert Marshall Balfour, visited Japan, China, Taiwan, Korea, Indonesia and the Philippines, before reporting back to JDR and the trustees of the Foundation. The final report titled *Public Health and Demography in the Far East* garnered considerable publicity, but it failed to produce the sweeping programme that JDR desired.[56] Disappointed but defiant, JDR, on the suggestion of one of his associates, called a conference in Williamsburg, Virginia to set out the goals and policies for a new population movement. This 'invitation only' two-day meeting, held in June 1951, was attended by many of the leading scientists, demographers and public figures on the population question.

The minutes of the meeting reveal some of the tensions that were to bedevil the population movement over the next two decades.[57] Should reforms include aid to underdeveloped countries or would this simply encourage greater progeny? (This was Malthus's anti-charity position recycled in Cold War parlance.) Should the population movement take a firm stance on immigration, which threatened to 'engulf' Western civilization? Disagreement also arose between those who wanted to pursue population-related research and those who demanded practical action. But perhaps the most interesting facet of the discussion was the rekindling of the old debate about population 'quality' versus 'quantity'. Demographer Kingsley Davis, author William Vogt, eugenicist Frederick Osborn (cousin of the author of *Our Plundered Planet*) and scientist Detlev Bronk worried that runaway population growth – especially in Asia – would contaminate the population profile of more developed countries and potentially unleash destabilizing political currents. As we shall see, JDR viewed the 'quality' issue differently, stressing the social and behavioural dimensions of reproduction in contrast to the crypto-eugenic arguments aired around the table.

Outside the roundtable, JDR was acutely aware that the Foundation, although supportive of the need to address the population problem, was wary of getting involved in such a controversial area. The desire not to alienate the Catholic Church was certainly one factor in the Foundation's stance, but no less pressing was the fear of 'scatteration': it was thought that the population problem was simply too big and too diffuse for one philanthropic organization to tackle.[58] Nevertheless, after a period of cautious deliberation, JDR established the Population Council (incorporated in 1951 but not publicly announced until 1953) with a personal gift of $100,000.[59] JDR assumed the presidency of the Population Council, but Frederick Osborn, as executive vice-president, was handed control over day-to-day affairs. In time, the Population Council was to become, in the words of historian Michael Connelly, 'not only the world's preeminent institute for policy-oriented research in demography and contraception, but also a nexus for all other major players in the field'.[60]

Ferment in Asia

As noted, JDR had a strong personal interest in Asia, but it is nonetheless revealing how frequently the region is referenced in the early proceedings of the Population Council. Indeed so frequently was Asia (and in particular India) mentioned during proceedings at Williamsburg that economist Isador Lubin, felt compelled to interject:

> At luncheon today I raised the question as to why it was that almost everybody who spoke this morning talked about India. What is there about India that makes this situation so acute? And I think unconsciously we are scared, and I think we have a right to be. In other words, that is where the ferment is taking place. That is where the pressure is greatest.[61]

As Lubin so succinctly put it, fear was the fuel driving this imaginative investment in Asia. In the same year that JDR established the Population Council, for example, a flagship advisory committee on agricultural activities – comprising the formidable brains of Elvin Stakman, Richard Bradfield and Paul Mangelsdorf (and also aided informally by J.G. Harrar, Harry Miller and Warren Weaver) – reported to the Foundation's trustees in ominous tones:

> The problem of population and food is no longer one of the future. It is upon us now ... Whether additional millions in Asia and elsewhere will become Communists will depend partly on whether the Communist world or the free world fulfills its promises. Hungry people are lured by promises, but they may be won by deeds. Communism makes attractive promises to underfed peoples; democracy must not only promise as much, but must deliver more.[62]

The report went on to note that global forces had unleashed a welter of seditious ideas among the poor.

> As a result of contacts with the more highly developed countries during and since the war [World War II] their leaders are becoming more conscious of the fact that there is a better way of life for them. The airplane and the radio are constantly reminding them of this fact. Agitators from Communist countries are making the most of the situation. The time is ripe, in places over-ripe, for sharing some of our technical knowledge with their people. Appropriate action now may help them to attain by evolution the improvements, including those in agriculture, which otherwise may have to come by revolution.[63]

It is interesting to note too that the report dramatizes the importance of modernizing peasant attitudes and mentalities. What the authors term 'the struggle for the minds of men' was clearly as important as the contest to control stomachs and reproductive organs – indeed all the more so, as the authors intimate, in countries where the prevailing conditions are at 'the same stage as it was in the more advanced countries 150 years ago'.[64] This perception of an 'historical lag' conditioned policy in interesting ways, not least in the recognition that while 'some need opportunity, others need *motivation*'.[65] This argument certainly appealed to JDR who was profoundly interested in the sociology of human action: what makes people *want* to produce more and conceive less? How is an 'unmodern demography', to use Sarah Hodges' term, transitioned to a modern, progressive society?[66]

Hence, while it is tempting to see the Rockefeller-sponsored Green Revolution as the roll out of a 'technological package' (comprising high-yielding seeds, regular irrigation and the application of large quantities of chemicals and hydrocarbons to crops), the reality is somewhat different since from the very beginning the Foundation stressed the importance of *social* as well as technical transformation. A high-level report on Indian agriculture authored by Harrar, Mangelsdorf and Weaver made this objective clear. The document begins in assured tones: 'Reduced to its simplest terms, the agricultural problem of India is that there are too many people on too little land.'[67] But this fundamental problem was compounded by cultural values that were transmitted and reproduced through the psychic environment of the Indian village:

> The villages are so overwhelmingly important in the agricultural economy of India, as well as in its social structure, that they merit a brief description. The villages may vary somewhat from region to region but within a region they are as uniform as so many ant hills. Indeed, from the air, where a number of villages may be seen simultaneously, they have the appearance of structures built by creatures motivated largely by inherited animal instincts, and devoid of any inclination to depart from a fixed hereditary pattern. The inheritance in this instance, of course, is social.[68]

Here the village is depicted as the spatial antinomy of the city and Western modernity.[69] The goal of modernization theory was to encourage an ontological shift from the fatalism and inertia that characterized traditional life toward a spirit of risk-taking and competitive exchange. In short, the goal was to *create a capitalist subject for a capitalist system*. Indians might be encouraged to advance, the authors note, only if reform programmes reached all the way down to the village-level reality of peasant life: 'The most serious problem faced by agriculture in India is not a technical one, but a cultural one [...] there has to be a departure from old customs and ways of thinking.'[70] Although reforming habits and conduct at the micro-level seemed a daunting prospect, the option of standing back and doing nothing was infinitely worse: '[U]nless the food problem is solved' the authors warned, 'South India will go Communist.'[71]

In the hyper-vigilant terms of the Cold War, a free Asia represented nothing less than an 'existential danger' for the US.[72] In a letter to Warren Weaver dated 23 October 1952, biochemist William Farnsworth Loomis depicted the region as a geographical pivot guarding the future security of Western civilization. Loomis was writing on the subject of world food problems, but he began by describing a magazine article he had read by the former First Lady, Eleanor Roosevelt. He recounts Roosevelt's description of three UN agencies – the 'hunger fighting FAO', the 'disease fighting WHO' and the 'ignorance fighting UNESCO' – and how each 'independently drew up a world contour map of their particular problem'. Loomis then noted 'how these three maps were superimposable, one on the other, all concentrating on the age-old highly populated civilization of Asia'.[73] The observation is indicative of the strong interest that was developing within the Foundation for a developmental programme that focused on Asia.[74]

JDR continued to develop his personal interest in the Far East. After one visit to Indonesia where he met with local dignitaries, he recorded how 'courage, determination and imagination could block a communist-inspired effort'.[75] He had also by this time met with Wolf Ladejinsky, the special attaché of the US Embassy in Tokyo and a formidable agricultural economist in his own right. Ladejinsky was a reformer in the mould of Jimmy Yen (whose Mass Education Movement, as we saw, was much admired by JDR) and he firmly believed that the peasant was the key to forestalling communism. 'An overworked and over-exploited peasantry that for centuries was inertly miserable is now alertly miserable,' Ladejinsky cautioned.[76] These trips, in conjunction with advice from staff at the Rockefeller Foundation, convinced JDR that the ferment in Asia required a unique, interconnected programme of action. It was no longer a choice between 'food producing' and 'population reducing' programmes. The solution would not be found in 'either/or' approaches; it must be sought through a 'both/and' agenda. Or to say this differently, progressive change meant cultivating modern citizens capable of producing more calories while also desiring fewer children. Perhaps unwittingly at first, JDR was bringing together Cornucopians and Malthusians in a development vision that promoted Western-style modernization as a protection against the descent into hardship, despair and insurrection.

It would take a bit more time to create programmes built on the understanding that lasting change comes from 'within' rather than 'without' – from changes to local culture and individual mindsets rather than from elaborately conceived technical projects – but an important step on the road to that realization was JDR's decision to establish in November 1953 a new organization originally named the Council on Economic and Cultural Affairs but later given the more fitting appellation, the Agricultural Development Council (ADC). Dr John Lossing Buck was hired as executive director of the new programme. Formerly a high-level operative at UNFAO and an authority on farming systems in China, Buck's appointment signalled the importance of the social sciences in the operations of the new Council.[77] Like the GEB, ADC's remit was broadly conceived as 'educational'. It would offer fellowships for the training of indigenous scientists in Western institutions, grants for Western scholars to spend time in overseas universities, training manuals and other didactic materials to disseminate the latest research and best practices, funding for pilot projects and, of course, informal agricultural training in the tried and tested formula of agricultural extension programmes.

The significant emphasis on extension work offers a direct link through to the work of Seaman Knapp who stressed the importance of competent demonstration agents who would travel to villages, immerse themselves in local traditions and mores, and coax change by urging farmers to actively participate in their own development. When Arthur Mosher succeeded Buck as executive director in 1957, the stress on the human dimensions of agricultural production kicked on a gear.[78] Mosher undertook his doctoral training with the Nobel prize-winning economist Theodore Schultz, and like his mentor he wanted to incorporate a deeper understanding of local conditions – especially the sociology of village life – in the programmes of ADC. The resulting village education programmes were elaborate in scheme, but the goal was rather straightforward: to turn traditional peasants – understood as conservative, inert and risk-averse – into forward-thinking, utility maximizing, risk-taking agents. This method of improving agriculture was not meant to supplant the traditional Green Revolution approach to technocentric development. The Council merely returned to an early philanthropic tenet; namely that for change to be effective it must rouse the poor and encourage them to depend on their own exertions. Much in the same way that Malthus believed that markets unleashed the positive spirit of 'self-love', Mosher and his team believed their village-level programmes would channel self-interest into greater productivity.[79]

The work of the Population Council – the other arm of JDR's effort to cultivate modern, responsible citizens – must be seen in this light too. Michael Connelly astutely observes that 'Population control presented itself as a charity like any other, helping less fortunate people. *But it was the only one that promised to make them go away.*'[80] Certainly, key philanthropic actors came to regard population control as fitting squarely within their remit of *catalysing permanent transformations*. Whereas ADC busied itself with one side of the peasant problem – that of food production and difficulties associated with manipulating what Ashis Nandy terms 'the village of the mind' – the Population Council directed attention to the issue of uncontrolled fertility.[81] With barely a dozen staff, the Council initially focused on fellowship programmes (heavily biased toward Asia) as well as demographic and contraceptive research, but by the end of its first decade it had noticeably increased the scope and ambition of its programmes. Mounting international concern about population growth undoubtedly helped to galvanize efforts. Demographers such as Kingsley Davis featured increasingly in the popular press and official reports on population matters were now frequent topics in public discussions.[82] In 1959, General William H. Draper Jr was tasked with leading the President's Committee to Study the United States Military Assistance, but much to the surprise and annoyance of many, not least the Catholic hierarchy, his report recommended US assistance for global family planning.[83] The same year the Draper report was published, the Ford Foundation, one of the first and largest funders of the Population Council, sponsored an influential report on *India's Food Crisis*. The report predicted a food crisis of 'overwhelming gravity' and recommended that the country's food production be placed on a 'war footing': '*The entire nation must be made aware of the impending food crisis and steps must be taken to meet it.* Adequate supplies of food may indeed be essential to [the] survival of democracy, because freedom from hunger is a prerequisite to the enjoyment of other freedoms. *If elementary wants, such as food and clothing, are not satisfied, other freedoms may be sacrificed for the promise of food enough.*' The panel of experts – who spent just ten weeks on what one critic described as a 'whirlwind tour' of the country – were clear in their minds as to the cause of India's food problems: 'Too many people are attempting to earn a living on the land.'[84] They were similarly unequivocal on the solutions to India's problems. First, yields should be increased by adopting the Green Revolution's technical package: 'with hybrid maize,' the Ford team announced, 'India can in 5 to 7 years make more progress in increasing yields than the U.S.A made in 20 years.'[85] In addition, the team echoed earlier recommendations that the peasant be made a central component of planned modernization: 'The individual cultivator is the key person in any programme to increase food production, but comparatively little is known about him and the basis for his decisions on what he will produce and how. He must be persuaded to change his present pattern of production if food targets are to be achieved.'[86]

Once again it was fear that gave meaning to efforts to reduce population numbers, increase food supplies, and address the 'motivational gap' observed in peasant societies. Shortly after the Draper and Ford Foundation reports, JDR delivered a speech to FAO officials that made full use of the affective charge embedded in population debates:

> [P]opulation growth is second only to the control of atomic weapons, as a paramount problem of our time. All of us hope and pray that the world's nuclear suicide can be avoided. But there is a cold inevitability, a certainty that is mathematical, that gives the problems posed by too-rapid population growth a sombre and chilling cast indeed. The grim fact of population growth cuts across all the basic needs of mankind and, more than any other single factor, frustrates man's achievement of his higher needs.[87]

The discreet 'behind-the-scenes' approach that marked the first years of the Population Council is here abandoned in favour of a more confident and emboldened stance. JDR also makes full use of Malthusian terms to describe population growth's 'mathematical' certainty. As the official history of the Population Council described the new mood, the question was no longer 'what is the problem?' but 'what can we do about it?'[88]

It was in India too that the Council made its first foray into 'technical assistance' – essentially the public health equivalent of farm demonstration work. In hindsight we can identify three studies that were key to this fundamental transition. The first was a study of population control in Punjab undertaken between 1953 and 1956. Funded by the Rockefeller Foundation (to the tune of $250,000) and supported by The Harvard School of Public Health, the 'Khanna study' (as it came to be known) hoped to learn 'how to implant this small family system in a peasant population'.[89] The researchers studied 8,000 people from seven villages (plus a further 8,000 individuals who served as the control group). The conclusions were arresting: after five years, the birth-rate was noticeably *higher* among the experimental population compared to the control group who had received no birth control assistance. It was clear that for population control to be effective, it would need to pay more attention to values, attitudes and aspirations of the target population. The emphasis needed to shift to the question of receptivity: how would programmes reach the unconvinced and ill-informed?

A second study in family planning, beginning in 1955 in Singur, West Bengal and funded by the Council, sought to determine whether an educational programme carried out by field operatives could stimulate greater use of contraceptive techniques.[90] Finally the so-called 'Taichung Experiment' in Taiwan in the early 1960s analysed methods for diffusing family planning services and information to target populations. The researchers tested what combination of communication tools – including posters, mass meetings, letters, focus groups, home visits, etc. – were most effective in attracting new 'acceptors' of contraception.[91] The study also presented an opportunity to offer cheap intrauterine devices (primarily the Lippes loop recently developed with Council support), as well as oral contraceptives, to the experiment's participants. The results showed a marked preference for IUDs and a subsequent attenuation of participants' fertility rates. As Bernard Berelson, a key leader of the Taichung Experiment and soon to be president of the Population Council, reflected in 1962: 'I have become persuaded that the problem now is more how to do it than how to study it, that we now need emerging techniques of *communication* more than those of communication *research*.'[92] Here, as Susan Greenhalgh has noted: 'Culture is seen as communication about contraception, while fertility decline is portrayed as a sociotechnical process spreading contraceptive technology.'[93]

Domestically JDR stepped up efforts to convince the US government to act on the threat of runaway population. With Draper's assistance, JDR met with President Lyndon B. Johnson and showed him preprepared charts predicting widespread famines in China, India and Pakistan by the early 1970s.[94] Johnson's subsequent declaration of a 'war on hunger' shows that the 'war footing' approach of the Rockefeller and Ford Foundations achieved traction in policy circles. By the mid-1960s, the Rockefeller Foundation had established its own population programme in addition to announcing a global 'Strategy for the Conquest of Hunger'.[95] Internationally, JDR demonstrated his acumen for charming foreign leaders and dignitaries who were, at least to begin with, profoundly suspicious of Rockefeller designs. The demographer Frank Notestein – who from time to time had disagreements with JDR over the aims and orientation of the Council – relates the story of JDR visiting the Tunisian President Habib Bourguiba. Although initially reluctant to even meet with JDR, Bourguiba quickly warmed to the American philanthropist and subsequently agreed to population control measures. The resulting programme in Tunisia was 'truly international', wrote Notestein, 'with Bulgarian physicians inserting American-made IUDs in Tunisian peasant women'.[96] It was a similar story about JDR's meeting with the president of Pakistan in 1963. The Council had been active in Pakistan since its foundation and when Notestein showed President Ayub Khan the Council's new IUD (the Lippes loop trialled in the Taichung Experiment discussed above), the president declared that he would have every midwife in Pakistan inserting them within two weeks.[97] In 1965, Kenya became the first African country to formally request the Council's assistance. Significantly, JDR had discussed population problems with President Jomo Kenyatta during a visit in 1963. It is difficult to overestimate the role of JDR and the Population Council in proselytizing for global population control.[98]

Inspiring purposeful change

Not everyone agreed with JDR's methods. Kingsley Davis derided family planning efforts as palliative. 'By stressing the right of parents to have the number of children they want,' he protested, 'it evades the basic question of population policy, which is how to give societies the number of children they need.'[99] In the late 1960s and early 1970s – the highpoint of the population movement – a vocal coterie of scientists openly called for compulsory birth control programmes. Paul Ehrlich argued that governments ought to consider adding a 'temporary sterilant to staple food, or to the water supply. An antidote would have to be taken to permit reproduction.'[100] Alternatively, Ehrlich suggested cutting off aid to countries in which leaders were not doing enough to limit human reproduction or where the 'population–food balance is hopeless' (India fell into the former camp: 'India, where population growth is colossal, agriculture hopelessly antiquated, and the government incompetent,' wrote Ehrlich, 'will be one of those we must allow to slip down the drain'). Garrett Hardin also supported a policy of triage. 'Clearly the worst thing that we can do is send food [as aid] … Atomic bombs would be kinder. For a few moments the misery would be acute, but it would soon come to an end for most of the people, leaving a very few survivors to suffer thereafter.' Kingsley Davis endorsed draconian forms of population control:

> [I]t can be done with knowledge already available,' he declared, 'a nation seeking to stabilize its population could shut off immigration and permit each couple a maximum of two children, with possible license for a third.

Accidental pregnancies beyond the limit would be interrupted by abortion. If a third child were born without a licence, or a fourth, the mother would be sterilized.[101]

It is undoubtedly correct that JDR was *not* aligned with this hard-line camp. And yet through his own efforts, and those of the Population Council, the issue of 'population quality' lurked in the shadows, suggesting that 'more people' might develop into a global problem of security and interstate harmony. The writer, Lewis Lapham, who accompanied JDR and Notestein on a trip to Asia in 1963 recorded an interesting episode on a crowded shore near the city of Dhaka that is worth citing in full:

> We reached the west bank of the river at dusk. The sun, setting through a mauve haze, squatted on the flat roofs of the town. A dhow moved laboriously upstream under oars and a red sail. On the stone stairs leading from the shore, a holy man, his hair matted with dirt, gestured unintelligently to an indifferent audience. The sand swarmed with people.
>
> Rockefeller said nothing for perhaps twenty minutes. He stood beside an overturned oil drum, confronted by the chaos so remote from the orderly presentations in the 56th floor of the RCA Building. Here at last was what he had come to see, the plain reality of the so-called 'population explosion'. No statistics, no high-flown sentiments, no handsomely-illustrated brochures or predictions of disaster for mankind; just a lot of people pushing down the edge of a warm river. 'The numbers,' he said, 'the sheer numbers of it ... the quality, you see, goes down.'[102]

Similar to Ehrlich's own 'Damascus moment' (when he first apprehended 'the *feel* of overpopulation'), this description of population pressure – with 'sheer numbers' threatening 'chaos' on the 'orderly' world and driving down population 'quality' – depicts libidinal Asians as a danger to the West, a threat made all the more tangible by the real prospect of communist insurrection.

However, if population 'quality' served an important diagnostic purpose (aiding the identification of threats to the vitality of life), it also helped to outline a more positive, *therapeutic function* by dramatizing the importance of subjective change ('the struggle for the minds of men'). Significantly, Harr and Johnson note that the 'quality of life' theme preoccupied JDR from the moment he first established the Population Council in 1952. It became an integral part of what they describe as JDR's 'moral philosophy' and it taught him to see population control in a positive rather than negative light. It was wrong, JDR thought, to see the issue in straightforwardly Malthusian terms; that is, numbers of people versus quantities of food. This perspective likened people with animals and food with fodder (JDR and Foundation officials liked to quote the biblical injunction: 'man does not live by bread alone').[103] 'There is a third dimension,' JDR wrote, 'an aspect that touches the very essence of human life. This overlooked dimension concerns man's desire to live as well as survive.'[104]

Harr and Johnson call this third dimension the 'fundamental element' in JDR's thinking, and it is true that it comes across strongly in his developmental programmes for agriculture and population. What JDR's biographers fail to see, however, is how this question of 'quality' undergirds a set of normative claims about *the appropriate direction for social change*. Just as Malthus takes the inviolability of property as his starting point, philanthropic action interprets development to mean the social reproduction of productive and profitable bodies. In this sense, terms such as 'overpopulation' and 'underproduction', far from being neutral descriptions of social conditions, are intrinsic components in a subtle regime of human sorting and classification. Behind the charge of 'overpopulation', for instance, lie assumptions about personal choice, self-discipline, foresight and social aspiration as well as judgements about the level of threat those conditions pose to others presumably more prudent and enlightened. Similarly, the identification of 'low yield' economies is part of a poverty discourse that characterizes underdevelopment as the *absence* of certain elements (credit, fertilizer, improved seeds, but also personal qualities such as perseverance, entrepreneurialism, self-interest, resiliency, etc.). Once this move is made, it is easy to see how development sets as its target the rapid remedy of those imputed deficiencies. Seen this way, modern philanthropy represents something more than simply a new social ethic for treating hunger, poverty and disease. Intent on advancing the 'quality of life', it is fair to say that American philanthropists also helped to define and strengthen what those very 'qualities' might be. It is in this broad sense that philanthropists not only 'imagined' but actively constructed the paradigm of a 'progressive society' in whose name they acted. To the extent that the philanthropist's vision of human welfare is based on the negation of existing attitudes and modes of living, it always harbours within itself the seeds of structural violence.[105]

Notes

1 Paul R Ehrlich, *The Population Bomb*, (New York: Ballantine Books, 1968), p. 223.
2 Ibid., p. 11.

3 Ibid., pp. 15–16. This passage is brilliantly discussed in Matthew Connelly, 'To Inherit the Earth: Imagining World Population, from the Yellow Peril to the Population Bomb', *Journal of Global History*, 1 (2006), 299–319, p. 315.

4 Nick Cullather, '"Stretching the Surface of the Earth": The Foundations, Neo-Malthusianism and the Modernising Agenda', *Global Society*, 28 (2014), 104–12, pp. 105–6. Ehrlich wrote: 'This man is trying to tell us that in the next eight years India is going to find a way to produce enough food to support some 120 million more people that they cannot feed today ... Millions of Indians will die because of governmental attitudes exemplified by Subramaniam.' Paul Ehrlich, 'Population, Food, and Environment', *Texas Quarterly*, 11 (1968), 43–54.

5 C. Subramaniam, 'India's Program for Agricultural Progress', in Rockefeller Foundation (ed.), *Strategy for the Conquest of Hunger: Proceedings of a Symposium Convened by the Rockefeller Foundation, April 1 and 2, 1968, at Rockefeller University* (New York: Rockefeller Foundation, 1968), pp. 16–22.

6 Andrew Pearse, *Seeds of Plenty, Seeds of Want: Social and Economic Implications of the Green Revolution* (Oxford: Clarendon Press, 1980).

7 Greg Grandin, *Fordlandia: The Rise and Fall of Henry Ford's Forgotten Jungle City* (London: Icon Books, 2010), p. 41.

8 'While Malthus does excise the passage [on nature's feast] it is relatively easy to show that the sentiments are merely transposed into his discussion of charity and the poor law.' Garrett Hardin, 'The Feast of Malthus', *The Social Contract*, 8 (1988), 181–7, p. 181.

9 For a contemporary consideration of this theme see J. Essex, 'Idle Hands Are the Devil's Tools: The Geopolitics and Geoeconomics of Hunger', *Annals of the Association of American Geographers*, 102 (2012), 191–207.

10 Connelly, 'To Inherit the Earth', p. 301

11 Pierre Desrochers and Christine Hoffbauer. 'The Post War Intellectual Roots of the Population Bomb: Fairfield Osborn's "Our Plundered Planet" and William Vogt's "Road to Survival" in Retrospect', *The Electronic Journal of Sustainable Development*, 1 (2009), 37–61. See also Cormac Ó Gráda, *Eating People is Wrong, and Other Essays on Famine, its Past, and its Future* (Princeton: Princeton University Press, 2015), p. 4.

12 Alison Bashford, *Global Population: History, Geopolitics, and Life on Earth* (New York: Columbia University Press, 2014), p. 11.

13 Ehrlich's choice of title – militarizing the population question (which he later regretted) – tapped into, and amplified, this sense of terror. Ehrlich, *The Population Bomb*, pp. 69–80.

14 The citation is from International Development Advisory Board, *Partners in Progress: A Report to President Truman by the International Development Advisory Board* (New York: Simon and Schuster, 1951), p. 12. The commission was established to report on the objectives and policies for President Truman's Point IV programme. The board was chaired by Nelson Rockefeller. In his 'Family of Man' speech, JDR echoes this view claiming that 'the antidote to despair is to be involved.' John D. Rockefeller III, *The Second American*

Revolution: Some Personal Observations (New York: Harper & Row Publishers, 1973), p. xv.

15 William Godwin, *Enquiry Concerning Justice and its Influence on Morals and Happiness, Vol II*, 3rd edn (Toronto: University of Toronto Press, 1946), p. 528. My thanks to Robert Mayhew for pointing me to this passage.

16 All references to Malthus's so-called 'second *Essay*' (comprising the editions of 1806, 1807, 1817 and 1826) are taken from T.R. Malthus, *An Essay on the Principle of Population*, ed. Patricia James (Cambridge: Cambridge University Press, 1989). The quotation above is from vol. 1, p. 317.

17 Ibid., vol. 1, p. 318.

18 Ibid., vol. 1, p. 319.

19 Ibid., vol. 1 pp. 316 and 321.

20 Isabell Lorey, *State of Insecurity: Government of the Precarious*, trans. Aileen Derieg (London: Verso, 2015), p. 17.

21 *Essay*, vol. 1, p. 335.

22 Ibid., vol. 1, p. 359.

23 Ibid., vol. 1, p. 378.

24 'All who were in want of food,' declared Malthus, 'would be urged by imperious necessity to offer their labour in exchange for this article, so absolutely necessary to existence.' Ibid., vol. 1, pp. 324–5.

25 See the discussion of Malthus in Ed Cohen, *A Body Worth Defending: Immunity, Biopolitics, and the Apotheosis of the Modern Body* (Durham: Duke University Press, 2009).

26 This segment draws from arguments in D. Nally and S. Taylor, 'The Politics of Self-Help: The Rockefeller Foundation, Philanthropy and the "Long" Green Revolution', *Political Geography*, 49 (2015), 51–63.

27 A. Carnegie, *The Gospel of Wealth and Other Timely Essays* (New York: The Century Company, 1900), pp. 18–23, my emphasis.

28 Rockefeller Foundation, *Five-Year Review and Projection, December 2–3, 1968* (New York: Rockefeller Foundation Publication, 1968).

29 J.G. Harrar, 'Preface', in Rockefeller Foundation (ed.), *Strategy for the Conquest of Hunger*, p. vii.

30 Grandin, Fordlandia pp. 55–76.

31 Rockefeller, *Second American Revolution*, pp. 79–80.

32 Ibid., p. 82.

33 J. Wilson, 'Fantasy Machine: Philanthrocapitalism as an Ideological Formation', *Third World Quarterly*, 35 (2014), 1144–61.

34 W. Weaver, 'People, Energy and Food', *The Scientific Monthly*, 87 (1954), 359. Rockefeller Archive Center, Record Group: 3.1 Administration, Program & Policy, Series: 915 Natural Sciences & Agriculture, Box: 3, Folder: 21.

35 Ibid.

36 Cited in Bashford, *Global Population*, p. 301.

37 *Essay*, vol. 2, pp. 127–8. Garrett Hardin, 'Lifeboat Ethics: A Malthusian View', in Ingolf Vogeler and Anthony De Souza (eds.), *Dialectics of Third World Development* (New Jersey: Allanheld, Osman, 1980), pp. 171–85.

38 Raymond B. Fosdick, *A Philosophy for a Foundation* (New York: Rockefeller Foundation, 1963), pp. 24–7; Raymond B. Fosdick, *The Story of the Rockefeller Foundation* (New York: Harper & Brothers, 1952), pp. 210, 280, 287.

39 For the conventional account see Population Council, 'On the Origins of the Population Council', *Population and Development Review*, 3 (1977), 493–502.

40 The GEB is extensively discussed in Nally and Taylor, 'The Politics of Self-Help'. See also Theodore Mitchell and Robert Lowe, 'To Sow Contentment: Philanthropy, Scientific Agriculture and the Making of the New South, 1906–1920', *Journal of Social History*, 24 (1990), 317–40.

41 The meeting is discussed in Raymond B. Fosdick, *Adventure in Giving: The Story of the General Education Board, a Foundation Established by John D. Rockefeller* (New York: Harper and Row Publishers, 1962), pp. 41ff.

42 S.A. Knapp, 'An Agricultural Revolution', *The World's Work*, 12 (1906), 7733–8. Rockefeller Archive Center, General Education Board, Series: 1.4, Box: 694, Folder: 7152; S.A. Knapp, *Effect of Farmers' Cooperative Demonstration Work on Rural Improvement* (1908). Rockefeller Archive Center, General Education Board, Series: 1.4, Box: 694, Folder: 7156.

43 J.A. Evans, *Extension Work Among Negroes Conducted by Negro Agents, 1923: United States Department of Agriculture Circular 355*, (Washington, DC: Government Printing Office, 1925). Rockefeller Archive Center, General Education Board, Series: 1.4, Box: 694, Folder: 7152.

44 A.C. Waterhouse, *Food and Prosperity: Balancing Technology and Community in Agriculture* (New York: Rockefeller Foundation, 2013), pp. 60ff. On his first trip to China, JDR also met with Jimmy Yen and saw first-hand his agricultural work. J.E. Harr and P.J. Johnson, *The Rockefeller Century: Three Generations of America's Greatest Family* (New York: Scribner, 1988), p. 292.

45 Michael Latham, *The Right Kind of Revolution: Modernization, Development, and US Foreign Policy from the Cold War to the Present* (Ithaca: Cornell University Press, 2011).

46 Mona Domosh, 'Practising Development at Home: Race, Gender, and the "Development" of the American South', *Antipode*, 47 (2015), 915–41.

47 J.E. Harr and P.J. Johnson *The Rockefeller Conscience: An American Family in Public and Private* (New York: Scribner, 1991), p. 64.

48 Kolson Schlosser, 'Malthus at Mid-Century: Neo-Malthusianism as Bio-Political Governance in the Post-World War II United States', *Cultural Geographies*, 16 (2009), 465–84, p. 466.

49 Marshall C. Balfour and Marston Bates 'Special Report to the Board of Scientific Directors of the International Health Division of the Rockefeller Foundation November 4, 1949', pp. 8–9. Collection: Rockefeller Foundation, Record Group: 3.2 Administration, Program & Policy, Series: 900 General Program and Policy, Box: 57, Folder: 312.

50 Letter from Fosdick to Dr George Vincent dated 7 October 1924. Collection: Rockefeller Foundation, Record Group: 3.1 Administration, Program & Policy, Series: 918 General Education Board, Box: 1, Folder: 1.

51 'Excerpt from Plans for the Future, November 1944', pp. 30–1. Collection: Rockefeller Foundation, Record Group: 3.1 Administration, Program & Policy, Series: 915 Natural Sciences and Agriculture, Box: 2, Folder: 13.

52 D. Fitzgerald, 'Exporting American Agriculture: The Rockefeller Foundation in Mexico, 1943–1953', *Social Studies of Science*, 44 (1986), 457–83.

53 John H. Perkins, *Geopolitics and the Green Revolution: Wheat, Genes, and the Cold War* (Oxford, Oxford University Press, 1997).

54 Letter from Paul Mangelsdorf to Warren Weaver, 24 August 1949. Collection: Rockefeller Foundation, Record Group: 3.1 Administration, Program & Policy, Series: 915 Natural Sciences & Agriculture, Box: 3, Folder: 20.

55 JDR's father 'Junior' helped establish the Bureau of Social Hygiene (incorporated in 1913), which among other things supported the establishment of birth control clinics and population studies. Significantly, many of Junior's financial contributions in those areas were made anonymously to avoid controversy. In his final year of school, Junior placed JDR on the board of the Bureau. Ibid., pp. 114–15, 190–1, 269.

56 Copies of the report were mailed (unsolicited) to influential persons. See John Sharpless, 'Population Science, Private Foundations, and Development AID: The Transformation of Demographic Knowledge in the United States, 1945–1965', in Frederick Cooper and Randall Packard (eds.), *International Development and the Social Sciences: Essays on the History and Politics of Knowledge* (Berkeley: University of California Press, 1997), pp. 176–200, p. 197.

57 The present paragraph is based on the detailed discussion of the Williamsburg meeting in Matthew Connelly, *Fatal Misconception: The Struggle to Control World Population* (Cambridge, MA: Harvard University Press, 2008), pp. 155ff. A full transcript of the conference can be found at Rockefeller Family Archives, Record Group: 5 John D Rockefeller III Papers, Series: 1 Office of the Messrs. Rockefeller Files, Subseries: 5 Population Interests, Box: 85, Folder: 720–3.

58 Concerns about 'scatteration' are discussed in Fosdick, *Philosophy for a Foundation*, p. 11.

59 Harr and Johnson, *Rockefeller Conscience*, p. 39.

60 Connelly, *Fatal Misconception*, p. 159.

61 Ibid., p. 158.

62 Advisory Committee for Agricultural Activities [Elvin Stakman, Richard Bradfield and Paul Mangelsdorf], *The World Food Problem, Agriculture, and the Rockefeller Foundation, June 21 1951*, pp. 3–4. Collection: Rockefeller Foundation, Record Group: 3.1 Administration, Program & Policy Series: 915 Natural Sciences & Agriculture, Box: 3, Folder: 21.

63 *The World Food Problem, Agriculture, and the Rockefeller Foundation* Collection: Rockefeller Foundation, Record Group: 3.1 Administration, Program & Policy Series: 915 Natural Sciences & Agriculture, Box: 3, Folder: 21, p. 7.

64 Ibid., pp. 4, 6. The assumption of Western privilege that attends these descriptions is not *sui generis* to philanthropic accounts, but strikes to the

very heart of population science as it was historically constructed. See Susan Greenhalgh, 'The Social Construction of Population Science: An Intellectual, Institutional, and Political History of Twentieth-Century Demography', *Comparative Studies in Society and History*, 38 (1996), 26–66; and Simon Szreter, 'The Idea of Demographic Transition in the Study of Fertility Change: A Critical Intellectual History', *Population and Development Review*, 19 (1993), 659–701.

65 *World Food Problem, Agriculture, and the Rockefeller Foundation*, p. 15, emphasis added.

66 Sarah Hodges, 'Governmentality, Population and Reproductive Family in Modern India', *Economic and Political Weekly*, 39 (2004), 1157–63, p. 1159.

67 J.G. Harrar, Paul C. Mangelsdorf and Warren Weaver, 'Notes on Indian Agriculture' (1952), p. 11. Collection: Rockefeller Foundation, Record Group: 1.2, Series 460, Box 1, Folder 4.

68 Ibid., p. 3.

69 Nick Cullather, '"The Target Is The People": Representations of the Village In Modernization and U.S. National Security Doctrine', *Cultural Politics*, 2 (2006), 29–48; Nicole Sackley, 'The Village as Cold War Site: Experts, Development, and the History of Rural Reconstruction', *Journal of Global History*, 6 (2011), 481–504.

70 Harrar *et al.*, 'Notes on Indian Agriculture', p. 12.

71 Ibid., p. 6. Note the authors (pp. 6–7) do add the caveat: 'Other observers are not certain that this is true. There can, however, be little doubt that India will remain a world danger spot so long as she has an acute food problem.'

72 Nick Cullather, *The Hungry World: America's Cold War Battle Against Poverty in Asia* (Cambridge MA: Harvard University Press, 2010), p. 2.

73 Letter from William Farnsworth Loomis to Warren Weaver, 23 October 1952. Collection: Rockefeller Foundation, Record Group: 3.1 Administration, Program & Policy, Series: 915 Natural Sciences & Agriculture, Box: 3, Folder: 21.

74 In a memo for the president of the Foundation, Stakman pointedly wrote: 'How much of the experience of Latin America can be projected into the future; how much of it could be applied to Asia? What factors should be taken into consideration in trying to make a perceptible impact on hundreds of millions of Asiatic people? What are the prospects that the situation can be alleviated?' Letter E.C. Stakman to Dean Rusk, 22 December 1953, with accompanying memorandum. Collection: Rockefeller Foundation, Record Group: 3.1 Administration, Program & Policy, Series: 915 Natural Sciences & Agriculture, Box: 3, Folder: 21.

75 Harr and Johnson, *Rockefeller Conscience*, p. 67.

76 Ibid., p. 66.

77 Russell Stevenson and Virginia O. Locke, *The Agricultural Development Council: A History* (Morrilton: Winrock Institute for Agricultural Development, 1989), p. 6.

78 Ibid., p. 13

79 For Mosher's views on modernization and agriculture, see A.T. Mosher, *Getting Agriculture Moving: Essentials for Development and Modernization* (New York: Praeger, 1966).

80 Connelly, *Fatal Misconception*, p. 191, emphasis added.

81 Ashis Nandy is cited in Sackley, 'Village as Cold War Site', p. 482.

82 For example, Kingsley Davis, 'Analysis of the Population Explosion', *New York Times*, 22 September 1957. A copy of this article is held in Collection: Rockefeller Brothers Fund, Record Group: Special Studies Project, Series: Subpanel 3, Box: 21, Folder: 236.

83 Connelly, *Fatal Misconception*, p. 186; Harr and Johnson, *Rockefeller Conscience*, p. 44.

84 Agricultural Production Team, *Report on India's Food Crisis & Steps to Meet it* (Delhi: Government of India, 1959), pp. 11, 22, 30, emphasis in original. For a trenchant critique see Daniel Thorner, 'Ploughing the Plan Under: Ford Team Report on Food Crisis', *The Economic Weekly*, July 1959, pp. 901–4.

85 Agricultural Production Team, *Report on India's Food Crisis*, p. 5.

86 Ibid., p. 101.

87 Harr and Johnson, *Rockefeller Conscience*, p. 165.

88 Population Council, *The Population Council: A Chronicle of the First Twenty-Five Years, 1952–1977* (New York: The Population Council, 1978), p. 45.

89 Connelly, *Fatal Misconception*, p. 171.

90 Population Council, *Population Council*, pp. 46–7.

91 Ibid., pp. 50–1.

92 Ibid., p. 51, emphasis in original.

93 Greenhalgh, 'Social Construction of Population Science', p. 58.

94 Connelly, *Fatal Misconception*, p. 255.

95 The culmination of JDR's domestic efforts was his chairmanship of the President's Commission on Population Growth and the American Future, which published its final report in 1972.

96 As recounted in Harr and Johnson, *Rockefeller Conscience*, p. 164.

97 Pakistan became the second country in the world to establish a state-led programme of population control, setting aside $7 million for family planning between 1960 and 1965. For its part, the Population Council undertook to manufacture and distribute the new IUD, investing more than $2.5 million by 1968. Connelly, *Fatal Misconception*, pp. 185, 205.

98 Harr and Johnson, *Rockefeller Conscience*, p. 165.

99 Population Council, *Population Council*, p. 79.

100 Ehrlich, 'Population, Food, and Environment', pp. 52–3. Ehrlich is aware that his suggestions are both unrealistic and unpalatable, but nevertheless he urged policymakers to be 'tough-minded'. See also Harr and Johnson, *Rockefeller Conscience*, pp. 407–8.

101 Hardin and Davis's comments are discussed in Barry Commoner, 'Poverty Breeds "Overpopulation"', In Ingolf Vogeler and Anthony De Souza (eds.), *Dialectics of Third World Development* (New Jersey: Allanheld, Osman. 1980), pp. 186–95, pp. 187, 195. In a special issue on the legacy of Malthus's

Essay, William Paddock updates many of the xenophobic assertions cited above: 'our leaders direct foreign policy with no understanding of the resource base of the world's poor. Efforts to stabilize governments or feed the hungry fail as troops are sent to Haiti and Somalia, food to Ethiopia, and fact-finding groups to Central America. Some may puzzle, "What's wrong with our help?" but no one asks, "What's wrong with the tropics?" What's wrong with the tropics is geography which so restricts the farmer he can't produce enough surplus to support even today's civilization ... After fifty years of development effort, including a trillion dollars in foreign aid, the recipient countries remain the *less well-developed, emerging, less privileged, have-not, catch-up, low income, needy, poorest third, recipient, expectant, restless* – all euphemisms for *tropical.*' William Paddock, 'Malthus: Right or Wrong?', *The Social Contract*, 8 (1998), 197–205, p. 198, emphasis in original.

102 Harr and Johnson, *Rockefeller Conscience*, p. 82.
103 Rockefeller, *Second American Revolution*, p. 181; Fosdick, *Story of the Rockefeller Foundation*, p. 237.
104 Harr and Johnson, *Rockefeller Conscience*, p. 165.
105 Here I am trading on a point made by James Vernon with regard to how power operates in and through programmes of social welfare. James Vernon, *Hunger: A Modern History* (Cambridge, MA: Harvard University Press, 2007), p. 166. See also James C. Scott, *Seeing Like a State: How Certain Schemes to Improve the Human Condition Have Failed* (New Haven: Yale University Press, 1998); Tania Lee, *The Will to Improve: Governmentality, Development, and the Practice of Politics* (Durham: Duke University Press, 2007).

CHAPTER 9

The publication bomb: the birth of modern environmentalism and the editing of Malthus's Essay

Robert J. Mayhew

Malthus, population and the birth of modern environmentalism

It has become a historiographical truism to locate the birth of 'modern' environmentalism in an era that at its longest runs from the 1950s until the mid-1970s and that is frequently more tightly delimited as the five years either side of 1970. This commonplace appears in histories of and on both sides of the Atlantic.[1] On a broader geographical canvas, both Borstelmann's 'global history' of the 1970s and Radkau's global history of environmental thought have reaffirmed the centrality of this era to the birth of modern environmentalism, the latter framing this as an 'ecological revolution' forged by what he sees as 'the great synchronization around 1970' of environmental writing, science, legislation and popular activism, whose timeline runs from 1965 to 1972.[2]

Central to this periodization is a demonstrable upsurge in anxiety about the environmental 'footprint' of a rapidly growing human population in these years. Obviously, population has been a subject of concern since antiquity, and recognizably 'modern' concerns about statecraft and demography long predate Malthus. What was new to this era was the concern that population growth would disrupt ecological systems, leading to some form of environmental collapse whose feedback loops would destroy the sustainability of human life on earth. As Bashford has shown, the first half of the twentieth century saw a preoccupation with questions of 'room' on the globe, these being directly derived from Malthus's *Essay*, and with a complex amalgam of resultant issues around food supplies, optimum population densities, eugenic matters of demographic quality and contraception.[3] As she points out, this generation of 'keepers of population knowledge' died in the years either side of 1970, but their efforts were already being overwritten by the new type of ecological demographic agenda that defined modern environmentalism's concern with population, this being led by Paul Ehrlich's phenomenally successful *The Population Bomb* (1968) which 'at once incorporated and obliterated the generations of work that preceded it'.[4]

The new environmental inflection of demographic anxieties might be seen merely as a part of the broader flourishing of environmentalism in these years, but Robertson has argued instead that changing attitudes to population were causally significant in the construction of modern environmentalism: 'the history of population concern can help explain why the environmental movement exploded exactly when it did'.[5] Elsewhere, he has pointed to the strong chronological conjunction between a peak in neo-Malthusianism in the period 1968–70 and the peak of environmentalism more generally.[6] As he summarizes matters, those who attended to population concerns were early adopters of an environmentally attuned attitude: '[D]espite their misjudgements, the Malthusian environmentalists identified and called attention to environmentally destructive patterns of modern American society ... far sooner and with more clarity than others.'[7]

Putting these arguments together, it is possible to frame one element of the emergence of modern environmentalism in terms of a shifting discursive construction of demography in general, and of Malthus's contribution in particular. On such a reading, as one generation's understanding of Malthus in terms of room, food and population density subsided, so a new 'green Malthus' emerged as the analyst of population's deleterious impact on ecosystems. And as a stronger hypothesis about the importance of this green Malthus, it is possible with Robertson to suggest that neo-Malthusianism was ahead of the game, being a vital catalyst to the 'great synchronization' of modern environmentalism rather than just one part of that assemblage. In order to examine this reading of events, this chapter looks at the ways in which Malthus's *Essay* was edited in the period from 1958 to 1976 to assess how Malthus's contribution was framed and to consider whether and when that contribution came to be keyed around an ecological reading of demographic issues.

Malthus's publication bomb

One other element of the birth of modern environmentalism was the 'eco-book boom' of the period; that is, the unprecedented number and sales of publishing ventures about the environment. Indeed, 'in July 1971, a bibliographer at the Library of Congress reported that more books about environmental issues had appeared in the year since the first Earth Day than in all of American history before'.[8] Malthus was very much a part of this. In an assessment of academic publishing about Malthus since 1933, for example, Waterman noted that 'reappraisal of Malthus ... [was] well under way by the mid 1960s' following a long dearth of interest.[9] Academic literature was not just focusing on Malthus as a scholar of population or economics, but also aligning him with questions about the underdeveloped world, American food production and the history of science.[10] And yet such publications were by their very nature only aimed at a small, specialist audience; they could not have targeted the sorts of mass market at which titles such as Ehrlich's *Population Bomb* were pitched. A 'mass market' Malthus would come via a different channel; namely, editions of his *Essay* aimed at a general audience.

Looking at editions of the *Essay* in strictly bibliometric terms, there is considerable evidence to support the idea of a 'publication bomb';[11] that is, a discernible upsurge in popular publishing of Malthus's works, which is chronologically coincident with the more historically extensive readings of the birth of modern environmentalism. In the 120 years after Malthus's death in 1834, there were only three complete editions of the *Essay* printed in English: a 'seventh' edition in 1872; an edition by G.T. Bettany published in 1890; and one edited by William Layton for the Everyman Library in 1914. This last edition went through a series of reprints until 1952.[12] There were other sources by which Malthus's *Essay* could be accessed, most notably a 1926 facsimile for the Royal Economic Society of the 1798 edition, annotated by the pioneering biographer of Malthus, James Bonar, and made using the copy from John Maynard Keynes's own library. There was also a book bringing together chapters from the first and the second edition of the *Essay* in a set of parallel readings that was published by Macmillan in 1895 and reprinted on several occasions into the twentieth century.

In the 120 years to 1955, then, English-language editions of Malthus were rare, averaging no more than one per quarter-century. By contrast, the Malthusian publication bomb saw the production of seven complete, new editions with original editorial apparatuses in the period 1958 to 1976.[13] The process began with a revamp of the Everyman Library's Malthus in 1958 with a new introduction by Michael Fogarty, this edition being superseded in quick time (for reasons that will become apparent) by one with an introduction from the historical demographer Thomas Hollingsworth in 1973. The year after the emergence of Fogarty's edition saw Kenneth Boulding introduce a modern spelling rendering of the 1798

Essay for the University of Michigan Press. One year later again, the historian Gertrude Himmelfarb produced an edition for Random House's Modern Library. And then in 1963, the US publisher R.D. Irwin produced an edition. While these editions were important and their framing of Malthus's achievement will be analysed shortly, it was the two other editions of Malthus that made his words more readily available to a mass audience by the very nature of their publishers. First, Penguin Books published an edition of the 1798 *Essay* edited by the philosopher Antony Flew in 1970/1.[14] Penguin was unequivocally the dominant publisher in the United Kingdom market: 'the dominion of Penguin ... was absolute. By 1969, Penguin's estimated annual sales amounted to around 27 million books, about a third of the entire market, and this was its *lowest* share since the beginning of the war.'[15] This edition, still in print today, has sold some 64,000 copies.[16] Second, W.W. Norton published the *Essay* in their series 'Critical Editions in the History of Ideas' in 1976, with notes and an introduction by Philip Appleman. Again because of Norton's centrality to the collegiate market in the United States, this edition was able to reach an unprecedentedly large audience. Going into a second, revised edition in 2001, the Norton Malthus has sold some 15,000 copies.[17]

Averaging a new edition every two and a half years in the era 1958 to 1976, and with well over 80,000 copies sold in total, there can be no question that the publication of and appetite for Malthus's *Essay* underwent a step change at this time, a time that coincides precisely with the surge of modern environmentalism. And yet, as Hume taught us in the generation before Malthus, constant conjunction does not prove causation; the mere fact that Malthus was published with unprecedented vigour at this time cannot demonstrate either that this was caused by or was part of an emergent mass environmentalism, nor can it show the validity of Robertson's causal argument in the other direction that a resurgent Malthusianism spurred on modern ecological awareness. The boom in Malthus publishing could easily reflect changes in the book business as opposed to a putative eco-book boom: the rapid expansion of university education and the flourishing of the affordable paperback industry on both sides of the Atlantic may explain the Malthus publication bomb with no need for recourse to environmentalism. To address this question demands that we attend to the content of these new editions of Malthus: how was Malthus's contribution framed and imagined by his editors in the years after 1958? Was he viewed as originating awareness of the relationship between population growth and ecological system stress that defined the new green Malthusianism of the Ehrlich generation?

Editing the *Essay* and imagining Malthus, 1914–76

For the general reader trying to access Malthus's *Essay* prior to the late 1950s, by far the most commonly available edition was that produced by Everyman. At the time when he acted as editor for Everyman, William Layton was a promising Cambridge-trained economist who shared rooms with Keynes.[18] The year 1914 was to prove the great turning point in Layton's career as he was seconded to the Civil Service at the outbreak of the war, something that made his name and changed his career path away from academia. Layton would serve the League of Nations and was a longstanding editor of *The Economist*, being made Lord Layton in 1946.[19]

Layton's introduction to the *Essay* resonated strongly with the concerns of 1914, but the ideas of population control, eugenics and race anxiety were remarkably long-lived. As such, Layton's introduction still had strong resonance with many of the debates about demography in the immediate postwar period. Elements of Layton's approach came from his roommate Keynes's lectures on population to the Cambridge economics department.[20] Thus Layton argued that the classic Malthusian problem of population pressing on the means of subsistence had been dissipated in Europe in the nineteenth century, but that 'there are some who are already suggesting that the rise in the cost of living in the last few years foreshadows keen competition on the part of industrial nations for the world's food supplies'.[21] He also noted with Keynes that in the developing world 'the actual checks to population ... are still those so well described by Malthus'.[22]

The rest of Layton's introduction moved from questions relating to population numbers to address twin anxieties about differential fertility that were staples of demographic and political discussion in this era. First, there was a racialized concern about fertility: on a global scale, if affluent white races controlled their populations while the rest of the world was under the aegis of classic Malthusian checks, 'a change will be brought about in the relative proportions of the white and other races of the world'.[23] For specific nations, this differential fertility could lead to 'race suicide': 'in the United States ... it is no exaggeration to say that the whole country would have become entirely black were it not for the tide of emigration from Europe'.[24] Second, the greater fertility of the poor and the less-intelligent raised eugenic questions around national strength, talent and wellbeing. Without adjudicating on either issue, Layton concluded that they showed that 'the problem he [Malthus] raises is now, as ever, one of the greatest practical importance'.[25] For all this framing of Malthus's modernity, Layton's introduction was clearly losing its relevance by its final iteration in 1952, its thematic preoccupations showing strong affinities with the concerns G.T. Bettany had raised in his edition of Malthus as long ago as 1890. It would certainly appear that the Everyman Library viewed matters thus, as they were the first to commission a new editorial apparatus for Malthus's *Essay* and thereby begin his publication bomb.

Antony Flew, the editor of the 1970 Penguin Malthus (to which we will turn in due course), was famously waspish in tone, and he surpassed himself in a note that condemned the 1958 Everyman Library edition by commenting that 'it is wryly appropriate that the Catholic General Editor of the Everyman Library chose a philoprogenitive fellow Catholic, himself of Irish origin, to edit their new edition of the Second Essay'.[26] While this might be dismissed as the standard stuff of academic backbiting, in fact Flew's caustic aside captures more than a grain of truth about the edition Michael Fogarty produced in 1958.

It is not entirely clear why Fogarty was chosen to replace Layton's introduction, as he had not written about Malthus or demography previously and his grasp of basic facts about Malthus's life was uncertain, re-treading as he did the claim that Malthus 'practised the principle of population to the extent of eleven girls'.[27] What Fogarty undoubtedly did achieve in his 'Introduction' was to position Malthus in close proximity to Catholic doctrine about marriage and the family. This was made most apparent when Fogarty argued that 'in modern debates on population the extreme positions are often the "Catholic" and the "Malthusian", and these seem mutually exclusive. Yet Malthus's view of sex was essentially that of the Catholic Church, and the country where his principles have been most literally and whole-heartedly applied is the Republic of Ireland.'[28] Fogarty drew on Malthus's well-known hostility to contraception as 'improper arts',[29] an orthodox position for an eighteenth-century Anglican, and implicitly made the assumption that Malthus would have retained the same position 170 years later and thereby held a Catholic viewpoint.

This was but the first move in a set that might be said to 'Catholicize' Malthus for Everyman's readership. Thus Fogarty drew attention to the fact that Malthus believed in natural law and ethics, the doctrine that 'the prime source of knowledge about our duties is ... the study of nature'. Fogarty dubbed this 'the "Catholic" philosophy of natural law', thereby aligning Malthus once more in a Catholic doctrinal landscape. Reverting to this topic and splicing Malthus with the present day, Fogarty later added that 'his ideas on sex and on the natural law are still very much sub-ject to argument, indeed even more so than in his time. Humanists as well as Catholics (or Protestants who hold the "Catholic" tradition) can accept his doctrine of the natural law. But many Reformed theologians, to-day [sic] and in the past, deny that the law can be read out of nature.'[30]

Even where Fogarty did not connect Malthus exclusively to a Catholic position, he firmly placed him with respect to denominational discourse. Thus commentating on Malthus's argument that the poor must be able to support their own children, Fogarty glossed that 'in proposing these aus-terities Malthus talks ... like a Non conformist minister'.[31] Fogarty con-joined Malthus's emphasis on the need for self-reliance with the efforts of evangelical missionaries and '[from] a very different theological back-ground, [with] the Young Christian Workers ... in the Brussels slums around the First World War'.[32] This last reference once more brought Malthus into conjunction with Catholicism, in this case the burgeon-ing twentieth-century political-cum-religious groups of Catholic Europe known collectively as 'Christian Democrats'.

Fogarty also framed Malthus as 'one of the founders of modern eco-nomics'.[33] What Fogarty impressed upon his readers was Malthus's scope, that his demography and economics were also wrapped up not only with an ethics of natural law, but also with 'a philosophy and psychology of sex' and with a 'political and social philosophy'.[34] And thus in conclusion, and in a rare nod towards emergent concerns about a population explosion, Fogarty depicted Malthus as someone we should read today 'as a more specialised commentary by a skilled and observant investigator on the problems of cultural change in an Early Industrial age; an age with whose hard problems and gloomy conditions the maps of Asia, Africa, and Latin American are littered to-day'.[35]

Why did Fogarty depict Malthus as he did? It is hard not to answer this question in terms of Fogarty's own preoccupations, albeit this explan-ation can be ventured somewhat more charitably than did Flew. Fogarty wrote an autobiography, *My Life and Ours* (1999), shortly before his death in 2001. While he does not mention his work editing Malthus, he does make clear his lifelong commitment to Catholicism. Fogarty had gone to the elite Catholic school Ampleforth, and it was here he learned about Catholic doctrine, including ideas about natural law. After Ampleforth, Fogarty went on to read philosophy, politics and economics at Oxford, taking a first in 1938. He was particularly interested in economics and was part of the first generation in Oxford to be influenced by Keynes's ideas (although whether Keynes's admiration for Malthus sparked Fogarty's interest is not clear).[36] In the 1950s, Fogarty began to move beyond economics, notably through studying Catholicism and its organizational networks. In 1957, Fogarty published perhaps his most significant academic book, a meticulously researched historical and political inquiry into the phenomenon of Christian Democracy, with which he would link Malthus a year later in his comments on the Young Christian Workers.[37] Fogarty noted that moving to Cardiff and studying industrial relations also led him to a broader conception than that of an economist, demanding that he bring together economics, politics, sociology and psychology, something that again seems to connect with his depiction of Malthus.[38]

While one might psychologize the situation as Fogarty projecting his views onto Malthus, we are on secure ground in at least suggesting that his autobiographical preoccupations explain why Fogarty's edition depicted Malthus as it did. We can also see that Fogarty's reading of Malthus, while in a different discursive arena from the eugenic debates of Layton, most definitely did not tie Malthus to matters environmental. If the mid-1950s had begun to see a concern with the 'population bomb', notably through the 1954 Hugh Moore Foundation pamphlet of that name, this was clearly not influencing Fogarty's reading of Malthus as a Christian/Catholic evangelist for an ethics of moral restraint. Only ten years prior to Paul Ehrlich's celebrated public letter to Pope Paul VI denouncing Catholic population policy in the name of neo-Malthusianism, Fogarty's Everyman edition placed Malthus on the opposite side of this ideological divide.[39]

The Everyman Library were clearly not satisfied with Fogarty's Catholic Malthus, commissioning a new edition that appeared only 15 years later in 1973 and went to the opposite end of the critical spectrum by cleaving closely to a rigorously historical reading of Malthus. The new Everyman edition was introduced by T.H. Hollingsworth, a demographer at the University of Glasgow. Hollingsworth had been trained in the ambit of the sociologist D.V. Glass at the London School of Economics and went on to pioneer a quantitative approach to historical demography.[40] This background was strongly pertinent to the type of Malthus Hollingsworth presented. Drawing up a historical demographer's balance sheet, Hollingsworth saw Malthus as lacking sufficient data and as 'too fond of general theories and not interested enough in empirical results'.[41] Such empirical work had shown Malthus was wrong about the impact of the Poor Laws on fertility.[42] Hollingsworth also criticized Malthus's binary of positive and preventive checks as too simple,[43] before launching a more complex mathematical-cum-economic critique of Malthus's understanding of the relationship between human ingenuity and population size.[44] On the other side of the balance sheet, Hollingsworth praised Malthus's awareness of the different demographic dynamics exhibited by different social classes[45] and, above all, for discerning that the European demographic system was unique by virtue of its late marriage pattern.[46]

In what was a long introduction, Hollingsworth only left historical issues to address Malthus's contemporary importance very briefly. Here, it was argued that even after World War II the globe's demographic predicament was not apparent, but that 'by 1962, all was clear. The Malthusian prophecy was resurrected.'[47] Hollingsworth viewed this predicament exclusively in terms of population numbers, not in terms of their environmental impacts despite writing in the wake of Ehrlich *et al*. Further, Hollingsworth's final move was to place Malthus himself clearly in the past by noting that if Malthus's prophecy had been resurrected it was 'in a form scarcely recognizable as Malthus's' because he could not have contemplated the rapid mortality declines seen in the twentieth century nor would he have countenanced the contraceptive responses now being advocated in his name. If the *Essay* had been written 'as though the principle it states were true for all time, it was in fact a tract for its own times'.[48]

Ten years before this Everyman edition, a similar editorial project had emerged. In this case the balance sheet on Malthus was drawn up by Mark Blaug, who viewed Malthus's achievements more in economic than demographic terms and came to a still more critical conclusion about Malthus's pertinence to the present day. Blaug had completed a doctorate about David Ricardo and had gone on to teach a history of economics course at Yale University, replacing William Fellner who edited the series in which Blaug's edition of Malthus emerged.[49] This course led directly to what Blaug described as 'my only well-known book, *Economic Theory in Retrospect* (1962)'.[50] This text assessed economists in what Blaug calls 'absolutist' terms, comparing their achievements to current arguments in economic theory rather than framing them in the context of their own times.[51] It was from Chapter 3 of this book that the introduction to Blaug's 1963 edition of Malthus was largely drawn.

True to his absolutist approach, Blaug assessed Malthus's achievements negatively for two main reasons. First, Malthus's ideas were deemed, 165 years later, to be rather primitive; Blaug noting the 'utter simplicity' of his concepts.[52] Second, and more original was Blaug's criticism of the conceptual status of Malthus's ideas. Blaug had a lifelong interest in methodological issues in economic analysis. Autobiographically, he related this to encountering Karl Popper's ideas in 1962 but argued he had absorbed these ideas even earlier.[53] Blaug's Malthus introduction emerged in an edition dated August 1963, so it is impossible to know whether this was before or after his formal acquaintance with Popper but he certainly adopted a Popperian binary between hypotheses capable in theory of refutation, which were scientific, and those that, being by their construction impossible to refute, were therefore 'metaphysical'. Blaug had no doubt where Malthus's ideas were located in this binary: 'the Malthusian theory of population is a perfect example of metaphysics masquerading as science ... [I]t purports to say something about the real world but what it says is true by definition of its terms.'[54]

Putting these two lines of criticism together, Blaug came to a damning conclusion about Malthus: that he had not been able to diagnose the demographic realities of his own era. Drawing on economic history and historical demography, Blaug argued Malthus had failed to notice a 'population explosion' in the last two decades of the eighteenth century such that 'Malthus makes a poor guide in coming to grips with the nature of the population explosion that gave such prominence to his views'.[55] And unsurprisingly, if Malthus had not seen the population explosion of his own age, he would be of even less utility in diagnosing the economic and demographic realities of the later twentieth century's population explosion. Acknowledging that it was rapidly expanding populations in developing nations that had 'brought Malthus back into favour', and that this made Malthus's 'one of the longest-lived social theories of all times', Blaug concluded that despite this 'it is difficult to believe that Malthusian theory has much relevance to the discussion of modern population problems'.[56] For Blaug as for Hollingsworth then, attending to the historical Malthus showed his irrelevance to the analysis of contemporary population problems, and these problems themselves were modelled in socio-economic terms only, not in terms of possible environmental impacts.

If the 'population bomb' was one leitmotif of modern environmentalism, another was 'spaceship earth', a term that gained currency through a 1966 paper by the economist Kenneth Boulding.[57] As Boulding had been developing an ecological side to his economic analysis since 1958, it might be anticipated that when he introduced an edition of the *Essay* in 1959, this would firmly connect Malthus to emergent environmentalism.[58] On a closer inspection, the truth turns out to be somewhat more complex.

Boulding's trajectory had much in common with Fogarty's. Born a year earlier than Fogarty, Boulding also read philosophy, politics and economics at Oxford and came under the spell of the new Keynesianism.[59]

Boulding's early years as an academic were those of a conventional economist, his first paper addressing population issues – 'The Application of the
Pure Theory of Population Change to the Theory of Capital' – emerging
in 1934.[60] Here, the populations in question were not necessarily human
but any 'aggregation of disparate items, or "individuals", each one of
which conforms to a given definition, retains its identity with the passage
of time, and exists only during a finite interval'[61] and Boulding's interest
in them was not substantive, but in their use as a model for how capital
flows. But Boulding would soon diverge from the role of the economist;
he dated his emergent interest in conjoining economics with sociological
and political analysis to the years after 1948, an interest reinforced by his
move to the University of Michigan in the following year.[62] A decade later,
and still at Michigan, Boulding published his edition of the *Essay* for his
university's press.

As with Boulding's career, there are elements in his 'Forward' to the
Essay that resonate with Fogarty's edition in framing Malthus's work in
Christian terms as 'almost like a modern Book of Job' in its 'contemplation
of a system which seemed to promise man perpetual misery on earth'.[63]
Likewise, Boulding could see with Fogarty that Malthus was (on a journey he himself had been taking over the previous decade) far more than an
economist *sensu stricto*. And yet in the main, Boulding's brief comments
created a significantly different vision of Malthus's contribution from
Fogarty's. Boulding praised Malthus, in conventionally Keynesian terms, as
'a great and insightful economist' whose reputation had paradoxically been
sustained despite the complete eclipse of his work by Ricardo.[64] Where
he diverged from mere 'Keynesianizing' of Malthus, was in why Malthus
was deemed great: 'from Adam Smith he had learned the great concept of
what we now would call equilibrium ... The crucial principle is that there
must be *some* limit to the number of mankind, and that growth of population, at no matter how slow a rate, must eventually bring the number to
this limit.'[65] As such, Boulding started to depict Malthus as realizing that
'an equilibrium population is a stationary population'[66] and thus to read
Malthus as establishing the need for a steady state system in demography.
In conclusion, Boulding returned to this point, making its relevance to
his own time more transparent: 'atomic and solar energy, nitrogen from
the air and magnesium from the sea give us at least the promise of a stable
high-level technology, but even if we achieve this, we must still achieve
population control. On this point the Malthusian logic is inescapable.'[67]
This was needed because of Malthus's 'remarkable insight' that '*room* as
well as nourishment might limit natural populations'.[68]

In its discussion of the need to reach a stationary global population due to the limits on room on our planet, Boulding's introduction obviously approaches the terminology of 'spaceship earth' that would be celebrated and seized upon by the environmental movement. And yet at this point in Boulding's trajectory, it is more accurate to see his framing of Malthus's insights as part of his fascination with the general systems science of von Bertalanffy. At Michigan, Boulding grew fascinated by systems theory as a way to draw meaningful connections and analogies between different inquiries.[69] This use of one system as a proxy by which to understand another was already prefigured by his first analysis of populations in 1934.[70] That Malthus's work could be viewed in systemic terms was made apparent as an aside in a 1953 essay on 'Economic Progress as a Goal in Economic Life' and at greater length two years later in 'The Malthusian Model as a General System'.[71] Material from both papers was directly recycled into Boulding's 'Forward' to his edition of Malthus.

In sum, Boulding's 1959 edition of Malthus does offer glimpses of the ideas of spaceship earth that would make him a doyen of the environmental movement a decade later in its attention to the need to move to a steady state population in a world of limited resources and finite room. And yet this was not an anticipation of these themes, but rather demonstrates the extent to which Boulding was preoccupied with the application of systems science to social phenomena and that both population dynamics in general and Malthus's analysis of them in particular were grist to this intellectual mill. Spaceship earth, of course, was simply another application of the same form of analysis but one that, in its fortuitous timing and its imagery, seized the environmental imagination and thereby became detached from its intellectual moorings in Boulding's broader concern with systems. Boulding's 1959 Malthus edition, then, did indeed tread a territory that would become closely tied to modern environmental consciousness in the near future, but its closest kinship was with the mathematical analysis of social systems, not with an environmental reading of that project. Boulding's spaceship of 1966 was most assuredly not yet flying in his 1959 reading of Malthus.

A year after Boulding's edition came a far more ambitious edition of Malthus in Random House's 'Modern Library', edited by the historian Gertrude Himmelfarb. Himmelfarb's introduction began in the present day with a sentence as arresting as that which opened Paul Ehrlich's *Population Bomb* at the end of the decade: 'the "Population Bomb" is beginning to usurp the place of the H-Bomb in the public imagination and conscience'.[72] Himmelfarb would return to the contemporary situation in rounding out her picture of Malthus, but the bulk of her introduction produced a very particular image of Malthus as a historical actor.

Himmelfarb's introduction was devoted to Malthus's intellectual journey between the first and last editions of the *Essay* that the book reprinted. She argued that debates about reform of the Poor Laws were 'the more immediate and urgent occasion behind the writing of the *Essay*' than the revolutionary fears of 1798.[73] The Malthus of 1798 was depicted as a successor to Adam Smith to be noted for his 'boldness in pursuing the logic of laissez-faire'.[74] But Himmelfarb's real interest, and the way in which Malthus would speak to the era of the 'population bomb', emerged in her tracing of how Malthus's ideas evolved. From the 1803 edition, the *Essay*'s incorporation of prudence as a check to population gave Malthus's ideas a wholly different complexion. By allowing that moral and social conventions could undercut the iron law of population outstripping resources, Malthus had achieved 'the de-naturalization or socialization of the lower classes'.[75] Further, Malthus's recognition that governments, via education and changed electoral practices, could encourage prudence in the lower classes led him to advocate an 'enlarged scope of government ... oddly inconsonant with the spirit of laissez-faire'.[76] While acknowledging Malthus 'would have been as much appalled by "birth control" ... as the most pious Catholic',[77] Himmelfarb did not, unlike Fogarty, thereby see in Malthus a Christian let alone Catholic ethic. On the contrary, she viewed Malthus's advocacy of prudence and moral restraint in resolutely secular terms. Malthus was a 'prophet of our times' for his recognition of the 'embourgoisement' of society[78] and his realization that governments could help to harness the social, political and economic aspirations of the poorer classes to achieve societal improvement.

It was Malthus the analyst of 'prudence' who would speak to our planetary concerns. In concluding her introduction, Himmelfarb reverted to the contemporary situation where 'population is already pressing uncomfortably upon the natural resources'.[79] Her conception of these resources was ambiguous by virtue of its brevity, but related more to the extraction of a living than to the degradation of environmental systems. It was an economist's understanding of nature, not an ecologist's. Within this frame, Malthusian moral restraint, suitably updated, offered a way to defuse the population bomb. History had shown that 'forces that once seemed outside our control ... were ... controllable; and nature itself (including human nature) was ... capable of being tamed and pacified'.[80]

Himmelfarb did not apply this insight in detail to the present day, but her reference to nature and human nature would appear to suggest that the twinning of agricultural and industrial planning to harness nature (as in the paradigmatic achievements of the 'Green Revolution') with birth control programmes to harness human nature would metal a road out of the Malthusian impasse, this being exactly the sort of approach advocated by US strategists at the time.[81]

Himmelfarb noted of the array of responses to Malthus that readers 'find in a book exactly what they expect to find in it'.[82] It is plausible to suggest Himmelfarb likewise found exactly the sort of book she wanted as she and her husband Irving Kristol built a platform that a decade later would be dubbed 'neo-conservatism'. While Kristol was less enamoured of Malthus than Himmelfarb, they shared a sense of Malthus as part of the tradition that neo-conservatism sought to cherish.[83] Himmelfarb's 1960 introduction framed Malthus as making the same journey neo-conservatism would a century and a half later: Malthus believed in markets and individual self-determination in 1798, but coupled this from 1803 onwards with an awareness of the need for a moral fabric – prudence – whose maintenance created an inescapable need for state intervention. And if it was this emergent awareness of the need to qualify the excesses of laissez-faire that made Malthus a prophet of our times, it also made him a neo-conservative *avant la lettre*. Himmelfarb's neo-conservative Malthus was assuredly not an ecological one, however, even if he was a prophet who could address the population bomb.

Uniquely, for Antony Flew's edition of the *Essay* we can compare the textual material Flew produced with the 'backstage' discussions and debates with and within Penguin Books thanks to their preservation in the Penguin Archive. Putting these two sides together gives us a rich insight into the politics of publishing Malthus in the age of environmentalism.

Flew submitted his editorial material to Penguin in January 1970. Coming a few months before Earth Day in the United States but after the impact of Paul Ehrlich's *Population Bomb* on both sides of the Atlantic, it is unsurprising that Flew at least mentioned the 'population explosions occurring now' in his introduction,[84] and yet the broader texture of Flew's work in fact addressed two rather different questions. First, Flew was preoccupied with the logical structure of Malthus's argumentation; something that befitted his status as an academic philosopher. Second, Flew made a series of interventions by asides and notes about the 'politics of population', jousting with both Marxist socialism in the context of the Cold War and with Roman Catholicism as we have already glimpsed through his criticism of Fogarty's edition.

By far the longest portion of Flew's introduction attended to the form of Malthus's argument. As Flew recalled in an autobiographical memoir, his interest in Malthus began in 1954 when he moved to the newly formed University of Keele.[85] Keele's approach, akin to a liberal arts college, demanded conceptual breadth from its philosophers and the Oxford-trained Flew threw himself into this by teaching Malthus and Darwin. The first fruits of this appeared in a 1957 essay about Malthus,[86] and Flew's subsequent writings about Malthus merely recycled material from this paper, including the analysis in the 1970 introduction for Penguin.[87] The thrust of all these versions of Flew's argument was to point out that, despite some logical inconsistencies, Malthus's argument in the first edition of the *Essay* was robust and allowed us to understand the dilemmas of the present-day population explosion because 'it is enormously easier to introduce modern methods of death-control than it is to introduce any methods of birth-control'.[88] And on these grounds, Flew revealed his hand in terms of the politics of population, arguing from a secular humanist perspective (Flew was a lapsed Christian whose father was a Methodist minister) for the necessity of contraception in both the developed and the developing world.

Flew added an important note to his Penguin introduction at this point, advocating that easy access to contraception should be prioritized in the United Kingdom, both because 'it ought to be intolerable that there still are unpremeditated pregnancies and unwanted children' but also, in a comment that is the most significant alignment between Flew and emergent environmentalism, because 'it would by at least stabilizing our population relieve all those growing pressures on amenity, space, and social services'.[89] And yet the surrounding text makes it clear that Flew's main targets in these comments were political and religious rather than environmental: controlling British population would allow the country 'to replace those existing schools which are out of date if only we could divert to this purpose some of the funds which are at present required to pay for the provision of new school places for additional children'.[90] Flew dated his transition from being a pure philosopher to being a politically engaged one to his disenchantment with the student uprisings of 1968 and the defence of quality schooling was to be a persistent theme.[91]

Fogarty was quite right that Malthus did not endorse contraception, but Flew viewed Malthus as a fellow traveller because of his advocacy of population control. And this guided Flew to two main targets he recurrently attacked in his edition, Marxist socialism and the Roman Catholic Church, the two normally being yoked together partly for their shared hostility to Malthus but also because of Flew's conception of Marxism as 'a great crusading religion … the secular Islam of the twentieth century'.[92] Flew could not resist returning to this theme in a later note to Malthus's text, likening Henry VIII's break from Rome in the Reformation to 'Marshall Tito's first breach with Stalin's secular and Russian Vatican'.[93] Flew also noted that at the 1954 World Population Conference, anti-Malthusianism meant that 'Roman Catholic and Communist ideologues kept finding themselves in Holy-Unholy Alliance'.[94] He also lambasted Ronald Meek's edition of Marx and Engels' writings about Malthus from 1953 as speaking throughout in 'His Moscow's Voice',[95] a parody of the dog on the HMV (His Master's Voice) record label aimed at Meek for publishing with Lawrence and Wishart, the official publishing house of the Communist Party of Great Britain.

From a secular humanist standpoint, then, Flew argued that the essential logical coherence of Malthus's position demanded that we embrace population control in the form of contraception. To the extent that socialism and Roman Catholicism refused to accept Malthus's argument on ideological not intellectual grounds, they were both religions driven by agendas that Flew, as a lifelong admirer of Enlightenment reason in the form of the work of David Hume,[96] deemed abhorrent because they were irrational and prevented individual and societal advancement. If this is the version of Malthus that Penguin got, their archive shows that this is certainly not the type of Malthus they had initially envisaged and that some were unhappy with Flew's use of Malthus to advance his post-1968 agenda as a philosopher provocateur. Penguin Books had already developed a reputation as a publisher with an interest in environmental matters, thanks to their publication of the UK edition of Rachel Carson's *Silent Spring* in 1962 and they would go on to publish an edition of the *Ecologist*'s bestselling *Blueprint for Survival*, 'one of the key documents of eco-activism', the year after the emergence of Flew's Malthus.[97] Both Penguin's founder, Allen Lane, and its charismatic commissioning editor in the mid-1960s, Tony Godwin, were engaged with green issues and supported this as a publishing priority.[98] And yet the commission for a Penguin edition of Malthus was never seen in these terms; on the contrary, Penguin's initial thoughts in September 1967 revolved around an edition that fitted into their publishing profile in the history of economic thought, with Carlo Cipolla to act as editor and with the edition to be published in parallel with one of Ricardo's *Principles of Political Economy*.[99] By December of that year, however, Flew had been approached.

When Flew submitted his manuscript, two problems emerged in his relationship with Penguin. First, it became apparent that Flew had not prepared a new edition, and that his copy text was Boulding's 1959 Michigan edition. This issue was tackled but the resultant changes delayed publication, explaining the discrepancy between the title-page's dating of 1970 and the actual publication date in January 1971. On this point, and tacitly acknowledging that Malthus could have been linked to environmental issues, Flew noted that 'a publication in 1971 will take some of the force out of any possible linkage with the European Conservation Year [of 1970], but the new marriage of inconvenience with [the publication of the Pelican edition of] David Ricardo is perhaps even more appropriate'.[100] As it had been envisaged on commissioning in 1967, Malthus would emerge framed as a contribution to the history of economics, not tied to matters environmental.

The other set of problems about the Penguin Malthus emerged via its proofreader, Carol Filby. As the book made its way from copy-editing to page-setting in September 1970, she wrote lambasting it to commissioning editor Dieter Pevsner as 'quite unprintable'. Expanding on her reasons for this judgement, Filby honed in on many of the textual elements already identified: 'the editor used the preface and footnotes throughout as a platform for his own personal prejudices, most of which have no connection whatever to the text itself ... the footnotes themselves are farcical'. That Filby was referring to Flew's anti-Catholic comments was made transparent by her statement 'that I am a Roman Catholic', but she concluded that books that are political soapboxes are 'just plain bad books, and there is no more to be said about it'.[101] Peter Wright responded by defending Flew's approach as part of the Penguin ethos: 'one of the purposes of the Pelican Classics Series is to point out the relevance of the book in question to the present time, and this is just what Flew is doing'.[102] And yet the troubled gestation of Flew's Malthus edition left a taint on the project for its publisher. Where Flew opined grandiloquently that his edition as the first to supply notes should 'be accepted as the standard edition', Wright offered a damning assessment of the book before it was even launched: 'In summary if we had our time over again, we certainly wouldn't ask Flew to do Malthus, but equally, now we that we've got it, its [sic] not by any means bad enough to warrant throwing it away and starting again. Incidentally you'd better not put my view of Flew's editing in writing; we don't want a libel action.'[103]

It has been said that 'each file in the [Penguin] archive ... has a story of its own'.[104] The story of Penguin's Malthus only features environmentalism as a relatively modest plotline; as we have seen, Flew did indeed discuss excess resource usage due to population increase but mainly to advocate contraception on humanist grounds. A marketing link to the European Year of Conservation was also ventured only to be dropped once publication was pushed back to 1971. Far more central to Penguin's initial scoping of the project was its connection to related titles in the history of economic thought. And at the heart of Flew's conception of the edition was a philosophical analysis of Malthus's argument to defend the necessity of contraception in the face of state socialist and Roman Catholic critiques. It would only be in 1976 that environmental issues would come to play a more central role in the story of an edition of Malthus's *Essay*.

It might seem incongruous that it was a poet and literary scholar who finally produced an edition of the *Essay* that resonated unambiguously with the environmental movement and its framing of the population question, but Philip Appleman's career, scholarly and creative, has been devoted to the furtherance of Darwinian (and by extension Malthusian) ideas. Appleman was born in 1926 and was thereby of the same generation as the group of scholars and activists who would define North American environmentalism. Growing up under the aegis of 'Midwestern fundamentalism' where 'church fathers and school boards had in effect abolished the natural law from the schools', Appleman's conversion experience came when he was in the merchant navy in 1948. As he adds, 'I was led to Malthus by reading Darwin'; it was via Darwin that Appleman was led to editing Malthus, not directly by the massive neo-Malthusian explosion of interest in population.[105]

Appleman's Darwinian epiphany and its Malthusian addendum were reinforced by his academic career in the 1950s and 1960s. He was employed at the University of Indiana, one of the first major US universities to develop environmental programmes in the 1960s,[106] and from that base was allowed to join the International School of America in 1960–1 and 1962–3. It was in this context that Appleman worked in India, a Malthusian *rite de passage* he shared with the doyens of neo-Malthusian environmentalism,[107] which led him to write a book about overpopulation in 1965, *The Silent Explosion*. The experience of India did not just lead to this factual tract, but also to new lines in Appleman's poetic career. Thus a 1968 poem, 'The Path of Redemption', was situated in Calcutta, fixating on 'Bony bodies dry as sticks' just as Ehrlich did in his famous opening to *The Population Bomb* in the same year. Again in 1968, Appleman's 'Middle of the Night', a poem about insomnia, noted the poet panicked at night, awake contemplating 'local politics,/demographic curves,/chronic aches/ and pains. Bad Nerves'.[108] And likewise as a novelist Appleman returned to overpopulation, most notably in his semi-autobiographical *In the Twelfth Year of the War* (1970), about a cerebral sailor, Ben. Ben sees the world, in an echo of the Vietnam conflict, as 'twelve years of GI's slogging through rice paddies, testing the support weapons of the forthcoming Holocaust on brown-skinned natives – the natives meanwhile breeding like rabbits'. Ben also exchanges letters with his too-worldly girlfriend Laura back in the US, who parodies Swift's *Modest Proposal* to suggest the 'irritating oversupply of babies' can be addressed by selling them as slave labour to American citizens.[109]

Malthusian themes had thus been recurring in Appleman's work for more than a decade after his experience of India when he published his edition of Malthus's *Essay* for Norton in 1976. Thus Appleman noted what Flew had called the 'Holy-Unholy' alliance of Roman Catholicism and socialism against Malthus, but took this point in a different direction. These groups, together with neo-conservatives (the likes, presumably, of Himmelfarb), were false optimists, 'whereas the "doomsayers," the so-called pessimists, are often the ones to raise an alarm, thus sometimes producing effective social action'.[110] In this category of socially transformative pessimists, Appleman spliced together Malthus with Rachel Carson, and in doing so framed Malthus as an ancestor of the modern environmental movement. This point was made still more clearly in the way Appleman envisaged Malthus's relevance to the modern age. Akin to Keynes (and thereby William Layton), Appleman thought Malthus's direct relevance to European societies had waned in the nineteenth century, but with rapid population growth 'after World War II … Malthus's handwriting once again appeared, clear and portentous, on the wall'. The new 'Malthusian crisis of vast proportions' was one of 'hidden, sometimes frightening, costs'. And those costs were measured in the coinage of environmental degradation: 'it is increasingly clear that the necessity of supplying food to very large and rapidly growing populations has pollution and resource-depletion effects that are more imminent and more destructive than they would be in a less densely populated world'.[111] Appleman also used his introduction to attack those who updated Malthus's hostility to social welfare schemes for an age of global food shortages and environmental stress by advocating 'food triage,' the selective use of food aid that would implicitly leave certain countries to face mass starvation. For Appleman, 'where Malthus was least humane, he was most wrong'[112] and this applied *a fortiori* to modern successors.

The environmental slant Appleman provided in his introduction was reinforced by the other contents of the Norton edition. The book offered not just Malthus's text but other supporting documents. While these documents covered a range of material, they included texts covering 'The Current Demographic and Environmental Situation', a titular conjunction itself redolent of the new environmental reading of Malthus, the section going on to excerpt Boulding's seminal essay, 'The Economics of the Coming Spaceship Earth'. A further and final selection of readings in the book covered 'Some "neo-Malthusian" proposals', and excerpted the luminaries of the new Malthusian moment who spliced together environmental and population concerns: the Paddocks, Hardin, the Ehlrichs and Lester Brown.

The Norton edition of the *Essay* addressed religious, political and economic readings of Malthus, but its main innovation and its Ariadnian thread was the conjunction of Malthus, population and the new environmentalism. In the quarter-century since his Darwinian epiphany, Appleman had been recurrently preoccupied by demographic questions of overpopulation and its impact on the globe in terms of warfare, quality of life, resource depletion and environmental degradation. In this conjunction, Appleman both reflected and was one of the creators of the distinctive intellectual filiations definitive of modern environmentalism. And turning these concerns to the framing of Malthus himself, Appleman created the first editorial apparatus to emphasize a green Malthus who spoke to the burgeoning environmental movement.

Conclusion: publishing Malthus and the Malthusian moment

The environmental historian Joachim Radkau has noted that we should beware reifying 'the' environmental movement of the 1960s and 1970s as if it were a singular, coherent platform.[113] A similar point holds good about the editing of Malthus in the same period: there were in fact many different discursive ambitions displayed in the editions of Malthus that emerged in this era. Above all, and putting these two points together, even if there was a temporal conjunction between an upsurge in environmental consciousness and the flourishing of new editions of Malthus's *Essay*, they were at best but tangentially connected phenomena. And that conjunction itself can be unpacked, the surge in Malthus editions being at its most intense in the five years either side of 1960, whereas the peak of environmental concern came a decade later.

Reviewing the evidence presented here, there were two recurrent thematics that appeared in the editing of Malthus. First, and perhaps surprisingly, Malthus remained interwoven with religious discourse throughout the period. This is most apparent in the Catholic reading of Malthus's intellectual achievements offered by Fogarty, yet it also informed Boulding and Himmelfarb. From the opposite side of the religious spectrum, Antony Flew, as one of the most prominent public atheists of his generation in the United Kingdom, could not resist polemics against Catholicism and against a state socialism he regarded as a form of religion manqué in his reading of Malthus. These, as we have seen, led to complex wranglings within his publishing house about the very notion of a worthy edition for the general public. Likewise Appleman's self-narrated journey was from a stifling religious bigotry to a Darwinian humanism with Malthus positioned as an emancipatory force despite his personal faith. As such, for a generation of editors born in the years either side of the First World War, religion, humanism and secularism remained fundamental issues, responses to which could be encoded through engaging with Malthus and Malthusianism.

Second, editions of Malthus remained tightly enmeshed in the context of the history of economics and demography. This is self-evident for the editions produced by Hollingsworth and Blaug, but is also relevant to other editorial projects. Thus for Fogarty and Boulding, Malthus offered a more interdisciplinary understanding of the task of the economist that was of enormous contemporary resonance. In both cases, it is hard not to see the continued spectre of Keynes's admiration for Malthus. This tied their editorial efforts with Malthus back to those at the beginning of the twentieth century as embodied in Leyton's 1914 edition. And while Flew's engagement with the ideas of Malthus exhibited a less economic trajectory, from the outset Penguin as Flew's publisher saw its edition of the *Essay* as a part of its history of economics list. Himmelfarb also engaged with Malthus as a political economist in her framing of his contribution as bringing the analysis of poverty into the social realm.

Taken in the round, Malthus was still predominantly read in terms other than environmental ones. Elements of the Malthus that interested the environmental movement were of course present in these editions of the *Essay*. Flew, Blaug, Himmelfarb and Hollingsworth in particular (and Fogarty to a lesser extent) understood the 'population explosion' as a simple fact, a backcloth for the continued interest of Malthus to a modern audience, although whether he was a useful guide to that fact was less than clear to Blaug and Hollingsworth. Likewise, the close filiations between Boulding's interest in systems theory, in Malthus as a systematic thinker and in the earth as a limited system long predated his celebrated spaceship earth essay of 1966 and were evident in his 1959 edition of Malthus. But it was only with Appleman's 1976 edition that Malthus was thoroughly editorialized as contributing to debates about resource depletion and environmental pollution, this at the very moment when, on both sides of the Atlantic, the environmental movement started to lose momentum in the face of economic austerity.[114] And none of these editions, of course, ever made Malthus an environmental superstar like Ehrlich, the latter selling an estimated two million copies of *The Population Bomb* while Malthus editions only sold in the tens of thousands.[115]

Malthus, then, was edited with different motivations in mind. Religious polemics, neo-conservatism and Cold War critiques of Marxism rubbed shoulders with historical demography, economic analysis and systems theory in the depiction of why Malthus was worth reading in the 20 years after 1958. One thread of this was indeed concerns about overpopulation and its environmental ramifications but we should not exaggerate either its dominance or the speed at which it rose to prominence in editorial depictions of the nature of Malthus's achievement and his contemporary relevance. In terms of the quantity of editions published, there can be no doubt that the period 1958–76 was a 'Malthusian moment'. And yet this publishing moment was certainly not the spearhead of a modern environmentalism and it was far more diverse in its aims and ambitions than can be comprehended by seeing in it a mere echo of the broader environmental moment. A green version of Malthus may have emerged during the era of environmentalism's upsurge, but it was both peripheral to that upsurge and by no means hegemonic as a vision of Malthus's achievement.

Notes

1 For the United States, see Samuel Hays, *Beauty, Health, and Permanence: Environmental Politics in the United States, 1955–1985* (Cambridge: Cambridge University Press, 1987), p. 55; Patrick Allitt, *A Climate of Crisis: America in the Age of Environmentalism* (New York: Penguin, 2014); Adam Rome, *The Genius of Earth Day: How a 1970s Teach-In Unexpectedly Made the First Green Generation* (New York: Hill & Wang, 2013). For Britain, see Dominic Sandbrook, *State of Emergency: The Way we Were: Britain 1970–1974* (London: Penguin, 2010), pp. 176–221; John Sheail, *An Environmental History of Twentieth-Century Britain* (Basingstoke: Palgrave, 2001), pp. 262–3; and Meredith Veldman, *Fantasy, the Bomb and the Greening of Britain: Romantic Protest, 1945–1980* (Cambridge: Cambridge University Press, 1994), p. 208.

2 Thomas Borstelmann, *The 1970s: A New Global History from Civil Rights to Economic Inequality* (Princeton: Princeton University Press, 2012), pp. 231–47;

Joachim Radkau, *The Age of Ecology: A Global History* (Oxford: Polity Press, 2014), pp. 79–113, quote at p. 79.

3 Alison Bashford, *Global Population: History, Geopolitics, and Life on Earth* (New York: Columbia University Press, 2014).

4 Ibid., p. 358 for previous generation and p. 364 for Ehrlich.

5 Tom Robertson, '"Thinking Globally": American Foreign Aid, Paul Ehrlich, and the Emergence of Environmentalism in the 1960s', in Francis Gavin and Mark Lawrence (eds.), *Beyond the Cold War: Lyndon Johnson and the New Global Challenges of the 1960s* (New York: Oxford University Press, 2014), pp. 185–206, p. 198.

6 Thomas Robertson, *The Malthusian Moment: Global Population Growth and the Birth of American Environmentalism* (New Brunswick: Rutgers University Press, 2012), pp. 152–3 and 221.

7 Ibid., p. 11.

8 Rome, *Genius of Earth Day*, pp. 209–10 and 240; cf. pp. 240–50.

9 A.M.C. Waterman, 'Reappraisal of Malthus the Economist, 1933–97', *History of Political Economy*, 30 (1998), 293–334, p. 325 (the long dearth is at p. 297).

10 John Pullen, 'The Last Sixty Five Years of Malthus Scholarship', *History of Political Economy*, 30 (1998), 343–52.

11 I borrow the term 'publication bomb' from the staunchly anti-Malthusian Julian Simon, who described the reaction to his *The Ultimate Resource* of 1981 in these terms: Julian Simon, *A Life against the Grain: The Autobiography of an Unconventional Economist* (New Brunswick: Transactions, 2002), p. 266.

12 Terry Seymour, *A Printing History of Everyman's Library, 1906–1982* (Bloomington: AuthorHouse, 2011). Seymour notes Layton and Fogarty but does not reference Hollingsworth's 1973 introduction (discussed below).

13 My argument only attends to the *Essay*. The sense of an explosion of interest in Malthus's writings is strengthened by noting that in the same time period Patricia James published *The Travel Diaries of T.R. Malthus* (1966), Bernard Semmel edited Malthus's *Occasional Pamphlets* for the first time since his death (1963), Malthus's *Summary View of the Principle of Population* (1830) was reprinted both as part of the New American Library volume on population (1960) and in D.V Glass's *Introduction to Malthus* (1953). Further, facsimiles abounded with a reprint of Bonar's annotated 1798 *Essay* in 1966 in the UK. This was also included in New York publisher Augustus M. Kelley's series of 'Reprints of Economic Classics' in 1965, a series that also included Malthus's *Pamphlets* (1970), *Principles of Political Economy* (1969), *Definitions of Political Economy* (1963) and *Measure of Value* (1957).

14 The title page states 1970 but the Penguin Archive at the University of Bristol gives a publication date of 28 January 1971: File DM1852/040/18. All subsequent references to the Penguin Archive are to this file, which is a copious A4 envelope file with no other internal referencing system. Thanks to Joanna Prior at Penguin Books for authorizing my use of this material and to Michael Richardson and Hannah Lowery in Special Collections at the University of Bristol for facilitating access.

15 Rick Rylance, 'Reading with a Mission: The Public Sphere of Penguin Books', *Critical Quarterly*, 47 (2005), 48–66, p. 52, emphasis in original. See also Steve Hare (ed.) *Penguin Portrait: Allen Lane and the Penguin Editors* (London: Penguin, 1995), pp. 278ff, and Jeremy Lewis, *Penguin Special: The Life and Times of Allen Lane* (London: Viking, 2005), p. 366.

16 Figures from Penguin courtesy of Simon Winder, email 10 January 2014. This edition emerged in the Pelican Classics series, which was founded in 1969 but was then shifted to the Penguin Classics series with no alterations to its text in 1985.

17 Figures from W.W. Norton courtesy of Rivka Genesen, email 19 May 2012.

18 David Hubback, *No Ordinary Press Baron: A Life of Walter Layton* (London: Weidenfeld & Nicolson, 1985), p. 40.

19 Ibid.; and Richard S. Grayson, 'Layton, Walter Thomas, first Baron Layton (1884–1966)', *Oxford Dictionary of National Biography*.

20 See John Toye, *Keynes on Population* (Oxford: Oxford University Press, 2000) for texts and commentary.

21 T.R. Malthus, *An Essay on Population*, ed. W.T. Layton (London and New York: Dent and Dutton, 1952), p. xi. Note this section is found verbatim in the 1914 edition. In fact, only one slight verbal change was made to the penultimate paragraph of the introduction in the 1952 edition.

22 Malthus, *Essay* (ed. Layton), p. xiii.

23 Ibid., p. xiii.

24 Ibid., pp. xiii–xiv.

25 Ibid., p. xiv.

26 T.R. Malthus, *An Essay on the Principle of Population*, ed. Antony Flew (Harmondsworth: Penguin, 1970), p. 278 n. 17. Flew made a similar comment in his essay 'The Structure of Malthus's Population Theory' in Bernard Baumrin (ed.), *Philosophy of Science: The Delaware Seminar: Volume 1: 1961–1962* (New York: John Wiley, 1963), pp. 283–307, p. 284.

27 T.R. Malthus, *An Essay on Population*, ed. Michael Fogarty (London: Dent, 1958), p. vi. Malthus had three children, only two of whom survived him, a fact that Layton was aware of in 1914.

28 Malthus, *Essay* (ed. Fogarty), pp. vi–vii.

29 This comment was made in the 1803 edition: see Patricia James, ed., *T.R. Malthus: An Essay on the Principle of Population*, 2 vols. (Cambridge: Cambridge University Press, 1989), vol. 2, p. 97.

30 Malthus, *Essay* (ed. Fogarty), p. ix.

31 Ibid., p. xiv.

32 Ibid., p. xvii.

33 Ibid., p. vi.

34 Ibid., p. vii.

35 Ibid., pp. xvii–xviii.

36 Michael Fogarty, *My Life and Ours* (Oxford: Thornton's of Oxford, 1999), pp. 16, 41–3 and 73–5.

37 Michael Fogarty, *Christian Democracy in Western Europe, 1820–1953* (London: Routledge and Kegan Paul, 1957).

38 Fogarty, *My Life and Ours*, pp. 82–4.

39 Robertson, *Malthusian Moment*, pp. 155–7.

40 T.H. Hollingsworth, *The Demography of the British Peerage* (London: Population Investigation Committee, 1965); T.H. Hollingsworth, *Historical Demography* (Ithaca, NY: Cornell University Press, 1969).

41 T.R. Malthus, *An Essay on the Principle of Population*, ed. T.H. Hollingsworth (London: Dent, 1973), pp. xv.

42 Ibid., pp. xxi–xxii.

43 Ibid., p. xv.

44 Ibid., pp. xvii–xviii.

45 Ibid., pp. xxiii–xxiv.

46 Ibid., pp. xiii–xiv.

47 Ibid., p. xxxi.

48 Ibid., p. xxxii.

49 For Blaug's life see his autobiographical essay, 'Not Only an Economist: Autobiographical Reflections of a Historian of Economic Thought', in Mark Blaug, *Not Only an Economist: Recent Essays by Mark Blaug* (Cheltenham: Edward Elgar, 1997), pp. 3–25; see also Denis O'Brien, 'Mark Blaug, 1927–2011', *Biographical Memoirs of Fellows of the British Academy*, 12 (2013), 25–47.

50 Blaug, 'Not Only an Economist', p. 11.

51 Ibid.

52 Thomas Malthus, *Principle of Population*, ed. Mark Blaug (Homewood, IL: Richard D. Irwin, 1963), p. vii. Cf. Mark Blaug, *Economic Theory in Retrospect* (London: Heinemann, 1968), p. 70.

53 Blaug, 'Not Only an Economist', pp. 18–19.

54 Malthus, *Essay* (ed. Blaug), p. ix. Cf. Blaug, *Economic Theory*, pp. 72–3.

55 Malthus, *Essay* (ed. Blaug), p. viii.

56 Ibid., p. ix.

57 Sabine Höhler, *Spaceship Earth in the Environmental Age, 1960–1990* (London: Pickering Chatto, 2014).

58 Nathan Keyfitz, *Kenneth Ewart Boulding, 1910–1993* (Washington, DC: National Academies Press, 1996), p. 7.

59 For Boulding's early life see Cynthia Kerman, *Creative Tension: The Life and Thought of Kenneth Boulding* (Ann Arbor: University of Michigan Press, 1974).

60 Fred Glahe and Larry Singell (eds) *The Collected Papers of Kenneth Boulding*, 4 vols. (Boulder: Colorado Associated University Press, 1971–4), vol. 1, pp. 9–32.

61 Ibid., vol. 1, p. 16.

62 Kerman, *Creative Tension*, p. 9; Keyfitz, *Kenneth Ewart Boulding*, p. 4.

63 T.R. Malthus, *Population: The First Essay*, ed. Kenneth Boulding (Ann Arbor: University of Michigan Press, 1959), p. viii.

64 Ibid., p. v.

65 Ibid., p. vi, emphasis in original.

66 Ibid.

67 Ibid., p. xi.

68 Ibid., p. xii, emphasis in original.
69 See Philippe Fontaine, 'Stabilizing American Society: Kenneth Boulding and the Integration of the Social Sciences', *Science in Context*, 23 (2010), 221–65.
70 Kerman, *Creative Tension*, pp. 40–1.
71 Glahe and Singell, *Collected Papers of Boulding*, vol. 3, pp. 53–86; vol. 1, pp. 453–63.
72 T.R. Malthus, *On Population*, ed. Gertrude Himmelfarb (New York: Modern Library, 1960), p. xiii. Himmelfarb reprinted an edited version in her 1968 collection, *Victorian Minds*, framing Malthus as a 'proto-Victorian'.
73 Ibid., p. xxii.
74 Ibid., p. xxiv.
75 Ibid., p. xxxii.
76 Ibid., p. xxxi.
77 Ibid., p. xxix.
78 Ibid., p. xxxii.
79 Ibid., p. xxxv.
80 Ibid., p. xxxvi.
81 The edited version of this text in *Victorian Minds* was even more opaque on this matter: Gertrude Himmelfarb, *Victorian Minds* (Gloucester, MA: Peter Smith, 1975), p. 110. For US strategy see especially Nick Cullather, *The Hungry World: America's Cold War Battle Against Poverty in Asia* (Cambridge, MA: Harvard University Press, 2010), and John Perkins, *Geopolitics and the Green Revolution: Wheat, Genes, and the Cold War* (New York: Oxford University Press, 1997).
82 Malthus, *On Population* (ed. Himmelfarb), p. xxxiv.
83 There are numerous versions of these arguments in Kristol's writings, but see especially Irving Kristol, *Reflections of a Neoconservative: Looking Back, Looking Ahead* (New York: Basic Books, 1983), pp. x–xi, 73–7, and his essay on 'Adam Smith and the Spirit of Capitalism', pp. 139–76, which discusses Malthus at pp. 169–71, explicitly drawing on Himmelfarb's 1960 introduction.
84 Malthus, *Essay* (ed. Flew), p. 18.
85 Antony Flew, *Philosophical Essays* (Lanham: Rowman & Littlefield, 1998), pp. 203–4.
86 Antony Flew, 'The Structure of Malthus' Population Theory', *Australasian Journal of Philosophy*, 35 (1957), 1–20.
87 For Flew's recyclings on Malthus, see his 1963 paper 'The Structure of Malthus's Population Theory' and the passing comments in Flew's work on Darwin, notably 'The Structure of Darwinism' in M.L. Johnson, Michael Abercrombie and G.E. Fogg (eds.), *New Biology Volume 28* (Harmondsworth: Penguin, 1959), pp. 25–44, and *Evolutionary Ethics* (London: Macmillan, 1967), p. 32.
88 Malthus, *Essay* (ed. Flew), p. 47.
89 Ibid., p. 43 n. 67.
90 Ibid., p. 42.
91 Flew, *Philosophical Essays*, p. 206.
92 Malthus, *Essay* (ed. Flew), p. 52.

93 Ibid., p. 282 n. 38.

94 Ibid., p. 53 n. 85.

95 Ibid., p. 52, n. 84.

96 Piers Benn, 'Antony Flew Obituary', *Guardian*, 14 April 2010.

97 Veldman, *Fantasy, the Bomb*, p. 221.

98 Lewis, *Penguin Special*, p. 348.

99 Penguin Archive, internal memo, 28 September 1967.

100 Penguin Archive, Flew to Wright, 18 August 1971.

101 Penguin Archive, Filby to Pevsner, 29 September 1970.

102 Penguin Archive, Wright to Pevsner, 26 October 1970.

103 Flew, *Philosophical Essays*, p. 204; Penguin Archive, Wright to Pevsner, 26 October 1970.

104 Hare, *Penguin Portrait*, p. xv.

105 Philip Appleman, *Darwin's Ark* (Bloomington: Indiana University Press, 1984), pp. xiii–xv; Philip Appleman email to the author, 22 November 2013.

106 Rome, *Genius of Earth Day*, p. 232.

107 See Robertson, 'Thinking Globally', p. 194.

108 Philip Appleman, *New and Selected Poems, 1956–1996* (Fayetteville: University of Arkansas Press, 1996), pp. 30 and 25.

109 Philip Appleman, *In the Twelfth Year of the War: A Novel* (New York: G.P. Putnam's, 1970), pp. 67, 56 and 99–102.

110 T.R. Malthus *An Essay on the Principle of Population*, ed. Philip Appleman (New York: Norton, 1976), p. xx.

111 Ibid., pp. xvi–xvii.

112 Ibid., p. xxiii.

113 Radkau, *Age of Ecology*, p. 98.

114 See Sandbrook, *State of Emergency*, p. 219; Veldman, *Fantasy, the Bomb*, p. 300; and Hays, *Beauty, Health, and Permanence*, p. 215.

115 Sales figures come from Paul R. Ehrlich and Anne H. Ehrlich, 'The Population Bomb Revisited', *Electronic Journal of Sustainable Development*, 1 (2009), 63–71.

CHAPTER 10

Malthus today

Derek S. Hoff and Thomas Robertson

At the 2014 World Economic Forum meetings in Davos, Switzerland, former American vice-president Al Gore – long a political lightning rod in the United States for his outspoken environmentalism – spoke about how population growth has exacerbated climate change and called for voluntary measures to lower birth-rates across the globe. According to second-hand accounts, Gore said the following: 'Depressing the rate of child mortality, educating girls, empowering women and making fertility management ubiquitously available – so women can choose how many children and the spacing of children – is crucial to the future shape of human civilization.'[1] These comments revealed much about the recent history of Malthusianism. Although Gore implied that lower population levels would help global ecosystems, he called for nothing more than increasing access to contraception, and while he advocated 'spacing children', he affirmed the right of women and couples to have as many children as they desire. Like many have since the 1970s, Gore combined his concerns about population growth with a rights-based feminist approach, mooring his environmental goals to the larger goal of empowering women.

Yet even these modest comments, which called for developments many of us find benevolent entirely apart from ecological concerns – more education and reproductive freedom for women – triggered a swift backlash. The conservative *Washington Times*, the capital city's number two paper, reported that 'Mr. Gore [may] have just made his most ridiculous comment to date ... That's right. According to the wit and wisdom of Al Gore, fertility management is the most effective way to fight global warming. We shouldn't be completely surprised by his defense of population control. This has long been part of his left-wing environmentalist agenda.'[2] The *Washington Times* then quoted the director of global warming and international environmental policy at the Competitive Enterprise Institute, an organization 'dedicated to advancing the principles of limited government, free enterprise, and individual liberty',[3] who remarked that

'Gore's eco-imperialism is uncomfortably close to the original racist goals of Margaret Sanger, the founder of Planned Parenthood, who advocated population control in order to control the number of black and brown people in the world'.[4]

Such overblown reactions to Gore's comments reflect the great distance that population politics have travelled since the late 1960s, when wealthy and developing nations alike took steps to lower their birth-rates, and, in the United States, an ecologically infused 'zero population growth movement' briefly catapulted to national prominence. Today, in contrast, Malthusians tilt at windmills. Even moderate Malthusianism earns a swift backlash from not just the right but also the left. Of course, several of the critiques of late-1960s Malthusianism that emerged from both sides of the political spectrum had merit, but Malthusianism also declined in the US because the divisive culture wars that emerged in the 1960s and 1970s hyper-politicized all reproductive matters. Increasingly, according to critics, to support population reduction was to support contraception access, abortion rights and new roles for women (anathema to the right), and to be anti-immigrant and misdiagnose the causes of poverty and ecological problems (anathema to the left). And increasingly, as the vilification of Gore reveals, merely to mention population risked being attacked as racist. Moreover, the economic rationales for population reduction – that it often promotes modernization in the developing world and enhances mass consumption in the wealthy world, where economies no longer rely upon the sheer body count – drew criticism too. As liberals critiqued Malthusians for blaming ecological woes on population instead of high-mass-consumption capitalism itself, conservatives constructed a neo-liberal consensus celebrating the economic virtues of population growth that largely prevails today across the American political spectrum.

Revisiting the Malthusian moment and its demise sheds important historical light on the postwar decades, especially the 1960s and 1970s. This chapter concentrates on the United States, and we make no claims that its experience is widely representative. To give just one example of contrast, the neo-liberal consensus supporting population growth is less strong in Europe than in the US. Support for population expansion in Europe is often simply a policy-oriented response to lower birth-rates and ageing populations, and thus tends to be less ideologically charged than it is in the still-rapidly growing United States – unless population expansion comes through the immigration of Muslims. The US case is also unique because of America's particularly virulent cultural politics, and its particularly high levels of faith in the virtues of markets.

Nonetheless, the US case is instructive because of America's global reach and prominence, and because of the leading role the nation played in promoting international family planning programmes. The basic contours of population politics over the past half-century share rough parallels not only on both sides of the Atlantic but even in many middle-income nations such as India and China: perception of a population 'crisis' significantly dissipated in the 1970s and 1980s and was replaced by support in some form or another for repopulation. Of course, the cultural, economic and political debates have played out differently in each national context. This chapter, then, traces the rise and fall of Malthusianism, primarily over the past 50 years and primarily in the United States, and in doing so seeks to explain how demographic debates arrived at the point where even brief, tame comments about population such as Al Gore's encounter widespread derision.

Before World War II, as Alison Bashford has shown us, population matters were central to global geopolitics.[5] After the war, continued high levels of population growth intersected with new economic and international concerns, as well as a budding ecological critique of industrialized society. In the US, population growth became both a domestic political concern and a national security issue. By the 1960s, a zero population growth movement calling for assertive state action to lower birth-rates emerged. In doing so, the population issue raised fundamental questions about the role of government: should the state set population targets and pursue diverse policies in support of them? Or can the market solve demographic problems better than the government? Although the overpopulation critique remained strong in the 1970s, waning political will to combat population growth mirrored declining faith in government and the collapse of the liberal consensus; indeed, an assertive pro-population growth set of ideas contributed to the rise of the 'New Right'. Although, of course, demographic, economic and environmental trends are always evolving, in many areas today's population debate looks strikingly similar to the debate circa 19803.

We argue that demographic changes only partially explain the collapse of concern about population growth since the late 1960s. True, the global rate of population growth did peak and began to decline in the late 1970s. The US birth-rate did drop to replacement level during the early 1970s, and if not for a bulge in the childbearing population and increased immigration, the nation's population might be declining today, as is the case in many highly industrialized nations. But demographic changes alone cannot explain the collapse of support for educational and policy efforts designed to lower birth-rates. After all, the population is still climbing, and no one can fully predict what the economic and environmental consequences of a world with eleven billion people will be.

Instead of emphasizing numbers in explaining the decline of postwar Malthusianism in the US, this chapter stresses the importance of cultural, political and intellectual–economic dynamics, in particular the fracturing of opinion about population growth on the left, even among environmentalists, and a coalescing of pro-population growth views on the right. These changes both mirrored and helped bring about a conservative ascendency in the past half century.

The history we tell in this chapter is often misunderstood on both sides of the political divide, and in these polarized times those who try to articulate a middle ground are often overwhelmed by voices that reduce population issues to caricatured extremes: the more people, the better for all time! We are doomed to suffer ecological–demographic collapse! Anyone who talks about the goal of lowering birth-rates is a racist troglodyte! Paul Sabin's recent study of a well-known 1980 wager regarding the future price of a basket of metals that Julian Simon, the most famous conservative anti-Malthusian, won against Paul Ehrlich, the most famous Malthusian, affirms our contention that the chasm between Malthusians and their enemies was essential to the current polarization of American politics.[6] Today, the global population is still decades from peaking and millions of people across the globe newly arrive at a mass-consumption lifestyle every year, but many on the right look at climate change through the lens of population politics of yesterday, mistaking the scientific consensus surrounding global warming for the same exaggerated and flawed doomsday thinking they associate with 1960s Malthusianism. Meanwhile, many on the left, including some environmentalists, continue to treat all Malthusians as if they are still advocating the positions of 1968, failing to see that most moderate Malthusians either never accepted those extreme views or that they softened their positions in response to the important race, class and gender critiques coming from the left in the 1970s. The cause of these moderates is hurt by the unreflective few who never took seriously either these critiques or important points from the right about how human ingenuity, market liberalization and technological progress have brought millions of people out of poverty since the late 1960s. Unless we understand the way population issues have been framed and often misunderstood in the past, it will be hard to stop talking past one another and to address the challenges of the future.

The United States played an unusually prominent role in population debates because during the eighteenth and nineteenth centuries it was the resource periphery for the expanding European economies and later, after World War II, it became the most important manager of global resources and politics. In the US, population concerns predated Malthus, but they did not take root for a century. In the middle of the eighteenth century, Benjamin Franklin worried that Americans would breed as prodigiously as fennel,[7] but a half-century later, Malthus's contemporary Thomas Jefferson captured the exuberant mood of the new nation when he predicted that America had land enough for a thousand generations of settlers. For most of the nineteenth century, the pell-mell exploitation of native peoples and the natural environment left little room for voices warning of natural or ecological limits. In the 1890s, however, surging immigration from Southern and Eastern Europe and the US Census Bureau's declaration that the frontier had 'closed' sparked a Malthusian revival in the United States.[8] Many elite Americans now feared that their nation had 'filled up', and filled up with the wrong people. And although the first generation of professional economists contested Malthusian notions of scarcity,[9] the leading historian Frederick Jackson Turner captured the prevailing mood when he proposed that the loss of the frontier threatened a social safety valve central to American democracy. Popular culture turned to a nostalgic celebration of the disappeared cowboy.[10]

By this juncture, Malthusianism was a conversation taking place on both sides of the Atlantic. A 'neo-Malthusian' (birth control) movement was firmly established in Britain and France. Malthusianism subsequently intersected in complicated ways with the eugenics movement, which, during the first third of the twentieth century especially, sought to breed 'better' populations by urging the supposedly genetically 'fit' to have more babies and securing laws allowing for the involuntary sterilization of the often institutionalized and supposedly genetically 'unfit' (almost always the poor, the disabled and the non-white). Eugenic thought was widespread and coexisted with ideas across the political spectrum, from racist anti-immigrationism – eugenics was crucial to the passage of restrictive immigration laws in the 1920s US – to a liberal and anti-racist international interventionism that demanded addressing global inequalities in population 'quality'. Eugenicists were often Malthusians, and Malthusians were often eugenicists, but not always. Eugenic thought, which focused on the class or racial composition of populations, often existed apart from Malthusian concerns about aggregate population size, but it also sometimes drew from them.

Malthusianism became more popular worldwide during the 1920s and 1930s, when ecological models began to shape thinking about human and animal population dynamics. In ways that would become common after World War II, population experts, social scientists and natural scientists around the world promulgated concepts at the meeting ground of demography and ecology, including carrying capacity, environmental degradation, the basic parallel between animals and human beings, and an emphasis on sex and reproduction. In the United States, for example, Harvard University biologist Edward Murray East pressed for a 'permanent' agriculture and expanded birth control access. East participated in the 1927 World Conference on Population, which called for more attention to population matters of all kinds, while displaying a diversity of opinion.[11] Like East, Indian economist Radhakamal Mukerjee belonged to the subset of Malthusians who worried about not only population growth but also the ecological question of how rising standards of living would accelerate resource depletion and degradation. Demonstrating that Malthusians were not always racist defenders of the colonial status quo,[12] Mukerjee provocatively argued that people from densely populated nations such as India and China should be allowed to migrate to less-populated ones, such as Australia. Although some experts used ecology to make Malthusian-based immigration-restriction arguments, Mukerjee and other scholars used ecology to make Malthusian-based arguments against immigration restriction.

Well into the late twentieth century, Malthusians around the world, including in the US and Europe, pushed against a socially and politically dominant culture profoundly opposed to birth control access and reproductive freedom, especially for women. For most of the twentieth century, traditional pro-natal beliefs and patriarchal structures combined to deny women access to contraception and to reject their desires to limit their families. In the 1910s, Margaret Sanger launched a movement for greater access to birth control technologies, but not until 1965 did the US Supreme Court identify the right of *married* citizens to use birth control, and even then doctors were selective. Accordingly, the women's movement and Malthusianism often overlapped. Indeed, it was those in the population limitation movement who helped create new technologies such as the birth control pill and the intrauterine device (IUD), as well as new legal rights. And it was population activists, along with environmentalists, who led the first major push for abortion rights in the 1950s, 1960s and early 1970s.[13]

After World War II, as global population growth rates approached their peak – and the wealthy democracies saw their own baby booms – Malthusian critiques grew into mainstream concerns. In 1948, two bestsellers by conservationists, Fairfield Osborn's *Our Plundered Planet* and William Vogt's *Road to Survival*, injected ecological ideas about (over) population into middlebrow American discourse and into policy discussions around the world. Although a few outliers, such as Vogt and wealthy American businessperson Hugh Moore, promoted a dire Malthusianism, a moderate tone pervaded the population discussion during the 1950s and early 1960s. For example, in his 1957 presidential address to the Population Association of America, 'The Aesthetics of Population', leading population economist Joseph Spengler 'called for a new aesthetically determined optimum level of population and concluded that "an overworked stork is the enemy of the beautiful" '.[14] The mainstream media also began connecting population growth and environmental degradation.[15] Well-established environmental organizations such as the Sierra Club cautiously dipped their toes into the waters of the population argument, and philanthropist John D. Rockefeller III spearheaded the creation of the Population Council, a research and advocacy organization dedicated to lowering birth-rates around the world and in the United States.[16]

Concerns about population growth became more mainstream as mounting populations in the developing world came to be seen as a Cold War security issue. When global population first emerged as an issue in the US in the late 1940s, the federal government showed little official concern. True, an assumption that overpopulation might potentially destabilize developing nations helped buttress new American foreign aid initiatives in the late 1940s under President Truman's 'Point Four' programme. Yet even as the Paley Commission, a high-level body that President Truman appointed in 1950, warned about resource scarcity around the world, it said little about population and ultimately placed its faith in Keynesian economic growth models and American technical-transfer programmes, calling for more 'growth and high consumption in place of abstinence and retrenchment'.[17] In 1959, President Eisenhower explicitly refused to involve the US government in population programmes.

But as foreign aid programmes seemed to stumble in the early 1960s in strategically important places such as India and Vietnam, and family planning became a more acceptable topic of conversation, more and more Americans called for new governmental action to address accelerating population growth. In 1966, a *New York Times* editorial warned that 'the Malthusian specter, more terrible than Malthus ever conceived, is so near to being a reality'.[18] A particular concern was the bulge of young people around the world who, lacking economic opportunity, might sow social and political instability. The rationale was partly humanitarian, but many top policymakers also saw national security implications: population reductions would help speed up economic development and encourage political stability, and thus help stave off communism. President John F. Kennedy allowed US international aid dollars to go toward the study of population programmes, but it was his successor, President Lyndon B. Johnson, who spoke most forcefully about a global population problem and supervised a revolution in policy. In 1965, Johnson announced that he would seek 'new ways' to combat 'the explosion in world population' and 'the growing scarcity in world resources', and his administration launched programmes that quickly made the US the largest provider of birth control around the world.[19] For others, however, the Cold War and population interacted in a separate way. To this group, which included many conservationists, concern about population showed the problems of narrow Cold War thinking and instead called out for new 'global' ways of viewing the planet. Either way, most population programmes at the time, like other programmes aimed at the developing world, tended to ignore the social and economic causes of poverty in favour of technical solutions.

Presidents Kennedy and Johnson also incorporated the mainstream consensus favouring slower population growth into their burst of liberal domestic policymaking. The 'War on Poverty' assumed not only that the bulging cohort of post-World War II Baby Boomers just then entering the labour force faced dire employment prospects but also that larger families reduced the upward mobility of the poor. These new demographic–economic assumptions, combined with the longstanding efforts of feminists and birth-control advocates, led to the first US government subsidies for domestic family planning clinics and programmes. Federal family planning policy predated the emergence of an 'urban crisis' paradigm to describe growing poverty and unrest among inner-city minorities, although it is also true that, following the 1965 rebellion among African-Americans in Watts, Los Angeles, some whites viewed birth control through a racist lens. Still, anxieties about population expansion extended well beyond matters of race. For instance, Johnson's 'Great Society' promoted rescuing beauty from the stultifying effects of industrialization, mass consumption, suburban sprawl and population growth. The preamble to the 1964 Wilderness Act begins:

> In order to assure that an increasing population, accompanied by expanding settlement and growing mechanization, does not occupy and modify all areas within the United States and its possessions, leaving no lands designated for preservation and protection in their natural condition, it is hereby declared to be the policy of the Congress to secure for the American

people of present and future generations the benefits of an enduring resource of wilderness.[20]

Johnson's new assertive population policy spurred a number of strong critiques. On the one hand, a new group of increasingly dire 'environmentalists' went well beyond the Johnson administration in both diagnosis and remedy. As they saw things, population growth had pushed the world to the brink of ecological and social catastrophe, if not already over the cliff. In *The Population Bomb* (1968), Stanford University biologist Paul Ehrlich predicted massive famines within a decade and called for 'crash' programmes to slash the birth-rate. Some of these proposed remedies – such as expanded non-maternal roles for women, better access to birth control and abortion, and more regulation of economic growth – appealed to many Americans, but others – such as taxes on diapers and consideration of forced sterilizations overseas – appeared draconian. In 1969, Ehrlich helped launch Zero Population Growth (ZPG), a national organization that addressed population–environment concerns and contraception rights in the US through a quickly sprouting network of local and largely autonomous branches. What distinguished Ehrlich's environmental camp from moderate Malthusians was a lack of faith that family planning programmes could compete with innate reproductive urges, profound concern that the 'green revolution' programmes that the Johnson administration celebrated as a way to increase food production would backfire because of their reliance on environmentally damaging chemical fertilizers and ecological models that predicted precipitous collapse when population numbers reached the earth's environmental 'carrying capacity'. Ultimately, Malthusian environmentalists feared, biology would trump technology.

Some radicals leapt beyond even Ehrlich. In a famous 1968 essay, 'The Tragedy of the Commons', biologist Garrett Hardin argued that individuals pursuing their own reproductive interests and desires would create a ruinously large population. Criticizing 'laissez-faire in reproduction', he warned that the 'freedom to breed will bring ruin to all'. Rejecting a 1967 United Nations declaration affirming the right to bear children, Hardin called for dramatic and direct state regulation of reproduction, or, as he put it, 'mutual coercion, mutually agreed upon by the majority of the people affected'.[21] In subsequent years, Ehrlich's and Hardin's analysis of population growth, immigration and the inequalities between rich and poor countries clashed, especially as Erhlich's arguments became much more nuanced than many who will forever associate him with 1960s radicalism imagine.[22]

Another forceful critique of American population policies came from conservative forces unhappy with President Johnson's support for birth control programmes. The most important came from the Catholic Church. In July 1968, just a month after Ehrlich's *Population Bomb* appeared, Pope Paul VI promulgated *Humanae Vitae* ('Of Human Life'), a declaration reaffirming the Church's total ban on birth control.[23] The pope based this argument on his view that procreation should be the sole purpose of sex, stating: 'Marriage and conjugal love are by their nature ordained toward the procreation and education of children.' Each and every marital act 'must of necessity retain its intrinsic relationship to the procreation of human life'. Birth control was morally unacceptable because it was 'specifically intended to prevent procreation'.[24] Pope Paul also warned about the potential for coercion in population programmes.[25] Many American Catholics ignored the new policy, yet the pope's injunction narrowed options for families in many countries around the globe.

Population programmes overlapped with American racial politics in complicated ways in the late 1960s and early 1970s. Some radical and black nationalist civil rights activists criticized population programmes as steps toward racial genocide, and this position occasionally appeared in mainstream African-American media. A March 1968 *Ebony* magazine article asked, 'Is birth control just a "white man's plot" to "contain" the black population? Is it just another scheme to cut back on welfare aid or still another method of "keeping the black man down?"'[26] Critics were correct that much of the rhetoric around population programmes in the US often targeted African-American communities (and non-whites in other countries), especially after racially charged riots erupted in US cities in the mid-1960s. Indeed, many population advocates had too narrowly blamed population growth for poverty, overlooking structural explanations such as the legacy of slavery and segregation, deindustrialization and racist governmental policies. Some environmentalists even pointed to biological theories of animal crowding to explain urban unrest, ignoring that many dense cities did not see much violence. Nonetheless, many population and family planning advocates had broad understandings of family planning and poverty, including congressional issue leaders Senators Ernest Gruening, Joseph Clark and Joseph Tydings.[27] And most mainstream civil rights organizations and leaders, including Martin Luther King Jr, whom Planned Parenthood awarded a prize, defended the programmes. Moreover, African-American women often supported population programmes. For instance, after a family planning clinic closed down in 1968 in the Homewood-Brushton neighbourhood of Pittsburgh because of complaints of 'black genocide' and threats of violence by male African-Americans, a group of black women organized in protest, arguing that male critics did not speak for 'the women of Homewood'. As one woman stressed: 'We should make the decision ourselves.'[28] Around the country, poor and middle-class African-American women expressed similar views.[29] As historians Johanna Schoen and Beth Bailey have shown, even when population and family programmes were designed based on politically narrow rationales, individual women were often able to make use of them for their own purposes.[30]

Moreover, the real target for most environmentalists had always been unbridled economic growth. Indeed, led by Ehrlich and ZPG, many 1970s environmental Malthusians directly critiqued the overconsumption of the middle class – that is, the mostly white middle class. The deep apprehension about the environmental consequences of unbridled economic growth drew from a deep reservoir in American thought. In *The Population Bomb*, for example, Ehrlich had pointed out that American babies were not just babies but 'superconsumers'.[31] In the wake of criticism from African-Americans, Malthusian environmentalists sharpened their racially neutral and consumption-oriented attacks. 'Each American child,' Ehrlich told *Time* in February 1970, 'is 50 times more of a burden on the environment than each Indian child.'[32] The revised 1971 edition of *The Population Bomb* referred to the US and Western European nations as ODCs: 'overdeveloped nations'.[33] An even more radical critique emanated from Herman Daly and the emerging field of ecological economists, which, insisting that natural resources on a finite earth pose 'limits to growth' and nodding to John Stuart Mill's 'stationary state', first demanded a path toward the 'steady state economy'.[34] Attacking middle-class consumption, however, did not win environmentalists and radical economists many friends given the politically powerful coalition promoting upward mobility through an ever-expanding economic pie.

Nonetheless, mainstream Malthusianism enjoyed its 15 minutes of fame during a brief window between 1968 and 1972. Zero Population Growth expanded rapidly to 400 branches, and Paul Ehrlich became a regular guest on Johnny Carson's *Tonight Show*. In Congress, Democrats and Republicans alike expressed concerns with America's dramatic population growth. The future president George Herbert Walker Bush headed a Republican Task Force on Earth Resources and Population and proposed renaming the Department of the Interior the Department of Resources, Environment and Population. On the floor of the US House of Representatives, Bush argued that the 'fantastic rate of [worldwide] population growth we have witnessed these past 20 years continues with no letup in sight. If this growth rate is not checked now – in this decade – we face a danger that is as defenseless as nuclear war … Unless this problem is recognized and made manageable, starvation, pestilence, and war will solve it for us.'[35] In a special message to Congress in 1969, in which he called for the creation of a special commission on population growth, President Richard Nixon insisted that 'many of our present social problems may be related to the fact that we have had only fifty years in which to accommodate the second hundred million Americans'.[36] The mainstream Malthusian consensus peaked around the first Earth Day, in April 1970, during which older environmental organizations joined ZPG in stressing the population–environment connection. In 1972, publication of the international bestseller *The Limits to Growth*, which predicted the collapse of the earth's systems within 100 years, seemed to augur the continuation of the Malthusian moment.[37]

At this very moment, however, President Nixon pivoted away from the overpopulation critique as part of a larger conservative reversal. In March 1972, the Commission on Population Growth and the American Future, chaired by John D. Rockefeller III (a scion of one of America's largest industrial fortunes), issued its final report, which called for several moderate measures to nudge the nation toward population stabilization, such as abortion rights, education and greater access to birth control. Nixon politely greeted the group at the White House – he did not want to anger John Rockefeller's brother Nelson, an important figure in the Republican Party's more liberal wing – but the president had already turned against the report behind the scenes. Speaking approvingly of a more negative draft of the speech on the occasion of the Commission's report than the one he would ultimately deliver, a draft written by young speechwriter Pat Buchanan, Nixon told his advisor John Ehrlichman that Buchanan was the only one capable of writing a speech 'to kick that population commission in the ass'.[38] Buchanan's draft had dismissed the idea that 'the American people are in danger of procreating themselves into poverty' as 'a chimera', and questioned 'the central conclusion of the commission – that there is nothing to gain from an expanding population'. Buchanan concluded that 'Malthusian specters, like the old soldier of the barracks ballad, as often as not just fade away'.[39]

Here Buchanan was tapping into a budding conservative counterattack bubbling beneath the Malthusian momentum. Since the 1930s, many across the mainstream political spectrum had argued that slowing population growth was not only entirely compatible with but might also contribute to economic growth in a personal consumption-driven economy. The state, not the stork, would fuel economic expansion. In the 1960s, however, the vanguard of a broader revival of conservative, market-oriented economic thought began articulating the pro-population growth economics that reign today. A new 'market-knows-best' demography argued that population growth generates long-term economic progress by generating economies of scale, spurring innovation (in part because temporary population pressures do demand responses) and even producing more geniuses. (Ironically, these ideas borrowed from, or perhaps wilfully ignored, Malthus himself, who described necessity as the mother of invention.) Just as an invisible hand ensures that the pursuit of individual gain benefits everyone in the aggregate, so too does an invisible hand ensure that millions of individual childbearing decisions result in a socially optimal population level. Another thread of conservative pro-natalism emphasized national security and greatness. The pages of the *National Review*, a leading conservative American magazine, documented the right's rapprochement with population growth. In 1965, *National Review* founder William F. Buckley Jr echoed the Malthusian consensus. 'Solutions for today and tomorrow are perhaps not so difficult to contrive,' he wrote of peaking global birth-rates: 'Send tractors to India, and hybrid corn to Egypt. But the day after tomorrow?' Buckley even assumed that the population crisis would come to American shores and concluded that 'that old dog Malthus turned out to be very substantially correct in his dire predictions'.[40] By 1970, however, the *National Review* had imbibed market-knows-best demography and was regularly printing pieces by leading neo-liberals, including Nobel Prize-winning economist Milton Friedman, emphasizing that population growth expands the market – and that the market, by inducing innovation and substitutions, can solve environmental problems better than regulation.

The hardening of the abortion wars in the United States also helped politicize the population question. In the 1950s and 1960s, many Republicans had supported family planning programmes along environmental and anti-poverty lines. Especially after the US Supreme Court legalized abortion in its 1973 *Roe vs Wade* decision, however, they abandoned this support because a new anti-abortion movement rejected any talk of overpopulation as a ruse to buttress abortion rights. Even before *Roe vs Wade*, Nixon had grasped the new political calculus surrounding abortion. Preparing to distance his administration from the Commission on Population Growth's pro-abortion rights 1972 final report, he said on tape: 'Those that vote for abortion, except for a few fanatical libs [liberals?], are not going to vote for Nixon because he comes out for abortion. Those who are against abortion, however, feel so strongly about it from a moral standpoint that they sure as hell will vote against Nixon because of that issue.'[41]

Meanwhile, new attacks on Malthusianism emerged from the left, especially as the Vietnam War eroded the centre-right Cold War consensus that had narrowed political debate in America since the late 1940s. One sign of a new contentious population politics was the bitter debate between America's two most visible environmentalists – Paul Ehrlich and Barry Commoner – in the year after the first Earth Day. A biologist at Washington University in St Louis, Commoner blamed environmental problems not on population but on harmful technology, more specifically the 'huge array of new substances' that unaccountable corporations had spread in the postwar decades, such as synthetic detergents, synthetic fabrics, aluminium, plastics, concrete, truck freight and non-returnable bottles.[42] The environmental damages from these products, he pointed out, far outpaced those from population growth. Commoner thus implied that society could live with the increased economic growth that Malthusian environmentalists had attacked since the late 1940s, as long as technological problems were eliminated. In addition, he attacked Ehrlich's calls for anti-natal measures as 'political repression'.[43] Although historians have often characterized the debate between the two ecologists as one pitting Ehrlich's biological models against Commoner's socialist-leaning analysis, in fact they both offered different critiques of capitalism. Commoner focused on faulty technology on the production side and Ehrlich focused on the ever-rising demand of 'superconsumers'.[44] Moderates tended to see merit in the less extreme versions of both.[45]

Just as domestic US population policies faced increasing pushback, so too did overseas policies. To be sure, even if President Nixon had moved away from domestic population programmes and the general Malthusian critique, his administration still saw population growth in the developing world as a significant economic and national security problem. A 1974 National Security Council report warned that the 'political consequences of current population factors' created 'political or even national security problems for the United States'.[46] At the World Population Conference in Bucharest in August 1974, the US delegation pushed for the United Nations' 'World Population Plan of Action', which called for specific birth-rate-reduction targets with specific deadlines. However, new and forceful criticisms of Malthusian positions emerged at the Bucharest conference. China and other developing nations rejected the Plan of Action as a new form of Western control, instead calling for restructuring the world's economy to correct exploitation by the West and to foster economic development. 'The best contraceptive,' the Indian minister of health Karan Singh proclaimed, 'is development.'[47]

Bucharest also displayed a growing feminist critique of conventional population planning, a critique that the mainstream population organizations took seriously. At the conference, prominent women's advocates such as Germaine Greer, Betty Friedan and Margaret Mead demanded that population programmes incorporate more awareness of womens' reproductive rights. In turn, Population Council founder John D. Rockefeller III, guided by his advisor Joan Dunlop, also directed attention to the gendered bias of many population programmes.[48] One early critic along these lines, journalist Barbara Seaman, reacted forcefully when she heard a well-respected doctor announce at a conference: 'The dangers of overpopulation are so great that we may have to use certain techniques of conception control that may entail considerable risk to the individual woman.' Shocked by this willingness to risk the health of individual women, Seaman began to argue for emphasizing reproductive rights above all when discussing population. 'It is a most basic violation of civil rights,' she wrote, 'for the group that is not at any risk from reproduction (male) to control the group that is at risk (female).'[49] Other intellectuals and activists, such as historian Linda Gordon, picked up the call, especially after reports of forced sterilizations in the US became public in 1973.[50] In 1976, news reports of a government-organized forced sterilization programme in India of horrifying proportions appeared to confirm feminists' worst fears.[51] Feminists thus stepped up attacks on the small subset of Malthusians, led by Hardin, who believed that women's control of their own bodies should yield before the greater good of national security, economic limits and protecting the environment. In response, many population advocates moved toward a position dominant today: emphasizing that planning one's family is a human right and hoping that growing acceptance of this stance will both empower women generally and reduce birth-rates.

Despite a new pro-women's rights emphasis with the population community, however, fewer women's groups aligned with Malthusians in the 1970s than in the 1960s. In part, the fraying of this alliance reflected the fact that the fringes of both camps received more societal attention and dug in. Some Malthusians offered consistent but isolated calls for coercive population policies, which, even if they had no chance of being passed, turned some feminists (and others) against the mainstream, family planning-oriented population movement. (No draconian policies to drive birth-rate reductions ever materialized in the wealthy industrialized democracies, although forced sterilizations, the legacy of eugenic and to a lesser degree Malthusian thought, continued in many American states.)

As the 1970s unfolded, disparate voices deepened the anti-Malthusian case. Market-oriented economists, led by former Malthusian Julian Simon, refined their argument that the market corrects for any short-term population problems.[52] On the other end of the political spectrum, liberals, who for decades had argued that Keynesian policies to stimulate mass consumption would allow the economy to grow with a stable population,[53] now responded to the combination of sluggish birth-rates, economic malaise and the breakdown of Keynesian economics by arguing that lower populations exacerbate economic inequality. But perhaps the most influential left-leaning critique of the conventional Malthusian analysis of 'Third World' overpopulation came from social activists Frances Moore Lappé and Joseph Collins's 1977 bestseller *Food First: Beyond the Myth of Scarcity*. Although concerned about population growth and environmental degradation, Lappé and Collins rejected the 'scarcity scare' that, they believed, drove Malthusian environmentalism. Too often, the authors argued, the concern about population growth boiled down to a fear of the poor. Instead, anticipating the arguments of the Nobel Prize-winning economist Amartya Sen (and building upon a longstanding left-wing critique of Malthus traceable to Marx), they insisted that the poor and their reproductive habits were not the cause of hunger. Noting that hunger existed in food-abundant countries such as the United States, and that, if distributed properly, more than enough food existed in poor nations like Bangladesh, Lappé and Collins blamed hunger and environmental damage on socio-economic disparities.[54] Income and wealth disparities, not food supply itself, explained why some people had access to food and others did not. Even doubling the world's food supplies, they theorized, would not eliminate hunger. In response, Ehrlich granted 'very grave problems of maldistribution and poverty that *must* be attacked' but stressed two points. First, even if poverty somehow were eliminated, continued population growth would bring 'problems of *absolute* scarcity [that] would far overshadow problems of maldistribution'.[55] Second, reducing the gap between rich and poor was simply no easy task. It would be far more realistic, he maintained, to reduce unwanted births.

Meanwhile, the population debate became ensnarled within a growing and contentious debate about immigration. America had liberalized its immigration policies in 1965, but the surge of interest in population in the late 1960s took place before immigration began to account for a sizeable percentage of the growth of the population, as it has ever since the 1970s. Zero Population Growth activists never emphasized immigration. By the mid-1970s, however, population and environmental groups were forced to decide whether they would call for limits on immigration – and thus come in for charges that they were racist (or at least that they undermined a liberal coalition increasingly dependent upon minority voters). Most mainstream organizations shied away from the issue, arguing that the earth hardly knows where someone lives. Still, some Malthusians argued that because Americans consume more than any other people, the nation should let in fewer people. Zero Population Growth was reluctant to enter this minefield, and so a number of new strident single-issue, anti-immigration groups emerged, such as FAIR (Federation for American Immigration Reform). These groups made all manner of Malthusian arguments – and in doing so helped narrow the constituency for Malthusianism. This issue would grow only more intense in subsequent decades, severely dividing the Sierra Club, a leading mainstream environmental organization, in the 1990s.

Despite the pivot under Nixon, the rise of the culture wars and the varied attacks against Malthusianism from both sides of the political spectrum, moderate and increasingly rights-based Malthusianism survived into the late 1970s in official circles. President Jimmy Carter was more of a Malthusian than Nixon or even Johnson, and he pursued an ambitious environmental programme, which included, at least initially, an embrace of anti-growth ideas. 'We have learned that more is not necessarily better', Carter stated in his 1977 inaugural address, tapping not only into concerns about population growth but also scepticism about the environmental and social consequences of economic growth and Americans' obsession with material gain. A year later, the White House convened a Conference on Balanced Growth and Economic Development, which included a visit from E.F. Schumacher, a British proponent of 'Buddhist economics' and author of the bestselling *Small is Beautiful*.[56] The last gasp of state-sponsored Malthusianism came in 1980 with the *Global 2000 Report to the President*, which urged stabilization of the American population and warned, 'If present trends continue, the world in 2000 will be more crowded, more polluted, less stable ecologically, and more vulnerable to disruption than the world we live in now.'[57] Conservatives maligned the report for epitomizing the doomsday mentality of population advocates and the general pessimism of the Carter years, and Carter had already learned through the sour economy of the late 1970s that questioning economic growth faced opposition even within his own party.

The *Global 2000 Report* disappeared without a policy trace, and indeed opposition to its assumptions and recommendations played a significant and under-recognised role in the rise of the 'New Right' and the landslide 1980 election of Ronald Reagan, who, as president, rolled back many of the population and family planning programmes of the Johnson and Nixon years. Despite his initial support for the prevailing view worried about overpopulation, Reagan had a long history of publicly taking issue with Malthusians. During his tenure as governor of California in the late 1960s and early 1970s, he had shaped his political personality in opposition to the population movement and the environmental–Malthusian position, and in so doing he helped unite the different wings of the Republican Party into a powerful conservative coalition. As early as 1971, Reagan contrasted the 'doomsday' view of the Malthusians – and their calls for new state regulation of fertility and the environment – with his distrust of the government, his faith in freedom, technology and the market, and his belief in the basic goodness of America, especially when compared to the Soviet Union.[58] Reagan also stressed exactly what many Malthusians saw as anathema: more economic growth. Reagan's arguments appealed to market- and cultural-conservatives alike, offering the sunny flipside to the doom and gloom of environmental Malthusians and Carter. Once in office, his administration famously declared at a 1984 United Nations conference on population that population growth had only a 'neutral' effect on economic growth, and he began to curtail abortion and even basic contraception programmes.

By the 1980s, then, most of the pieces of today's population puzzle had been put into place, and today's prevailing accord in favour of population growth had taken shape. The best that environmental Malthusians such as Al Gore could hope for was the feminist consensus forged at the UN Conference on Population in Cairo, Egypt, in 1994. There, building on the critiques first made by feminists in the early 1970s and in part responding to the unprecedented turnout of non-governmental organizations, especially women's rights groups, the participating governments at the Cairo conference stressed that population policies should focus on the needs of the individual, not aggregate policy goals; population programmes should emphasize access to contraception as part of general women's empowerment and contraception as part of a comprehensive health programme. Cairo 1994 was the last United Nations conference held specifically dedicated to population, perhaps because the policy positions that emerged from it, such as empowering women in fertility decisions, have become the reigning logic among non-conservatives.[59]

Perhaps the most important wrinkle in the debate since 1980 has been the much greater attention devoted to population ageing. Indeed, the politics of ageing currently dominates demographic discussion – and reinforces anti-Malthusian sentiment – in many wealthy nations. Ever since the American 'Baby Boom' (the large cohort born between 1946 and 1964) first captured attention in the early 1960s, policymakers feared that the Baby Boom would wreak fiscal havoc as a 'pig in the python', but the ageing issue has become more acute as the Boomers have retired and American budget deficits have returned to high levels. In the 1980s, conservatives seized upon the idea of a supposed 'ageing crisis' as a wedge through which to call for welfare state retrenchment along with repopulation, but the consensus became bipartisan in the 1990s. Accordingly, even many American pundits generally sympathetic to environmental causes, and sceptical of widespread exaggerations of a fiscal crisis, take it for granted that the nation has an ageing problem and urge Americans to have more babies (or welcome more immigrants) to pay the Social Security bill of the Boomers. Yet these pundits miss that the US is exceptional among the wealthy developed nations: its population is ageing but also growing at the same time. (We might also add that the US's debt-to-GDP ratio has dropped significantly since the Great Recession and is no longer high by historical standards.) The fears of ageing are even more acute in nations not expected to grow this century without immigration, such as Germany and Japan. Germany spends a remarkable $200 billion plus per year on measures to support families – €40 billion on child benefits alone[60] – but still has one of the lowest birth-rates in the world.[61]

Apprehension about an ageing population is only part of a broader pro-natalist revival. Popular cultures in nations with diverse demographic trajectories, economies and religions energetically promote the virtues of population growth and large families. In Denmark, a travel company recently launched a 'Do it for Denmark campaign' urging Danes to have more sex on holiday and offering 'three years of free baby supplies and a child friendly holiday for a couple who can prove that they conceived while on one of the company's holidays'.[62] Recently the Iranian regime reversed that nation's two-child policy, eliminated contraception programmes and called for Iranians to increase their population dramatically.[63] In Russia, where the population is expected to fall back to its 1950 level by the year 2100,[64] Vladimir Putin 'declared that state support for "motherhood" and multi-child families was an "unconditional national priority."'[65] In the United States, where population growth shows no signs of abating for the next century, television shows such as

John & Kate Plus 8 and its spinoff *Kate Plus 8* routinely celebrate large families. Even in India, where state-subsidized sterilizations remain widespread, the government extols the fact that the nation is about to become the most populous on earth.

Until its 2015 decision to abandon the infamous 'one-child' policy, China served as the major exception to the pro-natal trend, although its anti-natalist fervour had cooled before the official switch in policy. By the late 1970s, the Chinese fertility rate had dropped from over six children per woman to fewer than three,[66] yet Communist Party officials worried about the shortage of arable land and the large cohort then approaching childbearing age. Moreover, they believed that lowering the birth-rate would enhance the human capital of the population and thus promote economic modernization.[67] In 1979, the Party, encouraged by UN officials and outside organizations, announced the one-child and required local governments to enforce a system of limiting births. Exceptions were available for minorities, families in which a child was disabled, both parents worked in high-risk industries, or both parents were single-child children. Starting in 1984, special provisions were created for rural families. Officially the policy was based on persuasion, but non-compliant couples faced administrative, financial and occupation penalties. At times, numerous abuses such as forced abortions occurred. The one-child policy also exacerbated the problem of 'missing girls' – parents aborting foetuses when determined to be female.[68] China's anti-natalist policies received tacit and sometimes overt support from some Malthusians in the West, although many expressed grave concerns about human rights abuses, as did many conservatives who primarily saw in the Chinese case an example through which to stigmatize large population control efforts writ large. Overall, the authoritarian measures contributed to a lowering of the fertility rate, although not as much as might be gleaned at first glance, given that many urban Chinese wished to embrace a mass-consumption lifestyle made more affordable with one child.[69] Similarly, many demographers have concluded that the recent abandonment of the one-child policy will have modest aggregate effects at most, perhaps increasing the population by 23 million more than under the maintenance of the status quo.[70]

To be sure, Malthusian arguments remain an important part of discussion surrounding global ecological crisis, and many individual ecologists do express grave concerns about population growth in the wealthy world as well as in poorer nations, especially as average consumption levels march ever higher. (Indeed, the discussion about China usually focuses more on the ecological consequences of mass consumption than on birth-rates per se.) Ehrlich, for instance, maintains that although he got the timing wrong with earlier predictions, his concerns about unnecessary consumption, driven in part by population growth, still hold.[71] Others not so wrapped up in the polemics of the past have an easier time making this argument. Several small population-centric organizations – most notably the Population Media Center – discuss population more urgently and holistically and have adopted creative methods to get their messages across, such as inserting pro-birth control storylines into soap operas in several nations. Ecological economists, many associated with the Center for the Advancement of the Steady State Economy, continue to insist that the transition to sustainable or even zero economic and population growth will not only save the natural environment but, in fact, make us all richer and happier.[72] One can also find ample mentions of the perceived problem of global population growth in the climate change debate. In its November 2014 report, the Intergovernmental Panel on Climate Change (IPCC) pointed to population growth as one of several factors fuelling climate change, writing, 'anthropogenic greenhouse gas emissions have increased since the pre-industrial era, driven largely by economic and population growth, and are now higher than ever'.[73]

Many environmentalists sympathetic to Malthusianism look favourably upon such strong statements linking continued global population growth and climate change. Having learned from the criticisms that Barry Commoner and Frances Moore Lappé and others made in the 1970s, they are content to treat population as one variable among many others causing environmental problems. They also note that disparate organizations pursuing the Cairo agenda are already calling for proven ways to reduce population growth – greater access for birth control and more rights for women.

Not everyone agrees with the moderate, population-is-one-of-many-variables position. Some environmentalists are unhappy that climate activists even mention population; they tend to dismiss every reference to population as racist and imperial. Other environmentalists, however, want to emphasize population dynamics even more. These ardent Malthusians often complain that today's larger population organizations, such as the Population Council and the Population Connection (formerly ZPG), are timid and merely research-oriented. They call for new educational campaigns to separate sex and childbearing and stronger state population limitation measures such as tax incentives for smaller families, holding out that 'family planning is the single most cost-effective way to abate carbon dioxide emissions'.[74] Because of the contentious nature of demographic debates, larger mainstream environmental groups, such as the Sierra Club, have grown extremely cautious about engaging population matters.

Meanwhile, conservatives continue to reject even moderate women's rights-based Malthusianism, as Al Gore expressed in Davos. Despite recent projections that the US will increase by 100 million people to 417 million by 2060,[75] mainstream American conservatives often speculate that the US faces demographic decline (just as conservatives in many European and non-European nations call for repopulation along culturally nationalist lines). For example, conservative columnist Jonathan Last made a big splash recently when he wrote of a 'coming demographic disaster' as birth-rates sag.[76] Conservative denial of climate change (a uniquely American phenomenon) is often animated by the memory of 1960s Malthusians' erroneous predictions of impending massive global famine. A vocal minority of conservatives argues that today's warnings about climate ultimately will be judged as alarmist as Paul Ehrlich's predictions in *The Population Bomb* (1968). Indeed, anti-Malthusianism remains front and centre in the American right's blend of climate change denial, anti-environmentalism and anti-feminism. A lawmaker in Utah, for example, claims that growing acceptance of the science of climate change reflects a 'conspiracy to limit population not only in this country but across the globe'.[77] And whereas liberals still sometimes debate whether to emphasize population, conservatives take the supposed connection between population growth and economic progress as a matter of faith, rarely pausing to consider the more nuanced matter of how higher populations contribute to per capita growth and welfare.

Thus, Malthusianism as a viable political force is mostly spent in early twenty-first-century United States. After its high-water mark in the late 1960s and early 1970s, it became widely associated with extreme beliefs and high-handed policy recommendations that have been difficult to erase from political memory. Malthusianism is not dead, however. Tempered by useful critiques from both the right and left, moderate concern about population growth as one of many causes of poverty and environmental problems lives on and helps build support for programmes that many Americans endorse, such as greater education for women and expanded access to contraceptives, According to one's perspective, technological progress has either nullified or merely delayed the doomsday prognostications of a half-century ago. But at least one can reasonably ask whether we would be that much better-off had global population already peaked – and whether the planet is living on borrowed time as we approach eleven billion people. As the global population continues to grow, and as this growth acts as one multiplier driving resource depletion and climate change, it is not likely that Malthusian ideas will disappear completely, despite the current anti-Malthusian political climate.

Notes

1 Michael Taube, 'Al Gore's Latest Outlandish Outburst', washingtontimes. com. 25 February 2014.
2 Ibid.
3 https://cei.org/about-cei.
4 Taube, 'Gore's Outburst'.
5 Alison Bashford, *Global Population: History, Geopolitics, and Life on Earth* (New York: Columbia University Press, 2014).
6 Paul Sabin, *The Bet: Paul Ehrlich, Julian Simon and Our Gamble Over Earth's Future* (New Haven: Yale University Press, 2013).
7 See Chapter 4 in this volume.
8 David M. Wrobel, *The End of American Exceptionalism: Frontier Anxiety from the Old West to the New Deal* (Lawrence: University Press of Kansas, 1993).
9 Derek S. Hoff, *The State and the Stork: The Population Debate and Policy Making in US History* (Chicago: University of Chicago Press, 2012).
10 Wrobel, *End of American Exceptionalism*.
11 See, for example, Edward Murray East, *Mankind at the Crossroads* (New York: C. Scribner, 1923).
12 Radhakamal Mukerjee, *The Political Economy of Population* (London: Longmans, Green & Co., 1941), esp. pp. 30–1 and 61.
13 Hoff, *State and the Stork*, pp. 181–2.
14 Ibid., p. 131.
15 Ibid., pp. 170–1.
16 See Chapter 8 in this volume.
17 President's Materials Policy Commission, *Resources for Freedom: A Report to the President by the President's Materials Policy Commission: Volume 1: Foundation for Growth and Security* (Washington, DC: Government Printing Office, 1952), p. 21, also see p. 169.
18 'Johnson vs. Malthus', *New York Times*, 24 January 1966.
19 Lyndon B. Johnson, 'Annual Message to the Congress on the State of the Union', 4 January 1965. Online by Gerhard Peters and John T. Woolley, The American Presidency Project, www.presidency.ucsb.edu/ws/?pid=26907. Although much of the literature on Johnson's shift on population policy emphasizes the influence of the population movement, government officials were also crucial, including Secretary of Agriculture Orville Freeman and USAID's David Bell and Leona Baumgartner. See Thomas Robertson, *The Malthusian Moment: Global Population Growth and the Birth of American Environmentalism* (New Brunswick, NJ: Rutgers University Press, 2012), pp. 83–4 and ch. 4.
20 Public Law 88-557, 88th Congress 2nd Session, 3 September 1964.

21 Garrett Hardin, 'The Tragedy of the Commons,' *Science*, 162:3859 (1968), 1243–8, p. 1244.
22 Garrett Hardin, 'Living on a Lifeboat', *Bioscience*, 24:10 (1974), 561–8; Paul R. Ehrlich, Anne H. Ehrlich, and John P. Holdren, *Ecoscience: Population, Resources, Environment* (San Francisco: W.H. Freeman, 1977), p. 922.
23 Paul VI, '*Humanae Vitae*: Encyclical of Pope Paul VI on the Regulation of Birth', *Acta Apostolicae Sedis*, 6 (1968), 481–503, English translation from *The Pope Speaks*, 13 (1969), 329–46.
24 Ibid., pp. 334, 336.
25 Ibid., p. 329.
26 Mary Smith, 'Birth Control and the Negro Woman,' *Ebony*, March 1968, 29. For an excellent overview of African-American attitudes toward birth control and abortion in the late 1960s, see Jennifer Nelson, *Women of Color and the Reproductive Rights Movement* (New York: New York University Press, 2003), ch. 3. Also see Donald T. Critchlow, *Intended Consequences: Birth Control, Abortion, and the Federal Government in Modern America* (New York: Oxford University Press, 1999), pp. 60–1 and 141–45, and Bernard Asbell, *The Pill: A Biography of the Drug That Changed the World* (New York: Random House, 1995), pp. 234–8.
27 Hoff, *State and the Stork*, pp. 151–7.
28 'Women Rap Haden, Want Birth Control', *Pittsburgh Press*, 7 August 1968. Also see 'Negroes Fighting', *New York Times*, 11 August 1968.
29 For a primary source example, see Black Women's Liberation Group, 'Statement on Birth Control', in Robin Morgan (ed.), *Sisterhood is Powerful: An Anthology of Writings from the Women's Liberation Movement*, (New York: Vintage Books, 1970), pp. 360–1.
30 Beth L. Bailey, *Sex in the Heartland* (Cambridge, MA: Harvard University Press, 1999), pp. 109, 112–14.
31 Paul R. Ehrlich, *The Population Bomb* (New York: Ballantine Books, 1968), p. 149.
32 'Fighting to Save the Earth from Man', *Time*, 2 February 1970.
33 Paul R. Ehrlich, *The Population Bomb*, revised edn (New York: Ballantine Books, 1971).
34 See Herman Daly (ed.), *Toward a Steady-State Economy* (San Francisco: Freeman and Co., 1973).
35 Quoted in Hoff, *State and the Stork*, p. 185.
36 Richard Nixon, 'Special Message to the Congress on Problems of Population Growth,' July 18, 1969, *Public Papers of the Presidents of the United States: Richard Nixon, 1969* (Washington, D.C.: GPO, 1971), p. 529.
37 Donella H. Meadows, Dennis L. Meadows, Jørgen Randers and William W. Behrens, *The Limits to Growth: A Report for the Club of Rome's Project on the Predicament of Mankind* (New York: Universe Books, 1972).
38 Quoted in Hoff, *State and the Stork*, p. 214.
39 Ibid.
40 William F. Buckley, 'The Birth Rate,' *National Review*, 23 March 1965, p. 231.

41 Quoted in Hoff, *State and the Stork*, p. 214.

42 Barry Commoner, *The Closing Circle: Nature, Man, and Technology* (New York: Knopf, 1971), pp. 129–31 and 144. Quotation from p. 131.

43 Ibid., p. 214. For Ehrlich's response, see Paul Ehrlich and Richard Holden, 'One-Dimensional Ecology', *The Ecologist*, 2:8 (1972), 11.

44 Ehrlich, *Population Bomb* (1968), p. 149.

45 See Thomas Robertson, 'Revisiting the Early 1970s Commoner–Ehrlich Debate about Population and Environment: Duelling Critiques of Production and Consumption in a Global Age', in Corinna Unger and Heinrich Hartmann (eds.), *A World of Populations: The Production, Transfer and Application of Demographic Knowledge in the Twentieth Century in Transnational Perspective* (New York: Berghan Books, 2014).

46 National Security Council, *NSSM 200: Implications of Worldwide Population Growth for US Security and Overseas Interests* (Washington: National Security Council, 1974), p. 10.

47 Matthew Connelly, *Fatal Misconception: The Struggle to Control World Population* (Cambridge, MA: Harvard University Press, 2008), pp. 310–14, 317. Also see Critchlow, *Intended Consequences*, pp. 149–50 and 181–3.

48 Connelly, *Fatal Misconception*, p. 315, and Critchlow, *Intended Consequences*, pp. 149–50.

49 Barbara Seaman, *The Doctors' Case against the Pill* (New York: P. H. Wyden, 1969), pp. 45–6.

50 Linda Gordon, 'The Politics of Population: Birth Control and the Eugenics Movement', *Radical America*, 8 (1974), 61–97; Linda Gordon, 'The Politics of Birth Control, 1920–1940: The Impact of Professionals', *International Journal of Health Services*, 5 (1975), 253–77; and Linda Gordon, *Woman's Body, Woman's Right: A Social History of Birth Control in America* (New York: Grossman, 1976).

51 Connelly, *Fatal Misconception*, pp. 318–34; Ian Robert Dowbiggin, *The Sterilization Movement and Global Fertility in the Twentieth Century* (Oxford: Oxford University Press, 2008), pp. 188–192; and Davidson R. Gwatkin, 'Political Will and Family Planning: The Implications of India's Emergency Experience', *Population and Development Review*, 5 (1979), 29–59.

52 Julian Simon, *The Economics of Population Growth* (Princeton: Princeton University Press, 1977).

53 For a full discussion of stable population Keynesianism, see Hoff, *State and the Stork*, ch. 3. Also see pp. 124–9 for the place of population in postwar neo-classical growth theory.

54 Frances Moore Lappé and Joseph Collins, *Food First: Beyond the Myth of Scarcity* (Boston: Houghton Mifflin, 1977), p. 7.

55 Paul R. Ehrlich and Anne H. Ehrlich, 'ZPG: Where to Now?', *Zero Population Growth National Reporter*, 10 (1978), 4–5.

56 E. F. Schumacher, *Small Is Beautiful: Economics as if People Mattered* (New York: Harper & Row, 1973).

57 Council of Environmental Quality and the Department of State, *The Global 2000 Report to the President* (New York: Penguin, 1982), p. 1.

58 Ronald Reagan, 'Remarks to American Petroleum Institute', 16 November 1971, *Folder 'Speeches, 1970,' Box P18*, Ronald Reagan Library, Simi Valley, California. All quotations from p. 2.

59 Connelly, *Fatal Misconception*, pp. 363–9.

60 'A 200-Billion-Euro Waste: Why Germany is Failing to Boost its Birth Rate', www.spiegel.de/international/germany/study-shows-germany-wasting-billions-on-failed-family-policy-a-881637.html.

61 'Germany Passes Japan to have World's Lowest Birth Rate – Study', www.bbc.com/news/world-europe-32929962.

62 'Do it for Denmark! Low Birthrate Campaign Urging Danes to have More Sex', *RT.com*, 1 April 2014, http://rt.com/news/denmark-low-birthrate-sex-425. It is worth noting that *RT.com* is funded by the Russian state.

63 Palash Ghosh, 'Iran Scales Back Birth Control Programs, Seeks Baby Boom', *International Business Times*, 2 August 2012, www.ibtimes.com/iran-scales-back-birth-control-programs-seeks-baby-boom-737378.

64 Joseph Chamie and Barry Mirkin, 'Russian Demographics: The Perfect Stome', *Yale Global*, 11 December 2014, http://yaleglobal.yale.edu/content/russian-demographics-perfect-storm.

65 Valerie Sperling, *Sex, Politics, and Putin: Political Legitimacy in Russia* (Oxford: Oxford University Press, 2014), p. 150.

66 Yilin Nie and Robert J. Wyman, 'The One-Child Policy in Shanghai: Acceptance and Internalization', *Population and Development Review*, 31 (2005), p. 313.

67 Susan Greenhalgh and Edwin A. Winkler, *Governing China's Population* (Stanford: Stanford University Press, 2005), pp. 1–2.

68 Isabelle Attané, 'China's Family Planning Policy: An Overview of Its Past and Future', *Studies in Family Planning*, 33 (2002), 103–13, Susan Greenhalgh, 'Science, Modernity, and the Making of China's One-Child Policy', *Population and Development Review*, 29 (2003), 163–96; and Connelly, *Fatal Misconception*, p. 347.

69 Nie and Wyman, 'The One-Child Policy'.

70 'Now the Two-Child Policy', *Economist*, 7 November 2015, p. 39.

71 Paul Ehrlich and Anne Ehrlich, 'The Population Bomb Revisited', *Electronic Journal of Sustainable Development*, 1 (2009), 63–71.

72 See, for example, Brian Czech, *Supply Shock: Economic Growth at the Crossroads and the Steady State Solution* (Gabriola Island: New Society Publishers, 2013).

73 Intergovernmental Panel on Climate Change, 'Climate Change 2014, Synthesis Report: Summary for Policymakers', 5 November 2014, www.ipcc.ch/news_and_events/docs/ar5/ar5_syr_headlines_en.pdf.

74 Alisha Graves, 'Green Sex for Climate's Sake', *Bulletin of Atomic Scientists*, 16 December 2015, http://thebulletin.org/debating-link-between-emissions-and-population/green-sex-climates-sake.

75 For recent US Census Bureau projections, see 'New Census Bureau Report Analyses US Population Projections', 3 March 2015, www.census.gov/newsroom/press-releases/2015/cb15-tps16.html.

76 Jonathan Last, *What to Expect When No One's Expecting: America's Coming Demographic Disaster* (New York: Encounter Books, 2013).

77 Quoted in Hoff, *State and the Stork*, p. 7.

Afterword

Karen O'Brien

The essays in this volume amply confirm the editor's contention that Malthus's ideas have remained a touchstone of demographic debate in the more than two centuries since the first publication of the *Essay on the Principle of Population*. At the time of writing in 2015, the world has just learned of China's abrupt ending of its one-child policy, a policy that has been the greatest demographic experiment, on the Malthusian principle of the 'preventive' check, ever undertaken in human history. Alongside the official Chinese estimate of 400 million prevented births, that history will also record its human cost of forced sterilizations, infanticide, the gender imbalance resulting from these and from selective abortions, and the legacy of a vast ageing population with fewer working-age family members available to take care of them. The state enforcement of such a drastic preventive check has prompted many Malthusian reflections, over the years of its duration, on the distortions of well- or ill-meaning political management of poverty. Malthus would have had a great deal to say about this experiment, including the devaluation of girls that inevitably resulted from such a policy, just as he deplored the 'neglect and inconveniences attendant on the single woman' in his own time of excessive veneration for fecund marriages. Conversely, he would not have been entirely surprised by the low birth-rates among China's wealthier neighbours such as South Korea, Japan or Taiwan, since, like most writers of his era, he had observed a connection between wealth, or 'luxury', and low female fertility. He might have been bemused by the limited success or failure of the strategies of many of these states to redress low birth-rates by appealing, as Russia does, to the patriotism rather than to the self-interest of young women. In all these issues, Malthus's *Essay* has been a touchstone, not only for predicted disaster, but for the often counterintuitive, paradoxical patterns of reproductive behaviour, including those that fall out from the unintended consequences of pro- or anti-natalist state intervention.

Malthus remains everywhere the imagined interlocutor as we encounter and re-encounter the paradoxes of demography. In our immediate past, Google Ngram shows a steep rise in Malthusian bibliographic references in the early part of the twenty-first century, the latest in a long succession of peaks and troughs in Malthusian referencing. An article in *Science* (10 October 2014) by a group from the UN Population Division entitled 'World Population Stabilization Unlikely This Century', which gave an 80 per cent probability of an increase in global population to between 9.6 and 12.3 billion by 2100, prompted an outpouring of press coverage on explicitly 'Malthusian' themes. In the minds of the public at least, demographic science is never exempt from the need to explain the future in terms of answers to Malthus's questions. The figure of Malthus the monitory clergyman, once a theatrical caricature in the mode of the 'Machiavel' of Jacobean drama (literally so in William Cobbett's comic play *Surplus Population* of 1831), is no longer vivid to us. But the serious-minded author, regularly adduced to provide dark, underlying explanations for global disasters such as AIDs, Ebola or the Rwandan genocide, lives on.

Why should this still be the case? If, for the sake of argument, we were to play devil's advocate, we might ventriloquize those who say that Malthus is no longer relevant and that his blindspots were as large as his insights. We might easily list his shortcomings. He was not, for instance, fully *au fait* with the revolutionary economic changes of his own time. In the *Essay*, he demonstrated insufficient awareness of contemporary transformations in agricultural and industrial productivity, and in the use of fossil fuels, that were enabling his and other countries to support far greater population densities than ever before. To the extent that Malthus thought that the economic growth of his time might be at the expense of arable productivity, he wavered between laissez-faire and interventionism. He provided an acute but dubiously humane analysis of welfare dependency, asserting that the poor laws 'in some measure create the poor which they maintain', but he offered no clear road map for abolition, reform or change. He emphasized the deleterious effects of well-intentioned policy meddling and 'indiscriminate charity' on human happiness (for example, the generosity of the Lama in Tibet, which had created a 'mass of indigence and idleness') as much as those of despotism, tyranny and coercion.[1] Committed to an idea of social inequality as a motivator of worldly and spiritual endeavour, he did not sufficiently entertain the possibility that famine, even in highly populous countries, can be the effect of

socio-economic disparity and skewed wealth distribution, rather than of
scarcity. His problem of overpopulation was in part a middle-class anxiety
about the threat of the teeming and insubordinate labouring and urban
poor ('of all monsters the most fatal to freedom'). In the throes of this
anxiety, he had relatively little to say about middle-class overconsumption as a force for resource depletion (beyond some concerns about urban
meat-eating) or about the widely different ecological footprints of rich
and poor, or of advanced commercial nations and their underdeveloped
neighbours.

Malthus knew about the existence of contraceptive measures but did
not welcome them, even though they seemed to others the obvious instrument of the preventive check. This was less on account of Anglican prud-
ishness than out of preference for the social self-discipline of collective
population management. He followed Smith in advocating a national
system of education, but on grounds so instrumental to the promotion
of submissive 'peace and quietness' and 'instructing the people in the
real nature of their situation' as to be difficult to distinguish from the
Sunday School paternalism he deplored. In an age of large-scale emigration to North America and the colonies, he saw few opportunities either
for emigrants themselves or for the relief of overcrowding and poverty at
home, and he said so to a parliamentary Select Committee. His ideas were
anchored in traditional Christian pieties: those of Original Sin, the exhort-
ation to be fruitful and multiply, and the knowledge that 'for ye have the
poor with you always'. He was critical of contemporary social attitudes
towards women, and outspoken against forced marriages, and contempt
for 'old maids'. Yet his compassionate and mildly progressive gender outlook did not translate into a linkage (made by Mary Wollstonecraft and
others in Malthus's own time) between female education, reproductive
autonomy and child health.

With so many apparent blindspots and limitations, how is it that
Malthus's work remains, as the essays in this volume attest, such a rich
source of debate? How is it that his interpreters continue to find such
nuance and complexity in, for example, his account of poverty, of the
European impact on the new world or of the hidden history of humanity?
The answer must lie, as many of these essays intimate, in the intellectual
grounding of the *Essay* in a multifaceted British Enlightenment discourse
that linked economics, politics and ethics to a fundamental account of
the individual as actuated by justifiable self-regard. This follows from
Malthus's transformation of his heterodox, anti-radical polemic of 1798
into the 1803 quarto, a mature, and continually maturing, account of the

ways in which the Enlightenment vision of rising productivity, progress and the science of politics must be modified in the face of the population principle. Where Scottish and English Enlightenment writers such as Adam Smith, Hume and Gibbon, had identified despotism, religious intolerance, clerical interference in the state and commercial monopolies as the chief barriers to progress, Malthus revealed a deeper, structural impediment within the natural world itself. But, for Malthus, this impediment mobilized a debate within, rather than against, the master discourse of enlightened political economy. He may have brought about the Enlightenment's loss of innocence, and an end to the eighteenth-century dream of open-ended productivity and progress, but few would now agree with those who have argued that Malthus's work represents a profound epistemic shift to a post-Enlightenment worldview – a shift from an eighteenth-century engagement with the natural world through classification and control to an altogether different acceptance of man's participation in natural vicissitudes as the condition for his spiritual development.[2]

The impulse to classify, control and harness nature for the good of mankind remains. Most accounts of Malthus have emphasized his demographic predictions far more than his assertions about the finite and fragile nature of the environment. Yet here also, Fredrik Albritton Jonsson's chapter shows how Malthus reinserted political economy into the forms of global natural history inherited from Buffon, Linnaeus and Benjamin Franklin. Malthus identifies and predicts 'ecological strains' and threats to food security within a vision of the natural world as a source of supply of foodstuffs, materials, fuel and humans. His concern for environmental overstrain and degradation, although it had aspects in common with his Romantic critics, was not expressed in protectively aesthetic language. He does not offset environmental biocapacity against variations in human demand, or in ecological footprint; he is critical of the overconsumption of the rich ('luxury') but on grounds that 'national wealth and national happiness' should be more widely diffused down the social scale, but not on account of the exorbitant ecological impact of the wealthy few. Managed well, Malthus believed, a happy and prosperous society might claim the bounties of its natural environment both for necessities and luxuries for all.

Malthus's analysis of the environmental impact of the welfare-induced fertility of the poor was not accompanied by an analysis of the impact of the consumer behaviour of the wealthy. However, the 1803 *Essay* was, as Ted McCormick points out, strikingly different from preceding accounts of population growth in its articulation of the role of the individual in shaping human demographic destiny. Above all, it is this characteristically Enlightenment integration of the micro-scale of individual human psychological propensity, with macroeconomics, history and political science that has ultimately given the *Essay* its enduring ability to frame so much subsequent debate. At that micro-level, Malthus was in no doubt that human beings are fundamentally self-regarding and that the most important decisions and behaviours are not abstractly rational, although they may involve a degree of practical calculation about the best outcomes for oneself and one's family. Understanding those practical, adaptive behaviours required a critical engagement with Enlightenment historical notion of a natural course of human evolution through developmental stages towards social complexity and labour specialization.

The first two books of the 1803 *Essay* – little-read but essential to an understanding of the whole – draw upon a huge range of ethnographic and historical source material to reconstruct, from evidence and not abstract principles, the natural history of the human species. Conventional histories, which Malthus dismisses as those of only the 'higher classes', provide no insights comparable to those gained by looking beneath apparently linear history at constantly fluctuating and adapting human life at the margins of subsistence.[3] By doing so, Malthus is able to identify a number of human adaptations to environmental conditions that cut across different 'stages' of society and provide lessons for sustainable human development: he considers, for instance, the lower infant mortality rates and better health among Norwegian peasants who marry late.[4] The instruction that Malthus draws from this and other examples is not that late marriage should be legislated for. Instead he asserts, on explicit principles of utility, that educating and encouraging people to promote their own happiness by marrying late will naturally aggregate as general sustainability and happiness. 'No co-operation,' Malthus adds, 'is required.'[5] We are not expected, Malthus states firmly, to espouse abstract, ideological imperatives, or to control our biological goals for the good of the party, the motherland or the planet: 'It is not required of us to act from motives to which we are unaccustomed; to pursue a general good, which we may not distinctly comprehend.'[6] Salvation from the otherwise inevitable horrors of positive checks lies within us all, but should not be imposed upon individuals by the state or the Church. Conversely, he notoriously argued that the perverse incentives inherent in the English Poor Laws diverted men and women from that individual and collective salvation by rewarding irresponsibility, and enabling the parish or the state to assume the function of the head of the family.

The demographic transitions to below-replacement birth-rates experienced in the later twentieth and twenty-first centuries by many prosperous nations have been, as Malthus might have hoped, the outcomes of reproductive choice, rather than state interference, specifically the choices of informed, educated women, as well as men, opting for a more comfortable lifestyle. Malthus's belief that population bombs can be diffused by individuals making informed choices to wait and marry late was much derided in his day (in Cobbett's play, Parson Thimble castigates a young country girl: 'young woman, cannot you impose on yourself "*moral restraint*" for ten or a dozen years?').[7] For Romantic writers and their Victorian successors, the dark side of this individualism was that the poor and the unprovided-for might pathologically internalize this economic view of themselves as an unwanted guest at Nature's feast. Numerous poems, plays and novels poignantly dramatized the subjective experience of being a surplus or spare human being: one of a tribe of unmarried daughters, a vagrant, an orphan, a displaced migrant or an unmarried mother driven to infanticide. At the most extreme, in Thomas Hardy's *Jude the Obscure* (1895), the protagonist's son, Little Father Time comes to see his family's hardship and misery in Malthusian terms; and so he murders his two half siblings and kills himself leaving the suicide note 'Done because we are too meny'.[8] The Enlightenment viewed the connection between unforced and self-regarding individual action and social outcomes in terms of the laws of unintended consequences. Literary writers explored the lived, psychological consequences of being, oneself, an unintended consequence.

Malthus was undoubtedly far-sighted in his understanding of the cultural and lifestyle context shaping individual reproductive choice, and he was not, in the very long run, wrong to assert that, in aggregate, such choices could make an enormous difference to demographic outcomes. Book 4 of the *Essay*, however implausible and unpalatable in parts, is key to understanding the resilience of the work as a whole. By connecting the laws and principles of population to an account of human beings as spiritually autonomous and legitimately self-seeking, Malthus stayed true to his Anglican and Enlightenment intellectual heritage; and at the same time ensured an extraordinary legacy, far richer than the term 'Malthusian' implies.

Notes

1 E.A. Wrigley and David Souden (eds.), *The Works of Thomas Robert Malthus*, 8 vols. (London: Pickering and Chatto, 1986), vol. 2, p. 125. Malthus is here quoting approvingly from Samuel Turner's *An Account of an Embassy to the Court of the Teshoo Lama in Tibet* (London: W. Bulmer and Co, 1800).

2 For example, John Milbank, *Theology and Social Theory: Beyond Secular Reason*
   (Oxford: Blackwell, 1990), p. 42.
3 Wrigley and Souden, *Works of Malthus*, vol. 1, p. 18.
4 Ibid., vol. 2, p. 59.
5 Ibid., vol. 3, p. 484.
6 Ibid., vol. 3, p. 484.
7 William Cobbett, 'Surplus Population: And Poor-Law Bill. A Comedy', *The
   Political Register*, 28 May 1831, p.496.
8 Thomas Hardy, *Jude the Obscure*, ed. Patricia Ingham (Oxford: Oxford
   University Press, 2002), p. 325.

Bibliography

Agricultural Production Team. *Report on India's Food Crisis & Steps to Meet It* (Delhi: Government of India, 1959).

Albritton Jonsson, Fredrik. *Enlightenment's Frontier: The Scottish Highlands and the Origins of Environmentalism* (New Haven: Yale University Press, 2013).

'The Origins of Cornucopianism: A Preliminary Genealogy', *Critical Historical Studies*, 1 (2014), 151–68.

'Climate Change and the Retreat of the Atlantic: The Cameralist Context of Pehr Kalm's Voyage to North America 1748–51', *William and Mary Quarterly*, 72 (2015), 99–126.

Alexander, William. *The History of Women, from the Earliest Antiquity, to the Present Time*, 2 vols. (London: Strahan and Cadell, 1779).

Allitt, Patrick. *A Climate of Crisis: America in the Age of Environmentalism* (New York: Penguin, 2014).

Anonymous. *Certayne Causes Gathered Together, Wherin Is Shewed the Decaye of England* (London: Printed for Heugh Singleton, 1552).

The First Report from the Select Committee ... Appointed to Take into Consideration the Means of Promoting the Cultivation and Improvement of the Waste, Uninclosed, and Unproductive Lands (London: House of Commons, 1796).

A Clear, Fair, and Candid Investigation of the Population, Commerce, and Agriculture of This Kingdom, With a Full Refutation of Mr. Malthus's Principles (London: J. Mawman and J. Richardson, 1810).

'Johnson vs. Malthus', *New York Times*, 24 January 1966.

'Women Rap Haden, Want Birth Control', *Pittsburgh Press*, 7 August 1968.

'Negroes Fighting', *New York Times*, 11 August 1968.

'Fighting to Save the Earth from Man', *Time*, 2 February 1970.

Appleman, Philip. *In the Twelfth Year of the War: A Novel* (New York: G.P. Putnam's, 1970).

Darwin's Ark (Bloomington: Indiana University Press, 1984).

New and Selected Poems, 1956–1996 (Fayetteville: University of Arkansas Press, 1996).

Appuhn, Karl. *A Forest on the Sea: Environmental Expertise in Renaissance Venice* (Baltimore: Johns Hopkins University Press, 2009).

Arnold, D. *Famine: Social Crisis and Historical Change* (Oxford, Basil Blackwell, 1988).

Asbell, Bernard. *The Pill: A Biography of the Drug That Changed the World* (New York: Random House, 1995).

Ashwell, [Samuel]. 'Observations on Chlorosis, and its Complications', *Guy's Hospital Reports*, 1 (1836), 529–79.

Attané, Isabelle. 'China's Family Planning Policy: An Overview of Its Past and Future', *Studies in Family Planning*, 33 (2002), 103–13.

Avery, John. *Progress, Poverty and Population: Re-reading Condorcet, Godwin and Malthus* (London: Frank Cass, 1997).

Bailey, Beth L. *Sex in the Heartland* (Cambridge, MA: Harvard University Press, 1999).

Barlow, Nora (ed.). *The Autobiography of Charles Darwin, 1809–1882* (New York and London: W.W. Norton & Co., 1993).

Barrett, Paul H. (ed.). *The Collected Papers of Charles Darwin*, 2 vols. (Chicago: University of Chicago Press, 1977).

Barrett, Paul H., Peter J. Gautrey, Sandra Herbert, David Kohn and Sydney Smith (eds.). *Charles Darwin's Notebooks, 1836–1844* (Cambridge: Cambridge University Press, 1987).

Bashford, Alison. 'Malthus and Colonial History', *Journal of Australian Studies*, 36 (2012), 99–110.

  Global Population: History, Geopolitics, and Life on Earth (New York: Columbia University Press, 2014).

Bayle, Pierre. *Political Writings*, ed. Sally Jenkinson (Cambridge: Cambridge University Press, 2000).

Bayly, Christopher A. *Imperial Meridian: The British Empire and the World, 1780–1830* (London: Longman, 1989).

Bederman, Gail. 'Sex, Scandal, Satire, and Population in 1798: Revisiting Malthus's First *Essay*', *Journal of British Studies*, 47 (2008), 768–95.

Beier, A.L. *Masterless Men: The Vagrancy Problem in England, 1560–1640* (London: Methuen, 1985).

Belich, James. *Replenishing the Earth: The Settler Revolution and the Rise of Anglo-World, 1783–1939* (Oxford: Oxford University Press, 2010).

Benn, Piers. 'Antony Flew Obituary', *Guardian*, 14 April 2010.

Berg, Maxine. 'The Pursuit of Luxury: Global History and British Consumer Goods in the Eighteenth Century,' *Past & Present*, 182 (2004), 85–142.

Berry, Andrew (ed.). *Infinite Tropics: An Alfred Russel Wallace Anthology* (London: Verso, 2003).

Biller, Peter. *The Measure of Multitude: Population in Medieval Thought* (Oxford: Oxford University Press, 2001).

Black Women's Liberation Group. 'Statement on Birth Control', in Robin Morgan (ed.), *Sisterhood is Powerful: An Anthology of Writings from the Women's Liberation Movement* (New York: Vintage Books, 1970), pp. 360–1.

Blaug, Mark. *Economic Theory in Retrospect* (London: Heinemann, 1968).

'Not Only an Economist: Autobiographical Reflections of a Historian of Economic Thought', in Mark Blaug, *Not Only an Economist: Recent Essays by Mark Blaug* (Cheltenham: Edward Elgar, 1997), pp. 3–25.

Bloor, David, *Knowledge and Social Imagery* (Chicago: University of Chicago Press, 1992).

Bodin, Jean. *The Six Bookes of a Common-weale* (London: Adam Islip, 1606).

Bonar, James. *Theories of Population from Raleigh to Arthur Young* (1931; reprinted London: George Allen & Unwin, 1992).

Bonnyman, Brian. *The Third Duke of Buccleuch and Adam Smith: Estate Management and Improvement in Enlightenment Scotland* (Edinburgh: Edinburgh University Press, 2014).

Borrello, Mark. *Evolutionary Restraints: The Contested History of Group Selection* (Chicago: University of Chicago Press, 2010).

Borstelmann, Thomas. *The 1970s: A New Global History from Civil Rights to Economic Inequality* (Princeton: Princeton University Press, 2012).

Botero, Giovanni. *A Treatise, Concerning the Causes of the Magnificencie and Greatnes of Cities* (London: Printed by T. Purfoot for R. Ockould and Henry Tomes, 1606).

The Reason of State, trans. P.J. Waley and D.P. Waley, and *The Greatness of Cities*, trans. Robert Peterson (New Haven: Yale University Press, 1956).

Bowker, Geoffrey C. and Susan Leigh Star, *Sorting Things Out: Classification and Its Consequences* (Cambridge, MA: MIT Press, 1999).

Bowler, Peter. *Evolution: The History of an Idea* (Berkeley: University of California Press, 2003).

Bray, Elizabeth. *The Discovery of the Hebrides: Voyages to the Western Isles 1745–1883* (Edinburgh: Birlinn, 1998).

Briggs, Asa. *Victorian Cities* (London: Odhams Press, 1963).

Brown, Ford K. *The Life of William Godwin* (London: J.M. Dent, 1926).

Bruce, James. *Travels to Discover the Source of the Nile in the Years 1768, 1769, 1770, 1771, 1772 and 1773*, 5 vols. (Edinburgh and London: G.G.J. and J. Robinson, 1790).

Buchwald, Jed Z. and Mordechai Feingold. *Newton and the Origins of Civilization* (Princeton: Princeton University Press, 2013).

Buck, Peter. 'People Who Counted: Political Arithmetic in the Eighteenth Century', *Isis*, 73 (1982), 28–45.

Buckley, William F. 'The Birth Rate', *National Review*, 23 March 1965.

Burbridge, David. 'William Paley Confronts Erasmus Darwin: Natural Theology and Evolutionism in the Eighteenth Century', *Science and Christian Belief* 10 (1998), 49–71.

Burke, Edmund. *Thoughts and Details on Scarcity* (London: F. and C. Rivington and J. Hatchard, 1800).

Burkhardt, Frederick and Sydney Smith (eds.). *The Correspondence of Charles Darwin: Volume 1, 1821–1836* (Cambridge: Cambridge University Press, 1985).

(eds.). *The Correspondence of Charles Darwin: Volume 4, 1847–1850* (Cambridge: Cambridge University Press, 1988).

(eds.). *Correspondence of Charles Darwin: Volume 7, 1858–1859* (Cambridge: Cambridge University Press, 1992).

Burkhardt, Frederick, Janet Browne, Duncan M. Porter and Marsha Richmond (eds.). *Correspondence of Charles Darwin: Volume 8, 1860* (Cambridge: Cambridge University Press, 1993).

Butt, John (ed.). *The Poems of Alexander Pope* (London: Methuen, 1963).

Campbell, Mildred. '"Of People Either Too Few or Too Many": The Conflict of Opinion on Population and Its Relation to Emigration', in William Appleton Aiken and Basil Duke Henning (eds.), *Conflict in Stuart England: Essays in Honour of Wallace Notestein* (London: Jonathan Cape, 1960), pp. 169–201.

[Carlile, Richard]. 'What is Love?', *Republican*, 11 (1825), 545–69.

Carlyle, Thomas. *Selected Writings*, ed. Alan Shelston (Harmondsworth: Penguin, 1971).

Carnegie, A. *The Gospel of Wealth and Other Timely Essays* (New York: The Century Company, 1900).

Chaplin, Joyce. *Subject Matter: Technology, the Body, and Science on the Anglo-American Frontier, 1500–1676* (Cambridge, MA: Harvard University Press, 2001).

The First Scientific American: Benjamin Franklin and the Pursuit of Genius (New York: Basic Books, 2006).

Benjamin Franklin's Political Arithmetic: A Materialist View of Humanity (Washington: Smithsonian Institution, 2009).

Round About the Earth: Circumnavigation from Magellan to Orbit (New York: Simon & Schuster, 2012).

Chase, Allan. *The Legacy of Malthus: The Social Costs of the New Scientific Racism* (New York: Knopf, 1977).

Claeys, Gregory. 'The Concept of "Political Justice" in Godwin's *Political Justice*: A Reconsideration', *Political Theory*, 11 (1983), 565–84.

'The Effects of Property on Godwin's Theory of Justice', *Journal of the History of Philosophy*, 22 (1984), 81–101.

'The Reaction to Political Radicalism and the Popularization of Political Economy in Early 19th Century Britain: The Case of "Productive and Unproductive Labour"', in Terry Shinn and Richard Whitley (eds.), *Expository Science: Forms and Functions of Popularization* (Dordrecht: D. Reidel, 1985), pp. 119–36.

Thomas Paine: Social and Political Thought (London: Unwin Hyman, 1989).

'From True Virtue to Benevolent Politeness: Godwin and Godwinism Revisited', in Gordon Schochet (ed.), *Empire and Revolutions: Papers Presented at the Folger Institute Seminar 'Political Thought in the English-Speaking Atlantic, 1760–1800'* (Washington, DC: The Folger Library, 1993), pp. 187–226.

'The "Survival of the Fittest" and the Origins of Social Darwinism', *Journal of the History of Ideas*, 61 (2000), 223–40.

The French Revolution Debate in Britain (Basingstoke: Palgrave Macmillan, 2007).

'Paine and the Religiosity of Rights', in Rachel Hammersley (ed.), *Revolutionary Moments: Reading Revolutionary Texts* (London: Bloomsbury, 2015).

Clark, Gregory. *A Farewell to Alms: A Brief Economic History of the World* (Princeton: Princeton University Press, 2007).

Cobbett, William. 'Surplus Population: And Poor-Law Bill. A Comedy', *The Political Register*, 28 May 1831.

Rural Rides, ed. George Woodcock (Harmondsworth: Penguin, 1985).

Cody, Lisa Forman. 'The Politics of Illegitimacy in the Age of Reform: Women, Reproduction, and Political Economy in England's New Poor Law of 1834', *Journal of Women's History*, 11 (2000), 131–56.

Coen, Deborah R. 'What is the Big Idea? The History of Ideas Confronts Climate Change', *European Journal for the History of Ideas*, forthcoming.

Cohen, Ed. *A Body Worth Defending: Immunity, Biopolitics, and the Apotheosis of the Modern Body* (Durham: Duke University Press, 2009).

Cohen, Jeremy. *Be Fertile and Increase, Fill the Earth and Master It: The Ancient and Medieval Career of a Biblical Text* (Ithaca: Cornell University Press, 1989).

Cohen, Joel E. *How Many People Can the Earth Support?* (New York: W.W. Norton, 1996).

Collins, David. *An Account of the English Colony in New South Wales, with Remarks on the Dispositions, Customs, Manners, &c of the Native Inhabitants of that Country* (London: T. Cadell and W. Davies, 1798).

Commoner, Barry. *The Closing Circle: Nature, Man, and Technology* (New York: Knopf, 1971).

'Poverty Breeds "Overpopulation"', in Ingolf Vogeler and Anthony De Souza (eds.), *Dialectics of Third World Development* (New Jersey: Allanheld, Osman. 1980), pp. 186–95.

Conder, Josiah. '*Illustrations of Political Economy*. By Harriet Martineau. Nos I–V [and One Other Work]', *Eclectic Review*, 8 (1832), 44–72.

'*Illustrations of Political Economy*. By Harriet Martineau. Nos VI–VIII [and Two Other Works]', *Eclectic Review*, 8 (1832), 328–49.

Connell, Philip. *Romanticism, Economics and the Question of 'Culture'* (Oxford: Oxford University Press, 2001).

Connelly, Matthew. 'To Inherit the Earth: Imagining World Population, from the Yellow Peril to the Population Bomb', *Journal of Global History*, 1 (2006), 299–319.

Fatal Misconception: The Struggle to Control World Population (Cambridge MA: Harvard University Press, 2008).

Council of Environmental Quality and the Department of State. *The Global 2000 Report to the President* (New York: Penguin, 1982).

Critchlow, Donald T. *Intended Consequences: Birth Control, Abortion, and the Federal Government in Modern America* (New York: Oxford University Press, 1999).

[Croker, John Wilson, John Gibson Lockhart and George Poulett Scrope]. '*Illustrations of Political Economy*. Nos. 1–12. By Harriet Martineau', *Quarterly Review*, 49 (1833), 136–52.

Cullather, Nick. '"The Target is the People": Representations of the Village in Modernization and US National Security Doctrine', *Cultural Politics*, 2 (2006), 29–48.

The Hungry World: America's Cold War Battle Against Poverty in Asia (Cambridge, MA: Harvard University Press, 2010).

'"Stretching the Surface of the Earth": The Foundations, Neo-Malthusianism and the Modernising Agenda', *Global Society*, 28 (2014), 104–12.

Cunningham, John. *Conquest and Land in Ireland: The Transplantation to Connacht, 1649–1680* (Woodbridge: Boydell Press, 2011).

Curry, Kenneth (ed.). *New Letters of Robert Southey*, 2 vols. (New York: Columbia University Press, 1965).

Czech, Brian. *Supply Shock: Economic Growth at the Crossroads and the Steady State Solution* (Gabriola Island: New Society Publishers, 2013).

Darwin, Charles. *On the Origin of Species by means of Natural Selection, or the Preservation of Favoured Races in the Struggle for Life* (London: John Murray, 1859).

The Descent of Man, and Selection in Relation to Sex, 2 vols. (London: John Murray, 1871).

The Origin of Species, ed. Gillian Beer (Oxford: Oxford University Press, 1996).

Autobiographies, ed. Michael Neve and Sharon Messenger (Harmondsworth: Penguin, 2002).

The Origin of Species, ed. Jim Endersby (Cambridge: Cambridge University Press, 2009).

Darwin, Erasmus. *Zoonomia: Or the Laws of Organic Life*, 3rd edn, 4 vols. (London: J. Johnson 1801).

Dauvergne, Paul. 'Globalization and the Environment', in John Ravenhill (ed.), *Global Political Economy*, 4th edn (Oxford: Oxford University Press, 2014), pp. 372–97.

Davis, Kingsley. 'Analysis of the Population Explosion', *New York Times*, 22 September 1957.

de Beer, Gavin (ed.). 'Darwin's Notebooks on Transmutation of Species. Part I. First Notebook [B] (July 1837–February 1838)', *Bulletin of the British Museum (Natural History): Historical Series*, 2 (1960), 23–73.

De Bry, Theodor. *Grands Voyages* (Frankfurt, 1590).

Delumeau, Jean. *History of Paradise: The Garden of Eden in Myth and Tradition*, trans. Matthew O'Connell (Urbana: University of Illinois Press, 2000).

de Marchi, N.B. and R.P. Sturges. 'Malthus and Ricardo's Inductivist Critics: Four Letters to William Whewell', *Economica*, 40 (1973), 379–93.

Dentith, Simon. 'Political Economy, Fiction and the Language of Practical Ideology in Nineteenth-Century England', *Social History*, 8 (1983), 183–99.

Derham, William. *Physico-Theology: Or, a Demonstration of the Being and Attributes of God, from His Works of Creation*, 3rd edn (London: Printed for W. Innys, 1714).

Deringer, William Peter. *Calculated Values: The Politics and Epistemology of Economic Numbers in Britain, 1688–1738*. Unpublished PhD thesis, Princeton University (2012).

Desmond, Adrian. *The Politics of Evolution: Morphology, Medicine and Reform in Radical London* (Chicago: University of Chicago Press, 1989).

Huxley: From Devil's Disciple to Evolution's High Priest (London: Penguin, 1997).

Desmond, Adrian and James Moore. *Darwin: The Life of a Tormented Evolutionist* (New York: W.W. Norton, 1992).

Desrochers, Pierre and Christine Hoffbauer. 'The Post War Intellectual Roots of the Population Bomb: Fairfield Osborn's "Our Plundered Planet" and William Vogt's "Road to Survival" in Retrospect', *The Electronic Journal of Sustainable Development*, 1 (2009), 37–61.

Devine, T.M. *The Transformation of Rural Scotland: Social Change and the Agrarian Economy, 1660–1815* (Edinburgh: Edinburgh University Press, 1994).

Diamond, Jared. *Collapse: How Societies Choose to Fail or Survive* (London: Penguin, 2005).

Dick, Stephen. *Plurality of Worlds: the Extraterrestrial Life Debate from Democritus to Kant* (Cambridge: Cambridge University Press, 1984).

Dickens, Charles. *Hard Times*, ed. Grahame Smith (London: Dent, 1994).

A Christmas Carol and Other Christmas Writings, ed. Michael Slater (Harmondsworth: Penguin, 2003).

Dikötter, Frank. *Mao's Great Famine: The History of China's Most Devastating Catastrophe, 1958–1962* (New York: Walker, 2010).

Dolan, Brian. 'Malthus's Political Economy of Health', in Brian Dolan (ed.), *Malthus, Medicine and Morality: 'Malthusianism' after 1798* (Amsterdam: Rodopi, 2000).

Domosh, Mona. 'Practising Development at Home: Race, Gender, and the "Development" of the American South', *Antipode*, 47 (2015), 915–41.

Dowbiggin, Ian Robert. *The Sterilization Movement and Global Fertility in the Twentieth Century* (Oxford: Oxford University Press, 2008).

Drayton, Richard. *Nature's Government: Science, Imperial Britain, and the 'Improvement of the World'* (New Haven: Yale University Press, 2000).

Dugatkin, Lee Alan. *The Prince of Evolution: Peter Kropotkin's Adventures in Science and Politics* (Online: CreateSpace, 2011).

Dzelzainis, Ella. 'Charlotte Elizabeth Tonna, Pre-Millenarianism and the Formation of Gender Ideology in the Ten Hours Campaign', *Victorian Literature and Culture*, 31 (2003), 181–91.

'Feminism, Speculation and Agency in Harriet Martineau's *Illustrations of Political Economy*', in Ella Dzelzainis and Cora Kaplan (eds.), *Harriet Martineau: Authorship, Society and Empire* (Manchester: Manchester University Press, 2010), pp. 118–37.

Easley, Alexis 'Victorian Women Writers and the Periodical Press', *Nineteenth-Century Prose*, 24 (1997), 39–50.

East, Edward Murray. *Mankind at the Crossroads* (New York: C. Scribner, 1923).

Eastwood, David. 'Robert Southey and the Intellectual Origins of Romantic Conservatism', *English Historical Review*, 104 (1989), 308–31.

'Ruinous Prosperity: Robert Southey's Critique of the Commercial System', *Wordsworth Circle*, 25 (1994), 72–6.

Eden, Frederic Morton. *The State of the Poor: Or, a History of the Labouring Classes of England from the Conquest to the Present Period* (London: B. & J. White, 1797).

Ehrlich, Paul R. *The Population Bomb* (New York: Ballantine Books, 1968).
   'Population, Food, and Environment', *Texas Quarterly*, 11 (1968), 43–54.
   The Population Bomb, revised edn (New York: Ballantine Books, 1971).
Ehrlich, Paul R. and Anne H. Ehrlich, 'ZPG: Where to Now?', *Zero Population Growth National Reporter*, 10 (1978), 4–5.
   'The Population Bomb Revisited', *Electronic Journal of Sustainable Development*, 1 (2009), 63–71.
Ehrlich, Paul R. and Richard Holden, 'One-Dimensional Ecology', *The Ecologist*, 2:8 (1972), 11.
Ehrlich, Paul R., Anne H. Ehrlich and John P. Holdren, *Ecoscience: Population, Resources, Environment* (San Francisco: W.H. Freeman, 1977).
Eiseley, Loren. *Darwin's Century: Evolution and the Men Who Discovered It* (New York: Double Day, 1958).
Elliott, John. *Imperial Assumptions and Colonial Realities*. Keynote address given at 'The "Political Arithmetick" of Empires in the Early Modern Atlantic World, 1500–1807', Omohundro Institute for Early American History and Culture conference, the University of Maryland, College Park, 12 March 2012.
Elliot, Paul. *The Derby Philosophers: Science and Culture in British Urban Society, 1700–1850* (Manchester: Manchester University Press, 2009).
[Empson, William]. 'Mrs Marcet – Miss Martineau', *Edinburgh Review*, 57 (1833), 3–39.
   'Life, Writings and Character of Mr. Malthus', *Edinburgh Review*, 64 (1837), 469–506.
Endres, A.M. 'The Functions of Numerical Data in the Writings of Graunt, Petty, and Davenant', *History of Political Economy*, 17:1 (1985), 245–64.
Essex, J. 'Idle Hands Are the Devil's Tools: The Geopolitics and Geoeconomics of Hunger', *Annals of the Association of American Geographers*, 102 (2012), 191–207.
Favretti, Rudy and Gordon P. DeWolf Jr. 'Colonial Garden Plants', *Arnoldia*, 31 (1971), 172–249.
F.D. 'The Dressmaker's Apprentices: A Tale of Woman's Oppression', *Lloyd's Penny Weekly Miscellany*, 3 (1844), 433–4.
Finkelstein, Andrea. *Harmony and the Balance: An Intellectual History of Seventeenth-Century English Economic Thought* (Ann Arbor: University of Michigan Press, 2000).
Fitzgerald, D. 'Exporting American Agriculture: The Rockefeller Foundation in Mexico, 1943–1953', *Social Studies of Science*, 44 (1986), 457–83.
Flew, Antony. 'The Structure of Malthus' Population Theory', *Australasian Journal of Philosophy*, 35 (1957), 1–20.
   'The Structure of Darwinism', in M.L. Johnson, Michael Abercrombie and G.E. Fogg (eds.), *New Biology Volume 28* (Harmondsworth: Penguin, 1959), pp. 25–44.
   'The Structure of Malthus's Population Theory', in Bernard Baumrin (ed.), *Philosophy of Science: The Delaware Seminar: Volume 1: 1961–1962* (New York: John Wiley, 1963), pp. 283–307.
   Evolutionary Ethics (London: Macmillan, 1967).

Philosophical Essays (Lanham: Rowman & Littlefield, 1998).

Fogarty, Michael. *Christian Democracy in Western Europe, 1820–1953* (London: Routledge and Kegan Paul, 1957).

My Life and Ours (Oxford: Thornton's of Oxford, 1999).

Fontaine, Philippe. 'Stabilizing American Society: Kenneth Boulding and the Integration of the Social Sciences', *Science in Context*, 23 (2010), 221–65.

Fosdick, Raymond B. *The Story of the Rockefeller Foundation* (New York: Harper & Brothers, 1952).

Adventure in Giving: The Story of the General Education Board, a Foundation Established by John D. Rockefeller (New York: Harper and Row Publishers, 1962).

A Philosophy for a Foundation (New York: Rockefeller Foundation, 1963).

Franklin, Benjamin. *The Interest of Great Britain Considered, with Regard to Her Colonies, and the Acquisitions of Canada and Guadeloupe* (London: Printed by T. Becket, 1760).

Political, Miscellaneous, and Philosophical Pieces (London: J. Johnson, 1779).

'Observations Concerning the Increase of Mankind' [1751], in Leonard W. Labaree, *et al.* (eds.) *The Papers of Benjamin Franklin*, 40 vols. to date (New Haven: Yale University Press, 1959–), vol. 4, pp. 225–31.

Observations Concerning the Increase of Mankind, Peopling of Countries, &c. [1751], in Alan Houston (ed.), *The Autobiography and Other Writings on Politics, Economics, and Virtue* (Cambridge: Cambridge University Press, 2004), pp. 215–21.

Freeden, Michael. *The New Liberalism: An Ideology of Social Reform* (Oxford: Clarendon, 1978).

Fressoz, Jean-Baptiste and Fabien Locher. 'Modernity's Frail Climate: A Climate History of Environmental Reflexivity', *Critical Inquiry*, 38 (2012), 579–98.

Fryckstedt, Monica Correa. 'The Early Industrial Novel: *Mary Barton* and Its Predecessors', *Bulletin of the John Rylands University Library of Manchester*, 63 (1980), 11–30.

Fumerton, Patricia. *Unsettled: The Culture of Mobility and the Working Poor in Early Modern England* (Chicago: University of Chicago Press, 2006).

Furniss, Edgar S. *The Position of the Laborer in a System of Nationalism: A Study in the Labor Theories of the Later English Mercantilists* (1918; reprinted New York: Augustus M. Kelley, 1965).

Gaskell, Elizabeth. *The Life of Charlotte Brontë*, ed. Angus Easson (Oxford: Oxford University Press, 1996).

North and South, ed. Angus Easson and intro. Sally Shuttleworth (Oxford: Oxford University Press, 1998).

Gentleman, Tobias. *The Best Way to Make England the Richest and Wealthiest Kingdome in Europe, by Advancing the Fishing Trade and Imploying Ships and Mariners* (London, 1660).

Gerard, Bonnie. 'Victorian Things, Victorian Words: Representation and Redemption in Gaskell's *North and South*', *Victorian Newsletter*, 92 (1997), 21–4.

Ghosh, Palash. 'Iran Scales Back Birth Control Programs, Seeks Baby Boom', *International Business Times*, 2 August 2012.

Glahe, Fred and Larry Singell (eds.). *The Collected Papers of Kenneth Boulding*, 4 vols. (Boulder: Colorado Associated University Press, 1971–4).

Glass, D.V. *Numbering the People: The Eighteenth-Century Population Controversy and the Development of Census and Vital Statistics in Britain* (Farnborough: D.C. Heath, 1973).

Gleadle, Kathryn. *The Early Feminists: Radical Unitarians and the Emergence of the Women's Rights Movement, 1831–1851* (Basingstoke: Macmillan, 1995).

Godwin, William. *An Enquiry Concerning Political Justice* (London: G.G.J. and J. Robinson, 1793).

   An Enquiry Concerning Political Justice, 2nd edn (London: G.G.J. and J. Robinson, 1795).

   The Enquirer: Reflections On Education, Manners, and Literature: In a Series Of Essays (London: G.G. and J. Robinson, 1797).

   Of Population (London: Longman, Hurst, Rees, Orme and Brown, 1820).

   Enquiry Concerning Justice and its Influence on Morals and Happiness, Vol II, 3rd edn (Toronto: University of Toronto Press, 1946).

   An Enquiry Concerning Political Justice, 4th edn, 2 vols. (London: J. Watson, 1842).

   An Enquiry Concerning Political Justice, ed. Isaac Kramnick (Harmondsworth: Penguin, 1976).

   The Letters of William Godwin, ed. Pamela Clemit (Oxford: Oxford University Press, 2014).

Goldstone, Jack. 'The New Population Bomb: The Four Megatrends That Will Change the World', *Foreign Affairs*, 89 (2010), 31–43.

Golinski, Jan. *British Weather and the Climate of Enlightenment* (Chicago: University of Chicago Press, 2007).

Gordon, Linda. 'The Politics of Population: Birth Control and the Eugenics Movement', *Radical America*, 8 (1974), 61–97.

   'The Politics of Birth Control, 1920–1940: The Impact of Professionals', *International Journal of Health Services*, 5 (1975), 253–77.

   Woman's Body, Woman's Right: A Social History of Birth Control in America (New York: Grossman, 1976).

Gould, Stephen Jay. *Bully for Brontosaurus: Reflections in Natural History* (New York and London: W.W. Norton & Co., 1992).

Grainger, R.D. *Children's Employment Commission: Appendix to the Second Report of the Commissioners. Trades and Manufactures*, Part I (London: House of Commons, 1842).

Grandin, Greg. *Fordlandia: The Rise and Fall of Henry Ford's Forgotten Jungle City* (London: Icon Books, 2010).

Graunt, John. *Natural and Political Observations Mentioned in a Following Index, and Made upon the Bills of Mortality* (London: Printed by Tho. Roycroft for John Martyn, James Allestry, and Tho. Dicas, 1662).

Greengrass, Mark, Michael Leslie and Timothy Raylor (eds.). *Samuel Hartlib and the Universal Reformation: Studies in Intellectual Communication* (Cambridge: Cambridge University Press, 1994).

Greenhalgh, Susan. 'The Social Construction of Population Science: An Intellectual, Institutional, and Political History of Twentieth-Century Demography', *Comparative Studies in Society and History*, 38 (1996), 26–66.

'Science, Modernity, and the Making of China's One-Child Policy', *Population and Development Review*, 29 (2003), 163–96.

Groenewegen, Peter. 'Introduction: Women in Political Economy and Women as Political Economists in Victorian England', in Peter Groenewegen (ed.), *Feminism and Political Economy in Victorian England* (Aldershot: Elgar, 1994), pp. 11–15.

Grove, Richard H. *Green Imperialism: Colonial Expansion, Tropical Island Edens, and the Origins of Environmentalism, 1600–1800* (Cambridge: Cambridge University Press, 1995).

Grylls, Rosalie Glenn. *William Godwin and His World* (London: Odham Press, 1953).

Guest, Harriet. *Empire, Barbarism, and Civilisation: James Cook, William Hodges, and the Return to the Pacific* (Cambridge: Cambridge University Press, 2007).

Gwatkin, Davidson R. 'Political Will and Family Planning: The Implications of India's Emergency Experience', *Population and Development Review*, 5 (1979), 29–59.

Hacking, Ian. *The Taming of Chance* (Cambridge: Cambridge University Press, 1990).

Hale, Piers. 'William Morris, Human Nature and the Biology of Utopia', in P. Bennett and R. Miles (eds.), *William Morris in the Twenty-First Century* (Oxford: Peter Lang, 2010), pp. 107–28.

'Of Mice and Men: Evolution and the Socialist Utopia. William Morris, H.G. Wells, and George Bernard Shaw', *Journal of the History of Biology*, 43 (2010), 17–66.

Political Descent: Malthus, Mutualism and the Politics of Evolution in Victorian England (Chicago: University of Chicago Press, 2014).

Hardin, Garrett. 'The Tragedy of the Commons', *Science*, 162:3859 (1968), 1243–8.

'Living on a Lifeboat', *Bioscience*, 24:10 (1974), 561–8.

'Lifeboat Ethics: A Malthusian View', in Ingolf Vogeler and Anthony De Souza (eds.), *Dialectics of Third World Development* (New Jersey: Allanheld, Osman, 1980), pp. 171–85.

'The Feast of Malthus', *The Social Contract*, 8 (1988), 181–7.

Hardy, Thomas. *Jude the Obscure*, ed. Patricia Ingham (Oxford: Oxford University Press, 2002).

Hare, Steve (ed.). *Penguin Portrait: Allen Lane and the Penguin Editors* (London: Penguin, 1995).

Harmen, Oren. *The Price of Altruism, George Price and the Search for the Origins of Kindness* (New York: Norton, 2010).

Harr, J.E. and P.J. Johnson. *The Rockefeller Century: Three Generations of America's Greatest Family* (New York: Scribner, 1988).
The Rockefeller Conscience: An American Family in Public and Private (New York: Scribner, 1991).
Harrison, John *et al. The Malthus Library Catalogue* (Oxford: Pergamon Press, 1983).
Hartwick, John M. 'Robert Wallace and Malthus and the Ratios', *Journal of the History of Political Economy*, 20 (1988), 357–79.
Hawkesworth, John. *An Account of the Voyages Undertaken by the Order of His Present Majesty for Making Discoveries in the Southern Hemisphere*, 3 vols. (London: W. Strahan and T. Cadell, 1773).
Haygarth, John. *A Sketch of a Plan to Exterminate the Casual Small-Pox from Great Britain and to Introduce General Inoculation*, 2 vols. (London: J. Johnson, 1793).
Hays, Samuel. *Beauty, Health, and Permanence: Environmental Politics in the United States, 1955–1985* (Cambridge: Cambridge University Press, 1987).
Hazlitt, William. *Political Essays* (London: William Hone, 1819).
Heberden, William. *Observations on the Increase and Decrease of Different Diseases and Particularly the Plague* (London: T. Payne, 1801).
Hecht, Jacqueline. 'Malthus avant Malthus: Concepts et comportement prémalthusiens dans la France d'Ancien Régime', *Dix-huitième siècle*, 26 (1994), 69–78.
Herbert, Sandra. 'Darwin, Malthus and Selection', *Journal of the History of Biology*, 4 (1971), 209–17.
Hilton, Boyd. *The Age of Atonement: The Influence of Evangelicalism on Social and Economic Thought, 1785–1865* (Oxford: Oxford University Press, 1986).
A Mad, Bad and Dangerous People? England 1783–1846 (Oxford: Oxford University Press, 2006).
Himmelfarb, Gertrude. *Darwin and the Darwinian Revolution* (Chicago: Elephant, 1996).
Victorian Minds (Gloucester, MA: Peter Smith, 1975).
The Idea of Poverty: England in the Early Industrial Age (London: Faber & Faber, 1984).
Hindle, Steve. *On the Parish? The Micro-Politics of Poor Relief in Rural England, 1550–1750* (Oxford: Oxford University Press, 2004).
Hodges, Sarah. 'Governmentality, Population and Reproductive Family in Modern India', *Economic and Political Weekly*, 39 (2004), 1157–63.
Hoff, Derek S. *The State and the Stork: The Population Debate and Policy Making in US History* (Chicago: University of Chicago Press, 2012).
Höhler, Sabine. *Spaceship Earth in the Environmental Age, 1960–1990* (London: Pickering Chatto, 2014).
Hollander, Samuel. 'On Malthus's Population Principle and Social Reform', *History of Political Economy*, 18 (1986), 209–15.
'Malthus and Utilitarianism with Special Reference to the *Essay on Population*', *Utilitas*, 1 (1989), 170–210.

The Economics of Thomas Robert Malthus (Toronto: University of Toronto Press, 1997).

Hollingsworth, T.H. *The Demography of the British Peerage* (London: Population Investigation Committee, 1965).

Historical Demography (Ithaca, NY: Cornell University Press, 1969).

Hont, Istvan. *The Jealousy of Trade: International Competition and the Nation-State in Historical Perspective* (Cambridge, MA: Harvard University Press, 2005).

Hoppit, Julian. 'Political Arithmetic in Eighteenth-Century England', *Economic History Review*, 49:3 (1996), 516–40.

Householder, Michael. 'Eden's Translations: Women and Temptation in Early America', *Huntington Library Quarterly*, 70 (2007), 11–36.

Houston, Alan. *Benjamin Franklin and the Politics of Improvement* (New Haven: Yale University Press, 2008).

Hubback, David. *No Ordinary Press Baron: A Life of Walter Layton* (London: Weidenfeld & Nicolson, 1985).

Hulse, J.W. *Revolutionists in London: A Study of Five Unorthodox Socialists* (London: Clarendon Press, 1970).

Hume, David. *Essays Moral, Political and Literary*, ed. Eugene Miller, 2nd edn (Indianapolis: Liberty Fund, 1985).

Dialogues Concerning Natural Religion, ed. Dorothy Coleman (Cambridge: Cambridge University Press, 2007).

Huxley, Thomas. 'The Origin of Species', *Westminster Review*, April 1860.

'The Struggle for Existence: A Programme', *Nineteenth Century*, 23:132 (1888), 161–80.

Collected Essays of T.H. Huxley: Volume 9: Essays in Science (London: MacMillan, 1894).

'Evolution and Ethics', reprinted in James Paradis (ed.), *Evolution and Ethics: T.H. Huxley's Evolution and Ethics with New Essays on Its Victorian Context and Sociobiological Context* (New Jersey: Princeton University Press, 1989).

Huzel, James P. *The Popularization of Malthus in Early Nineteenth-Century England: Martineau, Cobbett and the Pauper Press* (Aldershot: Ashgate, 2006).

Hyndman, Henry Meyers and William Morris. *A Summary of the Principles of Socialism: Written for the Democratic Federation* (London: Modern Press, 1884).

Innes, Joanna. *Inferior Politics: Social Problems and Social Policies in Eighteenth-Century England* (Oxford: Oxford University Press, 2009).

International Development Advisory Board. *Partners in Progress: A Report to President Truman by the International Development Advisory Board* (New York: Simon and Schuster, 1951).

Jackson, H.J. and George Whalley (eds.). *The Collected Works of Samuel Taylor Coleridge, Marginalia Volume III: Irving to Oxlee* (Princeton: Princeton University Press, 1992).

James, Patricia (ed.). *The Travel Diaries of T.R. Malthus* (Cambridge: Cambridge University Press, 1966).

Population Malthus: His Life and Times (London: Routledge, 1979).

(ed.). *T.R. Malthus: An Essay on the Principle of Population*, 2 vols. (Cambridge: Cambridge University Press for the Royal Economic Society, 1989).

Jessop, Ralph. 'Coinage of the Term Environment: A Word Without Authority and Carlyle's Displacement of the Mechanical Metaphor', *Literature Compass*, 9 (2012), 708–20.

Johnson, Lyndon B. 'Annual Message to the Congress on the State of the Union', 4 January 1965.

Johnson, Walter. *The Morbid Emotions of Women: Their Origins, Tendencies and Treatment* (London: Simpkin, Marshall, 1850).

Jones, Greta. 'Alfred Russel Wallace, Robert Owen, and the Theory of Natural Selection', *British Journal of the History of Science*, 35 (2002), 73–96.

Jones, M.G. *The Charity School Movement: A Study of Eighteenth-Century Puritanism in Action* (Cambridge: Cambridge University Press, 1938).

Kaplan, Cora. 'Slavery, Race, History: Martineau's Ethnographic Imagination', in Ella Dzelzainis and Cora Kaplan (eds.), *Harriet Martineau: Authorship, Society and Empire* (Manchester: Manchester University Press, 2010), pp. 180–96.

Kerman, Cynthia. *Creative Tension: The Life and Thought of Kenneth Boulding* (Ann Arbor: University of Michigan Press, 1974).

Keyfitz, Nathan. *Kenneth Ewart Boulding, 1910–1993* (Washington, DC: National Academies Press, 1996).

Keymor, John. *John Keymor's Observation Made upon the Dutch Fishing, about the Year 1601* (London: Printed for Sir Edward Ford, 1664).

Keynes, John Maynard. *The General Theory of Employment, Interest and Money* (London: Macmillan, 1936).

The Collected Writings of John Maynard Keynes: Volume 10: Essays in Biography (London: Macmillan, 1972).

King, Helen. *The Disease of Virgins: Green Sickness, Chlorosis and the Problems of Puberty* (London: Routledge, 2004).

Kinna, Ruth. 'Morris, Anti-Statism and Anarchy', in Peter Faulkner and Peter Preston (eds.), *William Morris Centenary Essays* (Exeter: University of Exeter Press, 1999), pp. 215–28.

Kinney, Arthur F. (ed.). *Rogues, Vagabonds, and Sturdy Beggars: A New Gallery of Tudor and Early Stuart Rogue Literature* (Amherst: University of Massachusetts Press, 1990).

Klepp, Susan. *Revolutionary Conceptions: Women, Fertility, and Family Limitation in America, 1760–1820* (Chapel Hill: University of North Carolina Press, 2009).

Knapp, S.A. 'An Agricultural Revolution', *The World's Work*, 12 (1906) 7733–8.

Koerner, Lisbet. *Linnaeus: Nature and Nation* (Cambridge, MA: Harvard University Press, 1999).

Kristol, Irving. *Reflections of a Neoconservative: Looking Back, Looking Ahead* (New York: Basic Books, 1983).

Kropotkin, Peter. *Memoir of a Revolutionist* (New York: Grove Press, 1968).

Mutual Aid: A Factor in Evolution (London: Freedom Press, 1993).

Lansdowne, Marquis of [H.W.E. Petty-Fitzmaurice] (ed.). *The Petty-Southwell Correspondence, 1676–1687* (London: Constable & Co., 1928).

Lappé, Frances Moore and Joseph Collins. *Food First: Beyond the Myth of Scarcity* (Boston: Houghton Mifflin, 1977).

Last, Jonathan. *What to Expect When No One's Expecting: America's Coming Demographic Disaster* (New York: Encounter Books, 2013).

Latham, Michael. *The Right Kind of Revolution: Modernization, Development, and US Foreign Policy from the Cold War to the Present* (Ithaca: Cornell University Press, 2011).

Laycock, Thomas. *A Treatise on the Nervous Diseases of Women* (London: Orme, Brown, Green and Longmans, 1840).

Ledbetter, Rosanna. *A History of the Malthusian League, 1877–1927* (Columbus: Ohio State University Press, 1976).

Lehmann, William C. *John Millar of Glasgow, 1735–1801: His Life and Thought and his Contributions to Sociological Analysis* (Cambridge: Cambridge University Press, 1960).

Lepenies, Philipp. 'Of Goats and Dogs: Joseph Townsend and the Idealisation of Markets – a Decisive Episode in the History of Economics', *Cambridge Journal of Economics*, 38 (2014), 447–57.

Levy, D.M. 'Some Normative Aspects of the Malthusian Controversy', *History of Political Economy*, 10 (1978), 271–85.

Lewis, Jeremy. *Penguin Special: The Life and Times of Allen Lane* (London: Viking, 2005).

Locher, Fabien. 'Les pâturages de la guerre froide: Garrett Hardin et la Tragédie des communs', *Revue d'Histoire Moderne et Contemporaine*, 60 (2013), 7–36.

Locke, John. *Two Treatises of Government* (London: Awnsham Churchill, 1689).

Logan, Deborah A. (ed.). *Harriet Martineau's Writing on British History and Military Reform*, 6 vols. (London: Pickering & Chatto, 2005).

Lorey, Isabell. *State of Insecurity: Government of the Precarious*, trans. Aileen Derieg (London: Verso, 2015).

Lynch, William T. *Solomon's Child: Method in the Early Royal Society* (Stanford: Stanford University Press, 2001).

Maas, Harro. *Economic Methodology: A Historical Introduction* (London: Routledge, 2014).

Macdonald, Graham. 'The Politics of the Golden River: John Ruskin and the Stationary State', *Environment and History*, 18 (2012), 125–50.

Maclean, C.M. *Hazlitt Painted by Himself* (London: Temple, 1948).

[Maginn, William], 'Gallery of Literary Characters. No. XLII. Miss Harriet Martineau', *Fraser's Magazine*, 8 (1833).

Maines, Rachel P. *The Technology of Orgasm: 'Hysteria', the Vibrator, and Women's Sexual Satisfaction* (Baltimore: John Hopkins University Press, 1999).

Malthus, T.R. *An Essay on the Principle of Population, as it Affects the Future Improvement of Society* (London: J. Johnson, 1798).

An Investigation of the Cause of the Present High Prices of Provisions (London: J. Johnson, 1800).

An Essay on the Principle of Population, 2nd edn (London: J. Johnson, 1803).

An Essay on the Principle of Population, 3rd edn (London: J. Johnson, 1806).

A Letter to Samuel Whitbread, Esq. M. P. on his Proposed Bill for the Amendment of the Poor Laws (London: J. Johnson, 1807).

An Inquiry into the Progress and Nature of Rent (London: John Murray, 1815).

The Grounds of an Opinion on the Policy of Restricting the Important of Foreign Corn (London: John Murray and John Johnson, 1815).

An Essay on the Principle of Population, 5th edn, 3 vols. (London: John Murray, 1817).

Principles of Political Economy Considered with a View to Their Practical Application (London: John Murray, 1820).

An Essay on the Principle of Population, 6th edn (London; John Murray, 1826).

A Summary View of the Principle of Population (London: John Murray, 1830).

An Essay on Population, ed. W.T. Layton (London and New York: Dent and Dutton, 1952).

An Essay on Population, ed. Michael Fogarty (London: Dent, 1958).

Population: The First Essay, ed. Kenneth Boulding (Ann Arbor: University of Michigan Press, 1959).

On Population, ed. Gertrude Himmelfarb (New York: Modern Library, 1960).

Principle of Population, ed. Mark Blaug (Homewood, IL: Richard D. Irwin, 1963).

An Essay on the Principle of Population, ed. Antony Flew (Harmondsworth: Penguin, 1970).

An Essay on the Principle of Population, ed. T.H. Hollingsworth (London: Dent, 1973).

An Essay on the Principle of Population, ed. Philip Appleman (New York: W.W. Norton, 1976).

An Essay on the Principle of Population, in E.A. Wrigley and David Souden (eds.), *The Works of Thomas Robert Malthus*, 8 vols. (London: Pickering Chatto, 1986), vol. 1.

An Essay on the Principle of Population, ed. Patricia James, 2 vols. (Cambridge: Cambridge University Press, 1989).

Principles of Political Economy, ed. John Pullen, 2 vols. (Cambridge: Cambridge University Press for the Royal Economic Society, 1989).

An Essay on the Principle of Population, ed. Geoffrey Gilbert (Oxford: Oxford University Press, 1993).

Mandler, Peter. 'Tories and Paupers: Christian Political Economy and the Making of the New Poor Law', *Historical Journal*, 33 (1990), 88–103.

'The Making of the New Poor Law Redivivus', *Past and Present*, 117 (1987), 131–57.

Marouby, Christian. 'Adam Smith and the Anthropology of the Enlightenment: The "Ethnographic" Sources of Economic Progress', in Larry Wolff and Marco Cipolloni (eds.), *The Anthropology of the Enlightenment* (Stanford: Stanford University Press, 2007), pp. 85–102.

Marshall, Peter H. *William Godwin* (New Haven: Yale University Press, 1984).

Marshall, P.J. and Glyndwr Williams. *The Great Map of Mankind: Perceptions of New Worlds in the Age of Enlightenment* (Cambridge, MA: Harvard University Press, 1982).

Martineau, Harriet. *Illustrations of Political Economy*, 9 vols. (London: Charles Fox, 1834).

Autobiography, ed. Linda H. Peterson (Peterborough, Ontario: Broadview, 2007).

Marx, Karl. *Collected Works of Karl Marx and Friedrich Engels* (New York: International Publishers, 1975–2004).

Mayr, Ernst. *What Evolution Is* (New York: Basic Books, 2001).

Mayhew, Robert J. *Malthus: The Life and Legacies of an Untimely Prophet* (Cambridge, MA: Harvard University Press, 2014).

McAllister, William. 'Thought Experiments and the Exercise of Imagination in Science', in Melanie Frappiér *et al.*, *Thought Experiments in Philosophy, Science, and the Arts* (London: Routledge, 2013), pp. 11–29.

McCormick, Ted. *William Petty and the Ambitions of Political Arithmetic* (Oxford: Oxford University Press, 2009).

'Political Arithmetic and Sacred History: Population Thought in the English Enlightenment, 1660–1750', *Journal of British Studies*, 52 (2013), 829–57.

'Population: Modes of Seventeenth-Century Demographic Thought', in Carl Wennerlind and Philip J. Stern (eds.), *Mercantilism Reimagined: Political Economy in Early Modern Britain and Its Empire* (New York: Oxford University Press, 2014), pp. 25–45.

'Statistics in the Hands of an Angry God? John Graunt's Observations in Cotton Mather's New England', *The William and Mary Quarterly*, 72 (2015), 563–86.

McLane, Maureen. *Romanticism and the Human Sciences: Poetry, Population and the Discourse of the Species* (Cambridge: Cambridge University Press, 2000).

McNeil, Maureen. *Under the Banner of Science, Erasmus Darwin and his Age* (Manchester: Manchester University Press, 1987).

McRae, Andrew. *God Speed the Plough: The Representation of Agrarian England, 1500–1660* (Cambridge: Cambridge University Press, 1996).

Meek, Ronald (ed.). *Marx and Engels on Malthus* (London: Lawrence and Wishart, 1953).

Social Science and the Ignoble Savage (Cambridge: Cambridge University Press, 1976).

Milbank, John. *Theology and Social Theory: Beyond Secular Reason* (Oxford: Blackwell, 1990).

Milgate, Murray and Shannon C. Stimson. *After Adam Smith: A Century of Transformation in Politics and Political Economy* (Princeton: Princeton University Press, 2009).

Mill, John Stuart. *Autobiography of John Stuart Mill* (New York: Signet, 1964).

Mitchell, Theodore and Robert Lowe. 'To Sow Contentment: Philanthropy, scientific agriculture and the making of the New South, 1906–1920', *Journal of Social History*, 24 (1990), 317–40.

Mokyr, Joel. *The Enlightened Economy: An Economic History of Britain 1700–1850* (New Haven: Yale University Press, 2009).

Monro, D.H. *Godwin's Moral Philosophy* (Oxford: Oxford University Press, 1953).

Moore, James. 'Wallace's Malthusian Moment: The Common Context Revisited', in Bernard Lightman (ed.), *Victorian Science in Context* (Chicago: University of Chicago Press, 1990), pp. 290–311.

Moore, James W. '"Amsterdam Is Standing on Norway": Part II: The Global North Atlantic in the Ecological Revolution of the Long Seventeenth Century', *Journal of Agrarian Change*, 10 (2010), 188–227.

Moorehead, Alan. *The Fatal Impact: The Invasion of the South Pacific, 1767–1840* (1966; reprinted New York: Harper and Row, 1987).

Morris, William. *News from Nowhere and Other Writings* (London: Penguin, 1993).

Mosher, A.T. *Getting Agriculture Moving: Essentials for Development and Modernization* (New York: Praeger, 1966).

Mukerjee, Radhakamal. *The Political Economy of Population* (London: Longmans, Green & Co., 1941).

Mun, Thomas. *A Discovrse of Trade, from England vnto the East Indies* (London: Printed by Nicholas Okes for John Pyper, 1621).

Nally, D. *Human Encumbrances: Political Violence and the Great Irish Famine* (Notre Dame: University of Notre Dame Press, 2011).

Nally, D. and S. Taylor. 'The Politics of Self-Help: The Rockefeller Foundation, Philanthropy and the "Long" Green Revolution', *Political Geography*, 49 (2015) 51–63.

National Security Council. *NSSM 200: Implications of Worldwide Population Growth for US Security and Overseas Interests* (Washington: National Security Council, 1974).

Nelson, Jennifer. *Women of Color and the Reproductive Rights Movement* (New York: New York University Press, 2003).

Nixon, Richard. 'Special Message to the Congress on Problems of Population Growth', in *Public Papers of the Presidents of the United States: Richard Nixon, 1969* (Washington, DC: GPO, 1971).

Nyland, Chris. 'Women's Progress and "the End of History"', in Robert Dimand and Chris Nyland (eds.), *The Status of Women in Classical Economic Thought* (Cheltenham: Edward Elgar, 2003), pp. 108–26.

O'Brien, Denis. 'Mark Blaug, 1927–2011', *Biographical Memoirs of Fellows of the British Academy*, 12 (2013), 25–47.

O'Flaherty, Niall. 'Malthus and the History of Population', in Shannon Stimson (ed.), *An Essay on the Principle of Population*, by T. R. Malthus (Yale: Yale University Press, forthcoming).

Ó Gráda, Cormac. *Eating People is Wrong, and Other Essays on Famine, its Past, and its Future* (Princeton: Princeton University Press, 2015).

Paddock, William. 'Malthus: Right or Wrong?', *The Social Contract*, 8 (1998), 197–205.

Paradis, James (ed.). *Evolution and Ethics: T.H. Huxley's Evolution and Ethics with New Essays on its Victorian Context and Sociobiological Context* (New Jersey: Princeton University Press, 1989).

Parrinder, Patrick. 'Eugenics and Utopia: Sexual Selection from Galton to Morris', *Utopian Studies*, 8 (1997), 1–12.

Parthasasarathi, Prasannan. *Why Europe Grew Rich and Asia Did Not: Global Economic Divergence 1600–1800* (Cambridge: Cambridge University Press, 2011).

Paul, C. Kegan. *William Godwin. His Friends and Contemporaries*, 2 vols. (London: Henry S. King & Co., 1876).

Paul VI, '*Humanae Vitae*: Encyclical of Pope Paul VI on the Regulation of Birth', *Acta Apostolicae Sedis*, 6 (1968), 481–503.

Pearse, Andrew. *Seeds of Plenty, Seeds of Want: Social and Economic Implications of the Green Revolution* (Oxford: Clarendon Press, 1980).

Pender, Séamus (ed.). *A Census of Ireland, circa 1659: With Essential Materials from the Poll Money Ordinances, 1660–1661* (Dublin: Irish Manuscripts Commission, 2002).

Pennant, Thomas. *A Tour in Scotland and a Voyage to the Hebrides, MDCCLXXII* (Chester: B. White, 1774).

Perkins, John. *Geopolitics and the Green Revolution: Wheat, Genes, and the Cold War* (New York: Oxford University Press, 1997).

Petty, William. *Reflections on Some Persons and Things in Ireland* (London: Printed for John Martin, James Allestreye and Thomas Dicas, 1660).

A Treatise of Taxes and Contributions (London: Printed for N. Brooke, 1662).

Political Arithmetick (London: Printed for Robert Clavel and Henry Mortlock, 1690).

The Political Anatomy of Ireland (London: Printed by D. Brown and W. Rogers, 1691).

History of the Cromwellian Survey of Ireland, A.D. 1655–6, Commonly Called 'The Down Survey', Thomas Aiskew Larcom (ed.) (Dublin: Irish Archaeological Society, 1851).

Pichanick, Valerie Kossew. *Harriet Martineau: The Woman and Her Work, 1802–76* (Ann Arbor: University of Michigan Press, 1980).

Piketty, Thomas. *Capital in the Twenty-First Century* (Cambridge, MA.: Harvard University Press, 2014).

Plasmeijer, Henk W. 'The Talk of the Town in 1798', in Nora Fuhrmann, Eva Schmoly and Ravinder Stephan Singh Sud (eds.), *Gegen den Strich: Ökonomische Theorie und politische Regulierung* (Munich: Rainer Hampp, 2003), pp. 41–8.

Plattes, Gabriel. *A Discovery of Infinite Treasvre, Hidden since the Worlds Beginning* (London: Printed by I.L., 1639).

A Discovery of Subterraneall Treasure (London: Printed by J. Okes for Jasper Emery, 1639).

A Description of the Famous Kingdome of Macaria (London: Printed for Francis Constable, 1641).

Pocock, J.G.A. 'Gibbon and the Shepherds: The States of Society in the *Decline and Fall*', *History of European Ideas*, 2 (1981), 193–202.

Polanyi, Karl. *The Great Transformation: The Political and Economic Origins of Our Time* (New York: Beacon Press, 2001).

Pomeranz, Kenneth. *The Great Divergence: China, Europe, and the Making of the Modern World Economy* (Princeton: Princeton University Press, 2000).

Population Council. 'On the Origins of the Population Council', *Population and Development Review*, 3 (1977), 493–502.

The Population Council: A Chronicle of the First Twenty-Five Years, 1952–1977 (New York: The Population Council, 1978).

Porter, Roy. 'Erasmus Darwin: Doctor of Evolution?' in J. Moore (ed.), *History, Humanity and Evolution: Essays for John C. Greene* (Cambridge: Cambridge University Press, 1989), pp. 39–70.

Poynter. J.R. *Society and Pauperism: English Ideas on Poor Relief, 1795–1834* (London: Routledge and Kegan Paul, 1969).

Prendergast, Renee. 'James Anderson's Political Economy: His Influence on Smith and Malthus', *Scottish Journal of Political Economy*, 34 (1987), 388–409.

President's Materials Policy Commission. *Resources for Freedom: A Report to the President by the President's Materials Policy Commission: Volume 1: Foundation for Growth and Security* (Washington, DC: Government Printing Office, 1952).

Price, Richard. *Observations on Reversionary Payments: On Schemes for Providing Annuities* (London: T. Cadell, 1773),

An Essay on the Population of England, from the Revolution to the Present Time (London: Printed for T. Cadell, 1780).

Priestley, Joseph. *An Account of a Society for Encouraging the Industrious Poor* (Birmingham: Pearson and Rollason, 1787).

Pringle, Andrew. *General View of the Agriculture of the County of Westmoreland, with Observations on the Means of its Improvement* (London: J. Chapman, 1794).

Pujol, Michèle A. *Feminism and Anti-Feminism in Early Economic Thought* (Aldershot: Elgar, 1992).

Pullen, John (ed.). *T.R. Malthus: Principles of Political Economy* (Cambridge: Cambridge University Press for the Royal Economic Society, 1989).

'The Last Sixty Five Years of Malthus Scholarship', *History of Political Economy*, 30 (1998), 343–52.

Pullen, John and Trevor Hughes Parry (eds.). *T.R. Malthus: The Unpublished Papers in the Collection of Kanto Gakuen University* (Cambridge: Cambridge University Press, 1997–2004).

Pyle, Andrew (ed.). *Population: Contemporary Responses to Thomas Malthus* (Bristol: Thoemmes Press, 1994).

Rabelais, François. *Gargantua and Pantagruel*, trans. Sir Thomas Urquhart and Peter Motteux (New York: Digireads.com, 2009).

Raby, Peter. *Alfred Russel Wallace: A Life* (Princeton: Princeton University Press, 2001).

Radkau, Joachim. *The Age of Ecology: A Global History* (Oxford: Polity Press, 2014).

Reagan, Ronald. 'Remarks to American Petroleum Institute', 16 November 1971, *Folder 'Speeches, 1970,' Box P18*, Ronald Reagan Library, Simi Valley, California.

Rendall, Jane. *The Origins of Modern Feminism: Women in Britain, France and the United States, 1780–1860* (Basingstoke: Macmillan, 1985).

Report of the Select Committee on Petitions Relating to the Corn Laws of this Kingdom (London: James Ridgway, 1814).

Richardson, Angelique. *Love and Eugenics in the Late Nineteenth Century: Rational Reproduction and the New Woman* (Oxford: Oxford University Press, 2008).

Riskin, Jessica. *Science in the Age of Sensibility* (Chicago: University of Chicago Press, 2002).

Ritvo, Harriet. 'Possessing Mother Nature: Genetic Capital in Eighteenth Century Britain', in John Brewer and Susan Staves (eds.), *Early Modern Conceptions of Property* (London: Routledge, 1995), pp. 413–27.

Roberts, Lissa. 'Practicing Oeconomy During the Second Half of the Long Eighteenth Century: An Introduction', *History and Technology*, 30 (2014), 133–48.

Robertson, Thomas. *The Malthusian Moment: Global Population Growth and the Birth of American Environmentalism* (New Brunswick: Rutgers University Press, 2012).

'"Thinking Globally": American Foreign Aid, Paul Ehrlich, and the Emergence of Environmentalism in the 1960s', in Francis Gavin and Mark Lawrence (eds.), *Beyond the Cold War: Lyndon Johnson and the New Global Challenges of the 1960s* (New York: Oxford University Press, 2014), pp. 185–206.

Robin, Libby, Sverker Sörlin and Paul Warde. *The Future of Nature: Documents of Global Change* (New Haven: Yale University Press, 2013).

Rockell, Frederick. 'The Last of the Great Victorians: Special Interview with Dr. Alfred Russel Wallace', *The Millgate Monthly*, 7:83 (1912), 657–63.

Rockefeller, John D. III. *The Second American Revolution: Some Personal Observations* (New York: Harper & Row Publishers, 1973).

Rockefeller Foundation. *Five-Year Review and Projection, December 2–3, 1968* (New York: Rockefeller Foundation Publication, 1968).

(ed.). *Strategy for the Conquest of Hunger: Proceedings of a Symposium Convened by the Rockefeller Foundation, April 1 and 2, 1968, at Rockefeller University* (New York: Rockefeller Foundation, 1968).

Rockström, Johan, Will Steffen, Paul Crutzen, *et al.* 'Planetary Boundaries: Exploring the Safe Operating Space for Humanity', *Nature*, 461 (2009), 472–5.

Rogerson, John. *Old Testament Criticism in the Nineteenth Century: England and Germany* (London: SPCK, 1984).

Rome, Adam. *The Genius of Earth Day: How a 1970s Teach-In Unexpectedly Made the First Green Generation* (New York: Hill & Wang, 2013).

Ruse, Michael. 'Charles Darwin and Artificial Selection', *Journal of the History of Ideas*, 36 (1975), 339–50.

The Darwinian Revolution: Science Red in Tooth and Claw (Chicago: University of Chicago Press, 1979).

Ruskin, John. *Unto This Last and Other Writings*, ed. Clive Wilmer (London: Penguin, 1997).

Rusnock, Andrea. *Vital Accounts: Quantifying Health and Population in Eighteenth-Century England and France* (Cambridge: Cambridge University Press, 2002).

Russell, Bertrand. 'Population Pressure and War', in Stuart Mudd (ed.), *The Population Crisis and the Use of World Resources* (The Hague: W. Junk, 1964), pp. 1–5.

Russell, Colin. 'Richard Watson: Gaiters and Gunpowder', in Mary D. Archer and Christopher D. Haley (eds.), *The 1702 Chair of Chemistry at Cambridge: Transformation and Change* (Cambridge: Cambridge University Press, 2005), pp. 57–83.

Ryan, M[ichael]. *A Manual of Midwifery, and Diseases of Women and Children*, 4th edn (London, 1841).

Rylance, Rick. 'Reading with a Mission: The Public Sphere of Penguin Books', *Critical Quarterly*, 47 (2005), 48–66.

St Clair, William. *The Godwins and the Shelleys: The Biography of a Family* (London: Faber and Faber, 1989).

Sabin, Paul. *The Bet: Paul Ehrlich, Julian Simon and Our Gamble Over Earth's Future* (New Haven: Yale University Press, 2013).

Sachs, Jeffery D. *Common Wealth: Economics for a Crowded Planet* (London: Penguin, 2008).

Sackley, Nicole. 'The Village as Cold War Site: Experts, Development, and the History of Rural Reconstruction', *Journal of Global History*, 6 (2011), 481–504.

Salgado, Gamini (ed.). *Cony-Catchers and Bawdy Baskets* (New York: Penguin, 1973).

Sandbrook, Dominic. *State of Emergency: The Way we Were: Britain 1970–1974* (London: Penguin, 2010).

Sanders, Valerie. '"Meteor Wreaths": Harriet Martineau, "L.E.L", Fame and *Frazer's* [*sic*] *Magazine*', *Critical Survey*, 13 (2001), 42–60.

Schabas, Margaret. *The Natural Origins of Economics* (Chicago: University of Chicago Press, 2005).

Schlosser, Kolson. 'Malthus at Mid-Century: Neo-Malthusianism as Bio-Political Governance in the Post-World War II United States', *Cultural Geographies*, 16 (2009), 465–84.

Schofield, Robert E. *The Enlightened Joseph Priestley: A Study of His Life and Work from 1773 to 1804* (University Park: Pennsylvania State University Press, 2004).

Schumacher, E.F. *Small Is Beautiful: Economics as if People Mattered* (New York: Harper & Row, 1973).

Schwartz, Joel. 'Robert Chambers and Thomas Henry Huxley, Science Correspondents: The Popularisation and Dissemination of Nineteenth-Century Natural Science', *Journal of the History of Biology*, 32 (1999), 343–83.

Scott, James C. *Seeing Like a State: How Certain Schemes to improve the Human Condition Have Failed* (New Haven: Yale University Press, 1998).

Seaman, Barbara, *The Doctors' Case against the Pill* (New York: P.H. Wyden, 1969).

Sebastiani, Silvia. *The Scottish Enlightenment: Race, Gender, and the Limits of Progress* (New York: Palgrave, 2013).

Secord, James. *Victorian Sensation: The Extraordinary Publication, Reception, and Secret Authorship of Vestiges of the Natural History of Creation* (Chicago: University of Chicago Press, 2000).

Seymour, Terry. *A Printing History of Everyman's Library, 1906–1982* (Bloomington: AuthorHouse, 2011).

Shapiro, Judith. *Mao's War against Nature: Politics and the Environment in Revolutionary China* (Cambridge: Cambridge University Press, 2001).

Sharpless, John. 'Population Science, Private Foundations, and Development AID: The Transformation of Demographic Knowledge in the United States, 1945–1965', in Frederick Cooper and Randall Packard (eds.), *International Development and the Social Sciences: Essays on the History and Politics of Knowledge* (Berkeley: University of California Press, 1997), pp. 176–200.

Sheail, John. *An Environmental History of Twentieth-Century Britain* (Basingstoke: Palgrave, 2001).

Shelley, Percy. *A Philosophical View of Reform*, ed. T.W. Rolleston (1914; reprinted Honolulu: University of Hawaii Press, 2004).

Sherwood, John M. 'Engels, Marx, Malthus and the Machine', *American Historical Review*, 90 (1985), 837–65.

Short, Thomas. *New Observations, Natural, Moral, Civil, Political, and Medical on City, Town, and Country Bills of Mortality* (London: Printed for T. Longman and A. Millar, 1750).

Simon, Julian. *A Life against the Grain: The Autobiography of an Unconventional Economist* (New Brunswick: Transactions, 2002).

Sinclair, John (ed.). *The Statistical Account of Scotland: Volume 12* (Edinburgh: William Creech, 1794).

  Observations on the Means of a Cottager to Keep a Cow (London: W. Bulmer, 1801).

Skidelsky, Robert. *John Maynard Keynes: The Economist as Saviour, 1920–1937* (London: Macmillan, 1992).

Slack, Paul. *Poverty and Policy in Tudor and Stuart England* (Harlow: Longman, 1988).

  'Plenty of People': Perceptions of Population in Early Modern England (Reading: University of Reading, 2011).

Smith, Adam. *An Inquiry into the Nature and Causes of the Wealth of Nations*, 2 vols. (London: W. Strahan and T. Cadell, 1776).

  An Inquiry into the Nature and Causes of the Wealth of Nations, 2 vols. (Oxford: Clarendon Press, 1869).

  An Inquiry into the Nature and Causes of the Wealth of Nations, ed. R.H Campbell, A.S. Skinner and W.B. Todd, 2 vols. (Oxford: Oxford University Press, 1976).

Smith, Kenneth. *The Malthusian Controversy* (London: Routledge, 1951).

Smith, Mary. 'Birth Control and the Negro Woman', *Ebony*, March 1968, 29.

Smith, Vanessa. 'Crowd Scenes: Pacific Collectivity and European Encounter', *Pacific Studies*, 27 (2004), 1–21.

Sobri, Mohammed Helmi Mohammed, *The Establishment of the London University and the Socio-Cultural Status of English Liberal Education, 1825–1836*. Unpublished PhD thesis, University of London (2015).

Soloway, Richard. *Demography and Degeneration: Eugenics and the Declining Birthrate in Twentieth-Century Britain* (Chapel Hill: University of North Carolina Press, 1990).

Southey, Robert. 'Malthus's *Essay on Population*', *Annual Review and History of Literature*, 2 (1803), 292–301.

Essays, Moral and Political, 2 vols. (London: John Murray, 1832).

Letters from England, ed. Jack Simmons (London: Cresset, 1951).

Spary, Emma. 'Political, Natural and Bodily Economies', in Nicholas Jardine, James A. Secord and E. C. Spary (eds.), *Cultures of Natural History* (Cambridge: Cambridge University Press, 1996), pp. 178–96.

Spengler, J.J. *French Predecessors of Malthus: A Study in Eighteenth-Century Wage and Population Theory* (Durham, NC: Duke University Press, 1942).

Stedman Jones, Gareth. *An End to Poverty? A Historical Debate* (London: Profile Books, 2004).

Steffen, Will, Jacques Grinevald, Paul Crutzen and John McNeill, 'The Anthropocene: Conceptual and Historical Perspectives', *Philosophical Transactions of the Royal Society A*, 369 (2011), 842–67.

Stevenson, Russell and Virginia O. Locke. *The Agricultural Development Council: A History*, (Morrilton: Winrock Institute for Agricultural Development, 1989).

Stiles, Ezra. *A Discourse on the Christian Union* (Boston: Edes and Gill, 1761).

Stott, Rebecca. *Darwin and the Barnacle: The History of One Tiny Creature and History's Most Spectacular Breakthrough* (London: Faber & Faber, 2003).

Strange, Julie-Marie. 'Menstrual Fictions: Languages of Medicine and Menstruation, c. 1850–1931', *Women's History Review*, 9 (2000), 607–28.

Strangeland, Charles. *Pre-Malthusian Doctrines of Population: A Study in the History of Economic Theory* (1904; reprinted New York: Augustus M. Kelley, 1966).

Subramaniam, C. 'India's Program for Agricultural Progress', in Rockefeller Foundation (ed.), *Strategy for the Conquest of Hunger: Proceedings of a Symposium Convened by the Rockefeller Foundation, April 1 and 2, 1968, at Rockefeller University* (New York: Rockefeller Foundation, 1968), pp. 16–22.

Szreter, Simon. 'The Idea of Demographic Transition in the Study of Fertility Change: A Critical Intellectual History', *Population and Development Review*, 19(1993), 659–701.

Taylor, Barbara. *Eve and the New Jerusalem: Socialism and Feminism in the Nineteenth Century* (London: Virago, 1983).

Mary Wollstonecraft and the Feminist Imagination (Cambridge: Cambridge University Press, 2003).

Teitelbaum, Michael S. and Jay M. Winter. 'Bye-Bye, Baby', *The New York Times*, 6 April 2014.

Tellmann, Ute, 'Catastrophic Populations and the Fear of the Future: Malthus and the Genealogy of Liberal Economy', *Theory, Culture & Society*, 30 (2013), 135–55.

Thirsk, Joan. 'Enclosing and Engrossing, 1500–1640', in Joan Thirsk (ed.), *Chapters from the Agrarian History of England and Wales, 1500–1750: Volume 3: Agricultural Change: Policy and Practice, 1500–1750* (Cambridge: Cambridge University Press, 1990), pp. 54–109.

Thirsk, Joan and J.P. Cooper (eds.). *Seventeenth-Century Economic Documents* (Oxford: Oxford University Press, 1972).

Thomas, Brinley. *The Industrial Revolution and the Atlantic Economy: Selected Essays* (London: Routledge, 1993).

Thomas, D.O. *The Honest Mind: The Thought and Work of Richard Price* (Oxford: Oxford University Press, 1977).

Thomas, Julia Adeney. 'History and Biology in the Anthropocene: Problems of Scale, Problems of Value', *The American Historical Review*, 119 (2014), 1587–607.

Todes, Daniel. *Darwin without Malthus: The Struggle for Existence in Russian Evolutionary Thought* (New York: Oxford University Press, 1989).

[Tonna, Charlotte Elizabeth]. 'Politics', *Christian Lady's Magazine*, 1 (1834).

  The Perils of the Nation: An Appeal to the Legislature, the Clergy, and the Higher and Middle Classes (London: Seeley, Burnside and Seeley, 1843).

  Mesmerism: A Letter to Miss Harriet Martineau (London: Seeley, Burnside, and Seeley, 1844).

Tonna, Charlotte Elizabeth. *The Wrongs of Woman* (London: Dalton, 1844).

Toulmin, Camilla. 'The Orphan Milliners: A Story of the West End', *Illuminated Magazine*, 2 (1844), 279–85.

Townsend, Joseph. *A Dissertation on the Poor Laws: By a Well-Wisher to Mankind* (London: C. Dilly, 1786).

Toye, John. *Keynes on Population* (Oxford: Oxford University Press, 2000).

Turner, Samuel. *An Account of an Embassy to the Court of the Teshoo Lama in Tibet* (London: W. Bulmer and Co, 1800).

Tuttle, Leslie. *Conceiving the Old Regime: Pronatalism and the Politics of Reproduction in Early Modern France* (Oxford: Oxford University Press, 2010).

Valenze, Deborah. *The First Industrial Woman* (New York: Oxford University Press, 1995).

Veldman, Meredith. *Fantasy, the Bomb and the Greening of Britain: Romantic Protest, 1945–1980* (Cambridge: Cambridge University Press, 1994).

Vernon, James. *Hunger: A Modern History* (Cambridge, MA: Harvard University Press, 2007).

Waller, Charles. 'Lectures on the Function and Diseases of the Womb', *Lancet*, 25 January 1840.

Waterhouse, A.C. *Food and Prosperity: Balancing Technology and Community in Agriculture* (New York: Rockefeller Foundation, 2013).

Waterman, A.M.C. *Revolution, Economics and Religion: Christian Political Economy, 1798–1833* (Cambridge: Cambridge University Press, 1991).

  'Reappraisal of Malthus the Economist, 1933–97', *History of Political Economy*, 30 (1998), 293–334.

Watson, Frederick. *Historical Records of Australia: Series 1: Governors' Dispatches to and From England* ([Sydney]: The Library Committee of the Commonwealth Parliament, 1914).

Webb, R.K. *Harriet Martineau: A Radical Victorian* (London: Heinemann, 1960).

Webster, Charles. *The Great Instauration: Science, Medicine and Reform, 1626–1660* (London: Gerald Duckworth & Co., 1975).

Weiner, Myron and Michael S. Teitelbaum. *Political Demography, Demographic Engineering* (New York: Berghahn Books, 2001).

Whiteman, Anne (ed.). *The Compton Census of 1676: A Critical Edition* (Oxford: Oxford University Press, 1986).

Willis-Harris, H. 'The Survival of the Fittest', *Justice*, 28 April 1888, p. 2.

Wilson, J. 'Fantasy Machine: Philanthrocapitalism as an Ideological Formation', *Third World Quarterly*, 35 (2014), 1144–61.

Wilson, Kathleen. 'Thinking Back: Gender Misrecognition and Polynesian Subversion Aboard the Cook Voyages', in Kathleen Wilson (ed.), *A New Imperial History: Culture, Identity and Modernity in Britain, 1660–1840* (Cambridge: Cambridge University Press, 2004), pp. 346–8.

Winch, Donald. *Malthus* (Oxford: Oxford University Press, 1987).

Riches and Poverty: An Intellectual History of Political Economy in Britain, 1750–1834 (Cambridge: Cambridge University Press, 1996).

Wealth and Life: Essays on the Intellectual History of Political Economy in Britain, 1848–1914 (Cambridge: Cambridge University Press, 2009).

Wollstonecraft, Mary. *A Vindication of the Rights of Men and A Vindication of the Rights of Woman and Hints*, ed. Sylvana Tomaselli (Cambridge: Cambridge University Press, 1995).

Worster, Donald. *Nature's Economy: A History of Ecological Ideas*, 2nd edn (Cambridge: Cambridge University Press, 1994).

Wrigley, E.A. *Continuity, Chance and Change: The Character of the Industrial Revolution in England* (Cambridge: Cambridge University Press, 1988).

'Standing between Two Worlds', *Malthus and his Legacy: The Population Debate after 200 years*, conference papers, Australian Academy of the Humanities, www.naf.org.au/papers.htm.

Poverty, Progress and Population (Cambridge: Cambridge University Press, 2004).

Energy and the English Industrial Revolution (Cambridge: Cambridge University Press, 2010).

Wrigley, E.A. and David Souden (eds.). *The Works of Thomas Robert Malthus*, 8 vols. (London: Pickering and Chatto, 1986).

Wrobel, David M. *The End of American Exceptionalism: Frontier Anxiety from the Old West to the New Deal* (Lawrence: University Press of Kansas, 1993).

Yamamoto, Koji. 'Reformation and the Distrust of the Projector in the Hartlib Circle', *The Historical Journal*, 55 (2012), 375–97.

Yeo, Stephen. 'A New Life: The Religion of Socialism in Britain, 1883–1896', *History Workshop Journal*, 4 (1977), 5–56.

Young, Arthur. *The Question of Scarcity Plainly Stated and Remedies Considered* (London: B. M'Millan, 1800).

Young, Robert M. 'Malthus and the Evolutionists: The Common Context of Biological and Social Theory', *Past and Present*, 43 (1969), 109–45.

Index

1798, events in, 3, 6, 9, 75, 140–1

ageing population, 285
Aikin, John, 41
Albritton Jonsson, Fredrik, 6, 297
Alexander, William, 158
America in population thought, 32, 38–9, 79,
    81–2, 88, 106–8, 109, 110–11, 112, 114–16,
    121–3, 131, 267–89
American War of Independence, 111
Ampleforth, 246
Annual Review, 165
Anthropocene, 146
Appleman, Philip, 243, 257–9, 260, 261
Arbuthnot, John, 37
Australia in population thought, 117–20, 272

Baby Boom, 285
Bailey, Beth, 277
Bakewell, Robert, 138
Baconianism, 31, 33, 41
Balfour, Warren, 221
Banks, Joseph, 120
Bashford, Alison, 8, 240–1, 269
Bates, Henry, 192
Bayle, Pierre, 145
Bayly, Christopher, 140
Beddington, John, 17
Bederman, Gail, 156
Belich, James, 141
Bentham, Jeremy, 56
Berelson, Bernard, 229
Bertalanffy, Ludwig von, 251
Bettany, G., 242, 244–5
Bible on population, 27, 83, 106–8, 112–13, 114
birth control, 14, 81–2, 228–30, 253, 254, 272,
    274–7, 279–80, 296
Blaug, Mark, 248–9, 260
Bloor, David, 193
Blueprint for Survival, 255

Bodin, Jean, 27, 39
Bonar, James, 242
Borrello, Mark, 194
Borstelmann, Thomas, 240
Botero, Giovanni, 27, 39, 108–9
Bougainville, Louis Antoine de, 120
Boulding, Kenneth, 242, 249–51, 256, 259, 260–1
Bourguiba, Habib, 229
Bradfield, Richard, 223
British Association for the Advancement of
    Science, 194
Bronk, Detlev, 222
Brontë, Charlotte, 174
Brougham, Henry, Lord, 197
Brown, Lester, 259
Bruce, James, 84
Buccleuch, Duke of, 134
Buchanan, Pat, 278
Buck, John, 226
Buckley, William F. Jr., 279
Buffon, Georges-Louis Leclerc, Comte de, 297
Burke, Edmund, 56, 97, 99
Bush, George Herbert Walker, 277–8
Buttrick, Wallace, 217
Byron, Lord George Gordon, 12

Cambridge University, 3, 6, 18, 194, 195, 244
Candide, 40
Carlile, Richard, 164
Carlyle, Thomas, 12
Carnegie, Andrew, 214, 215
Carson, Rachel, 255, 258
Carter, Jimmy, 283
Center for the Advancement of the Steady State
    Economy, 287
Chalmers, Thomas, 188
Chaplin, Joyce, 8
charity, 60, 63, 87, 143, 214, 295
China, 12, 84, 218–19, 229, 269, 272, 280,
    286, 294

Christian Democrats, 246, 247
Churchill, Winston, 220
Cipolla, Carlo, 255
Claeys, Gregory, 3
Clark, Gregory, 17
Clark, Joseph, 276
climate change denial, 288
Cobbett, William, 11, 196, 197, 295, 299
Cold War, 217–19, 225–6, 254, 273–4
Coleridge, Samuel, 11, 52
Collet, John, 137
Collins, David, 119–20, 121
Columbus, Christopher, 107
Commoner, Barry, 280, 287
Compton Census, 30–1
Conder, Joseph, 155–6, 160
Condition-of-England novel, 157, 173–5
Condorcet, Marquis de, Marie Jean Antoine
        Nicolas de Caritat, 27, 40, 63, 74, 97, 111,
        112–16, 130, 140, 156, 157, 195, 212
Connelly, Michael, 222, 227
Cook, James, 80, 117–18, 120
Corn Laws, 8, 9–10, 142, 144
Critical Review, 54
Crocker, John Wilson, 156, 157
Cullen, William, 134

Daly, Herman, 277
Darwin, Charles, 1, 13, 62, 175, 182–202,
        257
Darwin, Erasmus, 139, 195, 196, 198
Darwinism, 12, 182–202
Davenant, Charles, 36
Davis, Kingsley, 222, 227, 230–1
Davis, Scott "Mac", 208–9, 211
De Candolle, Augustin, 184, 186–7
De Beer, Gavin, 184
De Bry, Theodor, 107–8
Delhi, 209
demography, historical, 247–8
Denmark, 137–8, 285
Derham, William, 37, 40
Descartes, René, 145–6
Desmond, Adrian, 183, 188, 189, 191, 195, 196
Diamond, Jared, 16
Dickens, Charles, 11, 173–4
Dodd, Norris, 216
Douglas, Thomas, 143
Draper, William, 227, 229
Drayton, Richard, 140
Dugatkin, Lee, 194
Dundas, Henry, 136

Earth Day, 253, 278
East, Edward, 272

East India Company, 30
Ebony Magazine, 276
Economist, The, 244
Economists on Malthus, 14–15, 248–51, 260
Eden, 106–8, 123
Eden, Frederick, 80
Edwards, Jonathan, 58
Egerton, George, 175
Ehrlich, Paul, 16, 208, 230, 231, 241, 242, 247,
        248, 251, 253, 257, 259, 261, 270, 275, 276,
        277–8, 280, 282, 287, 288
Ehrlichman, John, 278
Eisenhower, Dwight, 273
Eisley, Lauren, 184, 186
Elliot, George, 175
Elliott, John, 27
Elliott, Paul, 195
Empson, William, 157, 159–60
Engels, Friedrich, 12, 188–9
environmentalism, 231, 270, 280, 286–8
eugenics, 14, 175, 244–5, 271
Evangelicals, 166–9
Everyman Library, 242, 244–8
Evolution, theories of, 182–202
Evolution, anti-Malthusian theories of, 191–201

Fabian Society, 199–200
Factory Bill, 166, 167
famine, 4, 12, 58, 68, 75, 88
Fellner, William, 248
female labour, attitudes to, 165–73
feminism and population, 281, 296
Fenelon, François, 58
Filby, Carol, 256
First World War, 201, 244, 260, 271
Flew, Antony, 243, 245, 246, 253–7, 258, 260
Fogarty, Michael, 242, 245–7, 249, 250,
        252, 260
Food First, 282
food security, 9, 142, 144
Ford Foundation, 227–8, 229
Ford, Henry, 215
Fosdick, Raymond, 216–17, 220, 221
Franklin, Benjamin, 38, 39, 105, 106, 110–11,
        115–16, 121–2, 142, 145, 271, 297
Fraser's Magazine, 156, 163–4
Freeden, Michael, 191
French Revolution, 3, 4, 52, 139
Friedan, Betty, 281
Friedman, Milton, 279

Galton, Francis, 14
Gaskell, Elizabeth, 173, 174–5
General Education Board, 217–18
Genesis, Book of, 107

Gentleman, Tobias, 30
geopolitics, 216–19, 225–6
Gibbon, Edward, 297
Glass, D.V., 247
Global 2000 Report, 283
Godwin, Tony, 255
Godwin, William, 3, 27, 52–70, 74, 97, 111,
    112, 115, 130, 140, 156, 157, 164, 166,
    195, 212–14
Gold Standard, 9
Google, 295
Gordan, Linda, 281
Gore, Al, 267, 284, 288
Gould, Stephen Jay, 193
Grainger, R.D., 169–72
Grand, Sarah, 175
Grandin, Greg, 210
Grant, Robert, 196, 198
Graunt, John, 31, 35–6, 41, 110
Greece, ancient, 109, 117
Green Revolution, 209, 220–1, 224, 253
Greer, Germaine, 281
Groucy, Sophie de, 156
Gruening, Ernest. 276

Hale, Piers, 13
Hardin, Garrett, 216, 230, 259, 275, 281
Hardy, Thomas, 175, 299
Harmen, Oren, 194
Harrar, J. George, 220, 223, 224
Hartlib, Samuel, 31
Hawkesworth, John, 117
Hazlitt, William, 11, 54, 196
Heberden, William, 81, 89
Henry VIII, 255
Herbert, Sandra, 183, 184–5, 186–7
Himmelfarb, Gertrude, 184, 243, 251–3, 258,
    260
Hilton, Boyd, 75, 166
Hobbes, Thomas, 219
Hodges, Sarah, 224
Hoff, Derek, 16
Hollander, Samuel, 77
Hollingsworth, Thomas, 242, 247–8, 260
Home, Henry (Lord Kames), 134
Houston, Alan, 39
Hugh Moore Foundation, 247, 273
Hume, David, 3, 38, 79, 89, 99, 146, 243,
    255, 297
Hutton, James, 134
Huxley, Aldous, 14
Huxley, Thomas, 188, 189–93, 194

immigration, 282–3
improvement, discourse of, 31–2, 129–30, 134

India, 209, 224–5, 227–9, 257–8, 269, 272,
    281, 286
Indiana, University of, 257
Indonesia, 225
Industrial Revolution, 130, 133, 295
Intergovernmental Panel on Climate
    Change, 287
International School of America, 257
Ireland, 9–10, 29, 33, 86, 132, 245
Irish Rebellion, 3

James, Patricia, 196
Jefferson, Thomas, 271
Jevons, Stanley, 15, 146
Johnson, Joseph, 61
Johnson, Lyndon, 229, 274, 275
Johnson, Samuel, 2
Jura, 128–9, 130

Kalm, Pehr, 134, 136
Kennedy, John F., 274
Kenyatta, Jomo, 230
Keymor, John, 30
Keynes, John Maynard, and Keynesianism, 15,
    18, 242, 244, 246, 249, 250, 258, 260, 282
Khan, Ayub, 230
King, Gregory, 36
King, Martin Luther, 276
Knapp, Seaman, 217–18, 226
Knowles, James, 192
Knox, Robert, 196
Kristol, Irving, 253
Kropotkin, Peter, 182, 191–5, 198

labouring classes, 78–99
Ladejinsky, Wolf, 225
Lamarck, Jean Baptiste, 195, 196, 198
Lane, Allen, 255
La Pérouse, Jean, 120
Lapham, Lewis, 231
Layton, William, 242, 244–8, 258, 260
League of Nations, 244
Lennon, John, 208, 210, 211, 212
Levy, D.M., 77
Limits to Growth, The, 278
Linnaeus, Carl, 135, 297
Locke, John, 105, 108, 145
Loomis, William, 225
Lorey, Isabell, 213
Lubin, Isador, 223
luxury, 89–90
Lyell, Charles, 186, 188

Maas, Harro, 145–6
Maginn, William, 156, 157, 163–4

Malthus, Daniel, 61
Malthus, Thomas Robert, 3, 133
  checks to population, 4, 74, 77–8, 87–9, 90,
    91, 112–16
  colonialism, attitude to, 123–5
  early marriage, on, 86, 95
  education, views on, 90–1
  environment and, 81, 130–47
  Essay on the Principle of Population (1798), 3,
    53, 61, 74, 111, 136, 195
  Essay on the Principle of Population (1803 and
    other Great Quarto editions), 7–9, 40,
    68, 74–99, 116–24, 137–8, 142–4, 210–11,
    212–14, 298
  Essay on the Principle of Population (modern
    editions of), 241–61
  improvement, on, 91
  indigenous peoples, attitudes to, 106, 118–25
  Investigation (1800), 7
  Principles of Political Economy (1820),
    10, 15, 94
  as scientific, 76–7, 78
  Summary View of the Principle of Population
    (1830), 118, 124
  theology of, 6, 32, 41, 112–13, 114, 122, 245–7,
    259–60, 296
  travel writings, Use of, 8, 42, 77, 78–80, 112,
    116–24, 298
  travels of, 6–7, 8, 80, 84–5, 94, 137–8
  women, in *Essay*, 119–20, 159
Malthusianism, modern, 267–89
Malthusians and Malthusian League, 14, 17
Manchester Guardian, 188
Mandeville, Bernard, 145
Mangelsdorf, Paul, 221, 223, 224
Mao Zedong, 12
Marcet, Jane, 156
Marshall, Alfred, 15
Marshall, Peter, 65
Martineau, Harriet, 11, 13, 155–65, 168, 172, 174,
    175, 197
Marx, Karl, 1–2, 5, 12, 76–7, 188–9
Mather, Cotton, 39
Matthew, Patrick, 196
Mayhew, Robert, 16, 26–7
Mayr, Ernst, 187
McCormick, Ted, 2, 297
McRae, Andrew, 28
Mead, Margaret, 281
medical arithmetic, 38
medicine, advances in, 81
Meek, Ronald, 255
mercantilism, 25
Mexico, 209, 220–1
Michigan, University of, 250, 251

Mill, Harriet, 174
Mill, James, 155, 161
Mill, John Stuart, 15, 146, 158, 197, 277
Miller, Harry, 223
Milne, Patrick, 144
Montesquieu, Baron de, Charles Secondat, 39
Moore, James, 188, 191
More, Thomas, 28
Morris, William, 198–9
Mosher, Arthur, 226–7
Mukerjee, Radhakamal, 272
Myers, William, 215

Nally, David, 4, 16
Nandy, Ashis, 227
Napoleonic Wars, 10, 132, 144
National Review, The, 279
nature, laws of, 3, 245
New Wworld, 105–25
Newton, Isaac and Newtonianism, 3, 8
New York Times, 273
Neo-Conservatism, 253, 258, 269, 278–9,
    284, 288
Neo-Malthusianism, 146, 271
Nixon, Richard, 278, 279–80, 283
Norway, 84–5, 86, 91, 95, 137–8
Notestein, Frank, 221, 229
nuclear warfare, 15, 211, 230, 251–2

O ' Flaherty, Niall, 5, 8, 69
one-child policy, 286, 294
Osborn, Fairfield, 211, 273
Osborn, Frederick, 222
Otter, William, 61
Owen, Robert, 53
Oxford University, 194, 246–7, 249, 254

Paddock, Paul and William, 259
Paine, Thomas, 52, 55–6, 63, 97
Paley, William, 55, 68, 83, 99, 195
Parenthood, Planned, 276
Peace of Paris, 92
Pearson, Karl, 14
Penguin Books, 243, 253–7, 260
Pennant, Thomas, 128
Petty, William, 31, 33, 40, 41, 110
Pevsner, Dieter, 256
philanthropy, 214–32
Physiocrats, 6, 25, 132
Plasmeijer, Henk, 156
Plattes, Gabriel, 31
Popper, Karl, 248–9
Poivre, Pierre, 134, 135
political arithmetic, 30–1, 36, 110
Political Economy Club, 10

Polybius, 138
Pomeranz, Kenneth, 141
Pope Paul VI, 247, 276
population bomb, 15–16, 208, 217, 241, 247, 251–2, 260, 277, 288
Population Council, 222–3, 227–30, 273, 287
Population Media Center, 287
Poor Laws, 4–5, 7, 8–9, 10, 38, 42, 58, 60, 62, 75–6, 87, 92–7, 131, 166, 169, 196, 247, 252, 295, 298
Pope, Alexander, 1
poverty, 75–99
Poynter, J.R., 54, 76, 78, 93, 96
pre-Malthusians, 25–44
Price, Richard, 27, 38, 115, 121
Priestley, Joseph, 122
pro-natalism, 285–6, 294
Putin, Vladimir, 285

quantification of demography, 35, 80–1, 247–8
Quarterly Review, 156, 161, 163

Rabelais, François, 164
race, population and, 276–7
Radkau, Joachim, 240, 259
Reagan, Ronald, 284
reason-of-state, 108–9
Reform Act, 197
Ricardo, David, 10, 15, 53, 141, 248, 250, 255, 256
Rickman, John, 165
rights, 55–7, 63, 66, 68–9
Robertson, Tom, 16, 241, 243
Rockefeller Foundation, 209–11, 215, 229
Rockefeller, John D Sr., 215
Rockefeller, John D. Jr., 218
Rockefeller, John D. III, 215–16, 217, 218, 221–2, 223, 224, 225–6, 228, 229–30, 231, 273, 278, 281
Rockefeller, Nelson, 278
Roe, G. Hamilton, 170
Romantics, 11–12, 75, 196, 297, 299
Roman Catholicism, 245–7, 254–5, 258, 276
Rome, ancient, 109, 117
Roosevelt, Eleanor, 225
Rousseau, Jean-Jacques, 52, 61
Roxburgh, William, 136
Royal Economic Society, 242
Royal Geographical Society, 192, 194
Royal Society, 10
Royal Society of Literature, 10
Ruse, Michael, 185–6
Ruskin, John, 12
Russell, Bertrand, 15
Russia, 94, 192, 285, 294

Sabin, Paul, 270
Saint-Hilaire, Étienne Geoffroy, 195
Sanger, Margaret, 268, 272
Schoen, Johanna, 277
Schultz, Theodore, 226
Schumacher, E.F., 283
Science, 295
Scott, James, 30
Scotland, 86, 128–44
scriptural demography, 36–7
Seaman, Barbara, 281
Sebright, John, 185
Sen, Amartya, 282
Serres, Étienne, 195
Shaw, George Bernard, 200
Shelley, Percy, 11
Short, Thomas, 37–8, 41
Sierra Club, 273, 283, 288
Simon, Julian, 16, 270, 282
Sinclair, John, 129–30, 140–1, 142–4
Singh, Karan, 281
slavery, 110–11
Smith, Adam, 3, 6, 8, 9, 36, 42, 59–60, 63–4, 67, 69, 78, 83, 85, 89, 90, 98, 99, 129–30, 132, 134–6, 157, 252, 296, 297
Social Darwinism, 13–14
Socialism, 198–201, 253, 254–5, 258, 286
Southey, Robert, 11, 52, 54, 164–5, 168–9, 196
South Sea islands, 88, 120–1
spaceship earth, 249, 251, 259, 260–1
Spectator, 37
Spencer, Herbert, 189, 191
Spengler, Joseph, 273
Stakman, Elvin, 223
St Clair, William, 55
stadial theory, 32, 79, 91, 99, 106, 110–11, 114–15, 116–24, 145, 158, 159–60, 167, 298
Stalin, Joseph, 255
Statistical Society of London, 10
Stedman Jones, Gareth, 97, 158
Stewart, Francis, 128–9
Stiles, Ezra, 38, 115
Stott, Rebecca, 198
Strangeland, Charles, 25
Subramaniam, Chidambaram, 209–10
Sumner, John Bird, 41
Süssmilch, Johann, 39
Sweden, 84–5, 86
Swift, Jonathan, 165, 258
Switzerland, 84
systems theory, 251, 260–1

Tahiti, 80, 120–1
Taylor, Barbara, 158, 159
Thelwall, John, 52

Thomas, Brinley, 141
Thompson, William, 197
Time Magazine, 277
Tito, Josip, 255
Todes, Daniel, 194
Tonight Show, 277
Tonna, Charlotte, 166–73, 174
Torrens, Robert, 69
Townsend, Joseph, 2, 76, 97
Truman, Harry, 273
Turner, Frederick Jackson, 271–2
Turner, Samuel, 94
Tydings, Joseph, 276

Ulloa, Antonio de, 134
Unitarians, 10
United Nations, 225, 284, 295
Utilitarianism, 55, 57–8, 62, 66, 68–9

vagrancy, 29–30
Valenze, Deborah, 157
Vancouver, George, 120
Vico, Giambattista, 212
Vogt, William, 211, 222, 273

Wakley, Thomas, 196, 197
Wallace, Alfred Russel, 13, 62, 183–4, 188, 200
Wallace, Robert, 3, 38, 53

war, 82
Washington Times, 267–8
Waterman, A.M.C., 26, 69, 74, 242
Weaver, Warren, 216, 223, 224, 225
Whiston, William, 37
Whitbread, Samuel, 95, 98
Wilderness Act, 274–5
Wilkinson, John, 185
Willis Harris, J, 199–200
Winch, Donald, 55, 69, 168
Wollstonecraft, Mary, 156, 158, 159, 163, 164, 166,
        168, 296
Wordsworth, William, 11, 52
World Economic Forum, 267
World Population Conference, 280, 284
Wright, Peter, 256
Wrigley, E.A., 17, 86, 105, 133–4, 141
W.W. Norton, 243, 257–9

Yale University, 248
Yen, James, 218–19, 225
Yeo, Stephen, 198
Young, Arthur, 95–6, 129, 137, 140, 144
Young, Robert, 187–8, 191

Zero Population Growth movement/
        Population Connection, 269, 275, 277–8,
        283, 287